KERUX COMMENTARIES

1 PETER

———

KERUX COMMENTARIES

1 PETER

A Commentary for Biblical Preaching and Teaching

TIMOTHY E. MILLER

BRYAN MURAWSKI

KREGEL
MINISTRY

1 Peter: A Commentary for Biblical Preaching and Teaching

© 2022 by Timothy E. Miller and Bryan Murawski

Published by Kregel Ministry, an imprint of Kregel Publications, 2450 Oak Industrial Dr. NE, Grand Rapids, MI 49505-6020.

Unless otherwise indicated, the translation of the Scripture portions used throughout the commentary is the authors' own English rendering of the original biblical languages.

Italics in Scripture quotations indicate emphasis added by the authors.

The Hebrew font, NewJerusalemU, and the Greek font, GraecaU, are available from www.linguistsoftware.com/lgku.htm, +1-425-775-1130.

All photos are under Creative Commons licensing, and contributors are indicated in the captions of the photos.

Map on page 32 was designed by Shawn Vander Lugt, Managing Editor for Academic and Ministry Books at Kregel Publications

ISBN 978-0-8254-5841-5

Printed in the United States of America
22 23 24 25 26 / 5 4 3 2 1

Contents

HONORABLE SUFFERING AS THE FLOCK OF GOD (4:12–5:14)

PUBLISHER'S PREFACE TO THE SERIES

Since words were first uttered, people have struggled to understand one another and to know the main meaning in any verbal exchange.

The answer to what God is talking about must be understood in every context and generation; that is why Kerux (KAY-rukes) emphasizes text-based truths and bridges from the context of the original hearers and readers to the twenty-first-century world. Kerux values the message of the text, thus its name taken from the Greek *kērux*, a messenger or herald who announced the proclamations of a ruler or magistrate.

Biblical authors trumpeted all kinds of important messages in very specific situations, but a big biblical idea, grasped in its original setting and place, can transcend time. This specific, big biblical idea taken from the biblical passage embodies a single concept that transcends time and bridges the gap between the author's contemporary context and the reader's world. How do the prophets perceive the writings of Moses? How does the writer of Hebrews make sense of the Old Testament? How does Clement in his second epistle, which may be the earliest sermon known outside the New Testament, adapt verses from Isaiah and also ones from the Gospels? Or what about Luther's bold use of Romans 1:17? How does Jonathan Edwards allude to Genesis 19? Who can forget Martin Luther King Jr.'s "I Have a Dream" speech and his appropriation of Amos 5:24: "No, no, we are not satisfied, and we will not be satisfied until 'justice rolls down like waters, and righteousness like a mighty stream'"? How does a preacher in your local church today apply the words of Hosea in a meaningful and life-transforming way?

WHAT IS PRIME IN GOD'S MIND, AND HOW IS THAT EXPRESSED TO A GIVEN GENERATION IN THE UNITS OF THOUGHT THROUGHOUT THE BIBLE?

Answering those questions is what Kerux authors do. Based on the popular "big idea" preaching model, Kerux commentaries uniquely combine the insights of experienced Bible exegetes (trained in interpretation) and homileticians (trained in preaching). Their collaboration provides for every Bible book:

- A detailed introduction and outline
- A summary of all preaching sections with their primary exegetical, theological, and preaching ideas
- Preaching pointers that join the original context with the contemporary one
- Insights from the Hebrew and Greek text
- A thorough exposition of the text
- Sidebars of pertinent information for further background
- Appropriate charts and photographs
- A theological focus to passages

- A contemporary big idea for every preaching unit
- Present-day meaning, validity, and application of a main idea
- Creative presentations for each primary idea
- Key questions about the text for study groups

Many thanks to Jim Weaver, Kregel's former acquisitions editor, who conceived of this commentary series and further developed it with the team of Jeffrey D. Arthurs, Robert B. Chisholm, David M. Howard Jr., Darrel L. Bock, Roy E. Ciampa, and Michael J. Wilkins. We also recognize with gratitude the significant contributions of Dennis Hillman, Fred Mabie, Paul Hillman, Herbert W. Bateman IV, and Shawn Vander Lugt who have been instrumental in the development of the series. Finally, gratitude is extended to the two authors for each Kerux volume; the outside reviewers, editors, and proofreaders; and Kregel staff who suggested numerous improvements.

—Kregel Publications

EXEGETICAL AUTHOR'S PREFACE AND ACKNOWLEDGMENTS

For Peter & Elizabeth Rew,
elect-exiles who have suffered much and loved more

I am thankful for many who made this work possible. First, I thank Dr. Albin Huss, my seminary professor, who taught me to dig deeply into the Word. The model of block diagramming he taught me has been essential to my life work. Second, I thank my PhD advisor Dr. Radu Gheorghiță, who required me to memorize the text of 1 Peter. (I only wish I would have taken him up on his challenge to memorize it in Greek!) His further labor of helping me refine my dissertation on the use of Jesus's words in 1 Peter gave me a foundation for writing this volume. Third, I wish to thank my employer, Detroit Baptist Theological Seminary, which granted encouragement and time to complete this project. Fourth, I want to thank Bryan Murawski, the preaching author of this volume. As all who read this volume will see, he models what a pastor-theologian should be. Finally, I thank God for the opportunity to comment on his life-giving Word. May my feeble words magnify his.

—Timothy E. Miller
Allen Park, MI

PREACHING AUTHOR'S PREFACE AND ACKNOWLEDGMENTS

For Janice,
an imperishable beauty with a gentle and quiet spirit,
precious in God's sight and mine (1 Peter 3:4)

I am grateful for Tim Miller and the folks at Kregel for inviting me to contribute to this project. As a pastor and preacher, I have often struggled to find the balance between academic/exegetical resources and homiletical/practical books during sermon prep. I hope the reader will find this series well balanced between the two.

The members and regular attenders of Bethany Bible Church have been exceptionally helpful as I taught through 1 Peter in preparation for this commentary. They provided plenty of encouragement and challenging questions that strengthened every chapter of this commentary. Friend and colleague Gary Schnittjer gave me helpful advice and wise direction at a key point in this project. I am also grateful for the partnership in ministry with pastors Aaron Walters and Garrett Nimmo, who in many ways walked with me through the message of 1 Peter in the trials and sufferings we endured together in ministry as I worked on this commentary. My wife Janice helped provide feedback in many key areas as well. I thank the Lord for her wisdom, support, and friendship every day.

Preaching is a holy task, a high calling, as it undertakes to proclaim, explain, and apply the very words of God. The effectiveness of preaching directly correlates to its rootedness in Scripture. As such, I have striven to allow as many analogies, illustrations, and examples as possible to flow from Peter's text. Where Peter offers an image or metaphor rooted in everyday life, I attempt to allow that image or metaphor to motivate the creative applications and presentation of the sermon. In this way, the actual text of Scripture remains the highlight of the sermon.

I pray that the teacher and preacher will be able to benefit from the many exegetical insights here, and adapt the homiletical suggestions for his or her proper context. This, I hope, will lead to biblical, engaging, and relevant sermons, for the edification of the church, for the glory of God.

—Bryan Murawski
Belleville, MI

OVERVIEW OF ALL PREACHING PASSAGES

1 Peter 1:1–2

EXEGETICAL IDEA
Peter, an apostle of Jesus Christ, wrote to elect-exiles, who had become elect-exiles by the work of the triune God, whose first member chose them, second member sanctified them, and third member offered the sacrifice necessary that made their new identity possible.

THEOLOGICAL FOCUS
Believers in Jesus have a new identity as elect-exiles, eternally chosen by the Father, judicially sanctified by the Spirit, and graciously welcomed by means of the work of the Son.

PREACHING IDEA
The Born-Again Identity: The Triune God Transforms Our Identities from Lost Sinners to Elect Exiles.

PREACHING POINTERS
The first epistle of Peter opens with theological precision built on a Trinitarian foundation. Peter writes to a Gentile audience dispersed throughout Asia Minor and Galatia. They were spiritual exiles, temporary residents of earth. Though they shared no home or singular house of worship anymore, they united through a common identity. Peter's readers were among the elect, chosen by Father, Son, and Holy Spirit to multiply God's grace throughout the world.

Hardly more exciting news could begin a letter! Modern readers recognize that God counts us, too, among elect-exiles. The Father, Son, and Holy Spirit each had a role in our salvation, transforming our identities and giving us mission and purpose. We share the same identity as Peter's readers. We exist as exiles, dispersed throughout the world, far greater than the reaches of Galatia and Asia. Yet we unite as the elect in a faith founded in the foreknowledge of the Father, sanctified in the Holy Spirit, and purchased with the blood of Jesus Christ. The Trinity played a significant role in the lives of the first-century readers and continues to play a significant role in the lives of twenty-first-century Christians.

1 Peter 1:3–9

EXEGETICAL IDEA
God the Father was to be praised for granting new birth, for this new birth provided a living hope, guaranteed a secure inheritance, and produced rejoicing despite present trial.

THEOLOGICAL FOCUS

Believers should praise God the Father for the gift of the new birth, which provides a living hope, a secure inheritance, and a reason to rejoice despite trials.

PREACHING IDEA

The Born-Again Supremacy: Faithful Living Results in Supreme Rewards.

PREACHING POINTERS

The first-century church underwent heavy persecution as God's kingdom began its spread throughout the world. Persecuted believers couldn't help but ask themselves, "Is it worth it? Is this suffering worth the pain?"

Peter called the church to a future perspective, firmly rooted in the present hope of their salvation. Only by looking beyond their current trials could the early church see the reason for their pain. Believers have been born again to a living hope. God stores up for them an unfading inheritance far greater than anything they could accumulate in this life. Faithful perseverance through persecution results in praise and glory and honor when Christ returns. This gives reason to rejoice despite trials.

The twenty-first-century preacher must call the church to a similar focus. Though we may not all experience the same heat of persecution that the first-century church did, we have the same supreme hope and calling in our salvation. Faithful living results in glorious rewards. The modern believer must look beyond the here and now and realize that life is best lived for the future. This puts whatever trials or tribulations the church currently experiences into proper focus. By calling the church to look forward to the day of reward, believers have a sharper perspective on how to live today.

1 Peter 1:10–12

EXEGETICAL IDEA

The readers were to be envied, for they were experiencing the salvation accomplished by the suffering and glorification of Christ, which was predicted by the Old Testament prophets and was of great interest to the angelic beings.

THEOLOGICAL FOCUS

Church-age believers are privileged to know the fullness of the gospel, which the prophets desired to know, and the angels have great interest in.

PREACHING IDEA

The Born-Again Legacy: A Long Legacy of Prophets and Angels Magnifies the Mysteries of the Gospel.

PREACHING POINTERS

Suffering does not often feel like a privileged position. Peter's readers likely did not feel that they lived in a time of privilege or entitlement, especially as Christians in an increasingly anti-Christian society. Persecution plagued the church, threatening to scare believers away from their newfound faith. Believers suffered physically through imprisonment, beatings, displacement, and death.

Today, we might feel like we enjoy a variety of privileges for various reasons: we live in a period of unparalleled technological advancement; we benefit from a wealth of riches and luxury and comfort in our modern temperature-controlled mansions; diseases that would have been deadly just a few centuries ago can now be cured at the cost of a few dollars. The world is smaller than ever before, and we feel better off for it.

The preacher can show the church that these so-called privileges pale in comparison to the privileges of living on this side of the cross. Believers experience the fullness of the gospel, something both angels and prophets longed to comprehend for many millennia. To preach this passage is to preach the greatest privilege in the history of humanity, far eclipsing the glories of technology, comfort, travel, or earthly riches!

1 Peter 1:13–21

EXEGETICAL IDEA
In light of their new birth, Peter's readers had to set their hope fully on the coming of Christ, reject their old way of life by modeling God's holiness, and live in reverent fear, knowing God's impartial judgment and the overwhelming cost of their redemption.

THEOLOGICAL FOCUS
Believers must hope in Christ's coming, reflect the Father's holiness, and live in reverent fear.

PREACHING IDEA
Like Father, Like Sons: Be Holy, as God Is Holy.

PREACHING POINTERS
The first few paragraphs of Peter's letter focused on the "born-again identity" of the readers. Now, Peter transitions to tell his readers how they should expect to live in light of that new identity.

This passage offers the preacher the first passage packed with application in 1 Peter. Previous passages primarily built theological groundwork, laying the way for the imperatives to follow. Here, Peter launches into several commands, urging his readers to set their hope on God's grace, to be holy as God is holy, and to live in reverent fear. Then, in an explosive theological climax, he highlights the revelation of the gospel.

The passage may be the most exciting yet! Packed with clear commands and a ready-made gospel message in the text, few pericopes in the New Testament offer a clearer path to preach than this one. Peter stirs our hearts with his message, challenging believers to live in light of their identity as born-again Christians and to act according to the character of their holy Father.

1 Peter 1:22–25

EXEGETICAL IDEA
After hearing the living and abiding Word of God, Peter's readers responded in obedience to the truth and received the new birth, which worked in them a sincere brotherly love that they must earnestly exercise toward one another.

THEOLOGICAL FOCUS
Those who have experienced the new birth have been obedient to the truth of the Word of God, and they must now exercise the love natural to the new birth.

PREACHING IDEA
People Perish, but God's Word Persists!

PREACHING POINTERS
Nobody likes to think about how short life really is. Eighty years comes and goes too fast for our comfort. As children, death is hardly a thought. Toys and video games and movies distract from the harsh realities awaiting us in life. Teenagers hardly give their choices a second thought, living out their years in high school with reckless abandon, seemingly ignorant of any real consequences to their actions. College students fare no better, amping up the bad decision-making of their teenage years now that they are untethered from their parents' watch. Even young adults and early married couples rarely consider mortality, being too young, too healthy, and too in love to allow such thoughts to cross their minds. It isn't usually until middle age hits and our bodies begin to sag and slow down that our impermanence sinks in.

Peter knew the truth of this reality, as did the prophets before him. Peter's readers faced persecution and difficult trials. Peter has pointed them to the blessed hope of their salvation. They have been born again in Christ and now have a new calling and a means of facing their persecutors. But those facing the pressure of persecution may have felt like life as they know it was slipping away. In the first century, persecution often meant the loss of commerce and public rapport—and many times even imprisonment, bodily harm, or death. This caused many believers to consider their options. But Peter directs his readers' attention away from the transitory nature of life and roots their focus in the unfading Word of God. First Peter 1:22–25 calls readers to root their confidence not in their own longevity of life but in the enduring Word of God. Being born again means we become imperishable, though not in our earthly bodies. This gospel gives hope and encouragement through the difficulties of life. The preacher has opportunity to address the most common fear known to humankind: the fear of death. It impacts 100 percent of us, and therefore this passage is one of the most relevant in the entire epistle.

1 Peter 2:1–3

EXEGETICAL IDEA
As newborn babes, Peter's readers were commanded to long after the milk that causes them to grow up into salvation, while avoiding activities that are incompatible with their new life.

THEOLOGICAL FOCUS
Those given new birth through the Word must continue to desire that Word, thereby growing into salvation while also avoiding actions incompatible with the Word's teaching.

PREACHING IDEA
Born-again Believers Crave Pure Spiritual Milk.

PREACHING POINTERS
Peter's commands to the church in 2:1–3 come in two parts: a negative prohibition and a positive proscription. Negatively, the church must strip away five specific sins: malice, deceit, hypocrisy, envy, and slander. On the positive side, the church must feast on the pure nutrition of God's Word. This all assumes that believers in the church are truly born again.

For pastors looking to give their congregation a feast, 1 Peter 2:1–3 provides the perfect two-course meal. The first plate: "Avoid these sins!" And the second: "Eat this instead!" Too often sermons end up unbalanced—a lot of yelling at sin with very little grace, or urgent imperatives to "Avoid this sin!" without a proper balance of "Here's what to focus on instead." If preached correctly, congregants will leave feeling well fed and knowing how to feed themselves in the future.

1 Peter 2:4–10

EXEGETICAL IDEA
Peter indicated that his readers were in a privileged and honorable position, for they were priests who were being built into a spiritual house as a result of their divinely appointed acceptance of Jesus Christ as the cornerstone.

THEOLOGICAL FOCUS
Believers are chosen to be priests and are included in God's building program, for all those who recognize that Jesus is the cornerstone are granted the glorious benefits of being the people of God.

PREACHING IDEA
From Sinners to Stones, from Pagans to Priests: God's People Enjoy a Privileged Position.

PREACHING POINTERS
Imagine the surprise Peter's readers must have felt hearing words previously reserved for Old Testament Israelites now applied to them: "a chosen race, a royal priesthood, a holy nation, a people for his own possession" (2:9). Labels that once exclusively described the Jewish people, Peter now uses to describe even *Gentile* Christians! Through a skillful use of Old Testament quotations and allusions, Peter links believers with Jesus, showing strong continuity in God's program from one dispensation to another.

Today we can likewise join in these identifying characteristics. Christianity has no shortage of different denominations and labels that separate: Baptist, Presbyterian, Methodist, Charismatic, and so on. Even bigger denominations divide into further subcategories:

Southern Baptist, Freewill Baptist, American Baptist, and more. But Peter brings true believers together using metaphors that capture a common unity, built upon the foundation of Christ and his work. Preachers have the chance to use both Old and New Testaments in one sermon to help Christians understand their heritage and their common identity.

1 Peter 2:11–12

EXEGETICAL IDEA
Peter urged the exiled readers to abstain from sinful desires and to act honorably, with the hope that their accusers would see their good deeds and glorify God.

THEOLOGICAL FOCUS
Elect-exiles are to reject sin and live honorably before unbelievers, with the hope that their opponents would see and repent.

PREACHING IDEA
The Gospel Vocalized Is Ineffective without the Gospel Visualized.

PREACHING POINTERS
Building on the born-again identity of his persecuted audience, Peter provided another way for the believers to think of themselves: sojourners and exiles. This renewed focus on their identity should transform the way they interact with their culture. No longer should they be controlled by the passionate lusts that once characterized them. Now, their spiritual identity elevates their moral behavior to the extent that the pagan culture will take notice. Peter urged them to live in such a way that even their worst enemies would have no cause to speak ill of them.

Today, believers face the challenge of living a moral life amid an immoral society. It is much easier to blend into a secular workplace than to stick out against it. Business success often comes at the cost of integrity and honor. If believers think of themselves primarily as lawyers, farmers, construction workers, or teachers, then it becomes much easier to sacrifice godliness at the altar of corporate success. But this passage challenges believers to see themselves as exiles and sojourners, and to use opportunities where their morality clashes with the culture to share the gospel in both word and deed.

1 Peter 2:13–17

EXEGETICAL IDEA
Peter commanded the readers to submit to human authorities, live as freed slaves, and honor all people.

THEOLOGICAL FOCUS
Believers, as freed slaves of God, must submit to human authorities and honor all people.

PREACHING IDEA
Freely Live as Slaves to God-Ordained Authority Figures.

PREACHING POINTERS

It must have been difficult for believers in Peter's day to humbly submit themselves to the governing authorities. Nero ran the empire. His policies and anti-Christian agenda had potential to cause serious frustration to well-meaning believers looking to serve Christ in their newly established faith. Never before had the governing authorities taken such a proactive role in persecuting the church. It was never so dangerous to be a Christian.

Today's governing leaders pale in comparison to Nero's reign of terror. Believers sometimes get frustrated with government policies that seem to push against Christian values, but what we experience (at least in America) is far less severe than what the believers in Peter's day endured.

This should not diminish the reality of our persecution, especially when plenty of signs point to persecution continuing to ramp up, not diminish. Rather, if Peter's words to first-century believers encouraged humble submission to governing authorities, how much more should they impact twenty-first-century believers?

1 Peter 2:18–21

EXEGETICAL IDEA

Peter commanded slaves to be subject to their masters, even those who caused them unjust suffering, for in doing so they receive commendation from God as they follow the steps of Jesus.

THEOLOGICAL FOCUS

Believers should graciously endure sovereignly permitted unjust suffering, knowing that they are commended by God as they follow the steps of Jesus.

PREACHING IDEA

Being a Slave of Christ Means Submitting to Human Masters.

PREACHING POINTERS

Peter directly speaks to those in one of the most difficult situations imaginable: slaves suffering under a cruel master. How does a believer act as a born-again child of God while enduring unjust punishment as a slave? Instead of encouraging the believer to seek asylum or to attain freedom, his advice is to endure the sorrows while doing good. This aligns the believer's life with the unjust punishment Christ suffered, and has a sanctifying effect on the believer.

Most people today cannot directly identify with Peter's context. Though the sex-slave trade is growing in many parts of the world, the vast majority of people do not understand what it means to be held captive and forced to obey the will of another human being. But Peter's words still have relevance to the twenty-first-century Christian. Peter's point has more to do with living amid injustice than living amid slavery, and there is plenty of injustice going around. Believers can be encouraged to follow the footsteps of Jesus and endure suffering for the sake of maintaining a proper Christian testimony.

1 Peter 2:22–25

EXEGETICAL IDEA
Jesus, in his suffering on the cross, displayed a perfect model of innocent suffering as he took the sin of the elect readers, so that they, free from sin, would follow him and live righteously.

THEOLOGICAL FOCUS
Jesus's suffering on the cross has freed believers from sin and gives them opportunity to live for righteousness.

PREACHING IDEA
Jesus's Sinless Death Leads to Life for Sinners.

PREACHING POINTERS
Transitioning from commands given to slaves, Peter provides his first-century audience the perfect example of suffering for righteousness's sake. He gives the ultimate motivation to endure persecution or unjust treatment: Jesus endured the cross, bearing sin on his body in order to provide opportunity to live righteously. No greater example can be found than the example of Jesus and the gospel.

Followers of Christ today must recognize the foundation of the cross and the gospel in order to have proper motivation for obedience. Even most believers attempt to avoid any kind of suffering at any cost. When the opposing team insults us, we repay like with like and insult back. When a coworker threatens us, we look for opportunity to bring them down. But this is not the Jesus way. This passage motivates believers to imitate Jesus, even in how we respond to suffering.

1 Peter 3:1–7

EXEGETICAL IDEA
Peter instructed wives to submit to their husbands and display an inward beauty that attracts unbelieving husbands, that is honorable in God's sight, and that follows the example of prior godly saints; and Peter instructed husbands to live with their wives knowledgeably, honoring them as coheirs in the gift of life.

THEOLOGICAL FOCUS
Wives must follow the lead of their husbands, focusing on inward beauty, while husbands must live with their wives knowledgeably, honoring them as coheirs in the gift of life.

PREACHING IDEA
There's No Place Like Home . . . When Wives and Husbands Enjoy Their Proper Roles.

PREACHING POINTERS
Households of Peter's day typically upheld clear distinctions between husband and wife, child and parent, slave and free. This is true of both believing and unbelieving households.

Social norms controlled much of went on in the home and how husbands and wives interacted with each other. Peter speaks to these distinctions, upholding some of them and subverting others, in order to help the Christian husband and wife live out their God-given roles in the home.

Today's society has broken down many of these cultural distinctions, especially in the Western world. No longer can it be assumed that the husband is the head of the household or that the wife stays home and keeps house while the husband works for a living. Peter's commands speak to moderns just as he did to people in his day. The biblical truths he shares are timeless in their values and transcend culture in a way that help believers in the home, whether they share the bedroom with a Christian spouse or not. The preacher will find in this passage opportunity to speak biblical truth to families of all designs.

1 Peter 3:8–12

EXEGETICAL IDEA
Peter commanded his readers to cultivate positive social values and pursue righteousness, while rejecting detrimental social responses and turning from evil, so that they would acquire the blessing of loving life and seeing good days.

THEOLOGICAL FOCUS
Believers may acquire blessing by cultivating righteousness and rejecting unrighteousness.

PREACHING IDEA
God "Likes" True Social Networking.

PREACHING POINTERS
The pressure of persecution forces believers to determine their allegiance. When the heat is turned up, the church could either fracture in discord or unite stronger than ever. Peter's readers were facing the stress of persecution, which potentially could destroy their relationships with each other or cause bitterness and anger at the unbelieving world attacking them. But Peter challenged his readers to humble themselves and unite. He urged them to respond to evil with love, and by doing so to live out the call of the gospel in the midst of the hostile world around them.

Likewise, believers today face trials and temptations from many angles. Internally, many churches are fractured over mundane issues like tertiary doctrine or opinions on how to run a ministry. In our dog-eat-dog world, many believers have taken the worldly approach to trade insult with insult instead of returning love for evil. Those who desire to see good days search for them through self-help books and internet blogs instead of through God's Word.

Peter's words point to a better way of life. Through 1 Peter 3:8–12, preachers can address issues like church unity, responding to a hostile world, and pursuing the right kinds of goals in life. The passage speaks to various relationships, both in and outside the church, and orients the believer to live out the gospel in a Christlike manner.

1 Peter 3:13–17

EXEGETICAL IDEA
Peter encouraged the readers that if God willed their righteous suffering, they must consider themselves blessed, fear God above all else, and be prepared for evangelistic opportunities.

THEOLOGICAL FOCUS
Believers who suffer for righteousness must consider themselves blessed, fear God above all else, and be prepared for evangelistic opportunities.

PREACHING IDEA
Turn Periods of Persecution into Opportunities for Evangelism.

PREACHING POINTERS
Peter's readers knew suffering. Nero reigned terror on Christians, feeding them to wild beasts, lighting them on fire, crucifying them. Many of Peter's readers likely knew believers who suffered death—some friends, some family. Suffering for righteousness's sake was a reality for these Christians and in 1 Peter 3:13–17, Peter speaks directly to the persecuted church. How should one facing death on a daily basis love his persecutors? What perspective should such Christians have on their sufferings and trials?

Most believers in the Western world do not know such persecution. Some have had the unpleasant experience of losing a job because of their outspoken faith, or perhaps getting sued because of their business's moral stance. Very few believers face torture and death and only some have experienced suffering truly for doing what is good. But even if modern readers have not experienced persecution to the extent of Peter's original audience, the time is coming (Matt. 24:9; John 15:20; 2 Tim. 3:12) and this text prepares Christians for such unpleasantries.

Even more than that, it puts suffering and apologetic witnessing in the correct theological perspective. Most people desire immediate escape when undergoing pressure, but Peter's view is that it should not cause us fear, trouble, or even spiritual harm. In fact, with the right perspective, believers can turn times of persecution into opportunities for evangelism.

1 Peter 3:18–22

EXEGETICAL IDEA
Peter encouraged the suffering readers by pointing to the example of Christ, who suffered for a noble cause and was publicly vindicated.

THEOLOGICAL FOCUS
Suffering believers are to be encouraged by the example of Christ, who suffered for a noble cause and was publicly vindicated.

PREACHING IDEA
Christ's Vindication over Suffering Motivates a Christian's Victory over Sin.

PREACHING POINTERS

What motivates a believer to overcome suffering? Peter's readers must have wrestled with that very question. Why continue in the Christian faith if it only produced increased persecution and torment from maniacal dictators like Nero? When doing the right thing only gets you punished more severely, why do the right thing? Peter challenged his readers to consider Christ's example. Jesus suffered, died, and rose victorious over sin and death. His victory and perseverance through suffering motivates a Christian's victory through similar trials.

This holds true for modern Christians just as much as for those in Peter's day. Though 1 Peter 3:18–22 has more than its fair share of theological conundrums, it offers a clear path to application for believers. The preacher can encourage the church to suffer through the toughest of trials, seeing how Jesus did so first and now reigns victoriously. The passage has a bit of everything: a clear gospel message, challenging theology, and a motivating message.

1 Peter 4:1–6

EXEGETICAL IDEA

Peter commanded the readers to prepare to suffer for righteousness, knowing that such suffering is evidence of their cessation from sin, their obedience to the will of God, and their positive outcome in the future judgment.

THEOLOGICAL FOCUS

Believers must prepare to suffer for righteousness, knowing that such suffering is evidence of their cessation from sin, their obedience to the will of God, and their positive outcome in the future judgment.

PREACHING IDEA

Believers Must Arm Themselves to Suffer While Abstaining from Sin.

PREACHING POINTERS

Living righteously has consequences, both pleasant and unpleasant. Peter's readers learned quickly that sometimes living out the Christian life drew attention in all the wrong ways. Not only did they suffer persecution from Nero, but abstaining from the social connections of their life before Christ brought fallout as well. Believers found themselves maligned and suffering over their choices to cease from sin.

Christians today feel the same heat of persecution from colleagues and family members who don't understand their new lifestyle. Abstaining from alcohol leads the believer to incur great ridicule from his old drinking buddies. Abstaining from sex before marriage brings plenty of mockery from a woman's sorority sisters. Openly sharing the faith brings outright persecution and even shunning from certain family members. Christians face suffering for living like Jesus. Through the words of 1 Peter 4, preachers can challenge believers to persevere through such difficulties. Pointing the believer to Christ's example encourages the Christian to abstain from sin, even when the consequences continue to pile up in his or her social life.

1 Peter 4:7–11

EXEGETICAL IDEA
Peter commanded the readers to live rationally in light of the last days by loving, serving, and being hospitable to one another, for by doing so their prayers would be heard, and they would glorify God.

THEOLOGICAL FOCUS
Believers must live rationally in light of the last days by loving, serving, and being hospitable to one another, for by doing so their prayers will be heard, and they will glorify God.

PREACHING IDEA
Maximize Your Vertical Relationship with God by Deepening Horizontal Relationships with Believers.

PREACHING POINTERS
Peter's words to the first-century church conveyed an urgency not only due to the situation of persecution of his readers, but due to the dispensation in which they lived. Peter told them that "the end of all things is at hand" (4:7a), driving the commands that followed. The believers were urged to increase the effectiveness of their prayers by strengthening the quality of their relationships with each other and their impact on the local church. This would help them live as end-times believers, righteously prepared to meet their Savior when he comes.

If this was true of Peter's readers, it is all the more true and even more urgent two thousand years later for the modern church. This built-in urgency heightens the impact of the sermon from the very first phrase of the text. Peter provides other motivations for the church as well. Who doesn't want an increased prayer life? Who doesn't want to glorify God? Every believer wants both, and these motivations, placed within the pressure cooker of the end-times perspective, sound a clear alarm for believers to allow the gospel to work through their lives with powerful results.

1 Peter 4:12–19

EXEGETICAL IDEA
Peter commanded the readers to not be shocked or ashamed at suffering for righteousness; instead, they were to entrust themselves to God, rejoicing in suffering—because they knew that those who suffer for righteousness glorify God, are blessed in this life, and are vindicated in the next.

THEOLOGICAL FOCUS
Believers must not be shocked or ashamed at suffering for righteousness; instead, they are to entrust themselves to God, rejoicing in suffering—because they know that those who suffer for righteousness glorify God, are blessed in this life, and are vindicated in the next.

PREACHING IDEA
Flip the Script of Honor and Shame by Rejoicing in Righteous Suffering.

PREACHING POINTERS

If nothing else, the exposition of 1 Peter has established that the original readers experienced great persecution and suffering. They knew the difficulties of living life as a Christian and paying dearly for it. What kind of encouragement does a group like this need? Peter connects suffering to surprising phrases like "rejoice," "be glad," and "you are blessed." This upends expectations for his readers, giving them a new and renewed disposition to face their problems.

Believers today are not exempt from trials or persecution. In fact, they are to expect them (2 Tim. 3:12). When the cake shop owner is sued for refusing to compromise moral principles, how should she handle such suffering? When a college professor mocks a Christian student for his belief in God and the Bible, how should the student interpret this trial? How do third-world believers suffering physical imprisonment and even death react to such persecution? First Peter 4:12–19 reorients the minds and hearts of believers in any age going through righteous suffering, giving hope and promise to overcome such trials.

1 Peter 5:1–5

EXEGETICAL IDEA

Peter detailed duties within the community: elders must shepherd willingly and eagerly, serving as examples to the flock, nonelders must submit to the elders, and all must show humility to one another.

THEOLOGICAL FOCUS

Believers have duties within the community: elders must shepherd willingly and eagerly, serving as examples to the flock, nonelders must submit to the elders, and all must show humility to one another.

PREACHING IDEA

Humble Elders Lead Humble People toward a Humble Shepherd.

PREACHING POINTERS

Peter is near the end of his letter. He has addressed the issue of suffering in multiple parts of his writing. He applied Christian identity to various spheres of life, including what it looks like to act godly toward the government, in a master-slave relationship, and in the home between husbands and wives. Peter now turns to address the church, helping both the leaders (elders) of the church to understand what it looks like to lead and what it looks like for the followers to follow that leadership. Proper relationships within the church are essential if the Christian community is going to persevere under persecution.

Today, if the church is to succeed in her mission, such proper relationships remain essential. Too many examples abound of domineering or abusive pastors and leaders. The headlines are smeared with shepherds who have taken advantage of sheep by stealing money from the offering or worse, by leveraging their position for sexual satisfaction. Peter's words cut through this kind of unbiblical crassness and show what a true church leader ought to look like. He also addresses the congregation, encouraging a similar humility that reflects a submissiveness to both God and human leader. Churches today would do well to pay attention to Peter's admonitions to the flock.

1 Peter 5:6–14

EXEGETICAL IDEA
Peter gave final admonitions noting the need for humility, watchfulness, and enduring faith while the readers waited for God's coming climactic redemption.

THEOLOGICAL FOCUS
Believers must continue in humility, watchfulness, and enduring faith as they wait for God's climactic redemption.

PREACHING IDEA
Stand Firm in Faith, Watching for Christ's Coming and Wary of Satan's Schemes.

PREACHING POINTERS
The first-century church had suffered a lot. Persecution from Rome reached a pinnacle under Nero's leadership. In just five short chapters, Peter addressed the identity and calling of a believer under such circumstances. Now, at the close of his letter, he offered final words of instruction for the Christians. The devil still prowls the streets. Believers will continue to suffer. But Peter urged his readers to stand firm in their faith, awaiting the final glory of Christ's second coming.

The final sermon of any series can be a momentous occasion for the congregation. The preacher should feel the electric charge of Peter's closing instructions and translate that to a high-energy call to the church. If Peter's words were true back then, they are still so today: the devil continues to prowl, believers continue to suffer persecution, but *Jesus will return in glory!* This final passage gives believers hope for the future as they face the trials of the present day.

ABBREVIATIONS

GENERAL ABBREVIATIONS

A.D.	In the year of our Lord (*anno Domini*)
B.C.	Before Christ
LXX	Septuagint
MSS	Manuscripts
NA[27]	*Novum Testamentum Graece*, Nestle-Aland, 27th ed.
NA[28]	*Novum Testamentum Graece*, Nestle-Aland, 28th ed.
NT	New Testament
OT	Old Testament

TECHNICAL ABBREVIATIONS

ca.	circa
cf.	compare (*confer*)
e.g.	for example
etc.	and so forth, and the rest (*et cetera*)
et al.	and others (*et alii*)
idem	the same
i.e.	that is (*id est*)
n(n).	note(s)
p(p).	page(s)
rev.	revised
s.v.	under the word (*sub verbo*)
v(v).	verse(s)

BIBLICAL

Old Testament		*Old Testament (continued)*	
Gen.	Genesis	1 Kings	1 Kings
Exod.	Exodus	2 Kings	2 Kings
Lev.	Leviticus	3 Kgdms.	3 Kingdoms (LXX)
Num.	Numbers	4 Kgdms.	4 Kingdoms (LXX)
Deut.	Deuteronomy	1 Chron.	1 Chronicles
Josh.	Joshua	2 Chron.	2 Chronicles
Judg.	Judges	Ezra	Ezra
Ruth	Ruth	Neh.	Nehemiah
1 Sam.	1 Samuel	Esther	Esther
2 Sam.	2 Samuel	Job	Job
1 Kgdms.	1 Kingdoms (LXX)	Ps./Pss.	Psalm(s)
2 Kgdms.	2 Kingdoms (LXX)	Prov.	Proverbs

Old Testament (continued)

Eccl.	Ecclesiastes
Song	Song of Songs
Isa.	Isaiah
Jer.	Jeremiah
Lam.	Lamentations
Ezek.	Ezekiel
Dan.	Daniel
Hos.	Hosea
Joel	Joel
Amos	Amos
Obad.	Obadiah
Jonah	Jonah
Mic.	Micah
Nah.	Nahum
Hab.	Habakkuk
Zeph.	Zephaniah
Hag.	Haggai
Zech.	Zechariah
Mal.	Malachi

New Testament

Matt.	Matthew
Mark	Mark
Luke	Luke

New Testament (continued)

John	John
Acts	Acts
Rom.	Romans
1 Cor.	1 Corinthians
2 Cor.	2 Corinthians
Gal.	Galatians
Eph.	Ephesians
Phil.	Philippians
Col.	Colossians
1 Thess.	1 Thessalonians
2 Thess.	2 Thessalonians
1 Tim.	1 Timothy
2 Tim.	2 Timothy
Titus	Titus
Philem.	Philemon
Heb.	Hebrews
James	James
1 Peter	1 Peter
2 Peter	2 Peter
1 John	1 John
2 John	2 John
3 John	3 John
Jude	Jude
Rev.	Revelation

PERIODICALS

BBR	Bulletin for Biblical Research
Bib	Biblica
BR	Biblical Research
BSac	Bibliotheca Sacra
CBQ	Catholic Biblical Quarterly
CTM	Concordia Theological Monthly
JBL	Journal of Biblical Literature
JETS	Journal of the Evangelical Theological Society
JSNT	Journal for the Study of the New Testament
JTI	Journal of Theological Interpretation
Neot	Neotestamentica
NTS	New Testament Studies
RBL	Review of Biblical Literature
ResQ	Restoration Quarterly
RTR	Reformed Theological Review
TJ	Trinity Journal
TynBul	Tyndale Bulletin

WTJ	*Westminster Theological Journal*
ZNW	*Zeitschrift für die neutestamentliche Wissenschaft und die Kunde der älteren Kirche*

REFERENCE

BDAG	Danker, Frederick W., Walter Bauer, William F. Arndt, and F. Wilbur Gingrich. 2000. *Greek-English Lexicon of the New Testament and Other Early Christian Literature.* 3rd ed. Chicago: University of Chicago Press.
NIDNTT	Brown, C., ed. 1975–1978. *New International Dictionary of New Testament Theology.* 4 vols. Grand Rapids: Zondervan.
NIDNTTE	Silva, M., ed. 2014. *New International Dictionary of New Testament Theology and Exegesis.* 5 vols. Grand Rapids: Zondervan.

BIBLE TRANSLATIONS

CSB	Christian Standard Bible
ESV	English Standard Version
KJV	King James Version
LEB	Lexham English Bible
LXX	Septuagint
NASB	New American Standard Bible
NET	New English Translation
NIV	New International Version (2011)
NKJV	New King James Version
NLT	New Living Translation
NRSV	New Revised Standard Version

INTRODUCTION TO 1 PETER

OVERVIEW OF 1 PETER

Author: Peter, the chief apostle of Jesus Christ.

Readers: Peter writes to saints in the northern Roman provinces of Anatolia (Asia Minor and Galatia): Pontus, Galatia, Cappadocia, Asia, and Bithynia. They were likely Gentiles.

Provenance: Peter is in Rome (5:13).

Date: A date between A.D. 62–68 best fits the data.

Historical Setting: The Anatolian believers had experienced the new birth, and this set them apart from their countrymen. Their actions now appeared strange and resulted in persecution. Peter writes to encourage them to remain faithful, for their present rejection is a sure sign of God's acceptance.

Occasion: The immediate occasion for the epistle appears to be the sharp opposition the readers were facing because of their faith.

Theological Emphasis: The letter highlights the reader's identity, election, suffering, and holiness.

AUTHORSHIP OF 1 PETER

First Peter enjoyed early and wide support as being apostolic and therefore canonical. The case for Petrine authorship can be divided into internal and external evidence.

External Evidence

If, as many believe, 2 Peter 3:1 is speaking of 1 Peter when it said, "this is now my second letter to you," then that passage records the earliest record we have of 1 Peter.

Beyond the inner biblical testimony, early writers close to the apostolic era cite from 1 Peter. For example, Clement of Rome (A.D. 30–110), Papias (A.D. 60–130), and Polycarp (A.D. 70–155)[1] each have citations that appear

---

1   Clement of Rome (A.D. 30–110), Papias (A.D. 60–130), and Polycarp (A.D. 70–155). Clement was a bishop in Rome at the end of the apostolic period (A.D. 88–99). In his commentary, Elliott details the similarities between 1 Peter and 1 Clement, noting that "the numerous lexical and thematic affinities that they share make it likely that Clemens Romanus knew and alluded to 1 Peter" (Elliott, 2001, 138). Papias, a bishop of Hieropolis in Asia Minor, is recorded by Eusebius as using "testimonies from the first Epistle of John and from that of Peter likewise" (*Hist. eccl. 3.39.16*; trans. McGiffert). This latter book is believed to be 1 Peter. Finally, Polycarp,

to come from 1 Peter, though none of them actually identify the letter as being from Peter. Irenaeus (A.D. 140–203), Tertullian (A.D. 150–222), and Clement of Alexandria (A.D. 155–220)[2] coming just a few years later, do identify Peter as the author.

The Muratorian Canon (ca. 160–180)[3] appears not to have included 1 Peter (it also omits 2 Peter, Hebrews, and James), though due to the decay of the manuscript evidence we cannot be sure. Eusebius (265–340) categorized it among the books that are recognized by the church as authentic and canonical. He expressly states, "[it] was anciently used by the . . . fathers in their writings, as an undoubted work of the apostle" (*Hist. eccl.* 3.3; trans. McGiffert).

Internal Evidence

In the opening verse, the writer affirms that he is "Peter, an apostle of Jesus Christ." In 5:1 he calls himself a "witness of the sufferings of Christ," a statement that is true of the historical Peter (see the comments on the passage below). Further, in 5:13, the writer calls Mark, "my son." Such a designation is in accordance with early church testimony, which closely associates Peter and Mark.

The use of Jesus's words and actions in the body of 1 Peter should also be considered here. Of course, some might argue that someone falsely writing in Peter's name (a pseudonymous author) intentionally echoed the words and actions of Jesus to give the story more credibility. Nevertheless, we can say that the way the traditions concerning Jesus are used throughout the letter is consistent with Peter being the author.

Despite the traditional view, there are five main arguments against Peter's authorship. First, some have argued that the Greek is too good for a Galilean fisherman, especially since Peter is described in Acts 4:13 as "uneducated and untrained." Yet, the context of Acts 4 also shows the surprise of the Jewish leaders concerning Peter's skill despite the lack of formal

---

a second-century bishop of Smyrna, was also said by Eusebius to have "made use of certain testimonies drawn from the First Epistle of Peter" (*Hist. eccl.* 4.14.9; trans. McGiffert). Elliott has a helpful comparison of analogous points between Polycarp's *Letter to the Philippians* and 1 Peter (Elliott, 2001, 143).

2   Irenaeus (A.D. 140–203), Tertullian (A.D. 150–222), and Clement of Alexandria (A.D. 155–220). Irenaeus, though best known as a bishop in Lyons, had connections to both Asia Minor and Rome. He explicitly references Peter as the writer of the text as he cites 1 Peter 1:8: "Peter says in this epistle" (*Haer.* 4.9.2). Tertullian of Carthage also notes Peter as the author, for prior to quoting a section of the epistle he notes that "Addressing the Christians of Pontus, Peter, at all events, says" (*Scorp.* 12; trans. Alexander, Donaldson, and Coxe). Finally, Clement of Alexandria frequently ascribes comments from 1 Peter to the apostle Peter (e.g., *Paed* 1.6; 3.11; 3.12).

3   The Muratorian Canon (ca. 160–180). This document was discovered in the Ambrosian Library (Milan, Italy) by an Italian historian, L. A. Muratori. The anonymous eighth-century Latin document represents the first known collection of New Testament books. The fragment was published in 1740 and takes its name after its founder, Muratori. The fragment contains a list of twenty-two of the twenty-seven canonical books of the New Testament which are for "the whole Church" and which are deemed "apostolic" and may therefore be "publicly read in the Church." The following books are listed in Muratori's canon:

Matthew	Galatians	Titus
Mark	Ephesians	Philemon
Luke	Philippians	1 John
John	Colossians	2 John
Acts	1 Thessalonians	Jude
Romans	2 Thessalonians	Revelation
1 Corinthians	1 Timothy	
2 Corinthians	2 Timothy	

Saint Peter by Marco Zoppo. Public domain.

rabbinical training (Achtemeier, 1996, 7). Accordingly, such a passage says nothing about Peter's ability to write in Greek, and in fact may suggest he had language skills far beyond the average fisherman.

As for whether a Galilean *fisherman* could author the text, a few things may be said. First, some studies have suggested that those from Judea would have been trilingual, having some facility in Greek, Aramaic, and Hebrew (Gundry, 1964; Porter, 1993). Accordingly, Peter would likely have known Greek. Second, even if Peter's Greek was not good, he may have grown in his use of Greek through time as he functioned in

his leadership role within the early church. Finally, according to the quantitative textual analysis of Karen Jobes, the letter of 1 Peter is not outstanding Greek and it was likely written by someone whose first language was not Greek (Jobes, 2005, 325–38). These facts, though not requiring Petrine authorship, are consistent with it.

Second, some have suggested that 1 Peter is literarily dependent on the Pauline writings, which makes Petrine authorship unlikely since Peter was one of the original disciples of Christ. But the claim that 1 Peter is literarily dependent on Romans or Ephesians, though once popular, is very rarely argued today—and for good reason. It is much more likely that the early church was interconnected (Thompson, 1998, 49–70). Thus, the themes presented in 1 Peter share similarity with language in other Pauline epistles because the early church shared language more broadly. Indeed, 2 Peter 3:15–16 indicates that Peter knew Paul's writings. As both were apostles who had received revelation from the Lord, we should not be surprised to find echoes of the same themes from both.

Third, some have argued that the epistle lacks enough engagement with the words and life of Jesus to come from the fingers of Peter, an original disciple. But it is not clear there is a way to calculate how much Peter would engage the words and life of Jesus in a letter. Accordingly, an argument of this fashion is subjective. Additionally, there is much controversy concerning how much the author of 1 Peter does engage the words and works of Jesus. As for this commentary, we find much engagement, but others find less. Indeed, we find so much engagement that we have included this as one of the potential arguments for Peter's authorship (see below).

Fourth, some have argued that the persecution spoken of in 1 Peter only occurs after the lifetime of the apostle, whether during the reign of Domitian (A.D. 81–96) or Trajan (A.D. 98–117). Yet while some have argued that the persecution in 1 Peter is state-sponsored, there is little in the text to support this claim. Instead, the type of persecution described is social in nature (see the section on suffering as a theological theme of 1 Peter below). And even if there were some elements of state-sponsored persecution, such bouts of persecution need not be empire-wide. Far from indicating a post-Petrine date, the suffering context suggested by the letter of 1 Peter is consistent with nearly any period of the first century.

Fifth, some suggest that an author like Peter would not have used the Septuagint, but the author of 1 Peter clearly uses it as the choice for his Old Testament citations. It is clear, however, that the Septuagint was the Bible of the early church and especially that of the region to which Peter was writing. Accordingly, it is logical that Peter would reference the text known by all.

Those who find Peter's authorship doubtful generally suggest one of three other possibilities. First, some argue that the letter is pseudonymous/pseudepigraphal, attaching the name of the apostle in order to gain (illegitimate) authority for the epistle (Achtemeier, 1996, 41). Others argue that there was a "Petrine circle" that consisted of those faithful to the view of Peter, who after Peter's death published the letter in his name (Elliott, 2001, 131). Finally, some suggest the letter was written in an attempt by those at Rome to unite diverse strands of the Christian tradition and present a new synthesis of Christian tradition (Horrell, 2002, 29–60).

In conclusion, the external and internal evidence for authorship support Peter or are at least consistent with him being the author. And though other theories have been expressed, there does not seem to be sufficient reason to go beyond the bald statement of the text that Peter is the author. Of course, it is possible that Peter used an amanuensis, and some have suggested this to alleviate some of the difficulties noted

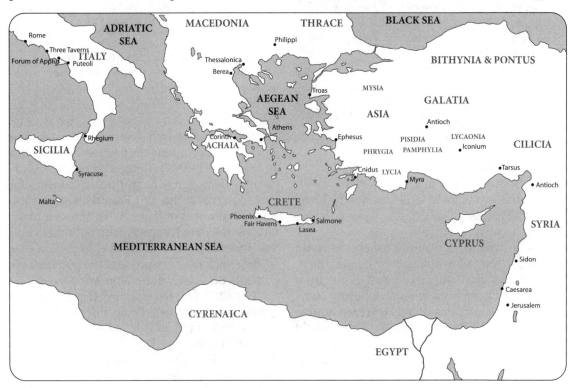

above (e.g., the quality of the Greek, the use of the Septuagint). In fact, it used to be argued that 1 Peter 5:12 gave evidence that Silas was an amanuensis for Peter. This has become more debated in recent scholarship (Richards, 2000). Regardless, the above argumentation shows that even without proposing an amanuensis, Peter's authorship can be fruitfully maintained.

RECIPIENTS

In one sense, the identity of the recipients is clear. They are those who were then residing in Anatolia, the northern Roman provinces of Asia Minor and Galatia: Pontus, Galatia, Cappadocia, Asia, and Bithynia.

The critical question, however, concerns their background, not their current location. More specifically, are they Jews or Gentiles? There are several arguments in favor of a Jewish audience.

First, the letter describes the readers as exiles in dispersion (παρεπιδήμοις διασπορᾶς; 1:1). While not demanding a Jewish audience, such a phrase certainly has historical connections with the Jewish people. Indeed, James 1:1 opens his letter to Jewish Christians describing them as the "twelve tribes in the dispersion" (διασπορᾷ).

Second, Peter applies terminology that is unique to Israel in the Old Testament Scriptures. This is seen most explicitly in 2:9–10, where the readers are referred to as a "race," a "nation," and a chosen "people." Third, 1 Peter cites the Old Testament with great frequency. Such citations suggest that his audience was familiar with and believed in the authority of these Scriptures. Finally, Scripture and church history confirm that Peter was an apostle to the Jews (Gal. 2:7–8). Accordingly, it is logical to assume that he would write to those he was commissioned to serve.

Alternatively, there are arguments in favor of a Gentile audience. First, the geographical regions to which the letter is written are predominantly Gentile. Accordingly, one would expect a Gentile audience if the letter does not make a Jewish audience explicit. Second, the vice lists present in the letter suggest a Gentile audience. For example, Peter speaks of the readers' past, which included "living in sensuality, passions, drunkenness, orgies, drinking parties, and lawless idolatry" (4:3). Of course, such past activities are not entirely absent from a Jewish audience, but they would have been characteristic of a Gentile audience.

Finally, perhaps the strongest argument in favor of a Gentile audience is Peter's description of the readers' past religious life. He indicates that they were formerly "ignorant" needing to be "ransomed from the futile ways inherited from [their] forefathers" (1:14, 18). Would Peter describe a Jewish heritage as "futile"? Of course, Peter could be referring to the unfaithful lifestyle passed down by unbelieving Jews, but the language seems to suggest that the entire path of the readers was wrong and needed to be redirected.

In our estimation, the evidence leans in favor of a Gentile audience, particularly because good responses can be given to the Jewish-audience arguments above.

First, while both James and Peter begin their letters with a statement about the dispersion, such statements are not parallel. James explicitly notes that he is writing to a Jewish audience by referencing the readers as "the twelve tribes." Peter lacks such a direct attribution. Further, Peter begins his letter with rich metaphorical emphasis. The readers are not physically exiles or strangers (1:1; 2:11; see the discussion below), yet they are these things spiritually. In the same way, Peter uses the image of diaspora not in a literal way, but to reference a dispersion away from one's spiritual homeland.

Second, that Peter uses terms once exclusively used of ethnic Israel is one of the most significant reasons to maintain a Jewish audience. Nevertheless, as Peter describes the significant place of the church in God's current program, he finds ready analogies between the relationship God had with Israel and the relationship he maintains with the church. Such attributions do not necessarily imply that the church replaces Israel (see the commentary below); all they suggest is that there is some rich analogy between the two groups.

Third, that Peter cites the Old Testament with great frequency says little about the audience for the simple reason that the Old Testament was the Bible of the church. The Old Testament was frequently read and consulted in the early church and Gentile converts would have been trained in its teachings. Accordingly, frequent use of the Old Testament would be expected whether the audience was Jewish or Gentile. In support of this point, we may observe that Romans has one of the highest frequencies of quotations of the Old Testament and is widely recognized to have been written to a Gentile audience.

Finally, while it is undoubted that Peter was the apostle to the Jews, this did not exclude his ministry among Gentiles (e.g., Acts 10:1–47), just as Paul's ministry to the Gentiles did not hinder his ministry among the Jews (e.g., Acts 17:1–2). Accordingly, ministry among Gentiles cannot be excluded on the basis of his primary calling.

So, in conclusion, while there were likely some Jews in the church, according to the evidence assessed above, the composition of the assembly appears to have been primarily Gentile.

PLACE OF WRITING

The location of writing is given cryptically in the second to last verse of the letter: "She who is at Babylon, who is likewise chosen, sends you greetings, and so does Mark, my son." The term "Babylon" has engendered debate. The following are options for understanding the term.

(a) *The ancient city of Babylon in Mesopotamia.* On a literal reading, Peter is referring to the city that has played a significant role in Israel's past. Nevertheless, due to that significant role and the fact that the

city was "virtually desolate in the first century CE" (Elliott, 2001, 132), it is better to take this as a metaphorical designation.

(b) *A city called Babylon in Egypt on the Nile.* This location would also allow the term Babylon to be taken literally. A few things make the location possible. First, there is a Coptic church tradition that says Peter wrote from there. Second, tradition also indicates that Mark evangelized Alexandria, establishing churches in the region. Peter, who calls Mark his son, may have been visiting these churches while he wrote the letter (Compton, 2019, 15).

(c) *The city of Rome.* Scholars almost unanimously support Rome as the place metaphorically described by the term Babylon. Such a designation is appropriate considering the increasing tension between Rome and Christians. Rome, like ancient Babylon, was antagonistic toward God's people. Further, church history associates both Peter and Mark with Rome. Finally, calling Rome Babylon is found within Jewish literature of the New Testament period (2 Bar. 11.1–2; 67.7; Sib. Or. 5.143, 159–61) and is found in the New Testament as well (Rev. 14:8; 16:19).

(d) *No specific city.* It is possible that Peter is not actually indicating a place of origin at all. Instead, the designation of Babylon simply highlights Peter's exilic status. Jobes, partially quoting Paul Achtemeier, gives voice to this position: "'Babylon' forms an inclusio with 'Diaspora' in the opening verse and thus functions 'to identify both the author and his Christian community as sharing with the readers such exile status'" (Jobes, 2005, 323).

In conclusion, while an entirely metaphorical designation not reflecting any particular city is possible, the feminine article (ἡ, "the") suggests a personification of the church in Babylon. And since this church sends greetings, it is likely that a specific location is meant, for what would it mean if the church at large—that is, all those in exile—sent greeting? The most likely specific designation is Rome, and that is the position that will be assumed in this commentary.

DATE OF WRITING

The date of the epistle is based chiefly on one's view of authorship and the type of persecution mentioned in the letter. For those who believe Peter did not write the epistle and believe the persecution spoken of in the letter is governmental, the likely date is during the reign of Domitian (A.D. 81–96). Any later date seems less probable due to the use of 1 Peter in 1 Clement (dated somewhere between A.D. 90–125).

Maintaining genuine authorship by Peter limits the possible date range significantly. Since Peter is reported to have died at the hand of Nero (*Hist. eccl.* 2.25.5–8), the latest date for the letter would be A.D. 68. Because the church does not appear to be new, a date somewhere in the 60s is most likely. The most likely date falls between A.D. 62–68.

HISTORICAL SETTING

Our exploration of the historical setting is organized into three parts. First, we must consider the rule of Nero and the effects of that rule. Second, we will examine the geographical regions addressed, seeking to understand the cultural and social situation of the readers. Finally, we will consider the religious setting, particularly the role of the imperial cult.

First, Peter wrote (ca. 64) while Nero was emperor of the Roman Empire. Nero had been adopted by his great-uncle Claudius and became Claudius's heir and successor. Like Claudius, Nero became emperor with the consent of the Praetorian Guard, and he began his rule in A.D. 54 at the age of sixteen. He was

nearing the end of his reign (A.D. 68). Though best known for the burning of Rome (July A.D. 64), during the latter part of his reign, the "Peace of Rome" (*Pax Romana*) was in jeopardy due, in part, to the Jewish riots in Judea (Bateman, 2017, 51–79). With Nero's death, the Julio-Claudian dynasty came to an end.

Julio-Claudian Dynasty
Augustus (27 B.C.–A.D. 14)
Tiberius (14–37)
Caligula (37–41)
Claudius (41–54)
Nero (54–68)

Despite the clear historical case for Nero's persecution of Christians, commentators have been reticent to suggest a state-sponsored form of persecution in 1 Peter. This is due to two factors. First, Nero's persecutions appear to have centered on Rome and there is sparse evidence it was empire-wide. Second, the text of 1 Peter offers no clear state-sponsored forms of persecution. Instead, the challenge they faced appears to have been local and personal rather than empire-wide and political.

Though the lack of state-sponsored persecution has been the consensus of scholarship over the last generation, some are beginning to propose an alternative interpretation. Travis Williams, for example, has argued for a "middle" way between personal, social suffering and state-sponsored persecution (Williams, 2012, 275–86). On this reading, the persecution begins as personal and social but can proceed to public and civil based on a verbal accusation. The crime would be the accused's identity as a Christian.

It seems to us most likely that this middle way is right. The events in Judea are upsetting things in Rome, and Peter's readers, situated between Rome and Judea, are not immune to the effects. Though the primary form of this persecution was personal and verbal, the Roman government had showed a willingness to oppose all that threatened the peace of Rome, including Christianity. Consequently, the threat for Peter's readers was primarily social, but could easily transition into the civil realm.

Our second area of historical interest is the geographical regions to which Peter wrote. The five locales Peter mentions in the first verse of the epistle (Pontus, Galatia, Cappadocia, Asia, and Bithynia) are representative of four Roman provinces (Pontus and Bithynia were united as a single province). The geographical breadth is 129,000 square miles and is roughly the size of the state of Montana (Elliott, 2001, 85). Prior to being integrated into the Roman Empire, these regions were composed of independent nations; they were conquered and annexed in the eastward progression of Roman rule beginning in 133 B.C.

Two of the provinces (Asia and Pontus-Bithynia[4]) had coastal access and thus were open to trade and experienced the cultural effects (i.e., Hellenization) that accompanied trade. The other two provinces (Galatia and Cappadocia[5]) were landlocked and mountainous,

resulting in sparser population. Overall, these areas are much more rural than the urban areas generally addressed by New Testament letters. In such settings, social identity is often tied to acceptance within the community. It is unsurprising then that identity is a central component of 1 Peter.

Before leaving the historical analysis, it is important to consider the religious milieu of Asia Minor. Religious belief in Asia Minor was diverse, and the Roman system made room for the belief systems of the various peoples, including the Jewish people. Differences of belief were tolerated to the degree that they did not cause social disruption or present a challenge to the political power of Rome. On the surface, then, one would imagine Christianity would be able to assert itself as a variant of Jewish belief and proceed without hindrance. However, the Romans did not look positively on religions that proselytized and changed the views and practices of Romans. Further, being viewed alongside Judaism had its own problems, as the opposition to Rome in Judea was intensifying.

---

4   Asia and Pontus-Bithynia. Asia was the most hellenized of the provinces to which Peter wrote. Previously, this area was the home of the kingdom of Pergamum, a chief kingdom of ancient Anatolia. Due to a lack of a successor, the last king of Anatolia granted the kingdom to Rome in 133 B.C. Because of its access to trade routes and its manufacturing, this province was the financial powerhouse of the region.

     Pontus and Bithynia were not always united. In fact, the kingdom of Pontus, which warred with the Romans for many years, was conquered and broken into sections that were annexed to the other provinces in 63 B.C. A major section was annexed with Bithynia, forming a Pontus-Bithynia province. Other areas were annexed to Cappadocia and Galatia. Some from Pontus were present in Jerusalem at Pentecost (Acts 2:9) and may have brought the gospel to this region. Around fifty years after the writing of 1 Peter, Pliny the Younger wrote a famous letter to Trajan (*Letters* 10.96–97) about how to handle Christian converts. The importance of the letter for our purposes is that it shows a large, seemingly growing population of Christians in the region. Further, it shows that the Romans were willing to persecute—even kill—Christians for their religious beliefs. Of course, we cannot draw a straight line between the situation of the letter and the situation of 1 Peter, but the parallels are interesting.

5   Galatia and Cappadocia. Galatia was named for the Gauls who migrated there from Europe. Over many years the territory was annexed to Rome, being completed in 25 B.C. The area was heavily rural and lacked significant hellenization. No major cities are spoken of in this region. The same can be said of Cappadocia, which was a mountainous region. It had many military outposts and was a substantial defense against invaders from the East. The province was once a central place in the Hittite Empire. Conquered and divided by the Persians, it later passed into the rule of one of Alexander the Great's successors. It was eventually conquered by Pompey but became an official province in A.D. 17.

More significantly for those in Asia Minor, however, was the role of the imperial cult and the way that it caused conflict with Christianity. The imperial cult was not a monolithic reality; rather, it differed from region to region and from emperor to emperor. The cult became prominent with the ascension of Julius Caesar. Though he did not allow people to worship him as divine, he allowed the building of temples in his name. And while there was no widespread demand for imperial worship in A.D. 60, its role in Anatolia was more prominent than most other places.

The importance of the imperial cult was due to the political and social situation of the region. Achtemeier indicates how the imperial cult operated for *both* Rome and Anatolia: "On the one hand, for Rome it provided a convenient way to allow various cities to show their loyalty to the empire.... For the provinces, on the other hand, it was a way to allow them to fit the political reality of their subjugation to Rome into the context of their ancient Greek culture, a culture that had provided a framework for subjugation in the form of cultic reverence for the gods" (Achtemeier, 1996, 27). In other words, Rome appreciated the imperial cult, for it allowed an avenue for Anatolia to show its political subjugation. Anatolia appreciated the cult for the way that it solidified the social identity of the region, which with its diverse background had little other social unity.

Understanding the imperial cult's influence in Anatolia helps to make sense of the message of 1 Peter. First, since the social cohesion of this region was at least partly formed by the imperial cult, Christians found themselves as outsiders socially. Knowing this background helps us to make sense of Peter's focus on the identity of the readers as chosen by God. Second, as noted above, the form of persecution suggested throughout 1 Peter is primarily social, and this background gives us some clue as to why that is. By rejecting the imperial cult, Christians were threatening the social unity of the region. And

since such actions could be viewed as a threat to Rome, for it was through the imperial cult that allegiance to Rome was symbolized, then the persecution could turn from social mockery to civil accusation quickly.

OCCASION FOR WRITING

Peter provides the occasion for writing in 5:12: "I have written briefly to you, exhorting and declaring that this is the true grace of God. Stand firm in it." The believers living throughout Anatolia were experiencing social estrangement and hostility due to their embrace of Christ. Peter was writing to confirm that such experiences are consistent with their calling in Christ, for they are following the same path as the Messiah. Accordingly, they must remain true to the gospel, recognizing that God is sovereign over their experiences and resting in the knowledge that one day they will receive eternal rewards for their faithfulness.

The most debated element of the occasion regards what Peter means when he calls the readers "exiles" (παρεπιδήμους; 1:1; 2:11) and "foreigners" (παροίκους; 2:11). The key question is whether these terms were intended to reflect the historical-social situation or the metaphorical-spiritual identity of the readers.

John H. Elliott has been the chief defender of the claim that these designations were *primarily* social in nature (Elliott, 2001, 2005). For Elliott, 1 Peter best makes sense when read in light of a historical situation in which people were displaced from their homeland. After they became believers, a metaphorical sense was also possible, yet such a metaphorical use is appropriate only because there is a true, social-historical foundation supporting it.

Jobes offers a similar argument, with one significant difference (Jobes, 2005, 28–41). For Jobes, the exiles in 1 Peter were believers *prior to becoming exiles*. As a result of the Claudian expulsion of Jews from Rome, these believers were resettled (in a colonization effort) to these regions of Asia. Such a historical explanation suggests why Peter would know the audience, for he was likely in Rome when the expulsion was carried out. Thus, Peter is connecting with those he already knew, who have now become exiles in a land that is not their own. Like Elliott, Jobes sees the metaphorical elements as extensions of the social-historical element.

The positions of Elliott and Jobes should not be dismissed lightly; nevertheless, there is some reason to read these terms in a primarily metaphorical sense (cf. Chin, 1991, 96–112). For example, 1 Peter is rich in Old Testament references, and this makes it possible that Peter used these terms to reflect the sociological unity that exists between these believers and their Old Testament forbearers. Further, many commentators have noted that Peter refers to his redeemed Gentile audience in terms once spoken regarding Israel (e.g., 2:9–10). In light of these facts, one could see Peter using these terms metaphorically in light of the Old Testament presentation of these terms.

The combination in 2:11 of "sojourner" (παρεπιδήμους) with "foreigner" (παροίκους) traces back to the same combination in Genesis 23:4 (cf. Ps. 23:4), which speaks of Abraham being in the land of promise without being at home there. In the words of Jobes, "The view that the terms . . . are used metaphorically of Peter's Christian readers is justified because these terms occur in the Septuagint to describe God's ancient people Israel in their various historical situations."[6] Indeed, if Peter is using this language metaphorically, he is using it in a similar way to Hebrews 11:13 (though Hebrews uses a translation equivalent [ξένοι instead of παροίκους]). There people of faith are described as those awaiting a city and homeland who have accepted their present status as exiles and foreigners on the earth.

THEOLOGICAL EMPHASES

First Peter is a rich document with many theological emphases that speak as powerfully today as they did when the letter was first written. Following Peter's Trinitarian emphasis, we will develop these themes in relation to the three persons of the Trinity. Accordingly, we will highlight the role of the Father in election, the Spirit in sanctification, and the Son in suffering. Following this triad, we will consider the readers as elect-exiles, which in 1 Peter is a result of Trinitarian action.

Election: God's Sovereignty in History

Peter began his letter by indicating that the readers had become elect-exiles "according to the foreknowledge of God the Father." Such language connected the readers to God's eternal plan of redemption. A few verses later, Peter indicated that Jesus was *foreknown* from the foundation of the world. The implication is that, like Jesus, the readers were foreknown in God's eternal redemptive plan (1:20). Peter also ended the letter by reminding the readers that they were chosen (5:13).

This eternal redemptive plan was communicated through the prophets, who knew they were serving a future audience. Peter indicated that the readers were that audience (1:12); they were the ones who experience the blessing of the fulfillment of prophecy. It is for them that the Father raised Jesus so that they might experience new birth (1:20–21).

In chapter 2, Peter contrasted believers in these Roman provinces with those who rejected Jesus. The readers were chosen and precious stones (2:5) who followed Jesus, *the* chosen and precious cornerstone (2:4). Jesus laid the foundation, and these readers were sovereignly selected to play a part in the building. Indeed, they were called a "chosen race," highlighting their identity based on the Father's sovereign choice

---

6   Gen. 15:13; 23:4; Exod. 2:22; Lev. 25:23; Deut. 23:8 (23:7 Eng.); 1 Chron. 29:15; Pss. 38:13 (39:12 Eng.); 104:12–13 (105:12–13 Eng.); 118:19 (119:19 Eng.).

(2:9–10). On the other hand, those who rejected Jesus did so because "they disobey the word, to which they were also destined" (2:8).

God's sovereignty was not limited to the blessings of salvation, however. We have already seen that God's sovereignty related to his building of the church (2:5) and this extended to his gifting people for the precise purposes he had within the church (4:10–11). God's sovereignty also encompassed the suffering of Christians. More will be said about the theme of suffering below. Here we simply note that 1 Peter stresses that God is sovereign over suffering. In 1:6 Peter noted that God plans the trials and suffering of his people in order to refine them, a theme he returned to in 4:12–16. In two places Peter explicitly spoke of suffering as a result of God's will (3:17; 4:19).

Suffering: Following the Steps of Jesus

While the Father sovereignly ordained the suffering of his people (see above), such suffering was directly connected to the work of Christ. The readers followed in the steps of Christ: "For to [suffering for doing good] you were called because Christ also suffered for you leaving you an example, so that you should follow in his steps" (2:21).

The logic of Peter proceeds in the following fashion. Since Jesus was the chosen stone who suffered, those stones chosen after him must likewise suffer. This follows the words of Jesus, who said that if he was persecuted, those who follow him must be persecuted as well (John 15:20). It is for this reason that Peter told his audience *not* to be surprised at the trials of persecution that came upon them (4:12). It is also for this reason that Peter could confidently say that the sufferings these saints were enduring were also being endured throughout the world by Christian brothers and sisters (5:9). Indeed, suffering was a necessity of Christian life (1:6).

Unique to the early church was the perspective shared by James (1:2), Paul (Rom. 5:3), and Peter (1 Peter 1:6) that trials and sufferings were to be a source of rejoicing. Of course, this idea derives ultimately from the words of Jesus, whose last beatitude indicated the blessing of those who suffered for righteousness (Matt. 5:10).

Peter offered substantial reasons to rejoice in suffering. First, rejoicing indicated that one was rightly related to God. As noted above, if Jesus suffered, those who follow Jesus should expect suffering as well. To the degree that one suffers, he or she identifies with Christ and, in the language of 1 Peter, "shares Christ's sufferings" (4:13). Indeed, those who were insulted for Christ could have confidence that "the spirit of glory and of God" rested on them (4:14).

Second, suffering had both eternal and temporal rewards. Just as Jesus said that those who were persecuted would have a "great reward" in heaven (Matt. 5:11), so Peter suggested the same. Those who suffered and passed the test of suffering would receive "glory, honor, and praise at the revelation of Jesus Christ" (1:8). On the temporal side, suffering was a part of the process God used to refine his people and show them to be righteous at the coming judgment (4:15–19).

The theme of suffering weaves through 1 Peter and appears in every chapter. Nevertheless, Peter began the letter and ended it with a reminder that suffering is only temporary. In 1:6, he indicated that the suffering was only for a "little while" (ὀλίγον). In 5:10, Peter used the same word when he noted that they must suffer for a "little while" (ὀλίγον) and then their redemption will come. Thus, while suffering may be the expected situation in this world, this world will pass away quickly and be replaced by eternal joy.

Holiness: The Work of the Spirit

Peter indicated that the readers were elect-exiles *through* (ἐν) the sanctification of the Spirit (1:2). By this Peter indicated that it was the work of the Holy Spirit that made these believers elect-exiles. While Peter infrequently drew direct attention to the Spirit (1:11, 12; 4:14), the work of the Spirit is assumed throughout the text wherever the call to holiness was extended, for it was the Spirit who sanctified.

After describing the change of the readers as a new birth, Peter indicated that as newborn children, they had to become holy as the Lord is holy (1:16). Further, he noted that such transformation is to be understood as a ransoming from the "futile ways" handed down from the readers' forefathers (1:18). The believers were newborn citizens of a new people, and they had to act like their heavenly Father.

Such a situation caused great friction in their age, for now these new believers rejected their former way of life along with its associated activities. Such a rejection was a fruit of the Spirit, and its result was suffering at the hands of unbelievers. Those whose way of life had been rejected recognized the implicit criticism in the rejection, and they responded initially with surprise and then with slanderous words (4:4). Accordingly, it is the work of the Spirit that made the readers exiles, for they had become new people because of the work of the Spirit.

Elect-Exiles: The Readers as the People of God

The identity of the people of God in 1 Peter brings together the themes we have addressed above. Indeed, the whole of 1 Peter was intended to emphasize the unique and important position the believers in Asia Minor had both historically and eschatologically.

They were sovereignly chosen by God to experience the new birth, which made them exiles in their prior homeland. The Spirit motivated the believers toward holiness, which created the distance between believers and their former relations. This led to suffering and persecution, which God used to refine his people. Nevertheless, the tension between the terms *elect* and *exile* was jarring, and Peter wanted to draw that contrast out.

In regard to God, they were chosen and precious. They were carefully selected stones that were being wisely set in their proper place by the Wise Builder. And though they were a holy nation (2:9), the earth was not their kingdom. Accordingly, they had to live honorable lives in exile, awaiting the redemption that calls them home (2:11).

In regard to men, the believers in Asia Minor were exiles. They were odd strangers whose actions were at one and the same time honorable and curious. Honorable, because they were the best citizens in many ways (they showed obedience to the emperor, submission to the law, and submitted to social customs). Nevertheless, they rejected what men generally crave—indeed, what the readers themselves once craved!

Thus, the life of the elect-exile was one of tension. The believers in Asia Minor were at one and the same time beloved (by God) and rejected (by men; cf. 4:6). They endured sorrow (because of persecution), but experienced true joy (because of the hope of the gospel; 4:13–16). They feared God, and thus had no one to fear (3:14).

The result of this paradoxical identity is that the readers were able to reflect God to the world. When they acted in righteousness, they acted as children of God showing the character of the Father. In the words of both Jesus and Peter, the readers could live in such a way that others saw their good deeds and gave glory to the heavenly Father (Matt. 5:16; 1 Peter 2:12). Accordingly, Peter did not directly tell his readers to take the gospel to unbelievers; instead, he assumed that as they were faithful to God, their unique lifestyle would cause unbelievers to question, opening the door for a proclamation of the gospel (3:13–17).

Peter finished the letter indicating that his point in writing was to encourage the readers to stand strong in the faith (5:12). He did so primarily by reminding them who they were. They were elect-exiles, and while their exilic identity was causing difficulty and pain, these would be short-lived. The Lord would return, and their short time of suffering would be worth it. For the time being, they had to focus on the positive side of exilic status. The tension they experienced was due to being chosen by God and was not evidence that they were rejected by God. Further, living rightly in the present led to reward and opportunity for witness.

While the roaring enemy prowled (5:8), Peter encouraged his readers that their endurance was a matter with which God involved himself. It is through God's power that they were guarded through faith for salvation (1:5). Indeed, the God they served is a "God of grace" and since he called them "to his eternal glory in Christ," he would also "restore, confirm, strengthen, and establish" them (5:10).

SOURCES

The two major sources for the letter of 1 Peter are the Old Testament and the words of Jesus.

Old Testament

First Peter is overflowing with Old Testament references, whether quotations, allusions,

or echoes (Glenny, 1987; Greaux, 2003; McCartney, 1989; Woan, 2008). Yet, only a few quotations are explicitly identified with words of introduction (1:16, 24–25; 2:6–8; 3:10–12). Other quotations are easily recognized by the strength of their lexical similarity with the Septuagint. Many more Old Testament passages are alluded to, and the nature of allusion makes an exact figure difficult to pin down, but scholars find somewhere between thirty and forty allusions (Carson, 2007, 1015). The least significant intertextual resonances are passages that merely echo the Old Testament. Due to their elusive nature, we will not seek to identify them. Nevertheless, D. A. Carson says that if we add together the three forms of reference, "scarcely a verse in this epistle would be exempt" from our study (Carson, 2007, 1015).

The following chart identifies where the references are located. They are not evenly distributed throughout the Old Testament; Peter showed a fondness for Isaiah and Psalm 34.

Old Testament Quotations and Allusions in 1 Peter (Modified from Woan, 2008, 269–70)		
1 Peter Reference	**Old Testament Source**	**Type of Reference**
1:16	Lev. 19:2	Marked Quotation
1:18	Isa. 52:3	Allusion
1:24–25	Isa. 40:6–8	Marked Quotation
1:25b	Isa. 40:9	Allusion
2:1	Ps. 34:13	Allusion
2:3	Ps. 34:8	Nonmarked Quotation
2:4c	Ps. 118:22	Allusion
2:4d	Isa. 28:16	Strong Allusion
2:6	Isa. 28:16	Marked Quotation
2:7	Ps. 118:22	Marked Quotation
2:8	Isa. 8:14	Marked Quotation
2:9a	Isa. 43:20–21 or Esther 8:12 LXX	Allusion
2:9b–c	Exod. 19:5–6 or Exod. 23:33 LXX	Allusion

Old Testament Quotations and Allusions in 1 Peter (Modified from Woan, 2008, 269–70)		
1 Peter Reference	**Old Testament Source**	**Type of Reference**
2:9e	Isa. 42:12; Job 12:22	Allusion
2:10	Hos. 1:6, 9; 2:1, 25	Allusion
2:11	Ps. 39:12 or Gen. 23:4	Allusion
2:12	Isa. 10:13	Strong Allusion
2:22	Isa. 53:9	Nonmarked Quotation
2:24a	Isa. 53:4, 12b	Strong Allusion
2:24b	Gen. 40:19; Deut. 21:22–23	Allusion
2:24d	Isa. 53:5b	Strong Allusion
2:25a	Isa. 53:6	Allusion
3:10–12	Ps. 34:13–17	Marked Quotation
3:14c–15a	Isa. 8:12–13	Strong Allusion
3:18	Isa. 53:12	Allusion
4:8	Prov. 10:12	Allusion
4:14	Isa. 11:2	Strong Allusion
4:18	Prov. 11:31	Marked Quotation
5:5	Prov. 3:34	Marked Quotation

Verba Christi: *The Words of Christ*

Another significant source for the thoughts and ideas in 1 Peter is the words of Jesus. This should come as no surprise to those who hold to genuine Petrine authorship. Indeed, it would be surprising if Peter did not use the words of Jesus as a source. Some have made this an argument in favor of Peter's authorship (Gundry, 1967, 1974), though others have argued that it is, at best, inconclusive (Best, 1970).

There are numerous significant challenges in determining the use of Jesus's words in 1 Peter. First, it appears that the early church preferred to refer to the words of Jesus through allusion and echo rather than explicit citation. These methods of reference are rhetorically more powerful than direct citation, but they increase the difficulty of determining precisely

where Jesus is being referenced. Another issue concerns language. If Jesus spoke in Aramaic, then the Greek Gospels have already translated his words. Peter, an eyewitness, may not translate the words the same way the Gospel writers did. Consequently, dependence may not be precisely lexical. Other challenges exist, but we mention these simply to indicate why there is such variance among the scholarly community concerning 1 Peter's dependence on Jesus's words.

Granted Peter's authorship and the early church's knowledge of Jesus's words, we should take an optimistic view of Peter's reference to this tradition. As with the references to the Old Testament, the references here are not evenly distributed. Peter shows a great affection for the Sermon on the Mount (Matt. 5–7; Luke 6).

Jesus's Words in 1 Peter (Modified from T. Miller, 2018)			
1 Peter Reference	**Gospel Parallel**	**Type of Reference**	**Probability of Reference**
1:2	Mark 14:23; Matt. 26:28; Luke 22:20b	Echo	Likely
1:2	Matt. 28:28–30	Echo	Possible
1:3	John 3:3–7	Allusion	Likely
1:4	Matt. 6:20; Luke 12:33;	Echo	Likely
1:6	Matt. 5:10–12; Luke 6:22–23	Echo	Very Likely
1:8	John 20:29	Echo	Likely
1:10	Matt. 13:16–17; Luke 20:23–24	Echo	Possible
1:11	Luke 24:25–27	Echo	Possible
1:13	Luke 12:35, 45	Echo	Likely
1:17	Matt. 6:9; Luke 11:2	Echo	Likely
1:18	Matt. 20:28; Mark 10:45	Echo	Likely
1:22	John 13:34–35; 15:12	Echo	Likely
1:23ff	Parable of the Sower (Matt. 13:1–23; Mark 4:3–20; Luke 8:4–15)	Allusion	Very Likely
2:3	Luke 6:35	Echo	Possible
2:4–8	Matt. 21:42–43; Mark 12:10–11; Luke 20:17–18	Echo	Very Likely
2:12	Matt. 5:14–16	Allusion	Very Likely
2:13–17	Matt. 17:25–27 (cf. Matt. 22:21)	Echo	Very Likely
2:18–21	Luke 6:32–35	Echo	Very Likely
2:25	John 10:11–18	Echo	Likely
3:9	Matt. 5:39–44; Luke 6:27–30	Allusion	Very Likely
3:14a	Matt. 5:10; Luke 6:22	Echo	Very Likely
3:14b	Matt. 10:26–28	Echo	Possible
3:16	Luke 6:28	Echo	Possible
3:13–17	Luke 21:12–19	Allusion	Possible
3:22	Matt. 26:64; Mark 14:62; Luke 22:69	Echo	Likely
4:10	Luke 12:42–48	Echo	Likely
4:13–14	Matt. 5:10–12; Luke 6:22–23	Echo	Very Likely
4:14	Matt. 10:20; Mark 13:11; Luke 12:10–12	Echo	Possible
5:2–4	John 21:15–17	Echo	Very Likely

Jesus's Words in 1 Peter (Modified from T. Miller, 2018)			
1 Peter Reference	**Gospel Parallel**	**Type of Reference**	**Probability of Reference**
5:2–4	Matt. 20:25–28; Mark 10:42–45; Luke 22:25–30	Allusion	Very Likely
5:5	John 13:1ff	Allusion	Very Likely
5:6	Matt. 23:12; Luke 14:11 (cf. 18:14)	Echo	Very Likely
5:7	Matt. 6:25–34; Luke 12:22–31	Echo	Likely
5:8–9a	Luke 22:31–32	Echo	Very Likely

OUTLINE

While 1 Peter could be divided into many different preaching units, we've chosen to divide 1 Peter into five major divisions with twenty preaching units.

LETTER OPENING (1:1–12)

- Greeting and Statement of Identity (1:1–2)
- Praise for the New Birth (1:3–9)
- The Believer's Privileged Knowledge (1:10–12)

NEW IDENTITY LEADING TO HOLINESS (1:13–2:10)

- Born Again for Holiness (1:13–21)
- Born Again to Love (1:22–25)
- Craving the Spiritual Milk (2:1–3)
- The Living Stone and the Living Stones (2:4–10)

HOLINESS APPLIED IN LIFE SITUATIONS (2:11–4:11)

- Elect-Exiles and Honorable Conduct (2:11–12)
- Submitting and Honoring (2:13–17)
- Honorable Conduct and Christian Slaves (2:18–21)
- The Example of Christ (2:22–25)
- Honorable Conduct and Christian Marriage (3:1–7)
- How to Live the Good Life (3:8–12)
- Suffering for Righteousness (3:13–17)
- Christ's Suffering Leading to Exaltation (3:18–22)
- Ceasing from Sin and the Future Judgment (4:1–6)
- Holy Living in the Assembly (4:7–11)

HONORABLE SUFFERING AS THE FLOCK OF GOD (4:12–5:14)

- Suffering as a Christian (4:12–19)
- The Flock of God (5:1–5)
- Final Admonitions (5:6–14)

LETTER OPENING
(1 PETER 1:1–12)

Peter began his letter with a relatively standard introduction, which introduced the writer as well as the audience. Peter, an apostle, was writing to believers in Asia Minor. The introduction went beyond simply naming the author and audience, for it also revealed the spiritual identity of the audience. In the first few verses (vv. 1–2), Peter laid the foundation for the rest of the book by naming his readers "elect-exiles" and by providing a Trinitarian description of how and why they had obtained this identity. Peter followed this introduction with a prayer of thanks to God (vv. 3–5), a statement of the reader's joy despite trial (vv. 6–9), and a recognition that all this had occurred just as the prophets predicted (vv. 10–12).

This first section may be divided into three preaching units: Greeting and Statement of Identity (vv. 1–2), Praise for the New Birth (vv. 3–9), and The Believer's Privileged Knowledge (vv. 10–12).

1 Peter 1:1–2

EXEGETICAL IDEA
Peter, an apostle of Jesus Christ, wrote to elect-exiles, who had become elect-exiles by the work of the triune God, whose first member chose them, second member sanctified them, and third member offered the sacrifice necessary that made their new identity possible.

THEOLOGICAL FOCUS
Believers in Jesus have a new identity as elect-exiles, eternally chosen by the Father, judicially sanctified by the Spirit, and graciously welcomed by means of the work of the Son.

PREACHING IDEA
The Born-Again Identity: The Triune God Transforms Our Identities from Lost Sinners to Elect Exiles.

PREACHING POINTERS
The first epistle of Peter opens with theological precision built on a Trinitarian foundation. Peter writes to a Gentile audience dispersed throughout Asia Minor and Galatia. They were spiritual exiles, temporary residents of earth. Though they shared no home or singular house of worship anymore, they united through a common identity. Peter's readers were among the elect, chosen by Father, Son, and Holy Spirit to multiply God's grace throughout the world.

Hardly more exciting news could begin a letter! Modern readers recognize that God counts us, too, among elect-exiles. The Father, Son, and Holy Spirit each had a role in our salvation, transforming our identities and giving us mission and purpose. We share the same identity as Peter's readers. We exist as exiles, dispersed throughout the world, far greater than the reaches of Galatia and Asia. Yet we unite as the elect in a faith founded in the foreknowledge of the Father, sanctified in the Holy Spirit, and purchased with the blood of Jesus Christ. The Trinity played a significant role in the lives of the first-century readers and continues to play a significant role in the lives of twenty-first-century Christians.

GREETING AND STATEMENT OF IDENTITY (1:1–2)

LITERARY STRUCTURE AND THEMES (1:1–2)

Peter began his letter in the same form as most New Testament letters, including his name, the identity of his readers, and a wish statement of grace and peace. What makes Peter's introduction unique is the developed description of the readers in three parts, each reflecting a member of the Trinity.[1] Having described the readers as "elect-exiles," Peter's three descriptive phrases indicated why, how, and to what end God has made them elect-exiles.

The major themes of these verses include: the identity of believers; the triune work of God to forge the believer's identity; and the purpose of the believer's new identity.

- **Introduction of the Author (1:1a)**
- **Description of the Audience (1:1b–2)**

EXPOSITION (1:1–2)

Letters in the ancient world normally began with an introduction identifying the author and the recipients, which would be followed by a greeting. Here Peter identified himself, giving further detail that he was an apostle of Jesus Christ. Peter's introduction is followed by an extended description of the readers. He first named them elect-exiles and then provided three prepositional phrases that further clarify that identity.

Introduction of the Author (1:1a)

Peter introduced himself, highlighting his role as an apostle of Jesus Christ.

1:1a. Peter opened the letter with a statement of identity, using the name "Peter" which was given to him by Jesus (John 1:42). The name means "rock,"[2] and was suggestive of the role Peter would play in the establishment of the church (Matt. 16:18). It appears that the readers from Asia Minor already knew Peter, but even if some did not, the narratives concerning him would have been known by any early Christian church. Peter was one of the central figures in the Gospels, being in Jesus's most intimate group with two others, James and John (Matt. 17:1; Mark 5:37).

Peter identified himself as an apostle of Jesus Christ. The term "apostle" (ἀπόστολος) could be used in a general sense referring to one who was a "messenger" or "delegate" (BDAG s.v. "ἀπόστολος" 122). Nevertheless, Peter used

---

1   Trinity. Some have suggested that it is anachronistic to title biblical triads such as this "Trinitarian." This is true to the degree that the term did not develop until after the New Testament period. Nevertheless, it is passages like this that are the very cause of Trinitarian language. Accordingly, we use it here even if it is technically anachronistic.

2   "Rock." While Jesus called Peter "the rock" upon whom the church was to be built (Matt. 16:18), he is not the cornerstone (Jesus). In light of this given name, it is not surprising that 1 Peter has one of the most extended considerations of the stone passages. There is the mention of the "living stones," the "priceless stone," and the "cornerstone" (2:4–10; cf. Rom. 9:30–33; 10:11) all of which have their foundation in the Old Testament (Ps. 18:22; Isa. 8:11–15; 28:16). This stone motif, begun in predictive prophecy in the Old Testament, is applied by Jesus to his own ministry (Matt. 21:42–44). Both Peter (Acts 4:11; 1 Peter 2:4–10) and Paul (Rom. 9:30–33; 10:11) capitalize on the motif. See the more detailed analysis in the exposition of 2:4–10.

it in a more official sense to refer to those who saw the living Christ and were called by him to proclaim the message of salvation and to play a pivotal role in the establishment of the church (Eph. 2:19–22; 3:4–5; 4:11–13).

By introducing himself as an apostle, Peter was indicating the authority by which the letter was to be read. This was not a mere letter from a contemporary; rather, it was the word of one specially called by Jesus to establish the church. Accordingly, his words carry divine authority and import.

Description of the Audience (1:1b–2)

Peter identified his readers as elect-exiles, noted their location, and provided further description of them through three loaded prepositional phrases.

1:1b. Peter began by highlighting the readers' spiritual status: "to the elect." As we will see, it is no mistake that Peter described the readers as those chosen by God. Many translations relocate the description to the end of verse 1 or the beginning of verse 2, allowing for a better flow with the prepositional phrases of verse 2 (NRSV, NASB, NKJV, NET). Moving the designation, however, loses some of the force that is provided by the fronting of the title. Further, as we will note, this designation is fundamental to understanding the rest of what Peter said about the readers.

Peter also described the believers in Asia Minor as "exiles in the dispersion." The word for exile (παρεπιδήμοις) speaks of one "staying for a while in a strange or foreign place," and can be translated "exile," "sojourner," or "temporary resident" (BDAG s.v. "παρεπίδημος" 775). Interpreters disagree concerning the nature of this identity, whether it refers to literal sojourners, as the word was generally used in the Greek culture, or whether it refers to a metaphorical and spiritual reality, as the word was sometimes used in the Septuagint (LXX Gen. 23:4; Ps.

38:13). As argued in the introduction, 1 Peter used the terms "sojourners" and "exiles" in a metaphorical way.

Septuagint (LXX)

The Septuagint was the Greek translation of the Hebrew Old Testament. It is clear that Peter used a Greek translation, for the similarity of his text to the Septuagint rendering is often too close to be accidental. Since 1 Peter is written to primarily Gentile congregations, their Old Testament text would have been the Septuagint. And since the early church's Bible was the Old Testament (much of the New Testament had not been written or circulated widely), the early church would have been quite familiar with the Old Testament narratives told in Greek language. It is for this reason that distinctive Greek words are important, for they are a primary vehicle to create associations between Old Testament texts and Peter's contemporary readers. In this case, "sojourner" (παρεπίδημος) is a loaded term, highlighting connections between Old Testament saints and Peter's readers (Gen. 23:4; Ps. 39:12). Peter makes this even more clear in 2:11, where he combines "sojourner" (παρεπιδήμους) with "exile" (παροίκους), a combination of terms used in two Septuagint texts—Genesis 23:4 and Psalm 39:12. Both are significant. The first highlights Abraham's plight as a stranger and a foreigner, and the second notes that David, though he is in the promised land, still sees himself as a stranger and foreigner. These textual links with the Septuagint would have been picked up by Peter's readers, and they suggest that Peter had a primarily metaphorical meaning in mind when he spoke of the readers as "exiles" or "temporary residents."

That they are "sojourners in the dispersion" has sometimes been used to argue for a Jewish audience. And while it is true that "dispersion" is sometimes used in a technical sense to refer to the Jewish people away from their homeland, here it is being used in its metaphorical sense. This is confirmed in that it is aligned with "sojourner" (παρεπιδήμοις), a term with rich theological import. In other words, the term is used "figuratively of Christians who live in dispersion in the world far from their heavenly home" (BDAG s.v. "διασπορά" 236).

How should we understand "elect" in relation to "exile"? Is it the elect who are in exile or the exiles who are elect? Better than either option is to see that Peter gave both descriptors equal weight. They were chosen to be exiles, and they were exiles because chosen. For this reason, we will speak of the readers as elect-exiles.

Peter's combination of disparate terms (one a word of favor, the other of alienation) served to highlight the way he thought about his readers, and more importantly, how he believed the readers should see themselves. They were chosen by God, yet in regard to the world they were exiles. For Peter, these were related, for it was God's choice that made them exiles among the world. Indeed, their exilic status came as a result of the changes God had made in them when he called them.

Peter concluded the first verse by indicating the various places the readers were located. It is quite possible, as C. J. Hemer (1978, 239–43) has persuasively argued, that Peter was ordering the names in light of the way a letter-carrier would have traveled. What is clearer, however, is that Peter was writing to a significantly broad geographical region. This accounts for the lack of specific names in the epistle, the general nature of the exhortation of the epistle, and the absence of any direct, personal communication.

1:2. Having already described his readers as elect-exiles, Peter now offered three phrases to further describe their identity. Peter's description was provided in a Trinitarian fashion, starting with the Father, moving to the Spirit, and ending with the Son. The first phrase indicated the grounds for the readers' elect-exile status, while the second indicated the means of that status. The third phrase is debated, but we will make the case that it provided the purpose of their being elect-exiles.

In the first phrase, Peter highlighted that his readers were elect-exiles "according to [κατά] the foreknowledge of God the Father." The word "foreknowledge" (πρόγνωσιν) can be used in a simple sense to refer to someone's knowledge of an event that will yet take place. But it can also be used in relation to God's predetermined plan, a sense more at home in the New Testament (see, e.g., Acts 2:23 where "foreknowledge of God" is used in parallel with "the definite plan of God") and particularly in this context. Accordingly, Paul Achtemeier translated the phrase as, "in accordance with the purpose of God the Father" (Achtemeier, 1996, 79). Later in this chapter (1:20), Peter used a cognate form of this word (προεγνωσμένου) to indicate that Jesus was foreknown "from the foundation of the world." Though not explicitly stated, there was an implication that the readers were likewise chosen from the foundation of the world. Their identity as elect-exiles, in other words, was not an accident of history, but was rather a part of the eternal plan of God. The sovereignty of God over the events in the lives of the readers is a recurring theme in 1 Peter (1:6; 3:17; 4:19). Since Peter's readers were experiencing some difficulty due to their newfound identity, Peter began by reminding them that such an identity was God's choice. That God was called "Father" highlights the intimacy that existed between the readers and God. It also began the family metaphor, which Peter will return to again when he called on the readers to love the brothers and sisters (1:22).

The second phrase focused on the work of the Spirit. Peter affirmed that the readers were elect-exiles "through [ἐν] the sanctification of the Spirit." Sanctification (ἁγιασμῷ) is most frequently thought of in its progressive sense, referring to the transformation of life that comes as a result of conversion and consistent dedication to the Lord. Nevertheless, the New Testament authors also spoke of sanctification as a completed reality (cf. 2 Thess. 2:13). Instead of the process of being made holy (progressive sanctification), it can refer to the fact that one has been made holy (immediate/initial sanctification) at the point of conversion. It is for this reason that the New Testament often refers to believers as "saints" (ἅγιος; Acts 9:13, 32; Rom. 8:27; 12:13; 15:25; 1 Cor. 6:1; 2 Cor. 1:1; Eph. 2:19; 3:8; Phil. 4:22; Col. 1:4; 1 Tim. 5:10; Heb. 6:10; Rev. 22:21). The sanctification referenced here is immediate. It "refers to the Spirit's illuminating the mind and heart of the elect, overcoming human depravity, convincing the elect of the truth of the gospel, convicting them of their sin, and equipping and enabling them to exercise repentant faith" (Compton, 2019, 38; cf. Spicq, 1966, 42). For Peter, the progressive sense was not unrelated to immediate sanctification, for progressive sanctification was only possible because of initial sanctification.

Having spoken of the work of the Father and the Spirit in the elect-exile status of the readers, Peter turned to the role of the Son. In this third and final phrase, Peter provided the purpose (εἰς)[3] for which the readers had become elect-exiles: "for obedience to Jesus Christ." The drawback of this interpretation is that it causes difficulty in understanding the phrase "of Jesus Christ" (Ἰησοῦ Χριστοῦ), which appears to be used in two apparently incompatible ways: obedience to Jesus Christ (objective genitive) and the sprinkling of the blood of Christ (possessive genitive). According to Achtemeier, this would be "something of a grammatical monstrosity and surely confusing to the reader/listener" (Achtemeier, 1996, 87).

Francis Beare (1947, 50–51), followed by Karen Jobes (2005, 72), provides a helpful solution. He suggests Peter is using a hendiadys, which means that he is using multiple terms in reference to a single idea. That Peter is using a hendiadys is supported by the unique language of "the sprinkling of blood." To those familiar with the Old Testament, the language would certainly bring to mind the establishment of the Mosaic covenant in Exodus 24:3–8. Jobes explains how the hendiadys comes from this Old Testament reflection: "The newly formed people of Israel first pledge their obedience (24:3, 7) and then are sprinkled with the blood of the sacrifice (24:8). In this ceremony both sides of the essential nature of the covenant are represented: the people pledge obedience to God, and the blood of the covenant is applied to them. Thus the phrase 'obedience and sprinkling of blood' can serve as a hendiadys to refer to God's covenant relationship with his people" (Jobes, 2005, 72).

Hendiadys

A hendiadys is a figure of speech that is defined as "the expression of a single idea by means of two nouns joined by the conjunction 'and,' rather than by a noun qualified by an adjective" (Baldick, 1996, 151). An English example is "nice and warm," which is a different way of saying "nicely warm." Another biblical example is given in Luke 21:15: "for I will give you a mouth and wisdom, which none of your adversaries will be able to withstand or contradict." Jesus is promising a

---

3 Purpose. Francis Agnew (1983, 68–73) has argued that the preposition (εἰς) is causal: "*because* of the obedience of Jesus Christ and the sprinkling of his blood." Such a reading balances the three phrases: The reader's elect-exile status is based on the Father's choice, is accomplished through the Spirit's sanctifying action, and is due to the obedient cross-work of the Son. Nevertheless, the preposition (εἰς) does not have a causal ("because") sense elsewhere in 1 Peter or even in the New Testament (Page, 2010, 295). Accordingly, it is better to follow most English versions in seeing Peter giving the *purpose* for which the readers had become elect-exiles: "for obedience to Jesus Christ."

"wise mouth" or "wise words" to his disciples. The function of the hendiadys is to lay stress on both words, instead of only the modified noun. In the latter example, the hendiadys emphasizes both the words and the wisdom. In reference to 1 Peter, the hendiadys speaks of an obedience-sprinkling. By using the figure of speech, Peter could emphasize both the obedience and the blood-sprinkling.

By speaking of obedience and the sprinkled blood of Christ, Peter was suggesting that the readers have entered the new covenant.[4] That is, just as the Mosaic covenant was entered by a pledge of obedience and was sealed with the sprinkling of blood, so these believers have pledged their obedience, and the sprinkled blood of Jesus has established the covenant.

In summary, the three prepositional phrases can be understood in the following way: Peter's readers were elect-exiles in dispersion due to God's predetermined plan, by means of being set apart in holiness by the Spirit, and for the purpose of becoming obedient members of the new covenant through the sacrifice of Jesus (cf. Achtemeier, 1996, 89).

Peter concluded the verse with a prayer wish that grace and peace would be multiplied among the readers. The combination of "grace" and "peace" is a standard greeting in New Testament documents (Rom. 1:7; 1 Cor. 1:3; 2 Cor. 1:2; Gal. 1:3; Eph. 1:2; Phil. 1:2; Col. 1:2; 1 Thess. 1:1; 2 Thess. 1:2; Titus 1:4; Philem. 3).

THEOLOGICAL FOCUS

The exegetical idea (Peter, an apostle of Jesus Christ, wrote to elect-exiles, who had become elect-exiles by the work of the triune God, whose first member chose them, second member sanctified them, and third member offered the sacrifice necessary that made their new identity possible) leads to this theological focus: believers in Jesus are elect-exiles, eternally chosen by the Father, judicially sanctified by the Spirit, and graciously welcomed by means of the work of the Son.

This Trinitarian work sets the stage for defining the identity of believers. God has chosen believers to be saints. This understanding provides a bulwark against the feelings and false ideals that threaten to attack when things do not seem to go the way we think they should. We might wonder whether God is really on our side. But Peter's introduction settles that issue, for the believer's status is not merely elect, but elect-*exile*. Accordingly, sanctification by the Spirit has made believers foreigners in the world in which they once were natives (4:3). That is, the Spirit has fundamentally changed those who are chosen to be different and distinct. This distinction is both the evidence of their election and the grounds for their estrangement from the world.

That believers are members of the new covenant is due to the cross-work of the Son. Being partners in the new covenant indicates that the church is beginning to receive some of the blessings promised in the Old Testament (Jer. 31:31–34). As Peter will later reveal, these

---

4   New covenant. While 1 Peter never uses the language "new covenant," many interpreters have found the new covenant as a basis for much of Peter's thought. For instance, in 1:2, Michaels notes, "Without speaking explicitly of a 'new covenant' or the 'blood of the covenant' (which may in his circles have been reserved for the Eucharist, cf. Mark 14:24; 1 Cor. 11:25), Peter relies on language that had perhaps become already fixed among Christians as a way of alluding to the same typology. To 'obey' was to accept the gospel and become part of a new community under a new covenant; to be sprinkled with Jesus's blood was to be cleansed from one's former way of living and released from spiritual slavery by the power of his death" (Michaels, 1988, 12–13). The connections between the major Old Testament texts concerning the new covenant and 1 Peter are further mined by Pryor (1986a, 1986b).

readers (and those believers who follow them) are in an envious position, for they know what previous generations longed to know (1:10–12). Indeed, we recognize that the unfolding of God's purposes has become evident and real.

The believer's identity is complicated, for on the one hand, it is to be desired (they are elect), while it is on the other hand filled with difficulty (they are exiles). Such difficulty is to be expected, for they are on a journey through a foreign land (in the dispersion) to their final, eternal homeland.

PREACHING AND TEACHING STRATEGIES

Exegetical and Theological Synthesis

Who are we? How did we get here? What is our purpose?

For millennia, philosophers have wrestled with those questions. Today, we have multiple ways of answering it, all wrong. Some find their identity in their occupation—I'm a lawyer, a pastor, a used car salesman, a blogger, a college student, a stay-at-home mom. Some find their identity in their relationships—I'm a father or a mother, a grandma or a grandpa, a husband or a wife. Some find it in their generational norms—I'm a Boomer, a Millennial, Gen X. Others look to their accomplishments or accolades to find themselves—I'm CEO of a Fortune 500 company, the manager of the state's largest bank, an influencer with a million followers on Instagram, bestselling author, MVP of the team.

Yet none of those things reveal the true condition of our hearts. At our best, we are sinners, unholy, desperately in need of a savior to repair our fallen condition. The Bible uses a number of terms to describe humankind's initial identity: enemies of the cross (Phil. 3:18); slaves of sin (Rom. 6:17); foolish, faithless, heartless, ruthless (Rom. 1:31); dead in our sin (Eph. 2:1) to name but a few. Our identity before salvation was nothing more than lost, hopeless, damned to eternal judgment.

Peter opens his letter by clearly stating that his readers have a new identity, not only in Christ but in the Father and Spirit as well. Who are we? We are elect-exiles. How did we get here? Through the Father's foreknowledge, the sanctification of the Spirit, and the sprinkling of the blood of Christ. What is our purpose? The rest of the letter will continue to address that question.

The gospel of Christ, made possible through the power of the Trinity at work in sinners, repairs the fallen condition of humanity. The gospel brings us from lost slaves and enemies of the cross to elect-exiles with renewed purpose and meaning. Without God, our identity can only flounder in meaningless, temporal, earthly things—titles that will vanish in the world to come. With God, we become something far more lasting and secure.

Preaching Idea

The Born-Again Identity: The Triune God Transforms Our Identities from Lost Sinners to Elect Exiles.

Contemporary Connections

What does it mean?

Not unlike the opening to other epistles in the New Testament, 1 Peter begins with an unusually dense vocabulary of words that modern-day congregants may struggle to understand. Even with only two verses to preach, pastors have their work cut out for them. Without proper guidance, many novices to biblical lingo will find themselves asking throughout the entire sermon, "What does *that* mean?"

Several terms introduce tricky theological concepts that are ultimately far too big to cover in a single sermon. Peter calls his readers "elect." He says they are elect "according to the foreknowledge of God." These terms are loaded! What does Peter mean by "elect" and "foreknowledge"? This text was not written to springboard the sermon into the five points of Calvinism, but a brief explanation of the terms in the text would be appropriate and necessary for exposition.

Even terms like "sanctification" and "sprinkling" may need brief explanation. As the commentary pointed out, "sanctification" normally refers to the ongoing process of making one holy, but the immediate reference here is to initial sanctification. Preachers must carefully distinguish between these two related concepts, as it will help put the rest of the letter into proper perspective. "Sprinkling" has Old Testament roots. Perhaps citing a verse like Exodus 24:8 may help illustrate this concept for the church. (See below for help on the geographical terms.) "Exile" and especially "dispersion" may also need brief historical explanation.

Finally, Peter roots the believer's identity in the work of the Trinity. Though the word "Trinity" is not used here (nor elsewhere in Scripture), the idea is clearly present and essential for an understanding of the passage. Again, preachers will likely want to avoid sidelining exposition for a fully orbed sermon on the theology of the Trinity, but the sermon should at least emphasize the certain individual roles of the Godhead that the text itself touches upon.

The preacher may find it helpful to put together a list of key terms with their definitions. It does not need to be anything fancy, but simply a concise guide to help young Christians navigate through the terms would suffice.

Key Terms in 1 Peter 1:1–2	
Elect	those chosen in God for salvation
Foreknowledge	God's predetermined plan for salvation
Exile	someone dispersed from their homeland (here metaphorical/ spiritual)
Dispersion	the metaphorical scattering of God's people
Sanctification	the Spirit's act of making God's people holy

Sprinkling	the Old Testament action of entering a covenant with the application of blood

Is it true?

The most challenging thing about this text may be getting Americans (or those who live in free countries) to think of themselves as exiles. We live in the land of the free! We love the idea of independence and self-reliance and eschew any notion that someone controls us. We are slaves to no one.

But that's not what the Bible says. The idea of living as exiles, even within our homeland, is not new to the New Testament. In Ezra, decades after the people returned from physical exile in Babylon, Ezra writes the words, "For we are slaves" (Ezra 9:9). Later, Nehemiah records similar sentiments (Neh. 9:36). Even after returning to the promised land, the people still viewed themselves as slaves. Clearly the physical reality of a situation was not the sole perspective of a spiritual community.

The preacher might want to point to such truths, or other passages that demonstrate the eternal perspective of spiritual exiles (cf. Phil. 3:20–21; Heb. 11:9, 13). Helping a modern believer view life from an eternal and heavenly perspective is no easy task, but it will be necessary to fully engage with Peter's words throughout his letter.

Now what?

Though the opening verses of 1 Peter function to set up the exhortations to follow, it still offers several potential avenues of application, even within the dense theology.

The preacher can focus the sermon on the concept of our twofold identity as elect-exiles based on the Trinity's work. Modern generations have an identity crisis. Being among the elect not only corrects those inclined toward self-pity and a bad self-esteem (how can we pity ourselves when we know the God of the universe has personally chosen us and made us his!), but it also gives special purpose and mission in life. Being an elect-exile gives us a spiritual perspective on any difficult situation we encounter. God has chosen us to be his; what could we possibly fear? Election, far from being a scary theological concept reserved for those in ivory towers, can actually be a great encouragement to believers in need of hope and love.

Second, our identity as exiles helps us break beyond the normal temporal perspective most people have in life and seek to live for eternal reasons. So many people live in order to work off their mortgage, to have a nice retirement, maybe a home down south. They want financial freedom, vacation pleasures, terrestrial pursuits. But none of these things last beyond our life here. We can't take our vacation home with us to heaven (nor would we want to, considering what God has in store for us!). We are but temporary residents here on earth.

Creativity in Presentation

In an attempt to be creative and helpful, some preachers and teachers have accidentally become heretics when trying too hard to explain the doctrine of the Trinity. The preacher would do well to avoid simplistic analogies (the Trinity is like an egg; the Trinity is like the three stages of H2O; the Trinity is like the threefold identity of a father, son, and husband). The potential for heretical teaching outweighs the potential for helpfulness with these analogies.

Instead, the preacher will want to lean on the focus of the text itself. Salvation comes through the Father's foreknowledge, the Spirit's sanctification, and the Son's shed blood. More need not be said (in this sermon).

Because this will presumably be the first sermon in an expository series in 1 Peter, the preacher may also want to give the church a glimpse forward at what is to come. The first two verses provide a good launch pad for the main themes that will be seen throughout the rest of the book—identity as elect-exiles, the need for sanctification and obedience, and so on. A brief outline of the book and overview of the letter would be helpful and appropriate. Some churches may even consider using a chart or graphic to give people an orientation in the text. Search the internet for The Bible Project's overview of 1 Peter as an example (https://bibleproject.com).

For handling the five geographical areas mentioned in the text (Pontus, Galatia, Cappadocia, Asia, and Bithynia), the preacher must assume that most congregants will be familiar with only one, and at most two, of these places. Displaying a map of the areas on PowerPoint could provide a visual reference for the church. Cull such maps from the many options in Logos or Accordance software, or perhaps even an open-source image from Wikimedia Commons (make sure to give credit where appropriate). Giving a visual of these areas will help people truly appreciate the extent of the "dispersion" mentioned in 1:1.

The sermon could be outlined based on a Trinitarian structure, as emphasized in the text:

- Introduction to 1 Peter (author, audience, purpose)

- Salvation according to the Father (election and foreknowledge)

- Salvation according to the Holy Spirit (sanctification)

- Salvation according to the Son (sprinkling)

- Conclusion/Application

DISCUSSION QUESTIONS

1. How does Peter use the concept of "elect-exiles"? How does this inform our identity as believers today?

2. How is the Trinity at work in our salvation? Why do some believers primarily only think of one member of the Godhead in relation to the gospel?

3. What does Peter mean that we are saved "according to the foreknowledge of God the Father"? How does this concept relate to election?

4. In what areas of life has the Holy Spirit been actively at work sanctifying you lately?

1 Peter 1:3–9

EXEGETICAL IDEA
God the Father was to be praised for granting new birth, for this new birth provided a living hope, guaranteed a secure inheritance, and produced rejoicing despite present trial.

THEOLOGICAL FOCUS
Believers should praise God the Father for the gift of the new birth, which provides a living hope, a secure inheritance, and a reason to rejoice despite trials.

PREACHING IDEA
The Born-Again Supremacy: Faithful Living Results in Supreme Rewards.

PREACHING POINTERS
The first-century church underwent heavy persecution as God's kingdom began its spread throughout the world. Persecuted believers couldn't help but ask themselves, "Is it worth it? Is this suffering worth the pain?"

Peter called the church to a future perspective, firmly rooted in the present hope of their salvation. Only by looking beyond their current trials could the early church see the reason for their pain. Believers have been born again to a living hope. God stores up for them an unfading inheritance far greater than anything they could accumulate in this life. Faithful perseverance through persecution results in praise and glory and honor when Christ returns. This gives reason to rejoice despite trials.

The twenty-first-century preacher must call the church to a similar focus. Though we may not all experience the same heat of persecution that the first-century church did, we have the same supreme hope and calling in our salvation. Faithful living results in glorious rewards. The modern believer must look beyond the here and now and realize that life is best lived for the future. This puts whatever trials or tribulations the church currently experiences into proper focus. By calling the church to look forward to the day of reward, believers have a sharper perspective on how to live today.

PRAISE FOR THE NEW BIRTH (1:3–9)

LITERARY STRUCTURE AND THEMES (1:3–9)

While 1 Peter 1:3–9 is the focus of this preaching unit, in Greek it is only part of a larger, complex sentence (1:3–12). The central consideration of the passage is the first statement: "blessed be the God and Father of our Lord Jesus Christ." Accordingly, this whole section is a doxology, indicating why God should be praised. But while the focus was formally on what God had done, Peter was also building up the reader's consideration of their own identity.

While the section is composed of one sentence, it breaks quite naturally into three sections (vv. 3–5, 6–9, 10–12).[1] The sections divide according to the persons of the Godhead and thus are formed in a Trinitarian fashion. John Elliott draws the comparison with the opening verses: "The triadic structure of vv. 3–12, focusing on God the Father (vv. 3–5), Jesus Christ (vv. 6–9), and Holy Spirit (vv. 10–12), echoes in modified sequence the similar triadic structure of v. 2 (God-Spirit-Jesus Christ)" (Elliott, 2001, 329).

Peter opened this section with a joyous consideration of the hope believers have due to Christ's resurrection and the confidence they have in their future inheritance (vv. 3–5). Peter

concluded, however, with a measure of realism. Despite the blessed new birth, the readers have and will experience diverse trials. Even in such suffering, however, God is sovereign, and he designs such testing to purify his people (vv. 6–9).

The themes of this section include the following: the new birth; the heavenly inheritance waiting for believers; divinely assisted perseverance through faith; the temporary suffering in this age; the reality that genuine faith is tested; and the overwhelming reward for those whose faith is tested and proved.

- ***The Blessings of the New Birth (1:3–5)***
- ***Trials, Rejoicing, and Salvation (1:6–9)***

EXPOSITION (1:3–9)

Peter was writing to believers who were socially estranged because they had embraced Christ. This estrangement resulted in hostility and verbal assault. Peter wrote to encourage them to remain faithful to God. Peter did this by reminding the readers who they were in Christ. And he reminded them that who they were was because of the incredible mercy of God.

Thus, while the entire sentence was an exposition of gracious work of the Father in granting the readers the new birth, such a statement had

---

1 Three sections (vv. 3–5, 6–9, 10–12). In terms of Greek rhetoric, this section of the letter is the exordium. Quintillian stated that the purpose of the exordium is "to prepare our audience in such a way that they will be disposed to lend a ready ear to the rest of our speech." Peter does this by providing a theological understanding of the identity of the readers. They are born again by the Father into a living hope, into a secure inheritance, and into a coming salvation. As we will note, each of the sections in the exordium highlights salvation and thus has a future-looking cast to them (Green, 1997, 22). The foundational nature of the exordium to the letter has been recognized in some specialized studies. R. T. Kendall, in an extended consideration of the exordium, suggests that 1:3–12 "provides the foundation for all of the author's subsequent remarks" (Kendall, 2010, 106). In support of Kendall's thesis, we note that the exordium serves to introduce many of the important themes that will be further developed throughout the letter (e.g., new birth, suffering, rejoicing).

the practical and intended effect of reminding the readers of the benefits they had been given in salvation.

Verses 3–5 highlighted that the new birth resulted in a living hope sourced in the resurrection of Jesus from the dead. Along with this hope was a secure inheritance. It was secure not only because it was being stored in a place that cannot be affected by this world, but also because the readers themselves were being guarded so that they would eventually find themselves in possession of the reward. Peter indicated that such guarding was the work of God, accomplished through the readers' faith. The result was that this new birth would end with salvation. Achtemeier cogently notes that these blessings were intended to be contrasted to the readers' former life "with its dead hope, its perishable inheritance, and its unreliable salvation" (Achtemeier, 1996, 92).

Verses 6–9 added a measure of realism, for despite the blessedness of their hope and inheritance, the readers' present experience was sometimes bleak. Nevertheless, Peter indicated that they could rejoice even amid trial, for God was sovereign over trials, and he designed them to purify his people. Remaining faithful through trials, as Peter assumed the readers would be, would result in praise, glory, and honor when Jesus returned. By noting that their present suffering was temporary ("a little while"), Peter suggested the contrast with the reward laid up for them. Indeed, their faith was more valuable even than refined gold. Stated differently, present trial and difficulty was a part of God's

sovereign plan and would ultimately result in God's rewarding his faithful people.

The Blessings of the New Birth (1:3–5)

Peter indicated that the Father was to be praised for giving new birth to the readers, leading to a living hope and a secure inheritance, along with the assurance that the Father would guard them through their faith for final salvation.

1:3. Peter began his letter with a statement of praise in a form found elsewhere in the New Testament: "Blessed be the God and Father of our Lord Jesus Christ" (2 Cor. 1:3; Eph. 1:3). Significantly, Peter defined God as the "Father" of Jesus and then proceeded to speak of the readers as being born again due to the Father's mercy. In this way, Jesus and the readers were aligned together as children of God, though Jesus maintained a distinctive place, as can be seen from his title as "Lord" (Kelly, 1969, 47).

Peter offered praise to God for the abundant mercy leading God to give the readers new birth. The mention of the Father's role in the new birth highlighted the gracious nature of the act, for just as one is incapable of contributing to his or her initial birth, so he or she is likewise dependent on another for this new birth. The term "born again" (ἀναγεννήσας) is unique to Peter in biblical literature, being used only here and in 1:23. The background for the term[2] is debated, but Jobes is correct that "The most immediate source for the new-birth concept is found in the first-century Christian

---

2   Background for the term. Where does Peter get the concept of "new birth"? At one time, some scholars believed the idea came from the mystery religions (Perdelwitz, 1911), but this is widely rejected today. Such a hypothesis both lacks evidence and is not as convincing as some closer tradition sources (Silva, 2014, 1:563). One possible source is the Jewish literature of the intertestamental period. Selwyn, for instance, traces the similar conceptions in rabbinic literature (Selwyn, 1946, 306). Even there, however, the conception is not used as it is by Peter, following Jesus. Brox summarizes the current state of arguments for sources different than the Jesus Tradition by noting that arguments "from Hellenistic religions (mystery cults) or a Jewish milieu do not succeed" (Brox, 1993, 61). The use of the tradition in 1 Peter is uniquely grounded in the teaching of Jesus.

tradition that originated in the teachings of Jesus himself" (Jobes, 2005, 83).

Jesus and the New Birth

Peter derived the idea of the new birth from the teaching of Jesus. The concept is clearly expressed in Jesus's conversation with Nicodemus (John 3:1–15). The exact language is different but similar. Where Peter had a compound word (preposition with verb; ἀνα-γεννάω), John's gospel has two distinct words (a verb followed by a preposition; γεννηθῇ ἄνωθεν; John 3:3, 7). The difference between John's gospel and 1 Peter is comparable to the following English: "he went *up* the hill" (two distinct words) or "he went *up-hill*" (a compound word). Justin Martyr, an early commentator on the New Testament, showed the closeness of the phrases when he cited John 3 using the compound word found in 1 Peter: "For the Christ also said, except ye be born again [ἂν μὴ ἀναγεννηθῆτε], ye shall not enter into the kingdom of heaven" (Justin Martyr, 1 *Apol.* 1.61).

This conception of new birth is developed throughout the epistle and was foundational to Peter's understanding of the readers' identity. They were a new people, being granted new life. Accordingly, they were different, and this made them exiles even among those whom they once were natives. It was this new birth that set them apart, and it was this new identity that Peter appealed to when he encouraged them toward righteous living. Indeed, they were children of God not merely because he was their creator, but more specifically because he was their spiritual progenitor.

This new birth resulted in three things,[3] which were signaled by the repetition of the same preposition (εἰς): a living hope, a secure inheritance, and a coming salvation. First, the new birth resulted in a living hope. The descriptor "living" not only contrasted with the dead hope of their past but was also a wordplay referencing the resurrection.[4] Their hope was living just as Jesus was living. He had conquered the grave and been shown victorious, and so they had a certain hope that they too would conquer death and be shown victorious. Such hope was not a subjective wish but was a statement of an objective reality. The resurrection of Christ, a historic event, gave grounds for their confident trust that their faith was not misplaced.

1:4. Having spoken of the living hope, Peter turned to a second result of the new birth: a secure inheritance.[5] The concept of inheritance was natural considering the readers' new identity as a

---

3   Three things. Achtemeier (1996, 92 n. 5) rightly notes Peter's emphasis on threes in this section: "this part of 1 Peter is marked by a predilection for groups of three, e.g., three prepositional phrases in 1:2; three alliterative adjectives in v. 4; three phrases beginning with εἰς in vv. 3–5; a triad of nouns in v. 7; even the division of this *prooemium* into three segments."

4   The resurrection. Some commentators have suggested that the phrase "through the resurrection of Jesus Christ from the dead" does not modify "living hope" but describes the new birth (Michaels, 1988, 19). Thus, Peter would be saying that one is *born again through the resurrection of Jesus from the dead.* Such a statement can be defended as apostolic doctrine; nevertheless, that does not seem to be Peter's point here. The living hope is living because Jesus is alive. Further, the word order and the unnecessary redundancy of "from the dead" suggest the connection between the living hope and the resurrection. Grudem offers a more extended defense of the perspective argued here (Grudem, 1988, 61). Kelly, on the other hand, offers an argument that the phrase has implications for both the new birth and the living hope (Kelly, 1969, 48).

5   A secure inheritance. That Peter is contrasting the inheritance of the old covenant (the land) with the inheritance of the new covenant (eternal rewards) is suggested by some commentators. For example, Schreiner says, "Peter understood the inheritance, however, no longer in terms of a land promised to Israel but in terms of the end-time hope that lies before believers" (Schreiner, 2003, 62; cf. Elliott, 2001, 335). While it is true that the

child of God. The term was used throughout the New Testament to refer to the believer's share in the coming age (Gal. 3:18; Eph. 1:14, 18; 5:5; Col. 3:24; Heb. 9:15). In sum, the inheritance was the readers' "portion in the new creation and all its blessings" (Grudem, 1988, 61).

By using three alpha-privatives to describe the inheritance (ἄφθαρτον, ἀμίαντον, ἀμάραντον), Peter showed rhetorical flair. Such a device was used when something was beyond one's descriptive ability and thus one had to "set forth what it is by declaring what it is not" (Trench, 1871, 239). Unfortunately, it is not easy to capture this in English. We can come close, however, if we are willing to stretch English on the first of the descriptions: unperishable,[6] undefiled, and unfading.

Peter first described the inheritance as unperishable (ἄφθαρτον). "Unperishable" was used to refer to realities that were impervious to destruction. For instance, it was used of God himself in reference to his immortality (Rom. 1:23; 1 Tim. 1:17), and it was used of the resurrected body (1 Cor. 15:52). Peter also used it in reference to the ever-abiding Word of God (1:23). Thus, the emphasis was placed on the eternal, unchanging nature of the inheritance.

The inheritance was also undefiled (ἀμίαντον). The word for defilement (μιαίνω) was used throughout the Old Testament in reference to ritual impurity and the defilement of the land through sin. The contrast here, then, was that the coming inheritance was not defiled by sin and is pure. Hebrews 7:26 used the word in reference to Jesus, who was undefiled. In sum, this word highlighted that the inheritance was unmarred by sin.

Finally, Peter indicated that the inheritance was unfading (ἀμάραντον). This word appears only here in the New Testament, but its meaning is suggested by its use in in the apocryphal Apocalypse of Peter where it refers to flowers in the eternal state that will never fade (BDAG s.v. "ἀμάραντος" 49). The word refers to the amaranthus flower, which had a rich red color (see image). The flower was popularly understood to be unfading in color. Unlike the things of this world that rust, fall apart, and lose their luster and beauty over time, the inheritance, Peter insisted, will never begin to fade.

Beare creatively captured the essence of Peter's three descriptions when he summarized them in this way: "the inheritance is untouched by death, unstained by evil, unimpaired by time" (Beare, 1947, 57–58).

This inheritance was "kept in heaven." The verb is a passive perfect, indicating the inheritance began to be kept by God in the past and continues to be safeguarded by him. Accordingly, Peter was emphasizing once more the divine nature of their experience of blessing. It was because of the Father that they were elected (1:1); it was because of the Father's great mercy that they were born again (1:3); and it was because of the Father that their inheritance was secure (1:4). That the inheritance was secured *in heaven* further confirms that the vicissitudes of this life cannot impact the waiting inheritance. Peter's transition to the second person ("reserved in heaven for *you*") had the effect of making the secured inheritance personal (Grudem, 1988, 62).

1:5. A living hope and a secure inheritance are the first two blessings Peter mentioned regarding the new birth. Verse 5 introduced a third—a coming salvation. The verse began, however, by further describing the readers in

terminology of inheritance would likely bring out such a contrast, it does not seem to be Peter's primary focus. His emphasis is on the distinction from the readers' past life with its perishable inheritance and the readers' present life and its imperishable inheritance.

6   Unperishable. While the normal English word would be "imperishable," the Oxford English Dictionary indicates that unperishable has a long history in English, despite its disuse today (Simpson, 1991, 19:138).

Amaranthus caudatus. Public domain.

Asia Minor. They were not only those whose inheritance was secure, but also they themselves were secure for the attainment of the future inheritance. This was because they were being guarded through faith for future salvation.

Peter used a passive verb[7] when referring to the readers "being guarded through faith," revealing that though the means of their endurance was faith, it was not the strength of the believers that kept them faithful. Instead, it was God's power that guarded them. In other words, God motivated the faith of these believers so that they remained faithful until the consummation of salvation. Peter Davids notes the underlying message indicated with Peter's use of military terminology: "The picture is that of a fortress or military camp. They are within. Outside the evil forces are assaulting them. But on the perimeter is the overwhelming force of 'the power of God.' He it is who protects them. They receive his protection simply 'through faith,' that is, through committing themselves in trust and obedience to God" (Davids, 1990, 53). This would surely have been an encouragement to beleaguered Christians who may have felt that their own strength was insufficient.

Peter indicated that God's power motivated the readers' faith until they received "a salvation ready to be revealed in the last time." The term for "salvation" (σωτηρίαν) could refer to deliverance from any difficulty. Nevertheless, it is clear here that Peter had a definitive, spiritual, and future vindication in mind. That it was future is clear from the language "in the last time." Nevertheless, the proximal closeness of that time was suggested by the readiness of the coming judgment. This was a theme Peter later returned to—namely, all that is necessary for the coming judgment has taken place, so judgment is ripe, ready, and coming. Throughout the biblical literature, the day of God's judgment was prominent. That day will reveal mercy, grace, and wrath. Peter indicated that these readers need not fear that day, for their vindication was sure. Because they were elected by the Father, born

---

7   Passive verb. Grammatically, the form is ambiguous and could be middle or passive. If middle, it has the sense of a believer using faith as the means of his or her endurance. Nevertheless, the stress on God's activity throughout this section and the proximity of the statement concerning God's power strongly suggest a passive reading here.

again through his mercy, and preserved by his power, they could stand confident.

Trials, Rejoicing, and Salvation (1:6–8)

Though the new birth led the readers to rejoice, they were also experiencing trials, designed by God to test and refine them so that they would be found worthy of praise. Peter indicated that these readers had shown themselves to be people of faith, who were filled with joy based on the knowledge that their faith resulted in salvation.

1:6. By the use of the word "now," Peter turned from their future hope to their present experience. Several interrelated exegetical matters affect the way one understands this verse. The first concerns what the relative pronoun "in this" refers to. The pronoun is grammatically ambiguous and can be taken as neuter or masculine. Those who take it as masculine must choose between three possible referents: "Jesus," "God," or "time." Due to the number of intervening words, the first two are unlikely. This leaves "time" as the most reasonable referent. But if "time" is the referent, one would assume that the associated verb would be future, since "this" refers to a future time: "in this you *will* rejoice." Peter, however, provided a present verb.

If we understand the pronoun to be neuter, then the pronoun's antecedent is conceptual, not grammatical. In other words, it refers to the general ideas presented in the prior verses. Accordingly, what the readers rejoiced in was not merely the future coming of the Lord, but in all the blessings associated with the new birth (the living hope, the secure inheritance, and the coming salvation).

A second grammatical challenge is that the verb can be either present or imperative. Three reasons are offered against an imperative interpretation. First, Peter has not yet introduced imperative verbs in the letter. Second, an imperative would be strange in this early portion

of the letter. Third, Peter used the same verb in verse 8 as an indicative. Thus, it is more likely Peter was using the word in the same way here.

Thus far, Peter indicated how the Christian readers had responded to the blessings of their new birth—they rejoiced. However, Peter knew another reality also faced them, so he addressed their experience of trials. Three temporal references are made in this verse. First, Peter spoke of trials as though they had already been experienced: "you have been distressed." Second, Peter added the word "now," making it clear that they were still experiencing these challenges. Finally, Peter mentioned that these trials were "for a little while." He was not indicating that the length of a particular trial was short; rather, he was comparing the time of trial to the future time of reward. As J. Ramsey Michaels notes, Peter was stressing that "the present ordeals are insignificant in comparison to the 'eternal glory' (5:10) that lies ahead" (Michaels, 1988, 28). This is a theme Peter returned to at the end of his letter, where he indicated that the readers must "suffer for a little while" until God fulfills his promises (5:10).

The statement "if necessary" assumes the truth of the statement for the sake of the argument. As the letter makes clear, Peter's readers were already experiencing such trials, so the assumption is true to reality. The verb "necessary" ($\delta\epsilon\hat{\imath}$) is used elsewhere in the New Testament to refer to the necessity of Christ's suffering (Mark 8:31). First Peter called the readers to follow the steps of Jesus (2:21), and here it indicated that the experience of trials is a divine necessity, just as it was in the life of Jesus. Such consideration was designed to inspire hope, for the same God who granted them the blessings of the new birth is the same one who sovereignly allowed their difficulties.

Peter called their difficulties "diverse, distressing trials." The word for "trials" could refer to temptations toward sin, but given the way Peter developed the image, the idea is of a test or trial, which determines the true nature of a thing. Clearly Peter did not have a solitary trial in mind, for he speaks of the *diverse* trials. The readers should expect to continue experiencing different types of distressing trials. All of this shows the significant contrast between what they had been given by God in Christ (election) and what they were presently experiencing (exile). This contrasting theme continues throughout the letter.

1:7. Having explained the reality of the trials the readers faced, Peter explained the divine purpose behind these trials. What was being tested was the readers' faith. In this context, faith was the quality of believing in and trusting in the gospel. That it was being tested suggests that there was a spurious type of faith, a "faith" that would fail the test of genuineness and be found wanting.

Peter assumed, however, that this would not be true of his readers, for he spoke of a tested and genuine faith. The word for "genuineness" (δοκίμιον) is derived from metallurgy, where a metal is purified by fire to be without alloy. Having gone through such purification, it is declared genuine. Peter explicitly brought this to the forefront by comparing a tested faith with tested gold. In the ancient world, as it still is today, gold was one of the most precious and valuable metals. Purified gold was of great worth. But Peter argued that even refined and genuine gold is not comparable to the value of a refined and genuine faith.

Peter returned to a future view when he indicated why genuine faith was more valuable than genuine gold. At the end of this age, when the Lord Jesus is revealed from heaven, genuine gold will perish,[8] while genuine faith will result in "praise, glory, and honor." There is some debate concerning the identity of those who receive this praise, glory, and honor. It could refer

to God, since elsewhere Peter indicated that glory belongs to him (4:11; cf. 5:10). It could also refer to Jesus, for glory was attributed to him as well (1:21; 4:13). Nevertheless, the context points to the readers as receiving these blessings. This thought is significant, for though the audience was presently experiencing rejection and societal shame, they would be the recipients of praise, glory, and honor when their Lord returned.

As Peter highlighted the divine purpose in trials, he also provided reason for rejoicing in trials. Though trials were grievous and distressing, they were the means of proving the genuineness of one's faith. Further, right responses to such trials resulted in praise, glory, and honor at the coming judgment. And though such trials were an ever-present reality, they would only last "a little while." Alternatively, the reward they received for faithfulness would last eternally in the age Jesus would institute when he returned.

1:8. The connection between verses 7 and 8 is not explicit. Most likely, verse 6 indicates the reality of trials, verse 7 indicates the purpose of trials, and verses 8 and 9 indicate what Peter

---

8   Gold will perish. Compton notes, "Gold is a stable element that does not decay with the passing of time. Yet, gold, along with all the other elements in the universe, will be destroyed with the destruction of the present heavens and earth (2 Peter 3:10; cf. Rev. 21:18)" (Compton, 2019, 53).

believed concerning the readers' response to trials (Compton, 2019, 55). In this way, Peter presented the readers in Asia Minor as those who have a genuine, tested faith.

Through two concessive clauses, Peter presented the situation of the readers. First, they were those who had not seen Jesus, yet loved him. The statement reflects a historical reality concerning the readers; they did not see Jesus when he walked the earth. Despite this lack, the readers nevertheless expressed a personal and deep affection for Jesus.

The second concessive clause indicated that the readers did not presently see Jesus, yet they believed and rejoiced. The addition of the word "now" (ἄρτι) indicates a temporal contrast with the prior clause. Peter used two different words to negate the clauses, and there seems to be meaning to his choice. Regarding the first clause, Peter used a rare combination to express the negation (οὐκ with a participle), while in the second, he used the more common negation (μή with a participle). Georg Winer suggests that "οὐ stands where something is to be directly denied (as matter of fact); μή, where something is to be denied as mere matter of thought (in conception and conditionally)" (Winer, 1882, 593).

Applying Winer's maxim to this passage, we see that Peter was saying their experience of not seeing Jesus *is not* open to change, but their present experience of not seeing him now *is* open to change. This coheres well with the broader context of 1 Peter, in which Peter told the readers to set their hope on the coming of their Lord (1:13). Though they can't go back to see Jesus, they have hope that they will in the future see him when he returns.

Peter indicated two present responses to their present lack of seeing Jesus: they believed in him and they rejoiced. Believing in Jesus is parallel in conception to having faith. Thus, Peter was saying that these believers were presently showing themselves to have a genuine faith, for they had expressed belief despite their difficulties. In fact, they were rejoicing in the face of these difficulties. By the repetition of the word rejoice, Peter intended to draw the reader back to verse 6 and suggest that trials produce joy, a point expressed elsewhere in the New Testament (Matt. 5:12; James 1:2).

The joy expressed by believers is an otherworldly joy. As Achtemeier notes, The joy is "clearly not of human origin: it cannot be expressed in human speech (the literal meaning of [indescribable] ἀνεκλαλήτῳ), and as a joy suffused with glory (δεδοξασμένη), it carries within itself a foretaste of the glorious future (cf. δόξα in v. 7) that awaits those who remain faithful to Christ" (Achtemeier, 1996, 103–4).

1:9. Peter here revealed why[9] the readers in Asia Minor were filled with overwhelming joy: they were receiving the due reward of their faith, the salvation of their souls.

Three interrelated questions arise in reference to this salvation: What is meant by "salvation"? When does this salvation occur? And what is meant by "souls"? We will handle each, starting with the last.

By "souls" Peter referred to the entire person. Later he spoke of the "eight souls" who were saved in the ark (3:20), by which he certainly referred to the whole person, not a separate spiritual aspect of a person's identity.

---

9   Revealed why. The verse begins with a participle, which could be construed in different ways. It could be temporal (as Michaels contends): "when you receive the outcome of your faith" (Michaels, 1988, 25). But such a reading misses the emphasis on present experience throughout verses 6–9. It could also be attendant circumstance (as Grudem suggests): "and you receive the outcome of your faith" (Grudem, 1988, 71–72). Such a reading is possible, but it leaves the reason for the rejoicing unstated. On the causal interpretation defended above, the participle gives the reason for the readers' rejoicing.

The timing of the salvation Peter speaks of initially appears to be a present salvation. That it refers to present experience is suggested by Peter's use of a present tense verb ("you are receiving"; κομιζόμενοι), by the parallelism with "love" in verse 8, and by the fact that Peter had been focusing on the readers' present experience since verse 6. Nevertheless, salvation is generally thought of in relation to future experience, something Peter also mentioned multiple times in the near context (1:5, 7). Further, Peter's use of "outcome" or "end" (τέλος) suggests a future interpretation.

A choice between the two is difficult. Thomas Schreiner suggests that Peter may have an already/not yet idea in mind: "Believers now enjoy salvation and yet will experience it fully at the revelation of Jesus Christ" (Schreiner, 2003, 70; cf. Elliott, 2001, 337). Achtemeier agrees, noting that because the participle depends on present tense verbs, the salvation "must be understood here as describing a present activity." Yet, he continues, "That it has a future orientation is nevertheless not to be denied; ['salvation'] σωτηρία is here an eschatological term." Thus, "Christians now obtain by faith what they will only fully enter into at the end; the power of the new age is already at work" (Achtemeier, 1996, 104).

A major part of salvation is the transformation of the person into the moral image of God, a work that is occurring through the refining fire of trial. Thus, the readers had cause to rejoice in that which caused them distress. Even the negative elements of their new birth—the accompanying, necessary trials—were reasons to rejoice.

THEOLOGICAL FOCUS (1:3–9)

The exegetical idea (God the Father was to be praised for granting new birth, for this new birth provided a living hope, guaranteed a secure inheritance, and produced rejoicing despite present trial) leads to this theological focus: believers should praise the Father for the gift of the new birth, which provides a living hope, a secure inheritance, and a reason to rejoice despite trials.

Just as believers in Peter's day needed to praise God for the new birth, so believers of every age should praise God for the same gift. Though the passing of years has led to the death of many earthly hopes, the resurrection of Jesus continues to inspire a living hope.

The passing of years has also led to the decay and destruction of many earthly treasures. The magnificent temples and marketplaces known to Peter's audience are now lying in ruins. The treasures once killed for are worthless today. In contrast, the inheritance of believers is untouched by the sin of this age (1:4) and is just as valuable today as it was in Peter's day. This is the inheritance God has promised to preserve for believers (1:5).

From the time of Peter to today, the world has seen many "saviors." Each, however, has died along with their associated promises and dreams. In contrast, the new birth promises a salvation, which God guarantees to those who truly believe. He does this by strengthening true believers in faith to persevere until they obtain final redemption (1:5). One means of strengthening believers' faith is through trials. Though these are grievous, they are designed by God's hand to refine his people like gold, removing the dross and showing them to be genuine in faith (1:7). In this way, as believers are sanctified by God's power, they begin receiving salvation, though the fullness of that salvation remains in the future (1:9).

Throughout this section, Peter contrasted the future with the present. In the future, there is a secure inheritance and a full salvation (1:7, 9). In the present, there are diverse, difficult trials (1:6). Nevertheless, God does not leave believers to themselves, nor is he absent in the present (1:7). Instead, the present prepares believers for the future. By means of the exercise of faith, these believers experience joy amid trial (1:6). This joy is not only over the future hope and inheritance, but also over the present experience of salvation they are privileged to experience.

PREACHING AND TEACHING STRATEGIES

Exegetical and Theological Synthesis

Humanity tends to obsess over the temporal. The automotive industry takes in nearly $1 trillion each year, all spent on vehicles that immediately begin to wear down upon leaving the lot. The real estate industry takes in about half of that, enslaving countless people to a debt many of them will never repay, to upkeep a home that will continually wear down. Collectors of stamps, coins, comic books, art, and other items spend money, time, and energy on amassing a collection of things that have little to no eternal value.

Humankind's obsession on the temporal reveals the level of our deception and self-infatuation. When something comes along to ruin our stuff—be it a natural disaster, a thief, or just the wear of time—it tends to upend our world.

But when our focus extends beyond this world and we find supremacy in Christ and his rewards, then when our earthly things rot and decay and get lost and stolen, we find ourselves still standing on solid ground. The fullness of our salvation is not in this life (1 Peter 1:3–4). God repairs the hurt of this existence with the glory of our eternal state. Our present salvation provides hope for our future, peeling our eyes away from the cheap, temporary prizes to the most valuable, eternal rewards. Only through the gospel of Christ can humanity find hope in our future. That future hope has a sanctifying effect on our present existence, causing us to rejoice in our faith even now (1:7–9).

Preaching Idea

The Born-Again Supremacy: Faithful Living Results in Supreme Rewards.

Contemporary Connections

What does it mean?

"Christianese" is a term used to describe church language that has become familiar to believers who have been in the church for some time but may be unfamiliar to someone new to the Bible or Christianity. Phrases such as "born again" are common lingo in the church, but put yourself in the position of an outsider. What does it mean to be "born again"? An unbeliever may be just as puzzled as Nicodemus was when Jesus used the term in John 3!

Preachers must be careful to explain such language. Do not think of it as "dumbing down" to explain such terms in the sermon; rather, in the same way God brought the New Testament to the world through the common ("koine") language of the everyman, so we ought to preach in such a way that all people can understand (1 Cor. 14:16).

The same goes even with the word "salvation," used here in verses 5 and 9. Peter's usage here may stump even seasoned Christians. If a Christian is asked, "What is salvation?" she might answer with a focus on forgiveness of sins and what Jesus has done in the past. This answer would not be wrong, but it would also not be complete. Here, Peter focuses on the *future* aspect of our salvation. This salvation is "ready to be revealed *in the last time*" (v. 5). As the exposition revealed, the description of salvation in verse 9 may enjoy both aspects of "already" and "not yet."

The preacher will also want to carefully explain the meaning of our future inheritance. Peter uses three "un-" words to describe it: unperishable, undefiled, unfading. The sermon can contrast these three words with earthly inheritance—which perishes, fades, and can become defiled. That nice house your parents left you? It will wear down. That large sum of money Grandpa gave in his will? You can't take it to heaven with you. That beautiful painting that your friend gifted you in her trust? It will eventually fade, no matter what efforts you make to keep it preserved.

But a believer's inheritance lasts far beyond any of these earthly treasures. Contrasting the nature of our eternal inheritance with the temporal nature of the earthly will bring out Peter's point clearly, even to those unfamiliar with the idea of heavenly rewards.

Is it true?

Is it truly possible to "rejoice with joy" (v. 10) even in the midst of trials and persecutions? Modern believers—many having never experienced true suffering for the Lord—may not warmly embrace this concept of rejoicing through trials. The church in many countries need not be convinced of such apparent truth, but in other countries that do not experience regular persecution, suffering for the faith may be seen as the greatest evil possible.

When we idolatrize comfort and ease of life, we seek to avoid suffering of any kind by any means necessary. But Peter urges believers to a higher way of living. We live with a faith that extends beyond the temporary trials of life. The preacher will need to point the church to the assurance of faith found only in the proven reliability of God and his people.

One means of providing such assurance is by using biblical examples, like the "hall of faith" in Hebrews 11. Each member of this group had "conviction of things not seen" (11:1), similar to Peter's readers. Or, the preacher may point the church to more modern examples of men and women who had faith beyond trials, such as missionary pioneers like Hudson Taylor or William Carey. These testimonies point to the possibility of rejoicing through trials with a mindset of salvation future.

Now what?

How do our future benefits in heaven, which are based on Christ's past work, impact our present reality as Christians? Think about an analogy with earthly inheritance in order to connect the dots between past, present, and future.

Suppose Grandma has just been diagnosed with stage 4 cancer. The doctor gives her a year to live, best-case scenario. Grandma sits the family down and lets them know—to their surprise—that they will each receive one million dollars from a series of investments she secretly built up over the years. How will that knowledge impact the way the family lives now? Rebellious grandson Joe might begin to rack up debt on his credit cards, knowing that a future payday is on the horizon and will eventually cover those expenses. Studious granddaughter Jane may set her sights higher on college, previously a goal unattainable due to lack of finances. Daughter Janet decides to forego the DIY home projects she had previously planned. Instead, she plans on hiring a handyman a year or two from now, whereas son-in-law John has a conversation with his employers about training someone for his position, knowing that he'll soon have plenty of funds to retire. A future inheritance has present impact, for better or worse depending on the wisdom and foresight of the steward.

The future inheritance and coming salvation of believers cause them to live in such a way that they reprioritize their present life. The preacher can point out the folly of living solely for this tiny blip on the everlasting line of eternity. Suddenly, sacrificing the comforts of America to live in a hut in Africa translating the Bible for an unreached tribe is not such a "sacrifice," when one considers the eternal rewards to come. Giving up a financially secure job as CEO in a large company in order to work for pennies on the dollar as a pastor makes more sense in light of our eternal future. Suffering through persecution brings joy instead of sorrow, for we know that we have pursued the right kind of things in this life, with heaven in mind.

Creativity in Presentation

Whenever possible, it is best to allow the text of Scripture to provide creative and engaging sermon illustrations for the preacher. The most notable possibility offered by 1 Peter 1:3–9 is the allusion to metallurgy in verse 7. Peter compares tested faith with tested gold. Most of his original readers would have picked up on the comparison rather quickly, needing little explanation. Today, most moderns are unfamiliar with such processes of refinement. The preacher may want to consider how to draw out this analogy with maximum effect. A simple description of the process works at a bare minimum, perhaps with a few visuals displayed if this fits the church environment. Smelting actual gold on the stage may be too expensive and dangerous (and distracting!) for a sermon, but even a short video clip of what the process might look like could help bring the text alive for readers. Plenty of such kind can be found on YouTube with a quick search.

The preacher may also want to consider the three "un-" words (unperishable, undefiled, unfading) as an opportunity to provide a visual for the church. My son and I collect coins. Collectors protect the highest graded coins behind hermetically sealed plastic or glass to keep them from fading or scratching. Otherwise, even something as refined and seemingly "permanent" as a shaped piece of metal will not last forever. Likewise (to my shame), I still have a few t-shirts from high school hanging around in my drawers, despite my wife's best efforts to rid me of them. I can't wear them out of the house anymore, and with each wearing and washing they fade even further.

Clothes fade. Coins tarnish. Show a few examples to the church. The best of what we have will one day perish. But the inheritance the Lord has for believers promises to last forever. Giving these examples (perhaps even visually with an object lesson on the stage) may help sharpen the contrast between what this world offers and what heaven promises. Heaven promises supreme rewards for those who live faithfully.

Preachers may want to outline the sermon according to the twofold structure of the paragraph:

- The Believer's New Birth (1:3–5)

- The Believer's New Trials (1:6–9)

DISCUSSION QUESTIONS

1. What do you think of the concept of an inheritance that is "unperishable, unde-filed, and unfading"? What most excites you about this reward?

2. What are some of the purposes of trials mentioned here in 1 Peter?

3. How can someone have an attitude of rejoicing even in the midst of trials and persecution? What kind of perspective does that take?

4. What trials are you currently enduring? How do Peter's words help you engage in a healthier, biblical way?

1 Peter 1:10–12

EXEGETICAL IDEA
The readers were to be envied, for they were experiencing the salvation accomplished by the suffering and glorification of Christ, which was predicted by the Old Testament prophets and was of great interest to the angelic beings.

THEOLOGICAL FOCUS
Church-age believers are privileged to know the fullness of the gospel, which the prophets desired to know, and the angels have great interest in.

PREACHING IDEA
The Born-Again Legacy: A Long Legacy of Prophets and Angels Magnifies the Mysteries of the Gospel.

PREACHING POINTERS
Suffering does not often feel like a privileged position. Peter's readers likely did not feel that they lived in a time of privilege or entitlement, especially as Christians in an increasingly anti-Christian society. Persecution plagued the church, threatening to scare believers away from their newfound faith. Believers suffered physically through imprisonment, beatings, displacement, and death.

Today, we might feel like we enjoy a variety of privileges for various reasons: we live in a period of unparalleled technological advancement; we benefit from a wealth of riches and luxury and comfort in our modern temperature-controlled mansions; diseases that would have been deadly just a few centuries ago can now be cured at the cost of a few dollars. The world is smaller than ever before, and we feel better off for it.

The preacher can show the church that these so-called privileges pale in comparison to the privileges of living on this side of the cross. Believers experience the fullness of the gospel, something both angels and prophets longed to comprehend for many millennia. To preach this passage is to preach the greatest privilege in the history of humanity, far eclipsing the glories of technology, comfort, travel, or earthly riches!

THE BELIEVER'S PRIVILEGED KNOWLEDGE (1:10–12)

LITERARY STRUCTURE AND THEMES (1:10–12)

First Peter 1:10–12 presents the end of the long Greek sentence[1] begun in 1:3. By means of a relative pronoun, Peter connected the conclusion of the sentence to the salvation spoken of in 1:5 and 1:9, a salvation that the readers were beginning to experience and were desiring to be completed.

This section breaks neatly into two parts. The first addressed the desire of the prophets to know more about the grace that was to be revealed in the future (1:10–11). The second part addressed the envious position of the readers, for the Old Testament prophets' labor was directed toward them. The privilege of their position was further highlighted by the statement that even the angels longed to know more about the gospel they were privileged to experience.

This paragraph appropriately concludes the opening of the letter. Just as 1:1–2 encouraged the readers in light of the future benefits of the new birth (living hope, secure inheritance, and a coming salvation), and 1:3–9 encouraged the readers in light of God's sovereign governance of trials, so this final section of the opening reminded them that what has come to pass was the will of God, which was harmonious with the predictions of the prophets long ago.

Themes of this section include: the careful investigation of Old Testament prophets into the details of God's plan for the Messiah; the relationship of Jesus to the Spirit who inspired prophecies concerning the Messiah; the beneficial position of the readers who are the focus of the prophet's predictions; and the interest of the angelic beings in the details of the gospel.

- ***The Prophets' Diligent Search (1:10–11)***
- ***The Envious Position of the Readers (1:12)***

EXPOSITION (1:10–12)

Peter concluded the opening by focusing on the reception of salvation. In these verses, Peter identified the privileged position of the Anatolian readers, for they were the recipients of the Old Testament prophets' labor when the prophets predicted the coming Messiah, his sufferings, and glory. Indeed, the readers were privileged because they knew what the prophets longed to know—they even knew what angels long to know! They had come to know this through the gospel, which was preached by the power of the Spirit sent from heaven—the same Spirit who inspired the prophecies of the Old Testament saints.

The Prophets' Diligent Search (1:10–11)

The salvation the readers were experiencing was prophesied by Old Testament prophets, who predicted the sufferings and glories of the Messiah and who desired to know more about the Messiah.

---

1 End of the long Greek sentence. Achtemeier notes the temporal balance Peter presented in this long sentence: "If the first part had major emphasis on the future results of God's act of begetting believers anew (especially inheritance and salvation), and the second part put emphasis on the present results (suffering, love, and joy), this part lays the emphasis on the past, in which the rudiments of this salvation were discerned, specifically through the intervention of the divine Spirit" (Achtemeier, 1996, 105).

1:10. In these verses, Peter confirmed a point he had been implicitly making. Namely, these readers had entered a spiritual heritage, which had been in the making from time immemorial. Regardless of their heritage (whether Jew or Gentile), these readers were the intended recipients of God's grace and favor, which was predicted in ancient times.

The note of God's sovereignty is repeated here when Peter indicated that such grace is "destined for you" (ϵἰς ὑμᾶς). The same construction is used in the next verse to speak of the sufferings "destined for Christ" (ϵἰς Χριστόν). This contrast emphasized the nature of the gospel, which began with God's divine elective choice and was accomplished through the suffering of Christ. The believer, then, is the recipient of grace, for such salvation could never be accomplished by oneself, nor could such a priceless payment be purchased.

Peter noted that the prophets searched their own prophecies. By using two words that have nearly the same meaning (ἐξεζήτησαν and ἐξηραύνησαν), Peter intensified the description of the search. Many English translations add the word "carefully" to express this point. For example, the ESV has "searched and inquired carefully" and the NRSV has "made careful search and inquiry."

Which Prophets?

Selwyn argued that the prophets spoken of here are New Testament prophets like Agabus (Selwyn, 1946, 134; cf. Warden, 1989, 12). But such an interpretation fails, for Peter speaks of "prophecies beforehand" or "predictions" (προμαρτυρόμενον) made by the prophets.

These descriptions suggest that what is prophesied was prophesied at some distant time in the past. Further, in verse 12 there is a clear contrast between those who prophesied and those who preached the gospel. Presumably the New Testament prophets both prophesied *and* preached. Finally, Peter cites numerous Old Testament prophecies concerning Christ, which suggests that the prophets he references here are the Old Testament prophets who made those prophecies.

1:11. What the prophets were searching for was revealed by two interrogatives in verse 11. These interrogatives have sparked debate. Two positions are taken. First, both interrogatives modify "time" (καιρόν), leading to the reading "what time or circumstances" (NIV, CSB, NLT). Second, the first interrogative (τίνα) is taken as substantival (referring to a person) and the second is adjectival, modifying "time" (καιρόν). This leads to the reading "what person or time" (ESV, NASB, NRSV, NET).

As can be seen by the diversity of translations, the correct reading is not explicitly clear. There are good reasons to argue for both positions. Jobes shows that by statistical analysis,[2] the personal reading (what person or what time) has word use in its favor. Further, if both interrogatives are adjectival, they appear redundant.

In favor of the entirely temporal reading is the fact that the Old Testament gives evidence of the prophets' interest in timing of prophecies (Dan. 9:2; 12:6–13; Hab. 2:1–4; Michaels, 1988, 42). Second, if the interrogatives have different senses, one would expect "and" (καί) instead of "or" (ἤ). Finally, though this reading requires redundancy[3] of the interrogatives, in

---

2   Statistical analysis. Jobes says, "Of the more than one thousand occurrences in the NT, the word [τίς] occurs less than twenty times as an adjective. Moreover, in all other occurrences in 1 Peter [τίς and its related words] function as pronouns" (Jobes, 2005, 102). But statistical analysis is rarely helpful in answering specific exegetical arguments, for following statistics would lead to eliminating all minor grammatical uses.

3   Redundancy. Michaels argues that they are not redundant. In his opinion, the second interrogative broadens the first. Thus, the first asks about the timing of the Messiah, while the second asks more generally about the timing of eschatological events associated with the Messiah (Michaels, 1988, 42).

this same context Peter recently used two words of nearly identical meaning for rhetorical effect ("searched and inquired" [ἐξεζήτησαν καὶ ἐξηραύνησαν]; v. 10). He could be doing the same here.

In the end, though a definitive answer is evasive, the temporal reading appears to be slightly favored by the evidence. Regardless of one's decision, the overall point is clear: The Old Testament prophets searched their own prophecies seeking to understand more fully what was being revealed. This may have had to do with the identity of the Messiah, but it certainly had to do with the timing of the Messiah.

Peter's mention of the Spirit was significant, for he referred to the Spirit as the Spirit of Christ. Such a designation was not unique to Peter, for Paul used identical language in Romans 8:9, and similar language was used in three other texts (Acts 16:7; Gal. 4:6; Phil. 1:19). Such passages highlight the unity of the Godhead. Further, Peter's association of Jesus with Old Testament prophecies implicitly affirmed the preexistence of Jesus.

The "Spirit of Christ" in Scripture	
Rom. 8:9b	Anyone who does not have the *Spirit of Christ* does not belong to him.
Acts 16:7	And when they had come up to Mysia, they attempted to go into Bithynia, but the *Spirit of Jesus* did not allow them.
Gal. 4:6	Because you are sons, God has sent forth the *Spirit of His Son* into our hearts, crying, "Abba! Father!"
Phil. 1:19	For I know that through your prayers and the help of the *Spirit of Jesus Christ* this will turn out for my deliverance.

The content of the Spirit's revelation was "the sufferings of Christ and the subsequent glories." The "sufferings of Christ" or the "Messianic sufferings"[4] were plural, referring primarily to the passive obedience of the Son, who in humility took the punishment of sin upon himself. In reference to such sufferings, Peter later spoke of Jesus as one who "bore our sins in his body on

---

4   Messianic sufferings. A few commentators have suggested that 1 Peter's outlook fits within an apocalyptic theme focused on messianic sufferings. Mark Dubis, who has written a monograph on the topic, defines it in the following way: "Early Jews and Christians anticipated a horrific period of suffering and tribulation that would precede the coming of the Messiah and the denouement of history. Stereotypical features of these woes include famine, earthquakes, war, apostasy, disease, family betrayal, rampant wickedness, cosmic signs, and (in some texts) the persecution of the righteous. These woes in early Judaism are 'messianic' not because the Messiah suffers them, but because they are a prelude to the Messiah's arrival. The crucifixion of Jesus, however, forced early Christians to adapt this Jewish scheme. In light of the cross, early Christians affirmed that, rather than bringing an end to the woes, the Messiah himself had inaugurated these woes in his first advent. Moreover, the church would continue to suffer these woes as it awaited the second advent of Jesus" (Dubis, 2001, 86).

     Some interpreters of 1 Peter have found the messianic woes a helpful guide for understanding some passages in the letter (Selwyn, 1946, 299–303; Michaels, 1988, 270). On the other hand, other interpreters are more critical, seeing that there is a danger that such a perspective can make an illegitimate intrusion on the text (Achtemeier, 1996, 110; Goppelt, 1993, 330). The most significant challenge in accepting the outlook is that the apocalyptic elements normally associated with such a view—earthquakes, famines, war—are missing from 1 Peter. And as Dubis notes, only some of "messianic woes" texts speak of the persecution of the righteous, which is the central element of 1 Peter. Accordingly, while some of the perspectives inherent to the messianic woe perspective are present in 1 Peter, they need not derive from a wholesale adoption of that perspective. Nevertheless, Dubis has highlighted many interesting connections. For a detailed defense, see Dubis's monograph (Dubis, 2002).

the cross" (2:24). The "glories that would follow" referred to Christ's present session at the right hand of the Father as well as the granted right to be the King of kings in the coming kingdom. Even prior to this kingdom, Peter spoke of Jesus as one who "who has gone into heaven and is at the right hand of God, with angels, authorities, and powers having been subjected to him" (3:22). The order of suffering followed by glory was an order repeated in 1 Peter (3:18–22) and one which, Peter would argue, was necessary for the readers to experience (2:21).

The Envious Position of the Readers (1:12)
These readers were served by the Old Testament prophets and by those who preached the gospel to them, and their consequent knowledge was of interest to past generations of God's people and was even of interest to the angels.

Israel and the Church

That 1 Peter was written primarily to Gentiles (see the introduction) creates a difficulty. Did the prophets write for the sake of future Gentiles or for the future nation of Israel? Indeed, one of the key questions throughout the history of the church concerns the role of Israel as a nation in God's unfolding plan of redemption. First Peter has been one of the battlegrounds in the discussion, for it appears clear that Peter is speaking to Gentiles, yet he attributes to them titles associated with ethnic Israel (e.g., 2:9–10), and aligns Old Testament statements concerning Israel to them (e.g., the readers as a part of the new covenant [1:2], which was to be with Israel [Jer. 31:31]). For some interpreters, Peter's transferring such titles and promises to elect Gentiles indicates that elect Gentiles have *become* Israel.

Accordingly, there is no more distinction between Israel and the church, for the church has become the new Israel, inheriting her promises.

But there is another way to understand the references in 1 Peter. This way maintains that the promises of the Old Testament were for Israel, and yet Peter was able to use the same language in reference to the church. Paul indicates that one of God's purposes in pouring out blessings on the Gentiles is to lead Israel to jealousy (Rom. 11:11). What could lead them to jealousy more than seeing another group enjoying the promises made to them? In this way, God is not replacing Israel with the church, for Israel still has a future (cf. Acts 1:6; Rom. 11:26). Instead, God is expanding the referent of his blessings, including those who God said would eventually receive blessings *through* Israel. It is for this reason Paul looks with great anticipation to the day when Israel will be restored, and the channel of blessing will be established just as God originally indicated (Rom. 11:15). For more from this perspective, see Vlach (2010).

1:12. The Spirit of Christ made known to the prophets two things. First, the Spirit revealed to them knowledge of the Messiah. Second, he revealed to the prophets that this knowledge of the Messiah was intended for the benefit of a future generation.[5] Peter now revealed that this future generation had come, and his readers were a part of that intended audience. By highlighting this fact, Peter was continuing the theme of the significance of the readers' position. From the beginning, God intended that *they* would be served by the prophecies.

The mention of the Spirit in the announcement of the gospel aligns this verse with the last.

---

5   Future generation. The text does not indicate the prophets knew which generation they were serving. Compton suggests that the book of Daniel and his prophecies concerning the timing of the coming of the Messiah may suggest that Peter is indicating that even the timing was revealed and recorded (Compton, 2019, 66). Nevertheless, Peter may simply be saying that they knew the revelation was for a future generation, though which one they could not be sure.

The same Spirit who inspired the prophesies is the same one who speaks through those who proclaim the gospel. Indeed, the content of the gospel is consonant with these past prophecies, though the preaching is accompanied with fuller clarity and content.

The final statement of the verse has been the source of great intrigue. What does it mean that the angels longed to look, and into what did they desire to look? Angels are not omniscient beings and elsewhere it is clear that they lack knowledge about God's plans (Mark 13:32). The full content of the gospel appears to have been a mystery hidden even from the angels (cf. Eph. 3:10). Accordingly, the angels are desirous to see the plan of redemption as it is worked out. They long to see the fullness of God's plan as it is revealed to God's people, for in this way they also learn of God's goodness. While many questions may yet remain, the overall point is clear—the readers were exceedingly blessed. What God has revealed to them has been the interest of angelic beings for ages past.

These verses show the centrality of Christ for the message of 1 Peter. It was Jesus's Spirit that inspired the prophecies, and the prophecies were about Jesus. The message of the gospel, by which the readers were saved, is all about the sufferings and glories of Jesus. Indeed, the path of Jesus from suffering to glory, Peter would later reveal, was also necessary for those who believe and follow Christ (2:21). They must suffer, yet glory will follow. From the first to last, 1 Peter is a text highlighting the significance of Christ for the present life of Peter's readers.

THEOLOGICAL FOCUS

The exegetical idea (readers were to be envied, for they were experiencing the salvation accomplished by the suffering and glorification of Christ, which was predicted by the Old Testament prophets and was of great interest to the angelic beings) leads to this theological focus: church-age believers are privileged to know the fullness of the gospel, which the prophets

desired to know, and the angels have great interest in.

Along with all the other benefits mentioned before (the living hope, the secure inheritance, and the coming salvation), Peter adds that all church-age believers have come to know what many generations of prophets longed to know. These prophets knew that their prophetic service was not for their own benefit, but they looked intently at their own prophecies to see what time these prophecies would ultimately unfold. In God's sovereignty, believers in this church age are the recipients of the full gospel message.

Despite the differences between church-age saints and the prophets, there is continuity among believers of all ages. The same gospel predicted *by the Spirit* is the same one that is still preached today *through the Spirit*. Despite the divide between Jew and Gentile, the Jewish messengers were divinely appointed to prophesy for the benefit of both Jews and Gentiles, all whom God would call in his elective grace.

Finally, while some mystery concerning the angelic interest in redemption remains, Peter is clearly indicating that the redemption of God's people is of cosmic interest. Thus, believers of all ages have entered God's wonderful and wise plan of redemption, which is a beautiful flower still in the process of blooming.

PREACHING AND TEACHING STRATEGIES

Exegetical and Theological Synthesis

From the very moment Adam and Eve ate the forbidden fruit, sin marred the perfect world that God had created. Every atom in the universe was impacted by this fateful decision. Sin changed everything.

But this is not to say that anything happened apart from God's sovereign plan. Ages before God breathed existence into humanity, God had a plan to redeem humanity from its sin through the death and resurrection of Jesus Christ. Peter himself will soon state that Jesus was "foreknown before the foundation of the world" and only revealed in the last times (1:20). Paul tells believers that they were chosen in Christ before the foundation of the world (Eph. 1:4). Elsewhere he says that the wisdom of the gospel was "decreed before the ages for our glory" (1 Cor. 2:7). Most tellingly, Peter preached to the people on the day of Pentecost that Jesus was crucified "according to the definite plan and foreknowledge of God" (Acts 2:23; cf. 4:27–28). Clearly, sin did not take God by surprise. God had a plan all along to deal with it through the shed blood of his Son.

God's solution to the problem of sin was foretold by the prophets. From Moses to Isaiah to Micah to Daniel, the Old Testament prophets eagerly looked forward to a future, permanent solution to the curse. God's judgment upon Israel during their forty years of wandering in the wilderness did not cure sin's effects; neither did seventy years in exile. The problem persisted and the people were left to long for a greater solution.

During this time, even the angels themselves eagerly longed to see how God would address the greatest problem the universe has ever known. What creation has longed for, what the prophets have written about, what the angels eagerly anticipated came to fulfillment in Jesus Christ's death on the cross and subsequent resurrection. As was planned before the foundation of the world, Jesus's blood atoned for the sin of all those who place their faith in him, and his resurrection defeated death and provides a future hope.

Believers on this side of the cross enjoy the greatest privilege of any believer in history: We experience the fullness of the gospel. We stand from a viewpoint where we see how God's plan has unfolded in all its beauty, for the benefit of humanity, to the glory of God.

Preaching Idea

The Born-Again Legacy: A Long Legacy of Prophets and Angels Magnifies the Mysteries of the Gospel.

Contemporary Connections

What does it mean?

The greatest challenge in preaching this text will likely come in offering a clear explanation of what Peter means when he says that the prophets "searched and inquired carefully" and that angels have "longed to look" into these things. The exposition above helped explain these concepts, slightly favoring the temporal reading that the prophets searched to understand the timing of the Messiah via their own prophecies.

The Bible offers several clear examples of this, which may be used for illustrative purposes. In Daniel 9:2, the prophet searches the prophecies of Jeremiah to see when the seventy years of captivity will end. At the end of the same book, Daniel inquisitively asks to have more information regarding the timing and nature of the end times. The angels deny his request. This is but one example of a prophet seeking more information about the prophecies in his own book.

An analogy with childbirth may also help. When a woman becomes pregnant, the doctor may give her a rough due date based on conception and the size of the baby. But this does not stop her from eagerly longing and guessing what the actual date will be. Did she tend to run early or late on her other pregnancies? How is the baby's growth progressing? Does she "feel" like the baby will come soon? She longs for what she knows will inevitably happen and looks for "signs" to clarify the exact "when" of the event.

Along the same vein, the preacher will also need to clarify Peter's words about angels longing to look at the revealed gospel. Though their position is one of privilege, with a spiritual perception far beyond ours, angels still relate to the cross differently than humans. Consider a servant in the queen of England's royal court. Certainly the servant has a privileged position, walking where most do not dare tread, seeing the royalty up close on a regular basis. But they still might look longingly—even jealously—toward those whom the royalty chooses to entertain and bless. Though the analogy is imperfect, it may lend an understanding toward how one can be in such a high position (angels) and yet still see things from an outsider's perspective.

Is it true?

The manner in which Peter speaks about angels might confuse some Christians. Our culture has a unique—and mostly wrong—fascination with angels, from the wrongheaded notion that babies become angels upon their death, to the cute little cherubs that hang on our Christian tree, to the egregious shows like *Lucifer* glorifying Satan himself. All of this has led to massive confusion about the true role of angels in God's redemptive plan. Even seasoned Christians have mistaken notions about what angels are and what they do.

Here, believers might be surprised to learn that angels are not omniscient. They do not know the future. There are aspects of God's plan that angels long to understand and perhaps even experience more fully. The preacher would do well to dispel some of the wrong ideas about angels, perhaps by contrasting some of these current shows or iconographic symbols with the biblical teaching on spirits. The sermon should not delve into an exhaustive discussion on angelology but cut through the false beliefs that angels are omniscient, omnipotent beings equal in power to God himself, in order to clarify Peter's words in 1:12.

Now what?

Being a Christian means we have a duty and responsibility to come to church, to share the gospel, to reach the unreached. The Bible certainly emphasizes this responsibility (Eph. 4:1; Phil. 1:27). But 1 Peter 1:10–12 does not challenge the reader with any imperatives; rather, it gives the privileged basis upon which these later imperatives will stand.

Enjoying such a privileged status in our era of redemptive history does not mean we walk around with heads held high, as if we earned it. Instead, knowing that we live in a time period that the prophets diligently sought to understand humbles us. Knowing that we experience the fullness of the gospel, something the angels have longed to look upon, causes us to praise God who has gifted us with such grace.

This privileged status should challenge us to live worthy of the gospel—not in some perverted attempt to earn salvation, but in such a way that demonstrates our gratitude for it. To paraphrase the poignant words of Spiderman's uncle, "With great privilege comes great responsibility."

I (Bryan) have four children. By virtue of my position in church, they all share the moniker "pastor's kids." They have not chosen this title for themselves, but it's theirs nonetheless. I often have to impress upon them the responsibility that comes with such a position. My daughter once asked me, "Dad, am I famous in our church?" The answer was, "Sort of." But with that so-called fame comes extra scrutiny and responsibility that does not normally come with being a child.

The child of God enjoys even greater privilege and consequently even greater responsibility. Challenge the church to recognize their status and live accordingly.

Creativity in Presentation

For a gripping introduction that would lead into the sermon, the preacher may want to consider tapping into some of the more creative individuals in his church. Open the sermon or the service with a short drama highlighting the longing of the prophets looking forward to the coming Messiah. Three short vignettes capturing the emotion and longing of the Old Testament saints can grip the attention of the audience from the get-go.

Consider Daniel—diligently searching Jeremiah's prophecies in his old age, hoping to foresee the conclusion of exile, yet looking ahead to the ultimate solution to the problem of sin, found only in the coming Christ.

Consider Isaiah—after decades of ministry, predicting the suffering servant: despised and rejected, yet the one who would bear the griefs of the nation and be pierced for the transgressions of sinners, ushering in peace and intercession.

Consider Micah—who prophesies about a ruler coming forth from the insignificant town of Bethlehem, a ruler predicted of old to reign in Israel and shepherd the lost flock.

Each of these (and many more) offer great "living" illustrations of the text. Writing a short, living drama based on several prophets can allow for the church to not only cognitively engage with the meaning behind Peter's words but emotionally engage with them as well. A consideration of these prophets will magnify the work of the gospel throughout the ages of redemptive history.

Preachers can organize the sermon based on the prophet/angel/readers motif in the text:

- The Search of the Prophets (1:10–11)

- The Search of the Angels (1:12)

- Application: The Search of the Church

DISCUSSION QUESTIONS

1. Why can believers on this side of the cross claim a more privileged status than prophets of the Old Testament? How does that make you feel?

2. Compare humans with angels. Which is the "greater" being? How does this passage inform our understanding of that question?

3. How does the privilege of being a Christian relate to the responsibility of being a Christian?

NEW IDENTITY LEADING TO HOLINESS
(1 PETER 1:13–2:10)

First Peter 1:13–2:10 serves as the body opening to Peter's letter. If the first section of the letter (1:1–12) was characterized by the indicative (stating who the readers are), this section is characterized by the imperative (stating what the readers should do). In fact, the imperative is based on the indicative, as can be seen from the first word beginning this section: "therefore" (διό). The main point of verses 13–21 is that the readers should be holy. They should do this because they have been purchased from the old way of life (v. 18) with an extremely costly sacrifice (v. 19) and now they have a new Father to emulate (vv. 14–16), a Father who will one day judge all people (v. 17). Verses 22–25 remind the readers of their conversion through the living Word and consequently call them to a sincere brotherly love. First Peter 2:1–3 furthers the newborn image by calling the readers to pursue the milk, meaning the Word of God. Finally, 2:4–10 returns to the privileged identity of the readers. This time, Peter indicates that the readers are like stones, built upon the Cornerstone, Jesus Christ. They are specifically chosen by God to create a new temple. Verses 9–10 multiply honorific titles on these believers, highlighting their favored status.

This major section, New Identity Leading to Holiness, is broken into four preaching units: Born Again for Holiness (1:13–21), Born Again to Love (1:22–25), Craving the Spiritual Milk (2:1–3), and The Living Stone and the Living Stones (2:4–10).

1 Peter 1:13–21

EXEGETICAL IDEA
In light of their new birth, Peter's readers had to set their hope fully on the coming of Christ, reject their old way of life by modeling God's holiness, and live in reverent fear, knowing God's impartial judgment and the overwhelming cost of their redemption.

THEOLOGICAL FOCUS
Believers must hope in Christ's coming, reflect the Father's holiness, and live in reverent fear.

PREACHING IDEA
Like Father, Like Sons: Be Holy, as God Is Holy.

PREACHING POINTERS
The first few paragraphs of Peter's letter focused on the "born-again identity" of the readers. Now, Peter transitions to tell his readers how they should expect to live in light of that new identity.

This passage offers the preacher the first passage packed with application in 1 Peter. Previous passages primarily built theological groundwork, laying the way for the imperatives to follow. Here, Peter launches into several commands, urging his readers to set their hope on God's grace, to be holy as God is holy, and to live in reverent fear. Then, in an explosive theological climax, he highlights the revelation of the gospel.

The passage may be the most exciting yet! Packed with clear commands and a ready-made gospel message in the text, few pericopes in the New Testament offer a clearer path to preach than this one. Peter stirs our hearts with his message, challenging believers to live in light of their identity as born-again Christians and to act according to the character of their holy Father.

BORN AGAIN FOR HOLINESS (1:13–21)

LITERARY STRUCTURE AND THEMES (1:13–21)

Having concluded a powerful description of the identity of the readers (1:1–12), Peter here provided guidance for how that identity should influence the lives of the readers. Peter structured these verses around three imperatives (set your hope [1:13]; be holy [1:15]; live in reverent fear [1:17]), each based on the character of God and the character of the audience as newborn members of God's family.

Peter highlighted the necessity of obedience, specifically a turning away from the former way of life and an imitation of the Father. Additionally, he gave concentrated consideration to the sacrifice of Christ, mentioning its value and cost. Finally, Peter once more highlighted divine election, showing that these readers were the recipients of grace in that they were included in God's eternal plan of redemption in Christ.

Themes of this section include: the believer's future hope; the necessity for those born again to emulate the holiness of the Father; the incalculable value of Christ's sacrifice; Jesus's role as the perfect, spotless lamb; and the central place God's elect enjoy in his divine plan.

- *Hope in Coming Grace (1:13)*
- *Conform to the Father's Holiness (1:14–16)*
- *Live in Reverent Fear (1:17–19)*
- *The Father's Plan Revealed (1:20–21)*

EXPOSITION (1:13–21)

Peter provided three commands in this section. First, he called the Asia Minor readers to set their hope fully on the coming grace that would be revealed when Christ returns (v. 13). They were to do this by preparing their minds for action and exercising self-control.

Peter's second command was preceded by a consideration of what they should not do. Those who had experienced the new birth must not be conformed to their past desires, which they once followed in ignorance (v. 14). But since they had been transferred into God's family, they now had to live as obedient children (v. 14). This leads to Peter's command that the readers were to imitate the holiness of the Father (vv. 15–16). To support this command, Peter introduced a well-known Old Testament quotation: "be holy, for I am holy."

The final command was that the readers must live in reverent fear during their time of exile (v. 17). Two reasons to obey this command were given. The first is that they had a Father who has promised to judge impartially according to each one's deeds (v. 17). Second, the costly price of their redemption required faithful living (vv. 18–19).

Peter concluded this section by once more considering the divine plan that led to the readers' redemption (vv. 20–21). Such a plan began in eternity past and included the election of Christ to the redemptive task, which led him from suffering to glory. Importantly, Peter highlighted that this eternal, redemptive plan was designed with these readers in mind ("for the sake of you").

Hope in Coming Grace (1:13)

In light of their new birth, Peter's readers must fully set their hope on coming grace.

1:13. As he turned from the introduction of the letter to the body opening, Peter offered the first command: set your hope fully on coming grace.

As with the other commands in this section, it is based on the indicatives of identity that have been developed throughout 1:1–12. It is best to see Peter's aorist imperatives as indicating a course of action that should be continued indefinitely.[1]

The command was accompanied by two participles, which are sometimes regarded as participles of means[2] but are best taken as attendant circumstance. Accordingly, they are coordinate with the verb and borrow imperatival force. The first, "prepare your minds for action" (ἀναζωσάμενοι), referred to the ancient practice of tying up one's garment so that it would not impede movement. Here it

was used metaphorically, for it spoke of tying up the loins of one's *mind*.[3] A modern equivalent would be, "roll up the sleeves of your mind" (Elliott, 2001, 355).

The second accompanying participle (νήφοντες) was also used metaphorically. In Koine Greek it referred to being sober but was used metaphorically in all its uses in the New Testament to refer to being self-controlled. More broadly, it referred to being "free from every form of mental and spiritual 'drunkenness,' from excess, passion, rashness, confusion, etc." (BDAG s.v. "νήφω" 672).

The two participles had a meaningful difference in tense. The first was given in the

---

1 Aorist imperative. First Peter shows a preference for aorist imperatives, particularly in exhortative contexts. While there is still some significant debate within Greek aspectual study, one area that seems to have general agreement is that the aorist (perfective) imperative is used for specific commands, which relate to a specific entity at a specific time and place. They may also reflect the need to begin or cease a certain activity. On the other hand, present (imperfective) imperatives are the default for general commands that are true across a range of contexts and times. The difficulty in 1 Peter is that our author seems to use aorist imperatives for general exhortation. As a result, Turner concluded, "One cannot pretend to see any principle behind the choice of tenses, and the lack of it militates against the author's supposed literacy" (Turner, 1978, 4:128)

Constantine Campbell, one of the chief voices in Greek aspectual study, provides another, more gracious way of viewing Peter's use of these aorist imperatives. Campbell believes that while the aorist tends to give specific instruction, it can also have "summary implicature." That is, since the perfective aspect is designed to express something in summary, it can do so in the imperative (Campbell, 2009, 87). Importantly, when an author uses the aorist for the summary implicature, it is well suited for general exhortation. Following the lead of some commentators on 1 Peter (Achtemeier, 1996, 340 n. 60; Michaels, 1988, 130), this may best be called a programmatic aorist imperative. Such a title indicates that these aorists "[set] a course of action to be continued" (Achtemeier, 1996, 340 n. 60).

Care must be taken, however, to consider each aorist imperative in context. While it may be that Peter is using an aorist in a programmatic sense, it is always possible that he is using it for another reason. Buist Fanning lists four other possible uses of the aorist imperative in 1 Peter: (1) Peter may use the aorist imperatives to express ingressivity, stressing the entry into an action; (2) Peter may use them to stress urgency and authority; (3) Peter may use these imperatives in a consummative sense, highlighting that the actions need to be done until brought to their appropriate end; (4) finally, Peter may have little choice in aspect since some of the commands are traditional and thus are usually given in the aorist (Fanning, 1990, 370–79).

2 Participles of means. By taking these as participles of means, the text would be indicating the way one would set one's hope on the coming grace. Of course, the participle itself does not indicate whether the nuance includes means or is attendant circumstance; only contextual factors are decisive. That these are means of setting one's hope is more difficult to sustain than that these are actions that accompany setting one's hope. Accordingly, we have taken the attendant circumstance position.

3 Loins of one's mind. Some have made much of the background of this language. It could point back to the Exodus, where the Septuagint uses the same word to refer to the preparation of the people to leave Egypt. Of course, such a background fits with the theme of exile being developed in this passage. Nevertheless, the language is common, being used also by Jesus (Luke 12:35). If there is an intertextual reference being made, it is not explicitly clear.

aorist, likely indicating prior action; while the second had the present, likely indicating coordinate action. Thus, the girding up of the mind precedes the setting of one's hope, while being self-controlled was coordinate with it.

The command to hope was intensified by the adverb "completely."[4] Thus the Asia Minor readers were to set their hope *fully* on the grace that would be brought[5] at the revelation of Jesus Christ. John Elliott suggests that the revelation of Jesus refers to the first advent, and thus the readers were to set their hope on the gospel that they had heard and believed (Elliott, 2001, 357). While Elliott is correct that Peter spoke of two comings of Jesus—past and future—Peter used different terminology in reference to each. In reference to Jesus's first coming, Peter spoke of Jesus being "made manifest [φανερωθέντος] in the last times for the sake of you" (1:20). In reference to the future coming, Peter spoke of "the revelation [ἀποκαλύψει] of Jesus Christ" (1:7). This latter term, the same used in this context, spoke of the last days. Accordingly, by using the same verb, Peter was calling for the readers to ground their hope on the future redemption promised them when Jesus returns.

The first command reminded the readers where they had to ground their confidence and expectation. While the present circumstances looked bleak and may have caused them to doubt their position, Peter called them to remember the gospel they accepted. The Father elected them and is preserving both them and their inheritance for the future day of redemption. That their path to such glory was not easy was suggested by the verbal ideas surrounding the command. The readers had to be prepared mentally and must always have been alert.

Conform to the Father's Holiness (1:14–16)
Peter commanded the readers to abandon their past desires and, as obedient children, to follow after the Father.

1:14. Peter prefaced his next command with a reminder to the readers about who they were. Since they experienced the new birth, they were now children of a heavenly Father. As such, they had to live obediently. Thus, while the phrase "as obedient children" served as a reminder, it also functioned as a ground for the following commands. Their new birth brought an obligation of obedience to the Father.

The negated participle, "do not be conformed" (συσχηματιζόμενοι), may be taken as an independent imperatival participle (Wallace, 1996, 650–52).[6] But since Peter used three other imperatives in the surrounding context,

---

4 "Completely." The adverb could modify the second participle and refer to the exercise of self-control: "be completely self-controlled." It seems more likely, and nearly all commentators agree, that Peter is modifying the main verb with the adverb.

5 Grace that would be brought. Though the participle "brought" (φερομένην) is present tense, it is being used here to refer to a future reality. Thus, nearly all modern versions translate it with a future force: "will be brought" (ESV, NLT, NET) or "to be brought" (NASB, NIV, CSB).

6 Independent imperatival participle. The existence of imperatival participles in 1 Peter has long been debated. If such a category exists in 1 Peter, there are nine places where they appear to be used (1:14; 2:18; 3:1, 7, 9 [twice]; 4:8, 10). Forbes provides a short and helpful survey of the issue in scholarship (Forbes, 2014, 6–7). At one time it was argued that imperatival participles were becoming common in the Koine period. Later interpreters challenged that perspective and argued that they were Hebraisms. More recently, Travis B. Williams has argued that the imperatival participle should be seen as a natural development in light of the inherent flexibility of the participle. The most important element of his article, however, is his argument that the imperatival participle bears the same semantic weight as the finite imperative (Williams, 2011, 59–78). Care should be made to distinguish between independent imperatival participles and dependent adverbial participles (whether means, manner, result, or attendant circumstance) that take on imperatival force from the verb they modify.

his choice of a participle and not an imperative here appears meaningful. By putting this negated command in participial form, Peter indicated that it is the means by which the following command could be carried out. In other words, one way by which one could be holy as God is holy was by not conforming to the old passions of life. The word "conform" (συσχηματιζόμενοι) was only used here and in Romans 12:2 in biblical literature. In both places it referred to being formed according to a mold. In Romans the mold was the world. Here, the mold was the readers' former desires. These conceptions were related, for Peter's readers were redeemed from the world's system of thought. The expression suggests that there was a natural, worldly pattern of thinking that must be avoided by believers.

Peter indicated that such passions should be put aside, for they were part of the convert's past life. Indeed, they were a core component of the "futile ways" passed down from the believer's forefathers (1:18). Later Peter spoke more explicitly about the futile ways, noting that the readers must live "no longer for human passions but for the will of God. For the time that is past suffices for doing what the Gentiles want to do, living in sensuality, passions, drunkenness, orgies, drinking parties, and lawless idolatry" (4:2–3). That these desires were sourced in ignorance suggests that the alternative was sourced in knowledge. They had come to know the truth; consequently, they must not return to a life of ignorance.

1:15. While verse 13 focused on the *future* grace that was coming, and verse 14 focused on the *past* life that must be avoided, verse 15 indicated the *present* life the children of God must live. The central command of verse 15 was a familiar one from the Old Testament: "be holy."

Before stating the command, however, Peter provided the grounds for the command. Appropriate to their new birth, the holiness of the Father provided the grounds for calling the believers to holiness. Nevertheless, there is some disagreement about exactly how Peter grounded the command. Two interpretations of the debated comparative phrase[7] can be seen by comparing English translations. Some translations have "just as the Holy One who called you" (NASB, NET), while others have "just as he who called you is holy" (ESV, NIV, NRSV, CSB). The latter, though more popular in modern translations, is less likely grammatically. In the end, the difference is of little meaningful significance, for both would indicate that the holiness of God stands as the standard of the believer's holiness.

By speaking of God's "calling" the readers, Peter once more highlighted the elective grace of God. The word Peter used to refer to God's action in calling believers (καλέσαντα) was used in the Septuagint and the New Testament to refer to choosing "for receipt of a special benefit or experience," especially in regard to salvation (BDAG s.v. "καλέω" 503). Thus, an implicit reminder of their beneficial place among God's people served as a further motivation to obedience.

Peter emphasized the command with the addition of the emphatic "yourselves" (αὐτοί).

This commentary does not find the category of the imperatival participle present in 1 Peter. Instead, since choice indicates meaning (Runge, 2010, 5–7), the choice of a participle form suggests dependence on a finite verb. Sometimes that dependence is not explicitly clear, and therefore many commentators default to the imperatival participle. This commentary will, on the other hand, seek to flesh out the significance of each of these participles.

7 Debated comparative phrase. The "just as he who called you is holy" reading is based on the participle as substantival with the word "holy" as a predicate. The "just as the Holy One who called you" reading takes "holy" as substantival and takes the participle as modifying the substantive. Michaels points out that the preposition (κατά) requires a noun like "holy" (ἅγιον) and not a verbal like "the one who called" (καλέσαντα) as its object. This suggests the former translation is correct (Michaels, 1988, 51).

He also extended the command to every area of life when he said that such holiness must be characteristic of "all" (πάσῃ) their conduct. More significantly, "What makes Peter's command both sobering and daunting is the fact that the standard by which they are to measure holiness in their pursuit is the absolute holiness of God" (Compton, 2019, 76). And it is such pursuit that made the readers different from the culture they previously identified with. Accordingly, it was the very act of becoming holy that made them subject to suffering. To the degree that they became like their Father, that is the degree to which they had become exiles even while remaining in their former homeland.

1:16. The conjunction that begins this verse (διότι) introduced an Old Testament quotation, just as it did two other times in this letter (1:24; 2:6). The quotation comes from the Septuagint of Leviticus, though since the statement occurs twice in Leviticus it is unclear which is being quoted (Lev. 11:44–45; 19:2). Leviticus 11 remembered the Passover event, while chapter 19 spoke of the ethical duties of God's people. Accordingly, the latter context was more appropriate to the context here and was thus the likely source.

The quotation had two parts. The first was the command; the second was the grounds for the command. The readers were to be holy *because* God is holy. Such a command and grounding fit perfectly with what Peter had just called his readers to in verse 15. By using a command given to Old Testament Israel in reference to the church, Peter showed the continuity between the people of God in all ages. Those who were called by God's name must be holy as he is holy.

Live in Reverent Fear (1:17–19)
Peter's readers had to live in reverent fear, for they had a heavenly Father who judged impartially, and they had been provided a costly redemption.

1:17. By starting this verse with a coordinating conjunction (καί), Peter aligned the command of this verse with those that came before. He had already called the readers to set their hope on coming grace and to imitate the holiness of the Father as they abandoned their old way of life, and now Peter indicated that the readers had to live in reverent fear. This verse provided one reason to do so, while the next verse provided another reason.

Peter's command was inserted into a conditional clause: "If you call on the Father . . .". Peter was not doubting whether they called on the Father. By using the first-class conditional, Peter was assuming the truth of the statement. Such a call was accomplished primarily through prayer (BDAG s.v. "ἐπικαλέω" 373), which highlighted the readers' personal relationship with the Father.

The designation "Father" naturally followed from the new birth analogy. Nevertheless, the source of the language, just as the source of the language concerning the new birth, came from Jesus's words. Often Jesus spoke of God as his Father, and he encouraged the disciples to pray to God as to a Father (e.g., Matt. 6:9). Thus, Peter was assuming a familial, gracious relationship. This should be kept in mind as we consider Peter's command concerning living in fear.

The central command was to conduct oneself with reverent fear during the time of sojourning. The word Peter used for fear (φόβος) could refer to causing dread and fright or it could refer to a deportment of reverence and respect. The concept of the "fear of the Lord" in the Scripture leans toward the latter (see the sidebar). Nevertheless, one's relation to the Lord should determine how to respond to him. Those who ignore his commands should have an appropriate dread of his judgment. On the other hand, those who obey him need not dread his judgment. Instead, they should tremble at his goodness. The combination of these is captured by the translation "reverent fear."

The Fear of the Lord

The English translation "fear of the Lord" does not communicate well the underlying meaning of the scriptural phrase. Unfortunately, no English equivalent perfectly captures the sense. In English, the sense often comes across as something that instills terror. Yet this is not what the phrase means, for Scripture reveals that Jesus experienced this fear, and it delighted him (Isa. 11:1–3). In fact, Moses contrasted such a terror with the fear of the Lord: "Moses said to the people, 'Do not *fear*, for God has come to test you, that the *fear of him* may be before you, that you may not sin'" (Exod. 20:20).

In a detailed study of the concept of the fear of the Lord, Michael Reeves concludes, "True fear of God is true love for God defined: it is the right response to God's full-orbed revelation of himself in all his grace and glory" (Reeves, 2021, 53). Such a knowledge leads to a trembling in the presence of such glory and results in a transformed life. It is for this reason that the Scriptures say this fear is the beginning of knowledge (Prov. 1:7) and the foundation of wisdom (9:10).

some find this contrary to a theology of grace, it need not be. As Thomas Schreiner says, "no dichotomy exists between judgment according to works and God's grace. Good works are evidence that God has truly begotten (1 Pet. 1:3) a person" (Schreiner, 2003, 83). This is the best way to resolve the perceived tension, for already in this letter Peter has spoken of divine grace numerous times (1:2, 3, 5, 10, 15).

Before turning to Peter's second reason to live in reverent fear, it is important to highlight the temporal limit Peter put on such fear. One day the readers would no longer live in reverent expectation of the coming judgment; rather, they would find themselves at home with their Father. But in the present, Peter described them as sojourners (παροικίας). The word is different from the word used in 1:1 to refer to their exilic status (παρεπιδήμοις), but it had a similar meaning. Peter used both words together in 2:11 to speak of the audience's current identity. By using this term, Peter reminded them that their current time of testing was limited.

This reverent fear was to be born out of a knowledge that God was an impartial judge, who would judge according to each one's deeds. That he was impartial indicated that the Father was not biased in his judgment as so many human judges were. Instead, his judgment would be appropriate and fair to all. Despite their calling him Father, he would not overlook their evil deeds. That the judgment would be according to works was the consistent testimony of Scripture (Matt. 16:27; Rom. 2:6; 1 Cor. 3:13; 2 Cor. 5:10; Rev. 2:23; 20:12–13). Though

1:18. Verse 17 indicated one reason to live in reverent fear: God would judge impartially. This verse and the next provided a second reason. Peter began the second reason by saying "for you know" (εἰδότες). This language indicated that he is speaking of tradition known by the readers. Apparently, this tradition concerned the necessity of redemption from their past life and the costliness of the redemption they gained.

The concepts of redemption and ransom[8] were central in these verses and require some

---

8 Redemption and ransom. The exact word for "redemption" (λυτρόω) that Peter uses occurs only two other times in the New Testament. The first occurs in Luke 24:21 where the disciples on the road to Emmaus say that they thought Jesus would redeem them. Clearly, they meant a political freedom from the Romans. The word also occurs in Titus 2:14, which speaks of Jesus "who gave himself for us to redeem us from all lawlessness and to purify for himself a people for his own possession who are zealous for good works." This latter passage fits quite well with Peter's emphasis here, for Peter is also calling on his readers to behavior appropriate in light of the redemption given by Jesus. Titus indicates why Jesus did it; 1 Peter indicates how believers should respond to it.

consideration. The concepts were used in broader Greek society to refer to the purchase of slaves or the buying back of people captured in war. In the Septuagint, the concepts referred to the freeing of slaves (Lev. 25:48). Other times, they were used to refer to salvation from a terrible situation (Dan. 6:17). They were also used in reference to the deliverance of the people of Israel from exile (Exod. 6:6; Isa. 51:11). Finally, such language was used in the New Testament to refer to Jesus's sacrificial death in payment for the sins of his people (Matt. 20:28; Mark 10:25; cf. Rom. 3:24–25; Eph. 1:7; 1 Tim. 2:6; Heb. 9:12, 15).

In light of the variety of uses of the word, Reinhard Feldmeier notes three potential motifs introduced by the redemption language: "redemption of slaves, freeing from exile, and atonement through Jesus's death" (Feldmeier, 2008, 117). The first is based on the broad use of ransom language in Greek culture, the second is partly based on Isaiah 52:3 and the thought of freedom from foreign exile, and the third is based on Jesus's statement in Mark 10:45 (cf. Matt. 20:28). After highlighting the possibility of each, Feldmeier suggests that Peter's "multiplicity of allusions that does not exclude one another can well be intended," for they "strengthen each other in their declarative effect" (117).

Certainly, the motif of freedom from slavery was used elsewhere in the New Testament (e.g., Rom. 6:6), and such a theme fits nicely with Peter's call to avoid the desires of the past life and to live holy lives. The redemption from exile also fits nicely into this passage, since one of the overall motifs of the letter is the readers' exile and foreignness until the coming kingdom. Clearly though, the language of the passage emphasized the third—atonement through Jesus's blood. Indeed, it is this third that made the other two possible.

Why the readers needed redemption was answered by the statement of what they were redeemed from. Their old life was described as "empty" (ματαίας), meaning it was "fruitless,

useless . . . lacking truth" (BDAG s.v. "μάταιος" 621). It was a futile way of life that would lead to a disastrous end at the judgment, and thus their only hope was to be redeemed from it. The way of life was further characterized as "inherited from your ancestors," indicating that such a way of life was passed down through the generations. Such a conception intentionally contrasted the new birth with their old life. Once they followed the course of their ancestors, which was empty and lacking truth. Now, they were born again by the divine power of God to a fruitful life, filled with divine truth.

Before addressing the cost of redemption, Peter highlighted what could not redeem them. By selecting gold and silver, some of the most precious and sought after things in his culture, Peter was indicating that even the most valuable human commodities are insufficient to pay the cost of redemption. That these things are "perishable" indicated why they are insufficient. As noted earlier, gold is a stable element (unlike silver, which tarnishes over time); nevertheless, it would be destroyed with the coming destruction of the heavens and earth (2 Peter 3:10). Accordingly, it had no lasting value and could not pay for the readers' redemption. Such consideration set the stage for the next verse, which highlighted a payment that was both nonperishable and of infinite value. Bruce Compton rightly notes an implication: "if all of these things are ruled out as acceptable payments, then the payment involves a price far beyond what the readers themselves could provide" (Compton, 2019, 88). Since all that men were able to provide was ultimately perishable, no human payment was sufficient for the needed redemption.

1:19. Having detailed what could not pay the redemption price, Peter turned to a positive statement of what had paid the price. Their redemption was purchased by the "precious blood of Christ." The phrase "blood of" was used as a shorthand to refer to the entire passion of the Son by which he brought redemption to his people. Referring to the blood was commonplace in the New Testament (Rom. 3:25; 5:9; Eph. 1:7; 1 John 1:7), and often, as here, refers to the sacrificial death of Christ. That the sacrifice was "precious" (τιμίῳ) speaks of the value of the sacrifice.[9] Peter was indicating that there was no comparison between the blood of Christ and "precious" metals (whether gold or silver). In terms of eternal significance, only the former had value.

References to the Blood of Jesus	
Rom. 3:25a	. . . whom God put forward as a propitiation by his blood, to be received by faith.
Rom. 5:9	Since, therefore, we have now been justified by his blood, much more shall we be saved by him from the wrath of God.
Eph. 1:7	In him we have redemption through his blood, the forgiveness of our trespasses, according to the riches of his grace.
1 John 1:7	But if we walk in the light, as he is in the light, we have fellowship with one another, and the blood of Jesus his Son cleanses us from all sin.

The comparison with perishable gold and silver indicated one reason Jesus's blood is more valuable. To that Peter added another:

The blood of Christ had inestimable value because it was the blood of a lamb without blemish or defect (Num. 6:14; 19:2). The comparison with a lamb pointed to the sacrificial value of Jesus's death. While Peter's Asia Minor readers were likely Gentiles, they were also likely well versed in the Old Testament[10] system of sacrifices, which required that the sacrifice be without blemish or defect. Peter was referring not to the physical body of Jesus, but to his moral quality, as Peter indicated in 2:22: "he committed no sin."

Agnus Dei by Francisco de Zurbarán. Public domain.

That Peter was pointing to Jesus as the ultimate fulfillment of the Old Testament sacrifices was made clear. Jesus was not simply *a* faultless lamb, but *the* perfect lamb. Further, what was pictorially presented by the flawless lamb was now made clear in the moral spotlessness of Jesus. Thus, Jesus was the fulfillment (antitype[11])

---

9 Value of the sacrifice. Clement, an early church father, was likely reflecting on this verse when he said, "Let us fix our eyes on the blood of Christ and understand how precious it is unto his Father, because being shed for our salvation it won for the whole world the grace of repentance" (Clement, *Epistles*, 7.2).

10 Well versed in the Old Testament. The early church saw themselves as part of the outworking of God's eternal redemptive plan, and consequently they embraced the Old Testament Scripture as their own. In fact, prior to the writing and distribution of the post-Christ Scriptures (i.e., what would later be called the New Testament), the early church only had the Old Testament and the traditions of the apostles. It is for this reason that New Testament authors, including Peter, could write to Gentile audiences and expect them to grasp Old Testament references.

11 Antitype. A type in biblical literature is a person, place, or thing that casts a shadow that is anticipatory of a later person, place, or thing. That the category exists is hard to deny; nevertheless, the extent to which typology is present in the biblical literature is debated. Some clear examples are Adam as the type and Jesus as the antitype

of the typological sacrificial system. While it is possible that Peter had a more specific application in mind—whether the Passover lamb or the lamb mentioned in Isaiah 53:7—it is probably best to see Peter as speaking broadly of the entire sacrificial system of the Old Testament.

The Father's Plan Revealed (1:20–21)
Peter revealed that in eternity, the Father planned the suffering of the Son for the benefit of the believers in Asia Minor, so that their faith and hope would be firmly fixed on God.

1:20. This verse and the next provided the third reason that readers should live in reverent fear before God during their exile: in sum, because God had included them in an eternal plan of redemption and had given them sufficient reason to hope and trust in him through the resurrection of Jesus.

Two major ideas were presented in this verse: Jesus was foreknown, and Jesus was revealed. First, Jesus was "foreknown before the foundation of the world." The word for "foreknown" (προγινωσμένου) is closely related to the word in 1:2 (πρόγνωσις) that referred to the reader's election: "according to the *foreknowledge* of God." There was great significance in this similarity, for just as Jesus was chosen beforehand for his role in suffering and then obtaining glory (1:21), so Peter's readers were also chosen beforehand to receive glory, and also to go through suffering.

The second portion of the verse provided the second truth: Jesus was revealed. The conjunctions used in the verse indicated that the first clause is concessive (μέν), while the second is emphasized (δέ; BDAG s.v. "μέν" 628). Accordingly, while the plan of the Father from eternity was of great interest to Peter and his

readers, the real point of emphasis was that this eternal plan has now been revealed.

Peter's temporal notations were important. The plan was made in eternity, before the world was created. And because God's plan was incrementally revealed through time, past generations of prophets longed to know more of it (1:11). This eternal plan had now been clearly revealed to the readers. Indeed, Peter emphasized the role of his readers, noting that this revelation was "for the sake of you" (δι᾽ ὑμᾶς). By such language, Peter indicated that his readers were at the center of God's eternal plans. They were truly a privileged people.

Peter indicated that this revelation had come in "the last times." This phrase indicated that Peter considered the timeframe of the readers as the last stage in history prior to the return of the Messiah and the coming judgment. The plan of God, which was hatched in eternity, was now in its final stages, and this had to influence the way the readers thought of themselves. That they were living in that final stage provided a motivation for action (4:7). Thus, while it was not explicitly given as a reason to live in reverent fear, understood rightly it provided such a motivation.

1:21. As noted above, two things were mentioned concerning Jesus in relation to the Father's action in verse 20: He was foreknown and he was revealed. Two more things were mentioned in verse 21: He was raised from the dead and he was given glory. Together, these four things indicated why Peter's readers should live in reverent fear before God.

Peter here indicated that it was through Christ that the readers had become believers in God.[12] In other words, the way God brought the readers to himself was through the revelation of

---

(Rom. 5:12–19); Melchizedek as type, with Jesus as the antitype (Ps. 110:4; Heb. 5:5–10; 6:19–20; 7:1–22); and the bronze serpent as type, and the cross as antitype (Num. 21:4–9; John 3:14–21).

12 Believers in God. The noun used here (πιστός) can refer to an active trust ("believe in God"; NIV, NRSV, CSB, etc.) or a passive trusting (are believers in God; ESV, NASB). The difference is not significant.

Jesus, whom he eternally planned to reveal for their sake. The two statements of what God did for Jesus—raising and glorifying—each had the readers in focus. The Father did these things "so that [the readers'] faith and hope are in God."

What Peter intended by the resurrection of Jesus is clear, but what he meant by "glory" is not clear. Peter seems to have included in "glory" all that was given to Christ due to his obedience. This included the position at the right hand and the future rulership as king over all nations. Peter spoke of the glorification of the Son later in the book, saying Jesus "has gone into heaven and is at the right hand of God, with angels, authorities, and powers having been subjected to him" (3:22).

In sum, Peter said that Jesus was foreknown for the readers, he was revealed for the readers, he was raised for the readers, and he was glorified for the readers. All was for them. How could they doubt God's loving intention toward them? Thus, the motivation for obeying the command to live in reverential fear before God was based on God's kindness. In the words of Wayne Grudem, "The God whom Christians fear is also the God whom they trust forever, the God who has planned and done for them only good from all eternity" (Grudem, 1988, 92).

THEOLOGICAL FOCUS (1:13–21)
The exegetical idea (in light of their new birth, Peter's readers had to set their hope fully on the coming of Christ, reject their old way of life by modeling God's holiness, and live in reverent fear, knowing God's impartial judgment and the overwhelming cost of their redemption) leads to this theological focus: believers must hope in Christ's coming, reflect the Father's holiness, and live in reverent fear.

These verses introduce the first imperatives in the letter. Just as the first section is characterized by the indicative (indicating who the readers are), so this section is characterized by the imperative (indicating how the readers should live in light of their identity). The key question that leads the imperatives of this section is, "How should we live in light of our exalted identity given through the new birth?"

In response to this unstated question, Peter gives his readers, and by extension all modern believers, four commands. The first is that believers must set their hope on the coming grace (1:13). They can do this by preparing their minds for action and then exercising self-control while they intentionally meditate on the truth that God's grace has prevailed and will prevail. Such consideration grounds them in truth and allows them to withstand the difficulties they face.

The second and third commands are related as two sides of a coin. On the one hand, Peter calls all believers to abandon their past way of life (1:14). The new birth offers a new beginning, and it requires all to forsake the old path, which was characterized by ignorance. On the other hand, Peter calls all believers to live out what they have come to know of the Father (1:15–16). Since he is holy, they must be holy. Continuing the theme of the new birth, Peter appeals to all believers to be obedient children as they imitate their heavenly Father. By grounding this command in the Old Testament, Peter is indicating that this is the requirement of all God's people, whether past or present. By implication, it is also true of all who have come to trust in Jesus today and in the future.

The final command—that all must live in reverent fear during the exile (1:17)—is accompanied by extensive consideration of why the command must be obeyed. He supports this command with three grounds. First, believers must live this way because God is an impartial judge who will treat each according to their works. Such a consideration is designed to remind believers that true children live like true children. Those who call God Father and yet do not conform to his holiness and live in light of his coming grace show that their faith is empty and fruitless. Accordingly, despite their apparent position among God's people, they will be judged severely (cf. 4:17–19).

The second reason that all believers must live in reverent fear before God during the time of exile concerns the costliness of redemption. Gold and silver, still some of the most sought after and costly elements in the world, are incapable of paying the price of redemption. A payment different in kind rather than quality is necessary. Jesus's blood, because it is the blood of *the* innocent lamb, has eternal value and is thus capable of paying for the redemption of all believers. That such a payment was given in exchange for the freedom of God's people logically requires obedience from that people.

The third and final reason to live in reverent fear concerns the place of believers in the eternal plan of God. Before the foundation of the world, God set a plan in motion that would lead Jesus to suffering and then glory. Such a plan was intended for all who would believe, inclusive of Peter's readers and modern believers. Accordingly, believers must recognize their privileged position and live in faithfulness to God's plan.

In sum, this section of 1 Peter calls all believers to obedience in light of their identity as elect-exiles chosen by the Father for new birth. They must set their hope on the coming grace, while abandoning the old way of life and seeking to live as their heavenly Father. As they do this, they must live in reverent fear, knowing the cost of their redemption, their place in the Father's eternal plan, and the fact that one day God will impartially judge all men.

PREACHING AND TEACHING STRATEGIES

Exegetical and Theological Synthesis
Humans tend to have too high a view of themselves. We readily boast in our accomplishments, our wealth, our status, our looks. We think that our technological achievements make us somehow superior to our dark-age ancestors.

But Peter teaches a different reality, one that sobers our minds to the hard truth of our true position before God. He describes life before Christ as one of "former ignorance" (1:14), not one of intellectual or technological superiority. He writes of believers being ransomed "from the futile ways inherited from your forefathers" (1:18). This provides an important connective with our descendants. Their ways were futile; ours are too. We have inherited not their wisdom or their wealth, but their futile way of living in opposition to God.

But if Peter was clear that our life before Christ was characterized by ignorance and futility, he is equally clear about how God's initiative and love brought us from this hopelessness to the hope we have now. Believers should set their hope on the grace "that will be brought to you" (1:13), not the grace that we earned (as if there is such a thing!). We did not call on God, but God called us (1:15). The only reason we can and should be holy is because God first set that standard (1:16). We did not purchase our own freedom from sin, but God ransomed us from our futile ways with the blood of Christ (1:18–19). Our vast technology did not uncover the mysteries of God, but God took action to reveal himself to us (1:20). Every line of this passage smacks of God's initiative and man's utter hopelessness apart from the Lord's work.

This should caution us against preaching the imperatives too smugly, as if we can accomplish the holiness God desires apart from his work and grace. It should remind us of our place in the cosmos: insignificant and helpless, destined for judgment had it not been for the merciful intervention of God. The gospel motivates every part of Peter's challenge to his readers.

Preaching Idea
Like Father, Like Sons: Be Holy, as God Is Holy.

Contemporary Connections

What does it mean?
The theological concept of holiness is paramount in this passage. "Holiness" is another

"Christianese" term, one that we often hear in church but rarely hear clearly explained. But "be holy" is the driving imperative in 1 Peter 1:13–21, which means that in order to properly preach this passage, the pastor must make sure he offers a clear explanation and illustration of holiness, rooted in the Old Testament law and fulfilled in Christ's perfect life. Jerry Bridges in *The Pursuit of Holiness* offers a concise, helpful definition: "To live a holy life, then, is to live a life in conformity to the moral precepts of the Bible and in contrast to the sinful ways of the world" (1978, 17).

Additionally, some explanation of the concept of "ransom" (v. 18) will be necessary to help bridge the gap between modern sensibilities and Peter's first-century world. Ransom (or "redeem," as some versions translate it) relates to the purchase and buying back of slaves. The sensitivity of Americans to any idea of slavery is heightened due not only to slave trade practices in the early centuries of our nation but also to the renewed considerations and calls for reparations. Eighteenth-century chattel slavery was steeped in racism, ignorance, and a disregard for humans made in the image of God.

The preacher must carefully distinguish the slavery that most Americans have a strong familiarity and rightful disdain of with the first-century slavery of Peter's day. No attempt should be made to excuse either institution, but in order to understand the all-important concept of ransom/redemption, the preacher must firmly set the minds of his audience not in past American practices but rather past Greco-Roman practices. A good explanation of slavery in the New Testament can be found in Rupprecht (1976).

Now what?

First Peter 1:13–21 asks the question, "How should we live in light of our exalted identity given through the new birth?" It is essential that the preacher realizes that the imperatives of this passage are based on the indicatives of (1) who God is, and (2) who God has made us to be. Because God is holy, we ought to be holy too. Because God has caused us to be born again to a new and living hope, we ought to act like grateful redeemed children of the heavenly Father.

Modern-day adoption illustrates both principles. Imagine a child born into the worst kind of poverty, addicted to heroin due to the choices of his mother, abandoned at the steps of the hospital with little care or love. The child spends years going through the system, bouncing from one foster home to another, struggling in school, making bad relationship choices—a product of neglect and a bad environment.

But then one day, hope shines when a family comes to adopt him. They take him from the poverty and abuse and bring him into a home filled with genuine love. He has not earned it; he has not even asked for it. Yet he finds himself immersed in love. They treat the child as one of their own. But along with this new life comes a set of new expectations. His parents are characterized by love and mercy, and the expectation is that he also acts in love and mercy. His parents have given him a new name, a new home, a new lease on life, and now he is expected to live and act accordingly. With the new life comes renewed hope, but also a higher hope. Better grades, better behavior, better goals—they expect more of him now than ever before.

The passage calls believers to renew their minds, set their hope on God, and live as obedient children in all holiness as a result of God's initiating love and the gospel. Call the church to be obedient children, but make sure they know why they are called to such a high calling.

Creativity in Presentation

The text presents several avenues of potential creative illustrations. Peter commands his readers to "prepare your minds for action," or more literally, "gird up the loins of your mind." Most moderns are unfamiliar with the imagery of "girding up the loins," the practice of tying up a garment around the hips to allow for greater movement and agility. Instead of simply explaining this concept, the preacher might want to go a step further and illustrate it with an appropriate robe or custom-made garment. The key is to demonstrate the freer mobility when one's loins are properly girded, then make sure to connect that with Peter's metaphor as it relates to the mind.

The participle "being sober-minded" may also give opportunity for creativity. Even Christians who grow up in a conservative church environment likely know what drunkenness looks like. Preachers need not make fools of themselves on the platform to act it out, but it won't take long to dig through the news to find examples of insobriety at its worst. A quick search on Google news with the term "drunk" pulled up more than eighty-six million hits on my computer: an Iowa woman was arrested for driving a school van with kids inside while intoxicated; Bruce Springsteen was arrested for drunk driving; an Oregon drunk driver was found to have a blood-alcohol level at nine times the legal limit. All of these hits appeared on the first page of my search. Using a few real-life (and recent) illustrations will help contrast the expected spiritual sobriety of the believer with the intoxicating sin of the world.

Finally, the command for believers not to be "conformed" to their former ignorance (v. 14) also has potential for a striking visual. As the exegesis showed, to be "conformed" means to be fitted to a mold. Many objects are made with a mold, but for me, the most striking (and tastiest) is chocolate. My (Bryan's) mother used to make chocolate lollipops and candies around certain holidays. She would heat the colored chocolate in the microwave or over the stove, then we would help her pour the liquid into a mold and wait for it to set before pulling it out and eating it. The preacher could use this concept of a mold as a reminder to congregants as they leave the church service. Handing out a small piece of chocolate—perhaps molded

in the shape of a cross—as church members exit could have a lasting effect on them by reminding them that we are to conform to God's holiness and be holy as he is holy.

Preachers can follow a simple outline of this text:

- Believers Hope in Christ's Coming (1:13)

- Believers Reflect the Father's Holiness (1:14–16)

- Believers Live in Reverent Fear (1:17–19)

- Believers Follow the Father's Plan (1:20–21)

DISCUSSION QUESTIONS

1. What does it look like to prepare our minds for action? How does this relate to being sober-minded? (1:13)

2. How do the imperatives in this passage relate to the character of God? How do they relate to the gospel and the born-again identity of a believer?

3. What does Peter mean when he tells the readers to "conduct yourselves with fear"? What kind of fear does he mean? What does this look like in our life?

4. How does Peter demonstrate God's initiative in salvation throughout this passage?

5. What does it look like for us to set our faith and hope fully in God and his grace? What does it look like when we fail to do so?

1 Peter 1:22–25

EXEGETICAL IDEA
After hearing the living and abiding Word of God, Peter's readers responded in obedience to the truth and received the new birth, which worked in them a sincere brotherly love that they must earnestly exercise toward one another.

THEOLOGICAL FOCUS
Those who have experienced the new birth have been obedient to the truth of the Word of God, and they must now exercise the love natural to the new birth.

PREACHING IDEA
People Perish, but God's Word Persists!

PREACHING POINTERS
Nobody likes to think about how short life really is. Eighty years comes and goes too fast for our comfort. As children, death is hardly a thought. Toys and video games and movies distract from the harsh realities awaiting us in life. Teenagers hardly give their choices a second thought, living out their years in high school with reckless abandon, seemingly ignorant of any real consequences to their actions. College students fare no better, amping up the bad decision-making of their teenage years now that they are untethered from their parents' watch. Even young adults and early married couples rarely consider mortality, being too young, too healthy, and too in love to allow such thoughts to cross their minds. It isn't usually until middle age hits and our bodies begin to sag and slow down that our impermanence sinks in.

Peter knew the truth of this reality, as did the prophets before him. Peter's readers faced persecution and difficult trials. Peter has pointed them to the blessed hope of their salvation. They have been born again in Christ and now have a new calling and a means of facing their persecutors. But those facing the pressure of persecution may have felt like life as they know it was slipping away. In the first century, persecution often meant the loss of commerce and public rapport—and many times even imprisonment, bodily harm, or death. This caused many believers to consider their options. But Peter directs his readers' attention away from the transitory nature of life and roots their focus in the unfading Word of God. First Peter 1:22–25 calls readers to root their confidence not in their own longevity of life but in the enduring Word of God. Being born again means we become imperishable, though not in our earthly bodies. This gospel gives hope and encouragement through the difficulties of life. The preacher has opportunity to address the most common fear known to humankind: the fear of death. It impacts 100 percent of us, and therefore this passage is one of the most relevant in the entire epistle.

BORN AGAIN TO LOVE (1:22–25)

LITERARY STRUCTURE AND THEMES (1:22–25)

This preaching unit could be divided into two sections. The first (1:22–23) has an imperative, which is supported by two participles. The two participles indicate the present reality of the readers (they had purified their souls and they had been born again), while the imperative indicates how they should live in light of their present reality (they must love one another). Like the verses that precede, these verses indicate what type of lifestyle is necessary in light of the new birth.

The second section (1:24–25) confirmed the assertion that "the Word of God is living and enduring" by means of an Old Testament quotation from Isaiah 40:6–8. By means of this quotation, Peter confirmed that the word of God spoken of by Isaiah is the same word they have heard in the gospel.

The major themes of this section include: the necessity of sincere brotherly love; the nature of the new birth that purified the soul; the natural outworking of the new birth leading to brotherly love; the perishability of human life; and the imperishability of the Word of God and consequently the imperishability of the life that derived from it.

- *Love One Another (1:22–23)*
- *The Living and Abiding Word (1:24–25)*

EXPOSITION (1:22–25)

Following the imperatives in 1:13–21, which focus on the readers' relationship to God, verse 22 added an imperative in reference to the readers' relationship to the Christian community: love one another. The command was supported by two facts. First, the readers had

purified their souls by obedience to the truth and this had led to a sincere brotherly love being planted in their hearts. Second, they had received the new birth from an imperishable seed.

The consideration of the Word as a seed led naturally to the next section (1:24–25), which provided a foundation for the previous assertion concerning the Word. It did so first by comparing "flesh," shorthand for humanity, to the grass and flowers of the field. Just as grass withers and the flowers fall, so humanity, seeded by a perishable seed, would also wither and fall. The broader contrast of the verses, however, was the contrast between perishable seed and imperishable seed. Thus, the new birth, because it was the product of the imperishable seed, led to a life that endures forever. This living and enduring Word, Peter clarified, is the gospel, which the readers had believed and embraced.

Love One Another (1:22–23)

Peter called the readers to love one another, grounding the command in their past obedience and new birth.

1:22. While the imperative of the verse (love one another) is the main focus of this passage, Peter began by indicating the reason the readers ought to obey the command. The participle "since you have purified your souls" is causal and is modified by two phrases that provided the means and purpose of the readers' purification.

Peter assumed that the readers had purified their souls. As elsewhere in 1 Peter, "souls" stood for the entirety of the person. That they are "purified" means that they had become holy, pure, and divinely acceptable. The participle, given in the perfect tense, indicated that the action of purification had taken place in the past and that its effects were ongoing in the present. In line with what Peter says in this epistle, the readers' purification took place at their new birth (1:3), when they accepted the word of the gospel (1:25). Therefore, the purification[1] referred to the reader's justification and initial salvation. In light of such purification, Peter indicated that believers must live in love.

Peter modified the participle with two phrases. The first indicated the means by which the readers purified their souls—"by obedience to the truth." Some interpreters find a tension between Peter's emphasis on divine action (election, new birth) and the implied role of the reader in this passage. In what sense was it their obedience that led to their purification? Such a concern seems to be responsible for the early addition[2] of the words "through the Spirit" to many Greek manuscripts.

But the testimony of the New Testament is that faith is itself a gift of God (Eph. 2:8; 2 Tim. 2:25). Thus, obedience, which flowed from faith, was divinely ordered. In other words, even the readers' obedience to the truth was due to the work of God. Accordingly, though the manuscripts that say the readers have come to "obey the truth *through the Spirit*" are wrong on a textual level, they nevertheless capture the essence of Peter's point.

The second phrase also modified the participle, indicating the purpose of the purification. The readers had purified themselves by obedience "for a sincere brotherly love." The word Peter used to refer to "love" (φιλαδελφίαν) concerned familial relations. This suggested that the purification in mind

was parallel in concept with the new birth, for it was the new birth that caused believers to have a new family. The point seems to be that just as there is a natural love flowing from family relations, so when one is born again there is a natural love that comes from that new birth. This is why Jesus said that the world will know believers by their love for one another (John 13:35).

The type of love Peter spoke of is defined as "sincere" or "genuine" (ἀνυπόκριτον). It was a type of love that is real, not hypocritical. The broader context of 1 Peter, with its call to follow the steps of Jesus, suggested that the love in mind was a self-sacrificial love. As Jesus said, "A new commandment I give to you, that you love one another: just as I have loved you, you also are to love one another." Accordingly, Jesus indicated that one of the central purposes of the readers' conversion was to create in them a genuine and sincere love. It is not surprising then that Peter called on them to exercise that love.

The indicative (you have purified your souls for the production of genuine love) led to the imperative (therefore love). Accordingly, Peter called on his readers to live out what they had come to experience. Since they had such love in them, they had to exercise it. The command was modified by a descriptor that could refer to fervency or constancy (ἐκτενῶς). The CSB takes it in the latter sense and has "love one another constantly." Most other translations take the word in reference to the depth of passion ("fervently," "eagerly"). A choice is difficult to make, and both seem appropriate to the context. Indeed, both translations flow

---

1   Purification. Grudem argues that the purification in view concerns sanctification (Grudem, 1988, 92–93). His five points of argument are answered by Schreiner, who makes the same argument as that in this commentary (Schreiner, 2003, 92–93).

2   Early addition. The majority of Greek MSS support this reading, but the earliest and most significant MSS do not (𝔓⁷² ℵ A B C Ψ). That these words would be intentionally omitted would be hard to explain, but their addition is easily explained as a clarification from 1:2. Accordingly, though the early textual support is strong, the contextual factors weigh in favor of the reading used in this commentary.

from the idea inherent in the word—that there should be a perseverance in love. Does such perseverance mean constancy even in times challenging to express such love? Does such perseverance mean depth of expression to fully fulfill the command? Though both are not easily captured by an English translation, both senses are likely being communicated by Peter. Perhaps "completely love one another" captures both senses.

Peter's Use of "Imperishable" (ἄφθαρτος)		
1 Peter 1:4a	**1 Peter 1:23a**	**1 Peter 3:4a**
and into an inheritance that is *imperishable*, undefiled, and unfading.	For you have been born again, not of perishable seed, but of *imperishable*.	Rather, it should be that of your inner self, the *imperishable* beauty of a gentle and quiet spirit.

The love must also be from a pure heart.[3] Thus, this love that derived from a purified soul must also express itself in a purified manner. By this command, Peter revealed that "acts of love" may not always be genuine or sincere.

1:23. This verse provided a second reason, given in parallel with the first, that readers should obey the command, "Love one another." In the last verse, Peter used a verb form (perfect causal participle) to indicate that the readers had experienced a purification in the past that had ongoing consequences (since you have been purified). Here he also used the same verb form (perfect causal participle) to indicate that readers had experienced a new birth in the past which had ongoing consequences (since you have been born again). These parallel conceptions suggest that the purification (justification) took place at the same time as the giving of new birth. Thus, there were two reasons the

readers should obey the command to love— they had been purified and they had been born again. The unstated agent in this new birth was clearly God the Father (1:2).

Two means of the new birth were mentioned. First, it was through an imperishable seed. The word "imperishable" (ἀφθάρτου) means "imperviousness to corruption and death" (BDAG s.v. "ἄφθαρτος" 155). The emphasis on the need for an imperishable seed highlighted the failure of anything within creation to accomplish this new birth. In other words, if the seed had to be imperishable and everything originating in creation was perishable, then the only hope resided in something outside creation.

The second means of the new birth was "the living and abiding Word of God." How did this relate to the first means—the seed? As Jesus said in his famous parable of the soils, "the seed is the Word of God" (Luke 8:11). Thus, the imperishable seed simply was the Word of God.

---

3   Pure heart. The adjective "pure" is textually problematic, being included in only some manuscripts. English versions show this, for while some include it (ESV, CSB, NET), some do not (NASB, NIV, NRSV). It is likely original and connects back to the purification of soul mentioned earlier. The external evidence for the inclusion of the word is strong, for it is present in the majority of MSS as well as some early and important MSS (e.g., 𝔓72 ℵ C P Ψ). That it is missing in some MSS may be explained by the repetition of the first two letters of the word "pure" (καθαρᾶς) and the word for "heart" (καρδίας).

Earlier Peter indicated that the new birth came about "through the resurrection of Jesus from the dead" (1:3). Which is right? Was the new birth through the imperishable seed or through the resurrection? Peter indicated that it was both. These two concepts were harmonious. The resurrection of Jesus was the grounds for the new birth; the Word of God was the instrument of the new birth. The former was the basis for granting new life; the latter was the tool used by the Spirit to bring about new life.

The adjectives "living" and "abiding" could refer to God: "through the word of the living and abiding God." And while this is grammatically possible, early Christian literature spoke of the Word as both living (Heb. 4:12) and abiding (1 John 2:14). Further, the following quotation from Isaiah 40 clarified that Peter was referring to the Word as that which was living and abiding.

That the Word was "living" referred to its life-giving quality. Just as a seed produced new life, so Peter says the Word produced new life. That it was "abiding" referred to its enduring nature. The next few verses revealed that there was a contrast with human seed, which produced only that which died and faded away.

The Living and Abiding Word (1:24–25)
Peter compared the eternal, life-giving Word of God to the temporal and fragile nature of humanity.

Comparing the Versions		
1 Peter (ESV)	**LXX (NETS)**	**Hebrew (ESV)**
All flesh is like grass and all its glory like the flower of grass. The grass withers, and the flower falls, but the word of the Lord remains forever."	All flesh is grass; all the glory of man is like the flower of grass. The grass has withered, and the flower has fallen, but the word of our God remains forever.	All flesh is grass, and all its beauty is like the flower of the field. The grass withers, the flower fades when the breath of the LORD blows on it; surely the people are grass. The grass withers, the flower fades, but the word of our God will stand forever.

A comparison between the New Testament and the Septuagint reveals much similarity, with some distinctive differences. First, Peter makes the comparison explicit in the first line with the addition of the comparative "as" (ὡς). The second line offers another difference. While the Septuagint clarifies that it is talking about the "glory of man," Peter uses a pronoun ("its glory") to refer back to "the flesh." The end result is the same, though the Septuagint is more explicit. Finally, in the last line a significant difference exists. Where the Septuagint has "the word of our God," Peter has "the word of the Lord." This is significant, because in the text of 1 Peter, "Lord" is used in reference to Jesus.

The major reason to believe Peter is following the Septuagint rather than the Hebrew here is the missing lines, "when the breath of the Lord blows on it" and "surely the people are grass".

1:24. This verse began with a conjunction (διότι) that marked it as giving support for what had just been stated. Here, as elsewhere, Peter supported his argument with an Old Testament quotation. But Isaiah 40:6–8[4] not only supported Peter's claim, but also moved the argument of the letter forward by comparing the nature of the Word with the nature of humanity.

The comparison was between "flesh" and "grass." By the former, Peter spoke of humanity. By the latter, he spoke of the common grass of the field. The central point of comparison was that both are fleeting. A second comparison was between the glory of man and the flower of the grass. In this latter comparison, Peter seemed to be speaking of the flower of the grass that sprouted quickly at the beginning of the growing season yet lasted only a little time before falling away. In the same way, man's glory is short-lived.

The final line of this verse indicated the fated end of grass and the flower of the grass: "the grass withers and the flower falls." Isaiah and Peter assumed the reader was able to make the connection. Men will rapidly wither away, and their glory will quickly fall. These truths were designed to encourage Peter's readers in their sojourning. Those who stood against them were not an eternal force. Those who seemed glorious in their radiance will one day be humbled in their fragility. Wicked men's honor would fall, and their life would fade. In contrast, the readers had an eternal hope, grounded in the eternal Word that gave them life.

1:25. In this verse, Peter concluded the quotation from Isaiah 40 and added a clarifying comment. The quotation ended with a contrast, signaled by the conjunction "but" (δέ). The contrast was between the nature of humanity and the nature of the Word of God. The former was temporary and would not endure. The latter was eternal and endures forever. The last line of the quotation was clearly why Peter quoted this text, for it agreed with Peter's assertion at the end of verse 23: the Word of the Lord endures.

Peter's point—the Word is abiding, while humanity is fleeting—may be fruitfully combined with his metaphor of new birth. The product of a perishable seed was perishable, while the product of an imperishable seed was imperishable. Humans, in their fallen nature, were subject to decay and would ultimately perish. Such a seed, therefore, had no lasting value. The Word, however, was imperishable, and therefore the new life it gave was also imperishable.

In light of the persecution context of 1 Peter, these words would have reminded the readers of what was lasting and what would ultimately perish. While those who stood against them appeared to have power and an unending reign, the truth is that they were like grass whose glory was bound to fade and whose life would ultimately perish. What the readers had been granted by the Father through his Word,

---

4   Isaiah 40:6–8. In the context of Isaiah 40, God was speaking to a future generation of Israelites who had experienced the covenantal promise of wrath for disobedience. They no longer needed to hear words of wrath; they needed words of comfort. The verses under consideration here give hope in the enduring nature of the Word of God, something Isaiah's listeners could depend on in uncertain times.

however, would make them endure beyond the lives and reach of their enemies.

At the end of this verse Peter indicated that the same word Isaiah spoke of is the same word the readers had preached to them. Peter was not saying that the same words were used; rather, he was indicating that the same source of authority—God himself—gave both. Words were a revelation of the one who spoke, and since God was eternal and unchanging, His words were eternal and had enduring significance. Thus, the same divine, life-giving Word that was spoken through Isaiah was the same as that spoken through the apostles and prophets of Peter's day. One significance of this fact was that there was continuity between the people of God in the Old Testament and the people of God in the New Testament. Both had access to the abiding Word of God.

THEOLOGICAL FOCUS (1:22–25)

The exegetical idea (after hearing the living and abiding Word of God, Peter's readers responded in obedience to the truth and received the new birth, which worked in them a sincere brotherly love that they must earnestly exercise toward one another) leads to this theological focus: those who have experienced the new birth have been obedient to the truth of the Word of God, and they must now exercise the love natural to the new birth.

This passage has numerous theological ramifications. First the new birth is accompanied by a purification, which leads those who have experienced the new birth to love. We expect brothers and sisters in a family to have love for one another, and Peter capitalizes on the new birth language to suggest something similar for believers. Those who have trusted in Christ have entered a new family, and they have new siblings. They must live out the natural love that is a part of belonging to a family.

Second, though this love is "natural," it must still be commanded. This suggests that love is not easy. Sacrifice of one's own desires for the

good of another is the very essence of love in the New Testament (1 John 4:10). Believers today, just as in Peter's day, must willingly set aside their own will to fulfill the needs and desires of brothers and sisters in the church.

Third, the seed that brought about the new birth is the Word of God. This seed is eternal, for it comes from an eternal God. Accordingly, those who have experienced the new birth have a new nature not limited by the frailties of humanity. While the "great people" of this world have glory, it will fall away shortly, just as the flower of the grass. And though men may appear to be impervious to all that stands against them, time is the mortal, ever-present enemy. Like grass, men wither and die. Not so for those who have experienced the new birth. Yes, they will die, but their true life is eternal, coming from an abiding Word.

Finally, the Word of God from the prophets of the Old Testament to the modern day has the power to bring new life. Isaiah spoke of the power of the Word in his day, Peter confirmed it in his day, and modern believers observe it as well. The Word of God endures for all time, being applicable in all ages, for it is the voice of the Creator and Redeemer, who calls for himself a people. Thus, to all who have believed in Christ—whether in Peter's day or our own—Peter says, "this [abiding] Word is the good news that was preached to you."

PREACHING AND TEACHING STRATEGIES

Exegetical and Theological Synthesis

We all face death. Though we do not like to think of it, oftentimes our bodies send us painful reminders that eventually we all wear down. Be it the gray hairs you see sprouting from your head in the mirror, the sudden appearance of a wrinkle, or the aches and pains of your joints that you never remember experiencing, our bodies have built-in reminders of our expiration date.

If we only focus on our mortality, life would be grim indeed. But Peter focuses his readers on a new birth: a spiritual birth through the imperishable seed of the gospel (1:23–25). Though the reality of death faces every person ever born, the hope of the gospel also extends to all people on earth. This hope has eternal endurance. There will never be a gray hair on the gospel!

Being born again through this living hope gives believers a new way of life: the way of love (1:22a). A new lease on life gives a new mission for life. Love stems from the pureness of our hearts, which were made holy by a holy God (1:22b). Just as Ebenezer Scrooge lived a newly transformed life after recognizing where the folly of his ways would lead him, so believers live a newly transformed life after being born again. The gospel changes us for the better, enabling us to love one another rightly. Christians can no more remain in their state of ungodliness after being saved than a baby can remain in the womb after being born.

Preaching Idea
People Perish, but God's Word Persists!

Contemporary Connections

What does it mean?
Reading this passage, one might wonder, "What does it mean that believers are born again through an imperishable seed?" To best explain this metaphor, contrast the imperishable seed with the perishable. Start with the latter. The church is familiar with a perishable seed.

When I (Bryan) was in second grade, we did a science unit on seed growth. To help us understand the concept, we were given jars of dirt in which we planted a sunflower seed. Imagine the delight of this class full of seven-year-olds when the seed began to sprout! Imagine the horror when—just days later—my fledging sprout began to wither. I was not the best gardener. But even if I had been, and had managed to cultivate a record-high sunflower, it eventually

would have withered at the end of the season. No amount of care can sustain such a plant past its season of growth. The grass withers and the flower fades.

Contrast the common imagery of farming and agriculture with the enduring quality of God's Word. Season after season it remains. We do not water it; we do not need to give it sunlight and soil. Yet it endures. It continues to be relevant, as the unending publication of commentaries such as this one attests to (I counted more than one hundred on 1 Peter catalogued on the website bestcommentaries.com!). The Bible remains a bestseller after all these years, and billions all over the world hold it as their dearest treasure. There is no reason to think it won't continue its relevance and abiding power for centuries to come, should the Lord tarry.

Is it true?
The church must be convinced of two essential truths by the time the sermon is finished: (1) the gospel transforms believers, enabling them to love one another; and (2) people's earthly bodies are temporary, but the Word of God and the gospel remain forever.

The preacher can easily illustrate the first essential truth through testimony. Hearing how a person went from an angry sinner to a loving saint illuminates the truth of Peter's statements. Using the testimonies of people within the church is always the best option, as it gives more immediate relevance and encouragement to the congregation when a "real-life" example shares. If no one is available, the preacher might want to consider a "testimony" from Scripture such as the apostle Paul, Rahab the prostitute, or Manasseh (the 2 Chronicles 33 portrait). The preacher can even utilize YouTube or a similar media source to share a testimony of a popular athlete, speaker, or media personality that might connect well with his audience.

The second essential truth—that flesh is temporary, but the Word of God lasts—is almost self-evident, but may still benefit from an analogy. There are countless ways to demonstrate the fragility of life. Read through an obituary. Find and share statistics from a funeral home director or hospital of the amount of deaths they handle each year. Or, perhaps a testimony from someone who unexpectedly lost a loved one could provide the right impact needed to help the church consider the temporary nature of life. Contrast this with the enduring nature of God's Word. The Bible remains the bestselling book of all time. During the worldwide coronavirus pandemic, many outlets reported the sales of Bibles surging. As people considered the possibility of death, they ran to an enduring source of life.

Now what?

The command in 1 Peter 1:22–25 is simple: "love one another earnestly from a pure heart." The simplicity of the command and the familiarity to most churchgoers may actually make it more challenging for the preacher to engage believers in a meaningful way.

Because of this, the preacher might want to emphasize the *way* in which Peter encourages believers to love. First, point out that "love" is *philadelphia* love, a brotherly or familial love. Just as a mother loves her children—no matter how many dirty diapers she changes, no matter how many times they paint the walls with peanut butter, no matter how many mistakes they make as teenagers or adults—so a believer must love another believer. Just as a father loves his daughter—even when she announces her unwed pregnancy, even when she forgets his birthday, even when she goes against her father's wishes and marries the wrong guy—so Christians must love other Christians. Family love is bonded with blood and should not be broken. Neither should the children of God break their love for one another.

Second, this brotherly love should be "sincere." As the exposition noted, "sincere" means "not hypocritical" or "genuine." Some profess an insincere love to whomever they tempt, only

to move on when it is convenient for them, leaving a ruined marriage in their wake. Christians demonstrate hypocritical love when they feign compassion after hearing of a prayer request, only to neglect actually praying for the individual and instead eagerly gossiping about the problem to others. Sincere love is patient, kind, selfless, not keeping record of wrongs, or boasting, but rejoicing in truth.

Finally, Peter tells believers that their love should be "earnest" and "from a pure heart." The purity of heart is a work completed by God. Love flows from it. To love "earnestly" is both a constant love and a passionate or an eager love. Use a testimony or example from a long-suffering Christian couple in the church. My own church had a couple that was married for seventy-six years before the husband passed away. Such longevity speaks to the earnestness of Christian love. Believers should eagerly express their love to one another. Preachers should not have to cajole congregations to love, but it should stem from a place of genuine eagerness to put others first.

With a focus on the qualifiers of the common command to "love," the preacher can help the church recognize the exact form of love Peter desires to see.

Creativity in Presentation

The text vividly compares flesh to withering grass in order to contrast the temporary nature of humanity with the permanence of God's Word. With some forethought and planning, the preacher can give a startling visual for the church to demonstrate the mortal nature of humanity and the imperishable nature of Scripture.

It would be far too gruesome to display images of necrotic flesh, unless one was preaching to a forensic conference. But the image of the withering plant—though it may offend the green thumbs and horticulturalists among the congregation—can offer a similar visual. Two weeks before the sermon, the preacher should purchase a dozen of the same kind of flowers.

Take care to tend to each flower equally, with one exception: stop watering the first flower with twelve days to go before the sermon. Stop watering the second flower with eleven days to go. The third flower with ten days, and so on.

If the science experiment is done right, the preacher will have a dozen flowers in twelve stages of decay. The withering plants can be displayed from one side of the platform to the other in decomposing progression. This visual can provide a striking illustration based on the metaphor in the text. People perish, but God's Word persists!

Preachers may want to adopt a structure similar to the following recommendation:

- An Untarnished Love (1:22–23)

- An Imperishable Word (1:24–25a)

- An Unstoppable Message (1:25b)

DISCUSSION QUESTIONS

1. How does verse 22 connect brotherly love with the truth of the gospel?

2. What does it look like, in practical terms, for Christians to "love one another earnestly from a pure heart" (v. 22)?

3. How does this world demonstrate that "all flesh is like grass"? How has history proven true the fact that "the word of the Lord remains forever"?

4. Read Isaiah 40. How does Isaiah's broader message relate to Peter's point in 1 Peter 1:22–25?

1 Peter 2:1–3

EXEGETICAL IDEA

As newborn babes, Peter's readers were commanded to long after the milk that causes them to grow up into salvation, while avoiding activities that are incompatible with their new life.

THEOLOGICAL FOCUS

Those given new birth through the Word must continue to desire that Word, thereby growing into salvation while also avoiding actions incompatible with the Word's teaching.

PREACHING IDEA

Born-again Believers Crave Pure Spiritual Milk.

PREACHING POINTERS

Peter's commands to the church in 2:1–3 come in two parts: a negative prohibition and a positive proscription. Negatively, the church must strip away five specific sins: malice, deceit, hypocrisy, envy, and slander. On the positive side, the church must feast on the pure nutrition of God's Word. This all assumes that believers in the church are truly born again.

For pastors looking to give their congregation a feast, 1 Peter 2:1–3 provides the perfect two-course meal. The first plate: "Avoid these sins!" And the second: "Eat this instead!" Too often sermons end up unbalanced—a lot of yelling at sin with very little grace, or urgent imperatives to "Avoid this sin!" without a proper balance of "Here's what to focus on instead." If preached correctly, congregants will leave feeling well fed and knowing how to feed themselves in the future.

CRAVING THE SPIRITUAL MILK (2:1-3)

LITERARY STRUCTURE AND THEMES (2:1-3)

Chapter 2 begins with "therefore," connecting the commands of this section with the new birth. Accordingly, Peter was indicating that the commands of this section were based on the reality that readers had been born again through the living and abiding Word of God.

Peter provided positive and negative commands, noting what should be done ("long for") and what should not be done ("rid yourselves of") in light of the readers' new birth. These commands were accompanied with a motivation and an assumption. The motivation to obey was that the readers would thereby grow into salvation. The assumption accompanying the command was that the readers would long after the milk because they had tasted the goodness of the Lord.

The themes of the section included the following: the necessity of growth after birth; the danger of sinful impediments to spiritual growth; and the natural desire for the Word, which was born out of an experience of the Lord's goodness.

- **What Must Be Put Away (2:1)**
- **Longing for the Word (2:2-3)**

EXPOSITION (2:1-3)

In these verses, Peter indicated what the proper response to the new birth should be.

There are positive and negative implications. Negatively, the readers had to avoid sinful activities (2:1). Positively, they had to long for the Word of God, which gave them new birth (2:2). Continuing the new birth analogy, Peter likened the Word to milk, a necessity in the growth of newborns. Capitalizing on this analogy, Peter indicated that growth through the Word was necessary for one's maturity into salvation. The command to long for the milk had a prerequisite; the reader had to have experienced the goodness of the Lord (2:3). In these verses, Peter assumed his readers had done so, and therefore the longing for milk would be natural.

What Must Be Put Away (2:1)

As recipients of the new birth, the readers had to avoid sinful activities consistent with their former life.

2:1. Peter began this new section with "therefore" (οὖν), signaling that his subsequent commands followed from the fact that the readers had been granted new birth through the Word of God (1:22–25). He began with the negative commands and then moved to the positive.

First, Peter commanded the readers to "put off"[1] certain sinful activities. The word for putting off was used of taking off a garment,

---

1   "Put off." Grammatically, Peter did not use an imperative. Instead, he used an adverbial participle, which borrowed the imperatival force of the verb it modified. Accordingly, the main command was the positive assertation to long for the milk (2:2), while the command to abstain from these sinful activities was coordinate with such action. The central focus, then, was on the positive command. Though some have suggested that this passage speaks of putting off one's garments in exchange for new ones in baptism, the use of this "putting off" language throughout the rest of the New Testament for ethical change (Rom. 13:12; Eph. 4:22, 25; Col. 3:8; Heb. 12:1; James 1:21) argues against such a position.

but it was used figuratively of removing certain activities from one's lifestyle (BDAG s.v. "ἀποτίθημι" 123–24). As was evident from the rest of the epistle, the readers were once engaged in sinful practices (4:3), and Peter's word choice suggested that these vices were once a part of their way of life. With the new birth, however, they had to no longer give place to such actions and attitudes.

Each element of this vice list referred to personal relations, specifically sins that would prevent the community of believers from loving one another. Accordingly, Peter seemed to still have in mind the love command of 1:22. As Schreiner aptly notes, "The sins listed tear at the social fabric of the church, ripping away the threads of love that keep them together" (Schreiner, 2003, 98).

Peter listed five sins to avoid. The first, "malice," referred to a "mean-spirited or vicious attitude or disposition" (BDAG s.v. "κακία" 500). Such a disposition was clearly destructive of community. The second vice was "deceit" and referred to living in a false way in order to gain an inappropriate advantage over others. "Hypocrisy" was the third vice, and it had already been mentioned as antithetical to love in 1:22, where Peter called for love to be sincere (i.e., without hypocrisy).

The fourth vice was envy, which consisted of "a state of ill will toward someone because of some real or presumed advantage experienced by such a person" (Louw and Nida, 1996, 759). Finally, Peter forbade his readers from "slander," which referred to evil speech designed to tear down others.

Longing for the Word (2:2–3)

In light of their positive experience of the goodness of the Lord through the new birth, the readers had to long for the Word of God, which would make them grow into salvation.

2:2. Turning from the numerous activities that were forbidden, Peter gave only one positive command—long for the pure spiritual milk. There is significant controversy over this analogy. On the one hand, it is clear that Peter was advancing the new birth metaphor in regard to newborn nutrition. On the other hand, the exact meaning of the metaphor is debated. What did Peter mean by milk?

The King James Version offered an interpretive translation, which sought to express the meaning of the metaphor: "desire the sincere milk of the word." And while there have been other proposals for the meaning of the milk metaphor,[2] aligning the milk with the Word of God has much to commend it (Miller, 2019). First, the word translated "spiritual" (λογικόν) in the ESV is only used twice in all biblical literature (here and Rom. 12:1), and its likely meaning is "pertaining to verbal communication" (McCartney, 1991, 128–32). In addition, it is obvious that the word is related to the word that means "word" (λόγος). This strongly suggests that the metaphor speaks about the Word of God. Second, the addition of the adjective "pure" (ἄδολον) also highlights the verbal nature of the analogy, for elsewhere Peter used the related "impure" (δόλος) to speak of verbal deceit (2:22; 3:10).

Third, the use of milk metaphors in Scripture and in early Christian literature is consistent with analogies to the Word of God. Finally, a word interpretation is consistent with the context of the passage, for Peter had just referenced the power of the Word in the new birth (1:23). In effect, Peter was calling his readers to long for that which caused the

---

2 Milk metaphor. Jobes has written on this topic, arguing that milk refers to all that "is consistent with life in the new reality that Christ's death, resurrection and ascension have created" (Jobes, 2012, 122; cf. 2002). In other words, milk should be taken more broadly than the Word, yet should include the Word. Contextually, however, the reader is led to believe the milk refers to the Word of God.

change in their lives, for the same power that gave them new life could also make them grow.

Milk Analogies in the New Testament

1 Cor. 3:2	I fed you with *milk*, not solid food, for you were not ready for it. And even now you are not yet ready.
Heb. 5:12–13	For though by this time you ought to be teachers, you need someone to teach you again the basic principles of the oracles of God. You need *milk*, not solid food, for everyone who lives on *milk* is unskilled in the word of righteousness, since he is a child.
1 Peter 2:2	Like newborn infants, long for the pure spiritual *milk*, that by it you may grow up into salvation.

The contrast of this command with the activities forbidden in verse 1 should be noted. The forbidden commands spoke of deceit and slander, the misuse of words among the community. In contrast, what they should long after is a nondeceptive word, which leads them to maturity in salvation. In other words, the Word would not mislead them but would guide them to full maturity, just as the mother's milk supplied the needed nutrients for an infant's growth to maturity.

Peter's word choice, "long for," indicated that the readers were to cultivate a "strong desire for something, with implication of need" (BDAG s.v. "ἐπιποθέω" 377). The metaphor likewise suggested this, as all who have heard the cry of a newborn for its mother's milk can attest. And while the analogy of an infant longing for milk may have suggested that the readers were recent converts, it need not have done so. The point of comparison was simply that they were to be *like* newborn infants in their desire for the milk. Additionally, while the metaphor of milk was used elsewhere in the New Testament in reference to elementary Christian teaching (1 Cor. 3:2; Heb. 5:12), that was not Peter's point here. For Peter, the milk was the entirety of the teaching of the Word of God, not just its elementary aspects.

The purpose of the longing was that the readers might by it "grow into salvation." The "it" refers back to the milk. Accordingly, Peter argued that it was through digestion of the Word-milk that the readers were to grow into salvation.

A concern over the language about growth into salvation might be responsible for the textual variant[3] that excludes "into salvation." Nevertheless, it is clear that Peter did not argue for works-based salvation here. The metaphor evidenced this, for one is never responsible for one's own birth. Further, Peter had already made clear that the readers' new birth was God's work (1:2–3).

Peter's language did, however, refer to eschatological salvation. That is, it was necessary for believers to grow in faith in order to obtain final salvation. A helpful way to think about Peter's language is to recognize that spiritual growth is not the cause of salvation; it is the consequence. Peter called the readers to faithful living consistent with the new birth. Those who had truly embraced Christ and had been born again through the Word were made new, and this newness of life led naturally to a changed life. Accordingly, growth into salvation is the *external change* of life consistent with the *internal change* God wrought in them. Seen in this way, Peter's command was that the readers continue their journey of faith to its natural end. In regard to the illustration

---

3   Textual variant. It is present in the best manuscripts ($\mathfrak{P}^{72}$ ℵ A B C K P Ψ). And the explanation that some scribes might have been uncomfortable with its teaching provides reason to think it may have been intentionally excluded from some MSS.

at hand, they were to be like newborn infants who long for the milk. Such a longing is natural, and when satiated leads to growth. In the same way, those born again through the Word have a new desire, and Peter indicated that they must pursue that desire. By means of such encouragement, God leads his people to obedience through the Word (Schreiner, 2003, 100–101).

2:3. The command of verse 2 had a prior assumption, one that Peter revealed in this conditional sentence. That assumption was that the readers had "tasted" that the Lord was good.[4] The use of the word for taste (ἐγεύσασθε) was intentional and capitalized on the metaphor of milk that has just been developed. Nevertheless, the word had a metaphorical sense of experiencing something. Such a metaphorical extension occurs in the English word as well, for we can speak of "tasting death" as experiencing death. Accordingly, Peter was assuming that the readers had experienced the goodness of the Lord. Indeed, it was a precondition of longing for the Word that one had experienced this goodness.

Many commentators have noted that Peter was reflecting Psalm 34:8, which encouraged readers to "Taste and see that the Lord is good." Of course, the quotation is not exact, for Peter left out "see." Nevertheless, the lack is explained in that Peter was using a milk illustration. The case for Peter alluding to this psalm is strengthened by Peter's use of this same psalm in 3:10–12. Significantly, Peter replaced the tetragrammaton (Yahweh, the unique name of God, which reflects his eternality and self-existence) with "Lord," which is used throughout 1 Peter in reference to Jesus. This replacement was surely not accidental, and it reflected Peter's view of the relationship between Yahweh and Jesus, a relationship of identity.

By noting that the readers experienced the goodness of the Lord by means of tasting the milk, Peter indicated that "there is a necessary link between God's word and the person of Christ" (Compton, 2019, 116). It is in the Word of God that one comes to know and experience the goodness of the Lord. Thus, longing for the Word is equivalent to longing for the Lord, for it is in the former that one experiences the latter.

THEOLOGICAL FOCUS
The exegetical idea (as newborn babes, Peter's readers were commanded to long after the milk that causes them to grow up into salvation, while avoiding activities that are incompatible with their new life) leads to this theological focus: those given new birth through the Word must continue to desire that Word, thereby growing into salvation, while also avoiding actions incompatible with the Word's teaching.

The new birth has implications for the lives of those who have experienced it, whether they experienced it in the first century or the twenty-first century. First, it calls on those newly born to avoid the community-destroying, sinful activities that are consistent with an unbelieving past life. Second, it calls them to further pursue that which brought them new life.

The grammar of the passage indicates that Peter's central command is to call his readers to long after the Word of God, here metaphorically referred to as milk. The metaphor is intentional and powerful. It shows that the Word of God is necessary for growth. Just as an infant needs milk to grow, so the spiritually newborn needs spiritual milk. The infant without milk cannot mature, so the one who has experienced the new birth must ingest the Word to grow into the maturity of salvation destined for those given the new birth.

---

4   The Lord was Good. The word for "good" (χρηστός) is very similar to the word for "Christ" (Χριστός), and likely would have been pronounced identically. Such an observation does not materially affect the interpretation, but may be another rhetorical element in the author's toolkit.

Significantly, Peter indicates that a maturing desire for the Word is grounded in a previous experience of the goodness of the Lord. This experience is the new birth itself, by which the readers come to know the Lord. Having come to know the Lord through conversion, they are given a taste that creates a desire to savor more. The content of the taste is not merely words, but a person—the Lord. Accordingly, it is through the Word that one experiences the Lord.

In sum, Peter calls the readers to long for the Word while avoiding sinful activities. In this way, they will grow into maturity and continue to experience the goodness of the Lord.

PREACHING AND TEACHING STRATEGIES

Exegetical and Theological Synthesis

Peter made it clear: His readers were born again to a living hope through the imperishable seed of God's Word (1:3, 22–23), inherited as obedient children (1:14), called to holiness (1:15–16), and ransomed from their previous life (1:18). This radical change in identity demands a radical change in behavior. One cannot be born again, called to holiness, ransomed from Satan's grasp, and continue to live exactly as before. New identity requires life change.

This is the context in which Peter commands his readers to put off all worldly sins (2:1). If seen in the light of the gospel, this command stems from a radical change within them and can be accomplished through the power of God's Word and through God's divine enablement. Apart from the Holy Spirit, it is a legalistic command that cannot be attained through humankind's own efforts.

The positive half of Peter's command follows: believers must long for the pure spiritual milk of God's Word (2:2–3). This command cannot be divorced from the imagery of the readers being "born again" (1:3, 23). Their new birth brings with it a hunger and thirst for spiritual things, not carnal or temporal or earthly things. As a newborn baby cannot help but desire its mother's milk, so a newborn Christian cannot help but desire God's Word. The longing for it is enabled by the Holy Spirit. Without this radical, internal, God-initiated change, any attempt to grow spiritually becomes a pharisaical attempt to better ourselves apart from the Lord's work within us. One must be truly born again before accomplishing anything Peter has to say in these verses.

Preaching Idea
Born-again Believers Crave Pure Spiritual Milk.

Contemporary Connections

What does it mean?
People who have grown up in church and speak fluent "Christianese" will have the hardest time understanding the driving metaphor of this passage. For many Christians, hearing the word "milk" applied spiritually sounds like a metaphor for the elementary or basic doctrines or teachings of Scripture. New believers must be fed milk, just like new babies are fed milk. Spiritually mature believers want a nice, juicy steak. They want the meat of deep Bible doctrine. Sounds good, right?

Unfortunately, that's not Peter's meaning at all here. Preachers must carefully help their congregation understand that metaphors are context-driven. Figures of speech vary their meaning depending on their context. The author of Hebrews might be making a contrast between milk and meat in regard to the elementary and deeper teachings of Scripture (Heb. 5:12–13). Paul may do something similar with milk as well (1 Cor. 3:2). But Peter uses the metaphor differently than these two authors. Peter intends for milk to stand for the entirety of the Bible's teaching, not just the "basic" doctrines for newborn believers.

To help the church understand this principle, illustrate using other metaphors common to our speech. Comparing someone to a beaver may be a compliment or an insult, depending on the context. Telling someone they are "as busy as a beaver" compliments their work ethic. Telling someone their teeth resemble a beaver's would be quite insulting. The same image can be used to insult someone, but in two totally different ways: you can eat like a pig, smell like a pig, look like a pig. Someone can be as unique as a snowflake, or their ego can be as brittle as a snowflake.

The Bible does the same thing. Just because a serpent is evil in one passage (Matt. 23:33) does not mean it is evil in another (Matt. 10:16), even within the same book. Give the church a few examples of these fluid metaphors in order to break down the conception that a figure of speech must mean the same thing in every context. Then, look at the text of Peter and carefully show how the image of milk is controlled by the way Peter uses it.

Is it true?

What if I don't *feel* like reading the Bible? Is it true that *all* Christians have an innate longing for the spiritual milk of God's Word? If I lack that longing, what does it say about my spiritual state?

Peter is unequivocally clear: Genuine born-again believers will have a natural, innate desire for spiritual things. Just as much as newborn babies are born with a desire for milk, so a believer will be born-again to spiritual desires. It is wise, then, for the preacher to lovingly—but truthfully—encourage those who call themselves Christians but have no relationship whatsoever to God's Word to reconsider the reality of their claim to be Christians.

At the same time, the preacher should also recognize the reality that even the most spiritual believer will sometimes go through seasons of depression, laziness, and apathy. This should not be the believer's permanent state, but just as a weightlifter doesn't always wake up wanting to hit the gym, so a believer

doesn't always wake up wanting to dig into God's Word.

But what advice would one weightlifter give to another? *Get to the gym anyway.* Push through it and you will be happy that you did. The same goes for the Christian. Even when you don't want to spend time with the Lord, do it anyway. You might be surprised at how much the Lord works in even the most reluctant heart.

Now what?

The application of this passage can be easily divided into two components: one negative, one positive. The negative side of the application—the sins to "put off"—comes in verse 1 and can be subdivided into five categories: put off malice, deceit, hypocrisy, envy, and slander. Each should be explained and illustrated in the context of the gospel. We do not remove these things by our own power or our own strength, but through the help of the Holy Spirit upon the foundation of our salvation.

Malice, or mean-spiritedness with the intent to do harm, can be illustrated using the example of phishing scams that collect information in order to sell it or siphon off funds from unsuspecting victims' accounts. Similar examples can be used for deceit. Consider more current examples, like the 2019 college admissions bribery scandal. One need only to look in politics to see plenty of examples of hypocrisy—green energy warriors flying around in multimillion-dollar fuel-guzzling jets, lawmakers breaking the very laws they create, and so on. Envy can also be seen all around us, with people buying bigger, better, faster, smarter toys not because they need them, but because their neighbors have them. Finally, slander: Though it is tempting to once more dip into politics, the preacher should make sure to eventually draw the examples toward application in the church. Tearing others down happens all too often in church board rooms when one person doesn't get his way. It may even happen through more subversive techniques, such as sharing a confidential prayer request in guise of spiritual virtue.

On the positive side, the preacher should allow verses 2–3 to supply the solution to the sin problem of verse 1. What does it look like to long for and pursue the pure spiritual milk of God's Word? The pastor should make sure to plug any and all Bible studies the church offers, giving people a clear path toward further learning. Consider providing a few Bible reading plans, challenging the congregation to read it through in a year, or read a portion of it by a certain time (Robert Murray M'Cheyne's plan is still helpful even after more than a century of use). Show the church a few apps that help keep one accountable to their devotions. Books like Hendricks and Hendricks' *Living by the Word* could also be recommended for those looking to learn how to dig deeper. Don't stop at *telling* the church to read more Scripture; *show them* how to do so and give them appropriate resources to help them along the way.

Creativity in Presentation

The text provides several opportunities for creative illustrations, based on the metaphors Peter uses for his readers. First, in verse 1 Peter commands the people to "put off" certain sinful activities. As the exposition noted, the word "put off" was commonly used of taking off one's clothes. Clearly, the preacher would not want to strip down in front of the congregation, but "putting off" a certain amount of one's clothes may help seal the illustration in the minds of the people.

Peter mentions five things to "put off": malice, deceit, hypocrisy, envy, and slander. The preacher might correspond an item of clothing with each of these five things. When speaking of malice, untie and take off the shoes. When condemning deceit, off goes the socks. Take off the jacket for hypocrisy, and so on. Of course, it (almost) goes without saying to only "take off" the clothing to an appropriate level.

The "sin" need not correspond directly with the article of clothing (which piece of clothing goes with "slander"?), but the point can still be made in a visual manner that these items should not hinder us. Perhaps to heighten the effect, the preacher might wear items not needed (a fanny pack, a gaudy belt, etc.), or perhaps quadruple up on sports jackets. The preacher can even have written or printed on successive shirts the sins mentioned and "take them off" one by one as he describes the dangers of each sin. We would caution, though, against making this too humorous an occasion, or denigrating the pulpit to silliness, but for some teaching contexts such a visual illustration may work well.

In addition, the imagery of infants longing for "pure spiritual milk" may offer some creative potential. One need only to ask a nursery worker to carry in one of the crying babies at the appropriate time to illustrate what it looks like to long for a necessity in life! If the parent allows, keeping the crying baby in the auditorium for but a minute will *feel* like ten minutes of torture and it will be sufficient to highlight Peter's point. In the same way this child cries for something pure and nutritious that only the mother can give, believers ought to long for the pure milk of God's Word. Do we hunger and thirst for our time in devotions with such a raw intensity? True believers will long for the pure spiritual milk of the Word.

Application should come easy in this sermon. Preachers may use an outline such as the following:

I. What Believers Must Put Away (2:1)
   A. Malice
   B. Deceit
   C. Hypocrisy
   D. Envy
   E. Slander
II. What Believers Must Long For (2:2–3)
   A. The Word!

DISCUSSION QUESTIONS

1. How do Peter's commands connect and flow from the believer's new identity in Christ, as developed in the first chapter?

2. What does it look like for you personally to "put away" all the sins mentioned in verse 1? Which of these five sins seem to cling to you the most?

3. Have you been longing for the pure spiritual milk of the Lord? What does that look like in your life?

4. How might we develop better habits of being fed spiritually nutritious food on a regular basis?

1 Peter 2:4–10

EXEGETICAL IDEA
Peter indicated that his readers were in a privileged and honorable position, for they were priests who were being built into a spiritual house as a result of their divinely appointed acceptance of Jesus Christ as the cornerstone.

THEOLOGICAL FOCUS
Believers are chosen to be priests and are included in God's building program, for all those who recognize that Jesus is the cornerstone are granted the glorious benefits of being the people of God.

PREACHING IDEA
From Sinners to Stones, from Pagans to Priests: God's People Enjoy a Privileged Position.

PREACHING POINTERS
Imagine the surprise Peter's readers must have felt hearing words previously reserved for Old Testament Israelites now applied to them: "a chosen race, a royal priesthood, a holy nation, a people for his own possession" (2:9). Labels that once exclusively described the Jewish people, Peter now uses to describe even *Gentile* Christians! Through a skillful use of Old Testament quotations and allusions, Peter links believers with Jesus, showing strong continuity in God's program from one dispensation to another.

Today we can likewise join in these identifying characteristics. Christianity has no shortage of different denominations and labels that separate: Baptist, Presbyterian, Methodist, Charismatic, and so on. Even bigger denominations divide into further subcategories: Southern Baptist, Freewill Baptist, American Baptist, and more. But Peter brings true believers together using metaphors that capture a common unity, built upon the foundation of Christ and his work. Preachers have the chance to use both Old and New Testaments in one sermon to help Christians understand their heritage and their common identity.

THE LIVING STONE AND THE LIVING STONES
(2:4–10)

LITERARY STRUCTURE AND THEMES (2:4–10)

These verses form the conclusion to the body opening. Verses 4–5 serve as introductory statements that are fleshed out in 6–10. More specifically, what Peter said in verse 4 is explained more fully in verses 6–8, while what he said in verse 5 is explained in 9–10.

In verse 4 Peter revealed that Jesus was a divinely chosen and precious stone that had been rejected by humanity. Peter gave evidence for this claim in verses 6–8 by quoting an Old Testament passage (Isa. 28:16) and applying its significance to both believers (v. 6) and unbelievers (vv. 7–8).

In verse 5 Peter indicated that those who had believed in Jesus, the stone, were themselves living stones being built into a temple to make a holy priesthood. This focus on the status of the readers was given further consideration in verses 9–10.

Six themes are evident in this section of 1 Peter. The first is the relationship between Jesus and his followers. While such a connection was never made explicit, it was assumed throughout. For example, that Jesus was a chosen and precious stone surely meant that the readers, who were "living stones," were also chosen and precious (cf. 1:1). Indeed, just as Jesus was rejected by men, so the readers should expect the same.

A second theme is the importance of the Old Testament for understanding the New Testament people of God. Throughout this section Peter quoted or alluded to the Old Testament no less than six times (Exod. 19:5–6; Ps. 118:22; Isa. 8:14; 28:16; 43:20–21; Hos. 2:23). Peter's combination of texts showed that he truly believed that the prophecies of old were written for believers in his day (1:12). Peter's use of these passages was in line with early Christian interpretation (see below). What was unique was his creative merging of them. This revealed his deep consideration of the relationship between the Scripture and those who have come to believe in Christ in this new epoch.

Third, up to this point Peter had focused primarily on the readers' identity individually in relation to Christ. Here, Peter indicated the readers' corporate identity through the analogy of the temple and the image of the priesthood. God's plan was not simply to redeem *a person* but to redeem *a people* for his name.

Fourth, Peter did not leave his focus on the Word of God. This is shown in that the difference between believers and unbelievers was grounded in their response to Christ. The believers, obeying the words of the gospel, accepted Jesus as the stone, but the unbelievers rejected him, disobeying the Word.

A fifth theme concerns the role of Jesus in God's plan of redemption. He is the very foundation on which God is creating a new people. Accordingly, we see a smooth transition from soteriology into ecclesiology, with Jesus being the key to the transition.

The final theme we will highlight concerns the activity of the people of God. Peter indicated that the people of God were a priesthood. Because of this priesthood, Peter indicated believers had the right to interact directly with God. As a priesthood, the people of God offered acceptable sacrifices to God, which in context appears to refer to verbal proclamation of God's acts and character (2:9).

- ***The Chosen and Rejected Stone (2:4)***
- ***Believers as a House and a Priesthood (2:5)***
- ***Honor for Those Who Believe (2:6–7a)***
- ***Shame and Stumbling for Unbelievers (2:7b–8)***
- ***The Honorable Position of Believers (2:9–10)***

EXPOSITION (2:4–10)

In these verses, Peter transitioned from the new birth analogy to two other analogies. First, he developed the temple analogy, with Jesus as the chief cornerstone (2:4–6). Believers are individual stones in the temple, which is being manufactured according to God's will for a place of his residence. Importantly, Peter aligned believers alongside Christ, noting that both were stones. Jesus was obviously more foundational, yet both Jesus and the believers were chosen by God for inclusion. The second analogy concerned being a holy priesthood (2:5, 9). The readers were chosen to perform priestly tasks, representing God before the world and making pleasing sacrifices. These two analogies highlighted the blessing of the readers' identity. Because they believed in Jesus, they would not trip over the stone as others were destined to do (2:7–8). Instead, they were granted unearned and unimaginable blessing and honor, as a result of God's choice of them and their accordant obedience to the Word in accepting the stone (2:6, 9–10). Peter

grounded each of his major statements in the Old Testament, confirming that the readers had come to have a place in God's unfolding redemptive plan.

The Chosen and Rejected Stone (2:4)

Peter indicated that Jesus was a living stone, rejected by men, though chosen by God and precious to him.

2:4. Verse 4 was transitional.[1] It connected with the previous verse by giving more detail concerning the Lord; namely, he was the one to whom the readers had come. The verse then introduced an important metaphor that guided much of the rest of the section. Just as the new birth analogy governed 2:1–3, so the cornerstone analogy governs 2:4–10.

Having shown how the verse connected to what preceded, we should also consider how it connected to what followed. Peter used a participle ("*coming* to him"), which is dependent on the finite verb in the next verse ("you are being built"). As with many participles, the meaning is ambiguous.[2] Nevertheless, it most likely suggested a temporal transition: "*as you come to him* you are being built up." This connects both with what comes before and what comes after. In regard to what comes before, Peter had just indicated his belief that the readers had experienced the kindness of the Lord, and surely they had done this by coming to him. It connects with what follows

---

1 Transitional. The existence of a logical or thematic connection between the theme of longing for God's Word due to the new birth and Jesus as a living stone has been a point of debate for commentators of 1 Peter. Achtemeier suggests seven possible connections in an excursus in his commentary (Achtemeier, 1996, 153). In the end, there will probably not be consensus, and this may reflect that Peter did not actually have a more meaningful reason than that he wanted to turn from one topic to another, and the shift in metaphor was an easy way of doing so.

2 Ambiguous. Two other options are possible. First, the participle may have conveyed the means of the verbal action: "*by means of coming to him* you are being built up." This is a possible interpretation, though less likely than the one suggested in the main text. Alternatively, the participle could have imperatival force and thus have meant "come to him and allow yourselves to be built up." While this final reading is possible, the main verb in verse 15 is better taken as an indicative verb than imperative, which means the participle does not have imperatival force.

in that it was a result of the readers' trust in Christ that they were now being built into a spiritual temple.

While Peter developed the stone analogy through multiple verses, it began with the simple statement that Jesus was a *living stone*. Both the adjective ("living") and the noun ("stone") were important. In regard to "the stone," Peter used a word for stone (λίθον) that was used to refer to a hewn stone, prepared for the role it was to have in a construction project. That Jesus was such a stone had significant connections to the Old Testament. In the verses that follow, Peter quoted three Old Testament texts that spoke of a stone and its role in God's unfolding plan.

The adjective "living," in combination with the readers' "coming to him," suggested that Jesus was a life-giving stone (Michaels, 1988, 98). An important reason he was designated as living, however, concerned his resurrection from the dead. In the words of 1 Corinthians 15:45, as a result of his work and resurrection, Jesus had become a "life-giving spirit."

That this living stone was "rejected by men" reflects the first of the three Old Testament passages cited. Septuagint Psalm 117:22 reads, "The stone that the builders rejected has become the cornerstone." Initially, one might think Peter was speaking of the rejection of the Messiah at the crucifixion. The language of "living stone," however, does not allow such an interpretation. Jesus was not the *living* stone when he was crucified. He took on the descriptor when he conquered the grave. Thus, the men who rejected this living stone are those who rejected him *after* the resurrection. This is confirmed in that Peter used a perfect verb (denoting a past event with present consequences), referring to the ongoing rejection of Christ (Achtemeier, 1996, 154). The ones who rejected, then, are among the readers' generation. Undoubtedly,

the original application of these texts referred to the Jewish people rejecting the stone, but Peter broadened the application by analogy to a broader audience.

The grammar of the passage[3] reveals that Peter's main point was not that Jesus was rejected, but rather that he was chosen and precious to God. The statement that the rock was chosen and precious plays double duty. It clearly referred to a select stone of great quality, but here, with the addition "to God," it also referred to God's subjective selection and opinion of Jesus.

That Jesus was a chosen (ἐκλεκτόν) stone was important, for it indicated that the Father had chosen the Son for a purpose. The word choice also reminded Peter's readers that they were "chosen" (ἐκλεκτοῖς; 1:1) as well. And lest the readers forgot, Peter reminded them once more in 2:9 that they were a "chosen" (ἐκλεκτόν) race. Such a perspective was critical for Peter's readers, for just as Jesus had been rejected by men, so Peter's readers were experiencing rejection by men as well. Their comfort was that just as Jesus was chosen by God, so they likewise were chosen. Both were rejected by men and chosen by God.

Believers as a House and a Priesthood (2:5)
Just as Christ was a chosen stone, so the readers were living stones, being built into a priesthood.

2:5. Peter began this verse with an emphatic "you also." In this way, he drew a direct line of relation between Jesus and the audience. The language of "living," which applied to both Jesus and the audience, further strengthens the connection. The order is important, for it was because Jesus was a living stone that the readers had become living stones. Their new life was

---

3   Grammar of the passage. This is accomplished with the correlative conjunction μέν . . . δέ in which the first line (introduced by μέν) is less prominent than the second line (introduced by δέ).

based on the resurrection-life Jesus had attained through the resurrection.

Capitalizing on the Old Testament stone passages, Peter offered a multifaceted building analogy. Jesus was the cornerstone on which the entire building was built. The readers, then, were individual stones, brought to life through Jesus, the living stone. Each stone was being intentionally placed in the building of this spiritual house.[4] The passive verb "being built up" referred either to Christ or the Father as the one doing the building.[5] It is best to see the Father as the one who chose each of the stones and to see the Son as the one who did the work of building, placing each stone in the structure as he saw fit. That Peter used a present verb suggested the ongoing action of Jesus building the church through the careful placement of each individual stone.

The analogy of the church as a building is common in Scripture (1 Cor. 3:10–15; Eph. 2:19–22; Heb. 3:2–6; 1 Tim. 3:15). But that Peter had more than a normal building in mind is confirmed as we examine his language. He called this a "spiritual house." The word for house (οἶκος) was sometimes used in reference to the temple in the New Testament (e.g., Matt. 12:4; John 2:16). The addition of language concerning priests and sacrifices confirms that Peter had in mind a temple where God dwells. Indeed, by the adjective "spiritual" Peter meant that such a place is where the Spirit of God resided. Scripture elsewhere used very similar language, calling the church a temple indwelt by the Spirit (Eph. 2:19–22).

What Peter said next has caused interpretive difficulty. Having just indicated that his readers were being built into a temple, Peter then revealed that God's purpose was to make the readers a holy priesthood. But how can the readers be both the individual stones of the temple while also being priests in the temple? Such a question reveals the limitations of analogies. Taking such limitations into view, it is best to see the analogies operating on two distinct planes: the analogy of the building addressed *who they were*, while the analogy of the priesthood addressed *what they did*.

Due to their role as a holy priesthood,[6] they were "to offer spiritual sacrifices." According to Peter, this was the purpose for

---

4   Spiritual house. Grammatically, there is some ambiguity concerning the function of the "spiritual house" in the sentence. The options can be seen in English with the following translations. The CSB takes the less popular position by translating the beginning of the verse as "you yourselves, as living stones, *a spiritual house*, are being built to be a holy priesthood." The ESV, along with most English translations, takes it as "you yourselves like living stones are being built up *as a spiritual house*, to be a holy priesthood." The first rendering takes the "spiritual house" as a descriptor of the audience, while the second takes it as an object. There are good grammatical reasons for this first rendering (i.e., the case of the noun is nominative and not accusative). Thankfully, however, there is little difference between the translations, for both indicate that the readers are a temple that is being built up.

5   Some see the verb as imperative. For example, the NRSV says "let yourselves be built into a spiritual house." Since the indicative and imperative share forms, this is possible. Nevertheless, it appears that there is a definite shift from the directives of 2:1–3 to the indicatives of 2:4–10. The function of the latter is to serve as an encouragement concerning God's choice of them and their incredible place in God's eternal plan of redemption. Inserting a command in this section would detract from the encouragement.

6   Holy priesthood. It is possible that Peter creatively modified Exodus 19:6 to come up with "holy priesthood." In that passage, God said to Israel that they would be "a kingdom of priests and a holy nation." Supporting this view is the fact that Peter later cites this very passage more directly, noting that the readers are a "royal priesthood" and a "holy nation" (2:9).

which they were made a priesthood. Clearly, these sacrifices were not physical sacrifices, yet that is not why Peter called them "spiritual." Both uses of the word "spiritual" in this text referred to the work of the Spirit. They were a "spiritual house" in that the Spirit made his dwelling among them. Similarly, the sacrifices were "spiritual sacrifices" in that they were sourced out of the work of the Spirit. Peter did not clarify the precise nature of these sacrifices. This may be because he could not adequately summarize their diversity. In other words, "spiritual sacrifices" may best be seen as any Spirit-motivated, obedient action.[7] Due to the parallelism of this verse with verse 9, Peter made it clear that one way readers could offer spiritual sacrifices was through the evangelistic proclamation of God's deeds.

Peter clarified that their sacrifices were acceptable to God "through Jesus Christ." Accordingly, such sacrifices were *not* acceptable unless through Christ. Earlier Peter indicated that it was "through Jesus" that the readers had believed in God (1:21). Later in the letter, Peter informed the readers that their acts of service bring glory to God "through Jesus Christ" (4:11). Together, these texts indicated that Jesus was the mediator between these priests and God. They further reminded the readers that their position and acceptability to God was only because of the work of Jesus.

Honor for Those Who Believe (2:6–7a)
Having chosen to establish their lives on Jesus, the cornerstone, believers had great honor and would never be put to shame.

2:6. This verse marks the third time Peter introduced an Old Testament quotation with "for" (διότι; 1:16, 24). As with the other two times, it was used here to give support to the preceding argumentation. In this case, it provided support for the claim that Jesus was the chosen and precious cornerstone.

The verb used to introduce the quotation was given in the perfect tense, indicating an action in the past that has ongoing consequences. For this reason, some versions have translated it as "*it stands* in Scripture" (ESV, NRSV, CSB). Such a translation captures Peter's view that the Scripture has perpetual authority.

The quotation came from Septuagint Isaiah 28:16,[8] and Peter combined it with Psalm 117:22 and Isaiah 8:14 to provide one of the most developed considerations of the Old Testament in the New Testament. As noted, Peter was not the only one to capitalize on the stone theme and its diverse expressions in the Old Testament. Jesus did so, and Luke and Paul followed him. Nevertheless, Peter's combination of the three texts was unique and was intentionally shaped for the present argument.

---

7   Spirit-motivated, obedient action. Michaels notes, "The two most pertinent New Testament parallels to the offering of 'spiritual sacrifices acceptable to God' use similar language either in reference to an all-out personal commitment to do the will of God (Rom. 12:1) or in reference to the two-pronged testimony of praise to God and good deeds to those in need (Heb. 13:15–16)" (Michaels, 1988, 100). The definition of these spiritual sacrifices agrees with the definition of Jobes, who recognizes the diversity and calls the spiritual sacrifices "all behavior that flows from a transformation of the human spirit by the sanctifying work of the Holy Spirit" (Jobes, 2005, 151).

8   Septuagint Isaiah 28:16. While the quotation follows the Septuagint generally, here Peter uses a different though related term to that used in the Septuagint. This could be Peter's own modification, for he will later use the same word in 2:8, providing a contrast between the positive election of Jesus and the negative rejection of those who do not believe. The problem with this, however, is that Paul also uses the same Greek word Peter does. Therefore, it is possible Peter and Paul are using a similar text, which has a different Greek word than the Septuagint tradition that has been preserved.

"Stone" Texts in the New Testament

Matt. 21:42	Jesus said to them, "Have you never read in the Scriptures: 'The stone that the builders rejected has become the cornerstone; this was the Lord's doing, and it is marvelous in our eyes'?" (cf. Mark 12:10; Luke 20:17)
Acts 4:11	This Jesus is the stone that was rejected by you, the builders, which has become the cornerstone.
Rom. 9:32–33	They have stumbled over the stumbling stone, as it is written, "Behold I am laying in Zion a stone of stumbling, and a rock of offense; and whoever believes in him will not be put to shame."
Eph. 2:19–20	So then you are no longer strangers and aliens, but you are fellow citizens with the saints and members of the household of God, built on the foundation of the apostles and prophets, Christ Jesus himself being the cornerstone.

The context of the Old Testament passage was significant to understanding Peter's use of the quotation. Due to Israel's breaking of the covenant and rejection of the Lord's guidance, Isaiah was revealing God's rejection of the religious and secular leadership in Israel. In light of this rejection, God was revealing a new plan of action. The quotation began with a word that called for the attention of those listening ("behold!"). What followed was a future event stated in the present tense ("I am laying" instead of "I will lay"). By using the present, Isaiah highlighted God's certain intention to lay the stone. The quotation is effective for Peter's readers, for what was stated by Isaiah as a *future* event has now *already*

taken place in the establishment of Jesus as the cornerstone.

In the context of Isaiah, the words chosen had great significance. There was to be a cornerstone laid in Zion, a reference to Jerusalem. But Isaiah chose not to say "Jerusalem." This choice was intentional and revealed that Isaiah was speaking of a coming Messiah *king*. This can be demonstrated from two significant psalms. Psalm 2:6 indicated that God places his king *in Zion*. Similarly, Psalm 110:2 indicated that God would give to the Messiah a scepter *extending from Zion*.

The location also reinforced the building analogy Peter was using. Zion was intended to remind the readers of the Holy Mount, where the temple resided. Calling the coming messianic king a cornerstone then suggested that he would be the foundation for a new temple. Within the context of Isaiah's prophecy, then, readers were to understand that God was rejecting the leadership of Israel but that he planned to establish a new order—one that was founded on the coming Messiah, and one that would potentially upset the entire religious structure then in place.

That the stone was a *cornerstone* was also significant. The Greek word can refer either to a headstone or a foundation stone. The latter reflects the text of Isaiah better, for in Septuagint Isaiah, the text speaks of a "stone for the foundations" (Elliott, 2001, 425). It also fits the present context better, for Peter's metaphor had Jesus chosen first and the individual believers chosen afterward, just as one would choose the foundation stone before selecting the subsequent stones that would be placed upon that cornerstone. Such a cornerstone was the most important stone in the building, for it determined the architectural soundness of the entire structure. By analogy, Peter was indicating the centrality of Christ in the church.

The cornerstone was described with two words (adjectives). The first was "elect" or "chosen" (ἐκλεκτόν). Within the building analogy, this suggested a stone carefully selected for its purpose. In reference to Christ, it referred to the Father's selection of Christ for the task of being the foundation of the church. As we noted above, Peter used election language multiple times in reference to his readers (1:1; 2:9; 5:13). As such, the readers were to understand that the Father not only chose Jesus as the foundation stone but he also carefully selected each of them for their role within the church.

The second description of the cornerstone (ἔντιμον) is less clear. It could be taken in reference to the value of the stone. If so, a translation like "precious" (ESV, NASB, NIV, NRSV, etc.) is appropriate. This is the way most English translations take the adjective, and it makes good sense in the context. Jesus, the cornerstone, was of excessive value, just as a good foundation stone was of great value.

But the word can also mean "valuable," speaking of something "being highly regarded because of status or personal quality." Accordingly, it could be translated with the words "honored" or "respected" (BDAG s.v. "ἔντιμος" 340). The CSB takes it this way ("a chosen and *honored* cornerstone"), as does the NLT ("chosen for great *honor*").

In light of the honor-shame dynamic[9] so prevalent in the Eastern world, the latter definition is most likely. This is confirmed in the very next line, where Peter indicated that believers will never be put to *shame*. And it is further confirmed when Peter noted, in the very next verse, that "there is *honor* for those who believe" (2:7). Of course, Peter may have been using a figure of speech called double entendre,[10] whereby he used the word in both ways at the same time. If so, Peter was saying that the cornerstone is *both* valuable and honorable.

Peter, following Septuagint Isaiah,[11] emphatically denied[12] that those who believe in God's cornerstone would ever face shame. The significance of this statement to Peter's audience can hardly be overemphasized. Having been given new birth in Christ, they had been changed by the Spirit, and this change had produced friction between the audience and their former relations, both familial and communal. Among Peter's audience, one of the quickest pathways to dishonor was to reject one's own family values and traditions, the very thing Peter's readers had done. By noting that the readers would *never, ever* face shame, Peter was encouraging them to look at life from a different, eschatologically informed perspective. True, they may have faced societal and familial shame, but they would never face the shame that really matters—the shame unbelievers would experience before their Creator.

---

9   Honor-shame dynamic. For more on this theme see Elliott, who argues that "the language of honor and shame, praise and blame, pervades the entire letter, as the public shaming to which Christians are exposed is contrasted to the honor that is theirs as God's elect and holy family of faith" (Elliott, 2001, 427).

10   Double entendre. While this literary technique is not frequent, it is sometimes present in contexts where there is a metaphorical element at play. For example, in John 3:3 Jesus said to Nicodemus that he must be "born again" or "born from above." Both of these translations come from the same combination of words (γεννηθῇ ἄνωθεν), and it is likely that Jesus is intending both at the same time.

11   Following Septuagint Isaiah. Peter finished the Isaiah quotation with the following words: "and the one who trusts in him will never be put to shame." There is a discrepancy in the textual traditions of the Greek (Septuagint) and the Hebrew (Masoretic) texts. The Septuagint says "those who believe *in him*." The Hebrew lacks the words "in him." The addition of the words appears to be an early interpretive translation that accurately recognized the metaphorical intention of Isaiah. It serves to indicate that the metaphor stands for a person. Accordingly, New Testament authors picked up on this passage, for it fruitfully expressed a central point of the gospel; namely, that it is through trusting belief in God's chosen stone that one gains honor.

12   Emphatically denied. He uses the most emphatic denial available in Greek (οὐ μή with an aorist subjunctive).

2:7a. In verse 7, Peter transitioned from the Old Testament reference to its application in the lives of believers and unbelievers. The first half of the verse focused on believers, while the second half focused on unbelievers. In regard to believers, Peter argued that they would not only avoid shame (as the quotation indicated), but they would positively experience honor.[13] Isaiah never explicitly said that believers would receive honor, but Peter rightly drew the implication from Isaiah's words. Such honor is consistent with what Peter had already said concerning his readers; they will receive honor at the coming of Jesus (1:7).

Shame and Stumbling for Unbelievers (2:7b–8)

In contrast to believers who had honor, those who did not believe had shame, for through disobedience they stumbled over Christ.

2:7b. The second portion of verse 7 focuses on those who refused to believe the Word of God. One might expect Peter to have said, "there is dishonor for those who do not believe." Peter did not provide such an explicit statement, but when properly understood, he was saying no less than that.

Those who believed received honor because of their relation to the stone, while those who did not believe received dishonor because of their relation to the stone. Accordingly, Peter was indicating that honor and shame were the product of one's relationship to the stone. Believers had rightly related to the stone, welcoming him and being built upon him. As a consequence, they were honored and would certainly avoid eschatological shame. Those who had rejected the stone, however, would find that the same stone that brought others honor would cause them to stumble.

Peter advanced his argument by referencing Psalm 118:22, which spoke of the rejected stone. Because of the limited context of the psalm, it is hard to determine who "the builders" were within the Old Testament context. Nevertheless, it took on greater clarity as it was used in the New Testament, especially as it was used in union with the other stone passages. Jesus referred to the builders as the Jewish leadership (Matt. 21:42; Mark 12:10–11; Luke 20:17), Paul spoke of those who rejected the stone and stumbled as the Jewish people (Rom. 9:32–33), and Peter appeared to have broadened it to refer to any and all people who rejected Jesus.

Consistent with Isaiah 8:14, Peter indicated that the stone related differently to people based upon their approach to the stone. Those who accepted the stone (i.e., believed in the stone) found the stone to be a stable foundation upon which a new life could be built. Those who rejected the stone (i.e., did not believe in the stone) discovered the stone to be an impediment, causing them to stumble. In both cases, however, Jesus was objectively the same; he was God's established cornerstone.[14]

---

13 Experience honor. The Greek word τιμή taken as "honor" here can also be translated "precious." Some argue that it should be since verse 16 uses a related Greek word (ἔντιμον) when it describes the stone as "precious." For example, the NIV has "now to you who believe, the stone is precious" (cf. NASB, NRSV). For the reasons mentioned in the commentary above, it seems evident that Peter's main point concerns honor and dishonor. Nevertheless, Peter's artistic skill, displayed elsewhere throughout the epistle, makes it possible that he is using double entendre here. If so, there is honor for those who believe and who find the stone precious. In regard to the analogy being portrayed (builders choosing a cornerstone), the meaning "precious" fits most naturally, but in regard to the image behind the analogy, the meaning "honor" fits most naturally.

14 God's established cornerstone. The passive verb highlights the Father's role in placing the cornerstone just as he intended. This is consistent with the rest of the passage, which focuses on the Father's plan being worked out through the obedient Son.

2:8. Having established that the unbelievers would find themselves stumbling over God's chosen cornerstone, Peter clarified the cause of their stumbling: they stumbled because they *disobeyed* the Word.[15]

The mention of "the Word" reminded the readers of the contrast between unbelievers and believers. In 1:22–23, Peter stressed both *belief* and *the Word* as he spoke of the readers' reception of God's grace: "Having purified your souls by your *obedience* to the truth for a sincere brotherly love, love one another earnestly from a pure heart, since you have been born again, not of perishable seed but of imperishable, through the living and abiding *Word of God*."

For Peter there were two categories of people: those who obeyed the Word, welcoming God's chosen cornerstone and being built up in him; and those who disobeyed the Word, rejecting God's chosen cornerstone and tripping over the stone.

Despite Peter's focus on the readers' response to the Word, Peter did not abandon his emphasis on divine election. Those who believed did so because of the Father's election (1:2). In like manner, though perhaps not in an equivalent manner, those who rejected the Word did so because they, the ones who disobeyed, had been destined to stumbling.

Unbelief, Disobeying, and Stumbling
There are at least four different interpretations of what Peter was saying about the stumbling of unbelievers (Compton, 2019, 132–35). The final three are exegetically possible, and one's overall theology will likely determine how one interprets Peter's meaning.

Peter is referring to national Israel. On this reading, it is not individual people who are rejected, but the nation of Israel, who is set aside because of their unbelief (Davids, 1990, 89). The strength of this position is that Jesus, Paul, and Peter elsewhere refer to Israel when speaking of stumbling over the stone (Matt. 21:42; Mark 12:10–11; Luke 20:17; Acts 4:11; Rom. 9:30–33). The chief liability of this view is that there is little reason to think Peter is referring to Jewish people, especially considering the broader context, which focuses on Gentile exclusion.

Peter refers to consequences being appointed, not individuals. On this reading, Peter is stating a simple fact: God has appointed that all who disobey the Word will stumble. Peter was not speaking of whether God appointed individuals to the unbelief, which leads to disobedience (France, 1998, 34).

Peter refers to God's appointing some to wrath. This reading suggests that just as God chose some to election, he also actively chooses some to condemnation (Schreiner, 2003, 112–14).

Peter refers to God's choice to pass over the non-elect. The difference between this view and the last concerns God's active choice. On this view, God elected some, but passed over others, allowing them to suffer the consequences of their sin (Compton, 2019, 133).

Before moving on, it is important to recognize the relationship Peter maintained between the Word and the stone. Those who obeyed the Word believed in the stone, resulting in honor. Those who disobeyed the Word rejected the

---

15 Disobeyed the Word. Some argue that the passage should be translated "they stumble at the word, because they disobey." While grammatically possible, such a view is less likely than connecting "the Word" to the participle "disobey." First, the Isaiah passage has no other object than the stone that causes stumbling (Compton, 2019, 130). Second, such an interpretation leaves "disobey" without an explicit object. What exactly do they disobey? In sum, it is much more likely that Peter would provide an object for the disobedience than the stumbling, for the stumbling already has an object—the stone.

stone, resulting in a tragic fall. Accordingly, the measure of one's obedience to the Word was one's belief in God's chosen stone. Those who accepted the Son and thus obeyed the Word were built on the Rock, while those who rejected him were thereby rejecting the Word that spoke of him.

The Honorable Position of Believers (2:9–10)

Peter expressed the extent of the honor given to believers by enumerating their honorific titles and functions.

2:9. By starting verse 9 with the contrastive conjunction[16] "but" ($\delta\acute{\epsilon}$), Peter continued the contrast between believers and unbelievers. Unbelievers were destined for falling, but Peter's readers were chosen for great honor. Indeed, this verse multiplied titles for believers in order to make fully evident the fullness of the honor reserved for them. This was especially relevant for Peter's readers who were experiencing persecution at the hands of those who rejected the Word. Peter was orientating their minds toward their true identity, while also showing them the terrible truth of the identity of those who presently had power over them.

Peter included four honorary titles for the readers, all derived from Old Testament statements about God's chosen people, Israel. The first and last title derived from Isaiah 43:20–21, while the middle two derived from Exodus 19:6. These honorific titles were accompanied by a statement of the purpose for which God had given them such honors.

The first honorable title given to the readers was "a chosen race." The word for "race" ($\gamma\acute{\epsilon}\nu o\varsigma$) was used in reference to a group that shared something significant in common, most often ancestry. Such a view fits nicely with Peter's readers, for in their regeneration they had been given new life and a new family. Having God as their father, they were granted many brothers and sisters. Though Peter's readers have no blood relation, they are spiritually united through their common birth by the Spirit of God. They are not only a "race"; they are a *chosen* race." The word for chosen ($\dot{\epsilon}\kappa\lambda\epsilon\kappa\tau\acute{o}\nu$) is the same word Peter used to refer to the audience as "*elect*-exiles" (1:1) and to Jesus as the "elect" stone (2:4). Accordingly, the readers were not only a united family by new birth; they were a specially chosen group.

The second title was "royal priesthood."[17] This title continues the theme of priesthood

---

16 Contrastive conjunction. The contrastive conjunction has been read by Elliott as pointing to a distinction between the Old Testament time period (when God said he would make Israel a priesthood in the *future*) and the New Testament time period (the church is *now* a priesthood; Elliott, 2001, 434–35). Such an interpretation is possible, but the passage flows much better if Peter has turned from a consideration of believers to unbelievers and then back to believers. This is the position taken in this commentary.

17 "Royal priesthood." There are other possible translations of this phrase. The debate rests primarily on whether both nouns should be taken as substantives or whether one should be taken as an adjective. Our translation above takes the first noun as an adjective: "royal priesthood." It is possible to take both as substantives: kingdom-priests. This is supported by the use of the phrase in Hebrew, where it is a combination of two substantives (Exod. 19:6). It is further supported by the fact that the other three adjectives connected to substantives in this grouping of four occur after the substantive. Nevertheless, this reading would make this second grouping stand out, as the others would have a substantive modified by an adjective. Second, the order issue is resolved by recognizing that 1 Peter follows the Septuagint and its ordering of words (Achtemeier, 1996, 165).

It is also possible to shift some of the punctuation (punctuation did not exist in the early manuscripts), resulting in "royal residence ($\beta\alpha\sigma\acute{\iota}\lambda\epsilon\iota o\nu$), priestly community ($\acute{\iota}\epsilon\rho\acute{\alpha}\tau\epsilon\upsilon\mu\alpha$ $\acute{\epsilon}\theta\nu o\varsigma$), and holy people ($\acute{\alpha}\gamma\iota o\nu$ $\lambda\alpha\acute{o}\varsigma$)" (Elliott, 2001, 435). While this is possible, 1 Peter has already shown a predilection toward balanced structures (e.g., 1:4). The use of four nouns with adjoining adjectives flows better and appears to reflect 1 Peter's style.

that Peter developed in the prior verses. That they were royal indicated their privilege of belonging to the king. Following Exodus 16, which envisioned Israel as set apart among the nations for unique service to God, Peter envisioned the church as set apart from the nations as unique servants to the king of the universe (Jobes, 2005, 161).

The readers were also called a "holy nation." That the redeemed were a "nation" did not suggest a present, earthly kingdom. Peter made this clear by calling the readers to obey the authorities over them, including the emperor (2:13). Nevertheless, they were a "*holy* nation." The word "holy" not only described the individuals within the nation (1:16; 2:4), but also reflected the nature of the nation itself. They were a set-apart nation, consecrated to the service of God (BDAG s.v. "ἅγιος" 10).

The final description noted that Peter's readers were a "people for his own possession." The NIV translated this clause as "God's special possession," reflecting Peter's emphasis on the purpose for which God had chosen the readers. Just as Israel was chosen among all the nations to be God's special possession, here Peter indicated that his readers were being called out from their own nations to be God's special people (Jobes, 2005, 162). All of the designations would

have encouraged the readers, but this one would likely have been most significant. Since the readers had been experiencing rejection at the hands of their own countrymen, they needed to be reminded that they were specially chosen by God.

"So that you may declare the praises [of God]" reveals the purpose for which God had bestowed these four identities upon his people. In other words, God chose this people in order for them to publicly make known his goodness,[18] particularly his grace in bringing the readers "out of darkness and into his marvelous light." Peter likely had in mind Gentile readers who were previously following the ways of ignorance (1:14) and to whom the light of the gospel provided new direction.

2:10. This verse concluded the opening of the letter and ended with another consideration of the Old Testament. The passage reflected, though it did not directly imitate, the language of Hosea 2:25c: "I will say to those called 'Not my people,' 'You are my people.'" By finishing this section of the letter with this Old Testament allusion, Peter reconfirmed his earlier claim that the prophecies of Scripture were directed to the benefit of the present readers (1:12). By parallelism, Peter showed that being called God's

You are [**A Chosen People**
A Royal Priesthood
A Holy Nation
A People for God's Possession] **that you may declare the praises of God**

---

18   His goodness. The Greek word used for praises can refer either to moral virtues or to mighty acts done that deserve recognition (Jobes, 2005, 163). Though the former is possible here, the latter is more likely for two reasons. First, it is consistent with Isaiah 43:21, which uses similar terminology to refer to Israel praising God for his deliverance from Babylon. Second, Peter made clear that it concerned their being delivered from darkness.

people was equivalent to being shown mercy.[19] Or, more specifically, it was by being shown mercy that the readers became God's people.

THEOLOGICAL FOCUS (2:4–10)

The exegetical idea (Peter indicated that his readers were in a privileged and honorable position, for they were priests who were being built into a spiritual house as a result of their divinely appointed acceptance of Jesus Christ as the cornerstone) leads to this theological focus: believers are chosen to be priests and are included in God's building program, for all those who recognize that Jesus is the cornerstone are granted the glorious benefits of being the people of God.

Just as Peter used a powerful birth analogy throughout the first portion of the letter, he uses two analogies here to encourage believers. First, he reveals that believers are a part of God's building project. Notably, they are *chosen* stones, just as Jesus was a chosen stone. And just as Jesus was rejected by men, so they too are rejected by men. Despite this, their chosen status includes them in God's glorious building, which is a house for his Spirit.

The consideration of the temple leads to the second analogy—believers are priests in the temple. Peter is not concerned about mixing illustrations, and he considers believers both the stones of the temple and the priests within the temple. Each illustration evidences different aspects of the believer's relationship to God. The building illustration shows the chosen nature of believers, and it shows that God has a place for each in his divine plan. The priest illustration highlights the role each believer is to have in God's program—namely, they are to offer spiritual sacrifices acceptable to God through Jesus Christ. These sacrifices come in many ways, but certainly include declaring "the praises of him who called [them] out of darkness into his wonderful light."

The reason believers are stones and priests, however, is based on their relation to Jesus Christ. Unlike those who reject the Word, stumbling over Jesus, the stone, they believe the Word and therefore trust in the stone. Accordingly, though they may face shame in regard to the rejection of men, they will never face shame as they stand before God. On the contrary, they are provided honorific titles that exceed one's imagination. More important than all of them, however, is the powerful declaration that those who once were not a people have now become God's people.

PREACHING AND TEACHING STRATEGIES

Exegetical and Theological Synthesis

First Peter 2:4–10 compares the believer to a spiritual house, with Jesus as the cornerstone. This is the highest of privileges for a people who have not earned it. The temple metaphor extends to include language usually reserved for the Old Testament people of God. This wording remarkably includes Gentile Christians, a people whose name was once practically a synonym for "sinner."

This gospel change—bringing a people who were once "not my people" into the kingdom and family of God—has implications for the believer. Why were the elect chosen? Why did God bestow such honorific titles upon his people? God's mercy didn't stop with the elect of Peter's day; rather, they were called out of darkness in order to share that same mercy with others. The

---

19   Being shown mercy. Peter used a perfect participle to refer to the readers' past (they had not been shown mercy), but he used an aorist passive to indicate their present experience (they received mercy). That he did not use a perfect with the second participle may simply show Peter's preference for the aorist (Forbes, 2014, 70). This is possible, but it is also possible that Peter used the aorist to draw extra attention to the past event that led to their having received mercy—namely, their new birth, which brought them into the new family.

links in the chain begin with Jesus, continue to the early church, and extend on down to believers of our time.

To be called out of darkness with a gospel of mercy means taking that same gospel to those others in need of that same mercy. The church's mission is wrapped up in the church's identity, founded upon the cornerstone of Christ.

Preaching Idea

From Sinners to Stones, from Pagans to Priests: God's People Enjoy a Privileged Position.

Contemporary Connections

What does it mean?

What does it mean that Christ takes us from sinner to saint, from pagan to priest? Peter uses a number of Old Testament images and metaphors to identify and describe the believer. Christians are like living stones being built up to a spiritual house (2:5), a holy and royal priesthood (2:5, 9), a chosen race (2:9), God's people (2:10). How do we know the meaning of each of these images?

The New Testament is not the starting place. Each phrase Peter uses to describe believers in this unit draws from the Old Testament. When handling Scripture's use of Scripture, the preacher must first take the congregation back to the original source. Read the original passage within context, offering brief explanation. Help them first understand how the Israelite audience would have understood the phrase. Then, let them feel the full impact of how applying these exclusively Jewish terms to a Gentile-Christian audience would have felt.

Even then, because many of us are so removed from a Jewish culture and Semitic religious thinking, the scandal of Peter's words will be lost on most secularized moderns. Using a contemporary analogy might help congregants understand the shocking nature of Peter's metaphors. What if, during the annual Army-Navy football game, the Army team came out wearing

Navy's uniform? What if Toyota began to adopt the slogan, "Built Ford Tough"? Imagine the shock if Burger King relabeled all their menu items with the letters "Mc" in front of each item!

As shocking (and perhaps offensive) as some of these might seem, imagine the shock (and certainly offense!) at Peter applying Old Testament Jewish phrases to Gentile Christians. Allow the phrases to have their full impact on contemporary audiences.

Is it true?

Is it true that modern believers are a chosen race, a royal priesthood, a holy nation? Evangelicals of certain traditions may wrestle with the appropriateness of those titles. The sharper a distinction drawn between the New Testament church and Old Testament Israel, the more difficulty one might have embracing such titles for themselves.

But Peter's words must not be shrugged off as mere analogies or surface-level metaphors. They mean something. They carry theological weight. If our churches are to understand the seriousness of their calling to take the gospel to the dark places of the world, they must also understand who they are in relation to Christ and the rest of God's people.

This is not to erase any distinction at all between the church and Israel. Whatever lens we view Scripture through, we must allow Peter's words to have their full force and understand this text within its proper context. But don't let the sermon turn into a theological argument between dispensationalism and covenant theology. Make sure to clearly exhort the church based on the commands of Peter, wherever you land theologically.

Now what?

How do we practice being stones and priests? I (Bryan) have at times heard well-intentioned congregants try to apply the priesthood analogy in some strange ways: "We must dress our best for church because after all, we are all priests, and the priests always looked their best when serving God." But far from being a roundabout way of commanding young pastors to wear a tie in church, Peter's metaphors must be controlled by context in their application.

Peter ties our priesthood to an action item: offer spiritual sacrifices acceptable to God through Jesus Christ (2:5). Spiritual sacrifices are obedient actions motivated by the Holy Spirit (Rom. 12:1–2). The parallel with 2:9 also indicates that being priests leads to proclaiming the gospel. So the priesthood of all believers, at the very least, should motivate us to obey God's Word and evangelize the lost. Encourage church members to identify unsaved members of their community, their workplace, and their family, and begin praying for opportunities to share Jesus with them. Challenge them to make a commitment to reach out to at least one unsaved person before the next week and share with them the message of salvation.

But what about being stones? How does that apply to our lives? Peter links the metaphor of believers being stones to Christ as the cornerstone. We are all part of one building, a spiritual house, a temple of the Lord. Remind believers that the church is not a physical building (even if it does have the word "church" in its name), yet we are all part of a spiritual building. Each believer has a unique place in the church, set there by Jesus himself, and should live with the recognition that the Holy Spirit resides within us (1 Cor. 3:16; 6:19). We would not dare profane a physical church building. How much more should we care for the spiritual vessels in which God dwells?

Creativity in Presentation

We all know what a house looks like. Many of us have even seen one being built. I (Bryan) remember when my parents were building their house. Over the course of several months, we visited the site a couple times a week, watching the builders clear the land, break the ground, lay the foundations, erect the walls, and put the finishing touches on a beautiful building.

Though most people are familiar with what a house looks like as it is built, many may be confused by the "cornerstone" analogy in Peter. Consider filming a brief interview with a builder or an architect (perhaps set against the backdrop of a half-completed structure). Ask him or her about the importance of a cornerstone, and use the illustration to highlight the importance of Christ in the church.

The preacher may also want to play off the "darkness" imagery toward the end of the pericope. What does it mean to be "called out of darkness into his marvelous light"? Turning off the building lights and shining light on the pulpit or the cross on the wall may have some impact. Perhaps a testimony from a congregant whom Christ brought out of a tougher lifestyle may also highlight the contrast between darkness and light. We are reminded of John Newton's conversion and lyrics to the well-known hymn "Amazing Grace": "I once was lost, but now I'm found, was blind but now I see." A clip from the movie *Amazing Grace* might put the verses into perspective.

These creative illustrations may help the preacher capture the privileged position of God's people, transforming them from sinners to stones, from pagans to priests. One way to structure the sermon is:

I. Two Metaphors (2:4–5)
   A. Believers as a House
   B. Believers as Priests
II. Two Outcomes (2:6–8)
   A. Honor for Believers
   B. Shame for Unbelievers
III. The Honorable Position of Believers (2:9–10)

DISCUSSION QUESTIONS

1. What is the connection between Christ as cornerstone and believers as living stones in a spiritual house?

2. Why is the Old Testament so significant for a New Testament Christian?

3. Is Peter simply using analogies to relate the church to the Israelites, or is he saying the church is to be identified with the Israelites? How much continuity exists between believers before and after the cross?

4. Knowing that we are a chosen race, a holy priesthood, a holy nation, a people for God's own possession, how does that change the way we live? How does that change the way we read the Bible?

HOLINESS APPLIED IN LIFE SITUATIONS
(1 PETER 2:11–4:11)

Having encouraged the readers by considering their blessed identity in the body opening (1:1–2:10), Peter turns to extended exhortation in the body middle (2:11–4:11). The fundamental command is that the readers, as sojourning citizens of heaven, would avoid sinful activity while acting honorably (2:11–12). They are to do this by submitting to every legitimate human authority and by honoring all people (2:13–17). These two directives provide specific application. For example, slaves are to submit to their masters (2:18–25), and wives are to submit to husbands (3:1–6). As it regards the directive to honor, husbands are to honor their wives (3:7), and the saints are to honor one another (3:8–12). Despite the readers' best efforts, Peter warns that unbelievers will still speak evil of their righteous conduct—yet this provides opportunity for evangelism and future reward (3:13–17). In such suffering, they are following the example of Christ, who suffered in the flesh, but now stands victorious over all his enemies (3:18–22). They are also to follow the example of Jesus by denying the flesh and living righteous lives (4:1–3), which inevitably will lead to estrangement from the culture they presently reside within (4:4). Nevertheless, they are to be encouraged, for God will come in judgment, to give both retribution to those who harm them and salvation to those who believe (4:5–6). In light of this coming judgment, believers are called to live expectantly, while loving one another and while using the Spirit-granted gifts they have been given (4:7–11).

This major section, Holiness Applied in Life Situations (2:11–4:11), is broken into ten preaching units: Elect-Exiles and Honorable Conduct (2:11–12), Submitting and Honoring (2:13–17), Honorable Conduct and Christian Slaves (2:18–21), The Example of Christ (2:22–25), Honorable Conduct and Christian Marriage (3:1–7), How to Live the Good Life (3:8–12), Suffering for Righteousness (3:13–17), Christ's Suffering Leading to Exaltation (3:18–22), Ceasing from Sin and the Future Judgment (4:1–6), and Holy Living in the Assembly (4:7–11).

1 Peter 2:11–12

EXEGETICAL IDEA
Peter urged the exiled readers to abstain from sinful desires and to act honorably, with the hope that their accusers would see their good deeds and glorify God.

THEOLOGICAL FOCUS
Elect-exiles are to reject sin and live honorably before unbelievers, with the hope that their opponents would see and repent.

PREACHING IDEA
The Gospel Vocalized Is Ineffective without the Gospel Visualized.

PREACHING POINTERS
Building on the born-again identity of his persecuted audience, Peter provided another way for the believers to think of themselves: sojourners and exiles. This renewed focus on their identity should transform the way they interact with their culture. No longer should they be controlled by the passionate lusts that once characterized them. Now, their spiritual identity elevates their moral behavior to the extent that the pagan culture will take notice. Peter urged them to live in such a way that even their worst enemies would have no cause to speak ill of them.

Today, believers face the challenge of living a moral life amid an immoral society. It is much easier to blend into a secular workplace than to stick out against it. Business success often comes at the cost of integrity and honor. If believers think of themselves primarily as lawyers, farmers, construction workers, or teachers, then it becomes much easier to sacrifice godliness at the altar of corporate success. But this passage challenges believers to see themselves as exiles and sojourners, and to use opportunities where their morality clashes with the culture to share the gospel in both word and deed.

ELECT-EXILES AND HONORABLE CONDUCT
(2:11–12)

LITERARY STRUCTURE AND THEMES (2:11–12)

First Peter 2:11–12 is the opening of the main section of the letter. It begins with emphatic negative and positive commands ("abstain from fleshly lusts" [2:11] and "act honorably" [2:12]), which are both based on the identity of the readers as elect-exiles. These commands are accompanied by a motivation—that those who presently accuse believers of wrongdoing would see the believer's good deeds and convert to Christ, giving honor to God (2:12).

The themes of this section include the following: how the believer's identity as an elect-exile ought to influence one's life; how believers should respond when they are falsely accused of wrongdoing; and how God may use attacks against believers for an evangelistic end.

- *How Not to Live as Exiles (2:11)*
- *How to Live as Exiles (2:12)*

EXPOSITION (2:11–12)

Having elaborately detailed the identity of the readers in 1:1–2:10, Peter turned to the practical implications of their identity. Since they were elect-exiles, they had to live in opposition to fleshly lusts that were inconsistent with their new life and live honorably within the communities they were sojourning among. This section of text detailed how believers would live in

such a way that the gospel message was visibly portrayed.

How Not to Live as Exiles (2:11)

Peter urged the readers to reject sinful desires that warred against their new identity.

2:11. Peter's use of "beloved" signaled a shift in the letter[1] from a description of the identity of the readers to a description of specific moral imperatives incumbent on them due to that identity (cf. 4:11). It is unclear whether the one who loves the reader is God or Jesus himself, though the former is more likely (making the translation "dear friends" [NET, NIV, CSB] less than adequate; Schreiner, 2003, 119). The use of "beloved" also focused attention on this verse, emphasizing the command of the verse.

Peter grounded the upcoming command in the readers' identity as "sojourners" (παροίκους) and "exiles" (παρεπιδήμους). For a broader discussion of these terms, see the introduction and the comments on 1:1. Peter's use of these words here reminded the readers of 1:1, where he initially established their identity as elect-exiles. Its use is also consistent with the use of the words in the Old Testament (LXX Gen. 23:4; Ps. 38:13). Both words referred to a people who were foreign to the culture in which they resided. In effect, Peter was saying, "In light of all that has

---

1 Shift in the letter. Grudem suggests that this section begins the "second half of the letter" (Grudem, 1998, 121). The first half focused on the identity of the readers (indicative focus) and was more theological, while the second half focused on the duty of the readers (imperative focus) and was more practical. This is not to say that the first section did not contain some practical advice, but it was given in a general way, while the admonitions in 2:11 and following were more specific.

been said about your identity as elect-exiles up to this point, here is how you must live . . .".

Instead of a simple imperative, Peter provided a word of strong emphasis ("I urge"; BDAG s.v. "παρακαλέω" 765), completed by another verb ("to abstain"; ἀπέχεσθαι). The net effect was to provide an emphatic command: "I urge you to abstain." What they must avoid is translated in various ways: "fleshly lusts" (NASB); "passions of the flesh" (ESV); "fleshly desires" (NET); "sinful desires" (NIV; CSB); and "desires of the flesh" (NRSV). Passions (ἐπιθυμιῶν) were not viewed negatively in the New Testament, but the addition of "of the flesh" (σαρκικῶν) signals that these passions were consistent with the readers' previous worldly lifestyle. Since they had abandoned that lifestyle with the new birth, they must now abandon all such activity.

The reason Peter urged them to act in conformity to their new identity was that Peter knew there was a spiritual war going on within each of his readers. By using language that called to mind actual physical warfare (στρατεύονται), Peter highlighted the serious nature of the conflict. No one takes war lightly, and neither should the readers take this conflict lightly. The battle is not physical, however, as was made evident by the statement "against your souls" (κατὰ τῆς ψυχῆς). The use of "souls" further highlighted the seriousness of the affair, for what was at stake was the very soul of the believer.

How to Live as Exiles (2:12)
Peter urged the readers to live such commendable lives before their accusers that God could use their honorable acts to lead the accusers to repentance.

2:12. Having stated what the readers must avoid (2:11), Peter here indicated what the readers must positively pursue. The way Peter gave the command (as a participle instead of an imperative), showed that this command was connected to the prior command. They are two sides of the same coin. One should not only avoid fleshly lusts, but one must also pursue "honorable conduct." The word "honorable" could also be translated as "good," for it speaks of conduct that meets "high standards or expectations of appearance" (BDAG s.v. "καλός" 504). Such positive pursuit of good conduct is done "among the Gentiles." Peter's use of "Gentiles" for unbelievers further highlights the identity of the readers, for they, as God's chosen people, are no longer to consider themselves members of that group.

Though the purpose statement of verse 12 ("so that they may see") has chiefly in mind the positive command ("maintain honorable conduct"), it also requires the prior negative command ("abstain from fleshly lusts"). In other words, in order for others to "see one's good deeds," it is necessary both to abstain from evil deeds and to engage in honorable conduct.

The response of the Gentiles may appear irrational. Why would they falsely accuse believers who pursue honorable conduct of doing wrong? It is likely that Peter assumed his audience recognized his allusion to the teaching of Jesus here. In the Sermon on the Mount, Jesus noted that his followers were the "light of the world" and gave the following command: "let your light shine before others, that they may see your good deeds and glorify your Father in heaven" (Matt. 5:14, 16). As the light of the world, believers expose the darkness of the world, and those in darkness prefer the darkness rather than the light because their deeds are evil (John 3:19). Stated differently: believers, with their honorable conduct and their avoidance of sin, reveal the sinfulness of those around them, just as a spotlight reveals dirt hidden in the shadow.

It is significant that Peter assumed the accusations were unfounded. Elsewhere in the letter, Peter highlighted that one should suffer for righteousness, not unrighteousness (2:19–20; 3:17; 4:15). Because the accusations were false, Peter envisioned that the accusers would observe the believers' good conduct, leading them to "glorify God on the day of visitation." Some argue that this is a statement of condemnation. On this reading, the mockers will one day be held accountable for their false statements and will be required to glorify God by admitting that believers were in the right.

Condemnation or Salvation?

Achtemeier argues that Peter envisioned condemnation for those who falsely accused believers: "The thrust of the verse is therefore not that the good works Christians do will deliver them from unjust oppression when those who observe them are led to conversion, but that at the time of the final judgment nonbelievers will be brought to the realization that the Christians did what they did at God's behest and with divine approval, and thus be led to glorify God" (Achtemeier, 1996, 178). He bases this primarily on the fact that "day of visitation" refers to the final day of judgment.

But even if we recognize that it refers to that final day, it need not refer to condemnation, for surely God will receive greater glory from those who repent than from those who are compelled to recognize their wrong conduct. We agree with Jobes, who says, "The day of visitation should probably be understood as a reference to the future final judgment, by which time Peter hopes that unbelievers who have observed the good works of the Christians they have slandered will have come to faith in Christ" (Jobes, 2005, 172).

That Peter was reflecting on the words of Jesus, however, suggests another interpretation. It is true that the "day of visitation" refers to the final judgment, but it appears that the present, honorable acts of believers have the potential of drawing those who speak falsely of believers into a consideration of the gospel. Having repented due to this exposure to the gospel, they will bring glory to God on that day that will publicly reveal all things. An evangelistic thrust is surely what Jesus was referring to when he noted that

his followers were the light of the world, who would lead others to give glory to God. Further, this interpretation matches Peter's later admonition that wives of unbelieving husbands should act honorably toward their husbands so that they may be "won without a word by the conduct of their wives" (3:1).

THEOLOGICAL FOCUS

The exegetical idea (Peter urged the exiled readers to abstain from sinful desires and to act honorably, with the hope that their accusers would see their good deeds and glorify God) leads to this theological focus: elect-exiles are to reject sin and live honorably before unbelievers, with the hope that their opponents would see and repent.

Believers in Peter's day were socially ostracized from their communities. Not much has changed since that time, for modern believers are likewise strangers and foreigners among their own countrymen. Having received the new birth and having been changed by the Holy Spirit, believers of all ages can no longer live among unbelievers as they once did. Recognizing their exilic identity, believers must reject the natural passions of the flesh, for believers now serve a different Master. At the same time, their relation to this Master demands that they live among their unbelieving countrymen in an honorable way. Since they have become sons and daughters of the living God, they are to represent their heavenly Father by embracing honorable conduct.

Despite the passing of time, the things that believers are to reject has remained the same. Technology may have opened new avenues of fulfilling the desires of the flesh, but it has not fundamentally altered twisted human desires. The same sins ancient readers waged war against are the same sins present readers wage war against. Peter indicates that men may reject their sinful desires, a point modern society has increasingly denied. On this point, Wayne Grudem says that Peter's command to abstain from the passions of the flesh "implies that inward desires are not uncontrollable but can be consciously nurtured or restrained—a needed rebuke to our modern society which takes feelings as a morally neutral 'given' and disparages any who would say that some feelings and desires are wrong" (Grudem, 1988, 122).

The same motivation Peter gave to his readers for obeying these commands is given to us today. The hope of all believers is that despite the way unbelievers treat believers, the light of the believer's good works exposed by their honorable conduct would lead to the repentance of the unbeliever. On that great day of judgment many people will say, "I spoke evil of God's people, but they were honorable. Seeing their righteousness, I was led to repent of my unrighteousness. Glory be to God!"

PREACHING AND TEACHING STRATEGIES

Exegetical and Theological Synthesis

The gospel changes lives. Accepting Jesus is not merely an intellectual exercise, mentally consenting to a list of proof texts in Romans. Becoming a child of God radically changes the fallen and lost nature of a person and brings him or her to a plane of new existence.

Peter appeals to his readers' identity as exiles and sojourners in order to help them reorient themselves to a hostile world. Their relation to God has been changed at their salvation (1:3–9); their relation to one another has already been touched upon (1:22). Now, their relationship to the world comes into focus. Though Peter will continue to help his readers fortify themselves theologically against the challenges of a persecuting society (3:8–22; 4:12–19), here he helps show them the benefit of godly living amid an ungodly people.

Living out the Christian life becomes increasingly challenging in a pagan world. It was true in Peter's day; it is true in our day. Much of the New Testament was written in a world

hostile to the faith. Paul tells Timothy that all who desire to live a godly life will be persecuted (2 Tim. 3:12). A skim through the book of Acts bears out the truthfulness of this statement. Paul's words were nothing new. Jesus already told his disciples to expect persecution (John 15:19–20). But the way forward was not to hide or shelter away from the world, but rather to be "in" it but not "of" it.

So Peter's challenge in this passage is consistent with his apostolic colleagues and the teaching of his rabbi. Passionate pursuit of God will catch the attention of our culture. But that does not have to end in persecution. Sometimes, unbelievers will look upon the actions of a believer, and that radical anticultural behavior will prove to them the truthfulness of the gospel we preach.

Preaching Idea

The Gospel Vocalized Is Ineffective without the Gospel Visualized.

Contemporary Connections

What does it mean?

What does it mean to visualize, not just vocalize, the gospel? We have all encountered or at least heard of examples where people seem to have the right message but say it in such a way as to repel rather than attract to the gospel. Whether the pro-lifer who screams hellfire and brimstone upon confused mothers walking into an abortion clinic, or the pharisaical fundamentalist who preaches a clear gospel while looking down through smug eyes, or the overzealous internet troll whose obnoxious posts communicate truth totally devoid of grace, we have seen gospel truth without gospel love in action.

Peter calls believers to keep their conduct honorable among unbelievers. Give non-Christians no occasion to speak ill about you. Match your deeds with what you believe. Live worthy of the gospel with which you were called. In a word, practice what you preach.

136

We are not advocating for a dilution of the gospel by extracting the "all have sinned" element or need for atonement. Rather, what we advocate aligns with Peter: the message of the gospel is best served with a side of love and humility and integrity. That way, people will see a changed life, a testimony of the real effects of the gospel.

Is it true?

"Preach the gospel at all times. When necessary, use words." Though no one is certain where it truly originated, the quote is often attributed to St. Francis of Assisi. The witty saying emphasizes the importance of living out the gospel not just in word, but in deed as well. Perhaps most often the gospel will be evident through actions rather than words.

We must be careful not to minimize the importance of words when sharing the gospel, though. After all, without the spoken truths of the gospel—that Jesus died a sacrificial, atoning death and was raised to life after a three-day burial, and that we must put our faith in him for salvation—one does not get saved. Without the substance of these doctrinal truths, the gospel has not been shared.

So is it true, then, that the gospel vocalized is ineffective without the gospel visualized? Of course, if one remembers to keep both actions and words properly balanced. If a Christian only preaches the gospel without living a life of love, their testimony is ruined. As another old saying goes, they don't care how much you know until they know how much you care.

On the flip side of the same coin, one cannot merely live a good life and expect that to substitute for the verbalized truths of the gospel. Sinners don't get saved by looking at saints. Sinners get saved by confessing Jesus as Lord and believing in their hearts that God raised him from the dead (Rom. 10:9–10). Without the preached gospel, one only has charity, and after all, even unbelievers can do that. Without a life of love, one only has hypocrisy, which repels unbelievers. So preach the gospel at all times with both life and word!

Now what?

Though only two verses, this pericope offers plenty of clear points of application for the sermon. The overall Preaching Idea, that the gospel should be visualized instead of just vocalized, should be a focus point for the preacher. Give examples of how love wins hearts, without deemphasizing the need to share the basic elements of the gospel when witnessing. If a church member has such a testimony, ask them to share it at the beginning, middle, or end of the sermon to accentuate Peter's point.

In addition to this main preaching point, the sermon can also home in on the other imperatives in the text. Abstaining from the passions of the flesh is not always the most fun message on a Sunday morning, but it is critically necessary for Christians to live out their journey as exiles. Give clear examples of what these passions look like, perhaps referencing a list like Galatians 5:19–21.

Illustrate what it looks like for a Christian to conduct themselves honorably among pagans. Use workplace examples from people in your congregation (I keep a list on my laptop of all the different occupations of my church members, which I refer to when needing such an illustration). What does proper conduct look like for a public schoolteacher when they are told to teach an immoral curriculum? What does proper conduct look like for a lawyer who regularly works among those critical of Christianity? What does proper conduct look like for the construction worker who has to endure foul language and ungracious habits all day long? Spell it out for the congregation. If you find yourself struggling to visualize what this looks like due to living in your vocational Christian bubble as a pastor, spend time with your members at their worksite, eat lunch together with their coworkers, walk the floor of their business. Perhaps it will give you proper perspective and plenty of fodder for the sermon.

Creativity in Presentation

A scene from the film *Les Misérables* (2012) illustrates Peter's point that the gospel lived out sometimes has eternal impact. In the movie (as well as the book), Jean Valjean is released after nearly two decades of false imprisonment. As can be true even in our society today, he struggles to find work after being paroled. He finally finds temporary shelter with a bishop. Valjean repays the bishop's hospitality by stealing his silver and fleeing. Valjean is caught by the police and is forced to confront the bishop. But instead of pressing charges, which would have surely sent Valjean back to prison, the bishop tells the police that he gave Valjean the silver. In fact, he even hands over his candlesticks, telling Valjean that he forgot them! This act of mercy and kindness has lasting impact on Valjean's life.

This short scene illustrates the gospel's impact on others. Christ showed us mercy when we deserved judgment. That gospel message should change us and cause us to act likewise to others. When we live out the gospel, others take notice and it ought to attract them to the faith.

It may be helpful to also emphasize that keeping one's conduct honorable among Gentiles does not *always* result in the sinner's salvation. After all, Peter says they "may" glorify God. The film *Unbroken* (2014) chronicles the real-life story of Louis "Louie" Zamperini, a WWII POW imprisoned by the Japanese. He undergoes terrible abuse at the hands of Japanese corporal Mutsuhiro Watanabe. Surviving the ordeal, Louie converts to Christianity upon his return home. Later, he travels back to Japan in order to forgive many of his captors. But though the war was over and Louie extended grace, Watanabe refused to ever meet with him.

Examples like these can put meat on the bones of Peter's commands. One from a well-known fictional account, one from a lesser-known real-life story, congregations should know what it looks like to live out the gospel in a hostile environment. Believers must live the gospel, not just preach it.

Preachers may want to add to the simple outline of these two verses for the sermon structure:

I. How Not to Live as Exiles
   A. Abstain from Passions of the Flesh
   B. Engage in the War against your Soul
II. How to Live as Exiles
   A. Keep Your Conduct Honorable
   B. Do Good Deeds
   C. Glorify God

DISCUSSION QUESTIONS

1. What does it mean to be a "sojourner" and "exile"? How does Peter intend for us to live in light of this analogy?

2. What "passions of the flesh" do you struggle with? What does abstention look like in regard to these struggles?

3. Has your conduct been "honorable" among the unbelievers in your home and workplace? How could you improve in this area?

4. Why is it essential to not just preach the gospel, but to live it too? What happens when either proper conduct or truthful words are missing from the gospel message?

1 Peter 2:13–17

EXEGETICAL IDEA
Peter commanded the readers to submit to human authorities, live as freed slaves, and honor all people.

THEOLOGICAL FOCUS
Believers, as freed slaves of God, must submit to human authorities and honor all people.

PREACHING IDEA
Freely Live as Slaves to God-Ordained Authority Figures.

PREACHING POINTERS
It must have been difficult for believers in Peter's day to humbly submit themselves to the governing authorities. Nero ran the empire. His policies and anti-Christian agenda had potential to cause serious frustration to well-meaning believers looking to serve Christ in their newly established faith. Never before had the governing authorities taken such a proactive role in persecuting the church. It was never so dangerous to be a Christian.

Today's governing leaders pale in comparison to Nero's reign of terror. Believers sometimes get frustrated with government policies that seem to push against Christian values, but what we experience (at least in America) is far less severe than what the believers in Peter's day endured.

This should not diminish the reality of our persecution, especially when plenty of signs point to persecution continuing to ramp up, not diminish. Rather, if Peter's words to first-century believers encouraged humble submission to governing authorities, how much more should they impact twenty-first-century believers?

SUBMITTING AND HONORING (2:13–17)

LITERARY STRUCTURE AND THEMES (2:13–17)

In 1 Peter 2:11–12 Peter provided emphatic negative and positive commands ("abstain from fleshly lusts" [2:11] and "act honorably" [2:12]), which were both based on the identity of the readers as elect-exiles. In this passage, those two commands were accompanied by five subordinate commands. The first was that the readers should submit to all legitimate authorities, whether the emperor or any sent by him (2:13–14). This first command was algo given with a motivation for obedience—by doing good the readers can silence the accusations of unbelievers (2:15). The final four commands are grouped together and highlighted the theme of honoring all people (2:16–17).

The major themes of this section include: the believer's relationship to civil authority; the believer's calling as a freed slave of Christ; God's purpose in calling his people to honorable conduct; and the responsibility of believers to those within the family of God and those outside the family.

- **Submission and Silence (2:13–15)**
- **Freedom and Slavery (2:16)**
- **Honor, Love, Fear, Honor (2:17)**

EXPOSITION (2:13–17)

In these verses, Peter provided three ways believers could act honorably. First, they must submit to the governing authorities. The government was designed to curb evil and commend good. Since believers were good-doers, Peter envisioned that their good conduct could silence their false accusers. Second, believers were to live as free servants of God. That is, they were to consider their freedom in Christ as an opportunity of service to righteousness, not a cover for sin. Finally, believers were to act with proper respect to all, showing love to fellow believers, reverence toward God, and honor toward the emperor.

Submission and Silence (2:13–15)

Peter commanded that the readers fulfill God's will by submitting to all legitimate authorities, silencing the false accusations of unbelievers.

2:13. The first way that Peter's readers were to live honorable lives before unbelievers was revealed in verse 13: "submit to all human persons." The command to submit (ὑποτάγητε) meant they were to place themselves under the authority of the emperor. That Peter had to clarify the relationship between believers and the emperor is easy to understand, for earlier he noted that the readers had become a "holy nation" when they were granted new birth (2:9). Thus, despite their lofty identity in God's coming kingdom, they were presently to live as respectful sojourners, submitting to the governing authorities.

In light of the prevalence of the imperial cult (see "Historical Setting" in the introduction of the commentary), one might think Peter would refrain from calling his readers to submit to the emperor. Two significant elements in the command mitigate such concern. First, Peter indicated that the readers must submit to "human persons." Though some translations have "human institutions"[1] (NASB, ESV, NRSV),

---

1   Human institutions. The translation "human institutions" may be defended by observing BDAG, which indicates that the word κτίσις can mean "created thing" or "system of established authority" (BDAG s.v. "κτίσις"573). The

there is no evidence that the word (κτίσει) was used in this way. Instead, throughout the New Testament and in the nonbiblical literature, the word referred to a created thing (e.g., Rom. 8:39; Col. 1:23). Peter clarified that the created thing was "human" (ἀνθρωπίνη). Accordingly, Peter was indicating that the emperor was a created person, clearly implying that he was no god.

The second way Peter mitigated the imperial cult interpretation of his command was by clarifying why the readers should submit to the emperor; they should submit "for the Lord's sake." The Lord referred either to Jesus or to the Father, and the clause indicated that obedience to the ruler of the state was predicated on obedience to God. Put simply, the reason Peter's readers were to obey the Roman king was because their heavenly King had commanded them to do so. The implications of this were significant. First, it highlighted that the Lord was superior to the emperor. Second, it implied that if there was a battle of authority between the emperor and the Lord, the Lord would supersede.

It should not be forgotten that the emperor in command at this time was Nero. Peter's command, then, was not to obey governing authorities when they are morally righteous and deserve one's obedience. Instead, recognizing that God is ultimately in control of establishing the nations and rulers that exist, believers were to submit to such authorities in deference to their Lord.

The command appears to have broader application than simply to this situation, for Peter indicated that the readers were to submit to *all* human persons. This same word for submission (ὑποτάσσω) is used in the next few sections of 1 Peter in reference to slaves in regard to their masters (2:18) and wives in regard to their husbands (3:1). It is likely Peter did not mean the command to be limited to these persons; instead, the point seems to be that God's people were to live honorable lives by submitting to all legitimate human authorities (e.g., including children obeying parents). By doing so, believers show themselves to be honorable people, shining the light of the gospel in the dark world.

Maison Carrée, Nîmes, France. Public domain.

2:14. Obedience was not due to the emperor alone, but was due to all those who were sent by the emperor.[2] The title "governors" (ἡγεμόσιν) was quite broad and would cover any Roman official who had a ruling capacity (BDAG s.v.

---

latter definition fits with "institution." Nevertheless, the only example used refers to the establishment of a city, which is not close enough to "institution" to defend such a translation. For more on this issue, see Williams (2014b).

2 Sent by the emperor. Some commentators suggest that the antecedent of "him" is the Lord from verse 13 (Best, 1982, 114; Hart, 1897, 59). On this reading, the Lord is the one who sends the governors to punish those who do evil and reward those who do good. Undoubtedly, this is a biblical conception, but it is grammatically suspect. The immediate prior reference is the emperor, and the passage makes perfect sense with him as the referent. Achtemeier believes Best's and Hart's interpretation flows from too closely aligning this passage with Romans 13 (Achtemeier, 1996, 183 n. 51).

"ἡγεμών" 433). Peter indicated that their ruling function included two elements: "to punish wrongdoers and reward good-doers." The first element—meting out retributive justice—is quite familiar in our present legal system, but the latter is not. Nevertheless, in Roman society, the ruler could seek to endorse good, civil conduct by rewarding faithful civilians with various honors and benefits.

2:15. The grammar of verse 15 allows for two different interpretations. Peter could be saying, "For it is God's will that by doing good you should silence the ignorant talk of foolish people" (NIV). On this reading, the will of God was that the readers would do good and put to silence their enemies. Alternatively, he could be saying, "Submit because this [the command to submit] is the will of God, with the result that you will silence the ignorance of foolish people by doing good" (Schreiner, 2003, 130). On this reading, the will of God was that the readers would submit, and this would ultimately result in the silencing of enemies. The difference is minor, for ultimately the entire process (submission, doing good, silencing opponents) was being revealed as the will of God.

Peter here used the same word for "doing good" that he did at the end of verse 13. Viewing the uses together, we see that Peter expected his readers to do good, placing them within the realm of receiving praise from those sent by the emperor. Whether Peter expected such praise to be publicly expressed is not clear. What is clear is that Peter viewed the honorable and good conduct of believers as a productive means to silence "the ignorance of foolish people." In other words, unbelievers may claim that believers are evil and morally bankrupt (cf. 2:12), but the believer's actions

prove otherwise. Such unbelievers are exposed by the light of the believer's good conduct. In such light, the unbeliever's words are shown to be based in ignorance and the unbeliever himself is shown to be foolish.

The Unbeliever's Ignorance

The word Peter used for "ignorance" in 2:15 speaks of "a lack of religious experience or lack of spiritual discernment" (BDAG s.v. "ἀγνωσία" 14). By using this word, Peter was indicating that unbelievers speak the way they do because they have not experienced what believers have experienced. More specifically, believers have experienced the new birth, which causes them to evaluate all of life differently. The unbelievers, not having such a transforming experience, speak from ignorance. Peter mentioned already that the readers once lived in the same ignorance (1 Peter 1:14). Such ignorance is explanatory but provides no justification for unbelievers. The only hope for those in ignorance is the new birth, which comes by the life-giving Spirit and the Word (1:3, 23).

Freedom and Slavery (2:16)

Peter commanded the readers not to use their freedom as a cover for sin but as an opportunity to live as slaves of God.

2:16. In Greek, this verse has no main verb. In such cases, the author assumes the reader knows the verb to supply. Unfortunately, there is debate here. The NIV, ESV, and NRSV supply "live": "Live as free people."[3] The CSB, however, supplies "submit": "submit as free people." Grammatically, this latter rendering is more likely, for Peter has just argued that the readers must submit to all human authorities. Accordingly, this verse answers how the readers should

---

3 "Live as free people." Michaels defends this interpretation by suggesting that the "as" clause connects with verse 17 (Michaels, 1988, 131). Thus, Peter is saying, "as free people . . . honor everyone, love the brothers, fear God, and honor the emperor." While this is possible, "as" clauses do not generally go with what follows; they naturally follow what they modify (Schreiner, 2003, 131).

view themselves as they submit. Peter noted that they should view themselves in two ways— as free people and as slaves of God.

The apparent contradiction between being free *and* slaves was not lost on Peter. Such a tension arose as a result of the readers' social situation. On the one hand, they were free from the things that once kept them in the bonds of ignorance (1:18) and they were free from the bondage of sin (2:24; cf. Romans 6). On the other hand, that freedom was gained only by becoming a bondservant of Jesus Christ. It is unclear whether Peter was continuing the direct consideration of government. If so, his point was that the readers were freed from the responsibility to obey any other king than Jesus (cf. Matt. 17:25–26), yet because they are servants of Jesus, they must follow his command to obey the governing authority God sovereignly allowed to rule over them.

Passages About the Believer's Freedom in the New Testament

Matt.

17:25b–26	Jesus spoke to him first, saying, "What do you think, Simon? From whom do kings of the earth take toll or tax? From their sons or from others?" And when he said, "From others," Jesus said to him, "Then the *sons are free*."
Luke 4:18–19	The Spirit of the Lord is upon me, because he has anointed me to proclaim good news to the poor. He has sent me to *proclaim liberty to the captives* and recovering of sight to the blind, to *set at liberty* those who are oppressed, to proclaim the year of the Lord's favor."
John 8:31–32	So Jesus said to the Jews who had believed him, "If you abide in my word, you are truly my disciples, and you will know the
	truth, and the truth will *set you free*."
Rom. 6:18	And, having been *set free* from sin, [you] have become slaves of righteousness.
Rom. 8:2	For the law of the Spirit of life has *set you free* in Christ Jesus from the law of sin and death.
1 Cor. 7:22	For he who was called in the Lord as a bondservant is a *freedman* of the Lord. Likewise he who was free when called is a bondservant of Christ.
2 Cor. 3:17	Now the Lord is the Spirit, and where the Spirit of the Lord is, *there is freedom*.
Gal. 5:1	For *freedom* Christ has *set us free*; stand firm therefore, and do not submit again to a yoke of slavery.
Gal. 5:13	For you were *called to freedom*, brothers. Only do not use your freedom as an opportunity for the flesh, but through love serve one another.

Peter clarified that though they were free, the readers must not "use freedom as a cover-up for evil." The word for "cover-up" (ἐπικάλυμμα) literally speaks of a veil, but it is used here figuratively to speak of using something as an excuse for evil behavior. It appears that Peter was warning that some might take their freedom in Christ as an excuse to cast off legitimate and healthy social values and customs (e.g., 1 Cor. 5:1–2; 6:12–15). By doing this, such believers would bring disrepute on Christ and the redeemed community. Such thinking was only possible to those who viewed their freedom in isolation from their service to Christ. Peter suggested a balanced perspective; the readers are free as servants of Christ. Indeed, they are free *because* they are servants of Christ. As Peter Davids notes, "Freedom is not release from bondage to a state of autonomy, but release from bondage to become a slave of God. Only in God's joyful slavery is there true freedom" (Davids, 1990, 102).

Honor, Love, Fear, Honor (2:17)

Peter summarized the requirement of believers to all people, fellow believers, God, and the emperor.

2:17. Peter concluded his general admonition to his readers with a staccato series of four imperatives. These short, pointed admonitions were given in an almost poetic way. They were also artistically designed, with a chiastic pattern[4] evident. Each of the commands has a different target audience in mind, though each reference how believers were to relate to others. The first and last referenced believers' relationships outside the family of God (everyone, the emperor), while the middle two referenced relationships within the family.

Members of the family household (lit. "brotherhood") were to love one another. Love was a central command in the New Testament letters (e.g., Rom. 13:8; Eph. 5:2; 1 John 4:11), and its centrality originated with Jesus (John 13:34; 15:17). Though Peter does not make it explicit here, the analogy of brotherhood was made possible because of the prior recognition that the church had become a family through the new birth. The third command may also be related to the family motif, as Peter called for the readers to "fear God." The word for "fear" (φοβεῖσθε) meant "to have a profound measure of respect for, to have reverence, respect" and it had special reference to "fear of offending" the one referenced (BDAG s.v. "φοβέω" 1061). In both Jewish and Greek culture, there was tremendous pressure to respect and live in fear of offending the father of the household.

Though the central commands in the chiastic pattern demand the most significant investment from the readers, it appears that Peter was emphasizing the outside commands. This is evidenced in numerous ways. First, chiasms of even proportions generally emphasize the outside elements (Beekman, Callow, and Kopesec, 2018, 103). Second, the outside elements of this chiasm share the same command: "honor" (τιμάω). Finally, the first command was given in the aorist tense, while the final command was given in the present tense. This imbalance of

Chiastic Pattern of Commands

Honor everyone.
    Love the brotherhood.
    Fear God.
Honor the emperor.

Inside Family of God   Outside Family of God

---

4   Chiastic pattern. The term "chiasm" refers to a "x pattern" in a literary document. One example would be where an author begins with a topic (A), moves to another (B), and then another (C). A fourth statement will be similar (lexically or thematically) with the third idea (C′), while a fifth statement will be similar to the second (B′), and a final sixth statement will parallel the first (A′). Many other forms exist, including some where a central element is emphasized by not being paralleled (e.g., A, B, C, B′, A′).

    These chiastic patterns are evident throughout the Old and New Testaments (Levinson, 2020). Some commentators find them with greater frequency than others, and there is always a danger of reading into a passage a chiastic pattern of one's own making.

aspect[5] likely drew attention to the first command as being the most significant of the four, with the following three expressing how that command could be carried out. That the first and last command were the same was likely an implicit critique of the imperial cult. While others were calling Caesar "lord," and some were speaking of his divine nature, Peter drew attention to the fact that he was to be honored just as other men. By once more referencing the emperor, Peter concluded this section where it began, putting bookends on this section and drawing it to a close.

THEOLOGICAL FOCUS

The exegetical idea (Peter commanded the readers to submit to human authorities, live as freed slaves, and honor all people) leads to this theological focus: believers, as freed slaves of God, must submit to human authorities and honor all people.

The government of Peter's day was largely antagonistic to the Christian faith. In the Western world many of our governmental structures have been open to Christian principles and the Christian way of life. If Peter commanded his followers to obey the governmental structures in such difficult circumstances, modern believers must do so in easier circumstances. As the Western world continues to move toward a post-Christian Western world, the church will be strengthened by remembering the context of our Christian forebearers. Whether the ruler of the government opposes God, or whether the structure of the government embraces immorality, God has called believers of all ages to obey the government *for*

the Lord's sake. That it is for the Lord's sake, however, makes all the difference, for believers who are called to obey their heavenly Master will disregard their earthly government. There can only be one Master, and as members of the holy nation called out by the heavenly Father, the believer's allegiance is predetermined.

Peter notes that God established government to punish evildoing and reward good-doing. Further, Peter reveals that God's will is that believers would be good-doers. Consequently, when the government is operating as designed and believers are acting as intended, believers of all ages *should* be commended by government. God designed that his established civil structure would work in tandem with his redeemed people to make God's character evident. Such commendation has the added benefit of shutting the mouths of those who would speak evil of believers.

Far from being limited and bound by their obedience to their sovereign Lord, the believers' pledge of allegiance to Jesus frees them to truly live. Peter's readers had experienced this in the new birth, as have all believers since then. Their relation to the Lord frees them from bondage to destructive desires and at the same time places them in a blessed bondage to righteousness. Some in Peter's day and in the modern church have become libertines, arguing that their freedom in Christ absolves them of moral scruples. Such people have simply replaced one set of fleshly lusts for another. Peter offers something much greater: the freedom that comes in living righteously, without guilt.

The responsibility of believers may be thought of in two categories: within the family

---

5   Imbalance of aspect. The reason for the imbalance is debated. One would have expected either all aorist imperatives or all present imperatives. Achtemeier argues that the first imperative was aorist because it was attracted to the tense of the verb in verse 13 (Achtemeier, 1996, 187), but this explanation does not resolve all the difficulties. Why were the other commands not in the aorist? Why wasn't the last command, which is the same command with a different target audience (emperor vs. everyone), in the aorist as well? It appears best to see the choice of the aorist as an emphatic marker on the first command, with the rest falling under that command. In other words, how can everyone honor all people? By loving the brotherhood, fearing God, and honoring the emperor.

and outside it. To those outside, honor is due and expected. Whether one speaks of the lowest peasant or the president of the country, all are mortals, made in God's image, and they deserve honor. Within the family, the heavenly Father ought to be reverenced, with a fear of dishonoring him by words and actions. In regard to brothers and sisters, believers are to love with a self-sacrifice reflective of the love that characterizes their shared Father.

PREACHING AND TEACHING STRATEGIES

Exegetical and Theological Synthesis
Someone once said, "Absolute power corrupts absolutely." The human heart is bent toward pride, selfishness, and lust for power. History is replete with examples of corrupt governments and dictatorial leaders who make their people suffer for their own gain. If it were not so, Peter would have no need to command his readers to be subject to "every human institution," for very few need extra encouragement to follow a benevolent and merciful leader.

The need for these commands reveals the sinful tendencies in humanity's heart. It also reveals that by doing good—even under corrupt leadership—the result can be beneficial, by silencing the foolish critics of Christianity (1:15). The gospel transformation in a believer causes proper submissiveness and behavior marked by integrity, which even the most stubborn of kings would admit is a benefit to the kingdom. The gospel, then, transforms not only individual people but benefits society as a whole.

Though many countries, like America, stress the value of individual freedom, Peter stresses the value of slavery to God over our individual freedom (1:16). Our freedom in the gospel of grace should not be used as a license or cover-up for evil, but rather the gospel should empower believers to enact good in society and the world, for the glory of our master Jesus. Rather than allowing power to corrupt, or allow

our individual freedoms to dictate our choices, believers should allow the gospel transformation to overflow in love, honor, and respect for all, based upon their fear of God rather than the emperor (1:17).

Preaching Idea
Freely Live as Slaves to God-Ordained Authority Figures.

Contemporary Connections

What does it mean?
What does it mean to freely live as slaves to governing authorities? And how far does that submission extend? To put it another way: Where is the line between appropriate civil disobedience and proper submissive obedience to an ungodly empire?

The key here is Peter's words "for the Lord's sake." He calls believers to "be subject *for the Lord's sake* to every human institution" (2:13a). Though we are free in Christ from our sin (Gal. 5:1, 13), God expects us to recognize his sovereign choice of the human government in which we were saved (Rom. 13:1–7). Our governing leaders may not make decisions that honor God or benefit Christians, but when Christians respect and obey these laws anyway, it does in fact honor God.

Only when the government's laws require believers to violate God's laws should believers practice civil disobedience. Grudem's thoughts may help: "God does not hold people responsible to obey the civil government *when obedience would mean directly disobeying a command of God himself*" (Grudem, 2018, 437 [emphasis original]). If the governing leaders told churches not to meet, then Hebrews 10:24–25 compels us to meet anyway, perhaps in secret. God's law trumps man's law. If the civil law allows (or in the case of some countries, requires) abortion, it does not mean that Christians should obey (see the Hebrew midwives and Moses's parents in Exodus 1–2).

But mere disagreement with a law does not constitute appropriate grounds for disobedience of a law. We may not like the 25-mile-per-hour speed limit, but as Christians we honor God if we observe it. We may not agree with the college curfew, but as Christians, we honor God if we return to our dorms by 11 p.m. And when we disobey and get caught by the authorities (because, after all, we *are* fallible humans!), we treat the police officer or supervisor with respect and dignity, knowing that they are acting as God's servant.

Is it true?

Does God really ordain authority figures and governments and require Christians to honor them? This is a truth that both believers and unbelievers alike may have a hard time swallowing. After all, there is always a 50/50 chance that the elected official was not whom we voted for, whose policies are not what we desire to follow. What about governments that support (with our tax money!) the murder of preborn babies and advocate for (also with our tax money!) anti-Christian policies?

To demonstrate the truthfulness of Peter's point, it would help first to turn to Scripture. The Bible offers plenty of examples that demonstrate God's sovereignty over the human governments of the earth. We can look to Daniel, who proved time and again that God knows the beginning from the end and sets up and deposes kings as he wishes. When King Nebuchadnezzar thought he established his own kingdom, God set him straight with a long period of insanity (Daniel 4). The book of Ezra begins by establishing that God moved the heart of King Cyrus to do his bidding with the Israelites (1:1–3). Truly, Scripture's voice is unified and clear: "The king's heart is a stream of water in the hand of the Lord; he turns it wherever he will" (Prov. 21:1).

For those more suspicious of God's sovereignty over the nations, who will not so readily accept Scripture's message, the preacher might want to point to "fortuitous" occasions in history that show the hand of God at work even in the darker times. One thinks of Antiochus IV Epiphanes, the great persecutor of the Jews in the second century B.C., who was suddenly struck down with a deadly disease at the height of his terror. If God's providence works among terrible kings like Antiochus, we can have confidence that God still providentially works in our own politicians and officials.

Now what?

Submitting to human institutions or governing officials is not always easy, especially when they have an anti-Christian agenda. But giving examples of those who have successfully done so may help the modern believer better respond to their specific situation.

The Bible is a good place to start, for it offers multiple examples (not the least of which is Peter himself!). Shadrach, Meshach, and Abednego (Daniel 3) all faced Nebuchadnezzar, Babylon's evil king who demanded they bow to his idol under penalty of death. They chose death, but still did so with respect and honor. The story of Ezra–Nehemiah also shows many examples of the postexilic people living under the thumb of Persia and how they relied on God, not on violence or shows of arrogance, to help them reach their goals. The apostle Paul showed supernatural restraint and humility when he went before the Jewish council in Acts 23. After realizing he had mouthed off to the high priest—even though that very priest was part of the council that had him flogged, jailed, and tried for the death penalty—Paul apologized and showed appropriate honor for the God-appointed office.

Sometimes seeing biblical principles worked out *outside* of Scripture can have a significant impact too. Consider the example of William Wilberforce, the British politician. Wilberforce believed strongly against the practice of slavery. Instead of resorting to violence or inciting hateful speech in rebellion against the ungodly practice, he used his influence in the government through lawful means to campaign against it. Just days before his death, Wilberforce saw the Slavery Abolition Act 1833 abolish slavery in parts of the British Empire. Similarly, Martin Luther King Jr. encouraged an entire generation to avoid violent rebellion and instead engage in peaceful civil disobedience. He carefully stood for the rights and freedoms inherent to all people while at the same time encouraging respect for the government. Before either of their time Justin Martyr, in his *First Apology*, argued that Christians are the most exemplary of all citizens and should not be treated as the rest of the criminals.

This perspective should characterize believers today. When the city raises our taxes, we pay them without rebellion or cheating on them, knowing that God ordained the government in place. When the police officer writes a ticket, gracefully accept it (even if you don't agree with it), knowing that she was put in her position by the Lord. When the country elects a new president, whether or not you agree with his politics, prayerfully honor him in the Lord. Giving examples of obedience to the empire in the Bible, church history, and in the modern day will help believers personalize the meaning of this passage.

Creativity in Presentation

It is one thing to preach that we need to "Honor the emperor," but it is another thing altogether to actually do it. Paul urges us to pray for those in authority over us (1 Tim. 2:1–2), which is one way to live out Peter's words to honor emperors and governors.

Consider projecting pictures of governors, police officers, first responders, mayors, and presidential officials. As a conclusion to the text, pray for them by name. Even better, invite local officials to church for a ceremony to honor

them. Bring them up and have the leaders of the church lay hands on them and pray for their safety, their difficult decisions, and for them to honor God. One church I (Bryan) know makes this an annual event, complete with a breakfast before the service.

Avoid making it a political event. Don't only invite Republicans or only Democrats. In fact, inviting officials whose policies and platforms most in the church *wouldn't* agree with could fit more in line with Peter's words. Also avoid letting the officials speak, unless they are members of your church. Politicians can't seem to keep from saying *something* partisan that could jeopardize the spiritual nature of the event.

Another way to "honor the emperor" might be to pray for an official at each service. Make a list of fifty-two government employees and/or positions and each week—starting with when you preach 1 Peter 2:13–17—and make it part of the service to pray for that official. Many churches regularly pray for members or missionaries in need. Others pray for national crises or current events. Why not routinely pray for the people who serve this country? Making this a regular part of the church's service will show the congregation that the text is not meant to be preached once and disregarded, but instead lived out week by week. Preachers should regularly remind the church the need to freely live as slaves to God-ordained authority figures.

Preachers can modify the following outline to structure the sermon:

- Submit to Human Authorities (2:13–14)

- Silence Ignorant Fools (2:15)

- Serve God Freely (2:16)

- Surrender in Love (2:17)

DISCUSSION QUESTIONS

1. What is the most difficult part of Peter's instruction to be subject to every human institution and ruler (2:13–14)? How does Peter's context in Nero's reign help us with application today?

2. How does doing good silence the ignorance of foolish people (2:15)? What does Peter mean by "foolish people"? Who are such people in our lives?

3. How do some Christians allow their freedom in Christ to cover up their evil (2:16)? What does living as freed slaves look like for you in your workplace or home?

4. Which of Peter's final four commands do you struggle with most (2:17)? How does each of these commands relate to our identity as freed slaves?

1 Peter 2:18–21

EXEGETICAL IDEA
Peter commanded slaves to be subject to their masters, even those who caused them unjust suffering, for in doing so they receive commendation from God as they follow the steps of Jesus.

THEOLOGICAL FOCUS
Believers should graciously endure sovereignly permitted unjust suffering, knowing that they are commended by God as they follow the steps of Jesus.

PREACHING IDEA
Being a Slave of Christ Means Submitting to Human Masters.

PREACHING POINTERS
Peter directly speaks to those in one of the most difficult situations imaginable: slaves suffering under a cruel master. How does a believer act as a born-again child of God while enduring unjust punishment as a slave? Instead of encouraging the believer to seek asylum or to attain freedom, his advice is to endure the sorrows while doing good. This aligns the believer's life with the unjust punishment Christ suffered, and has a sanctifying effect on the believer.

Most people today cannot directly identify with Peter's context. Though the sex-slave trade is growing in many parts of the world, the vast majority of people do not understand what it means to be held captive and forced to obey the will of another human being. But Peter's words still have relevance to the twenty-first-century Christian. Peter's point has more to do with living amid injustice than living amid slavery, and there is plenty of injustice going around. Believers can be encouraged to follow the footsteps of Jesus and endure suffering for the sake of maintaining a proper Christian testimony.

HONORABLE CONDUCT AND CHRISTIAN SLAVES
(2:18–21)

LITERARY STRUCTURE AND THEMES (2:18–21)

Peter began the heart of his epistle with 2:11–12, which included the dual-sided command to abstain from sinful desires and to act honorably. Then in 2:13–17 Peter provided general commands for all believers. From 2:18–3:12, Peter provided specific directives to certain segments of his readers. He began, in the text under consideration here, by addressing the slaves (2:18–21). He offered one directive: "submit to your masters with respect." The rest of the paragraph is Peter's clarification of and support for the command. He first explained that submission is necessary even to unjust masters (2:18). The grounds for such obedience are that one is "conscious of God," meaning that the reason for obedience is one's relation to God. The motivation for obedience was multifaceted: God called the readers to unjust suffering (2:21), God would reward them for unjust suffering (2:19–20), and their experience of unjust suffering followed the steps of Jesus (2:21).

The themes of this section include the following: the duty of Christian slaves to their masters; the believer's response to unjust suffering; and the role the example of Jesus should play in the believer's consciousness of his own suffering.

- *Be Obedient Slaves (2:18)*
- *Commendable Suffering (2:19–20)*
- *Following the Steps of Jesus (2:21)*

EXPOSITION (2:18–21)

Peter directed those in the congregation who were household slaves to submit to their masters. Obedience was required not only to the good masters but also to those who inflicted suffering unjustly. Peter encouraged readers that God looked positively on those who suffered unjustly, and that God was sovereign over such suffering. Believers should not be surprised at unjust suffering, for Jesus suffered unjustly, and his followers must walk in his footsteps.

Be Obedient Slaves (2:18)

Peter called the slaves in his audience to submit to both gentle and harsh masters.

2:18. Having given some general instruction on how believers were to live honorably as elect-exiles, Peter here turned to instruction specific to certain segments of his readers: He began by addressing the master-slave relationship (2:18–25), then moved to the husband-wife relationship (3:1–7). Such moral instruction to groups within a household was a normal pattern in Greek literature, and occurs with some frequency in the New Testament (Eph. 5:21–6:9; Col. 3:18–4:1; 1 Tim. 2:8–3:13; and Titus 1:5–2:10). Such ethical guides are popularly known as "household codes."

Peter's household codes were unique in multiple ways. First, Peter *began* by addressing the master-slave relationship. The normal pattern began with the highest social position and worked downward. Thus, the codes would normally begin with the husband-wife relationship, move to the parent-child relationship, and then conclude with the master-slave relationship (Elliott, 2001, 513). Peter's flipping of the norm appears intentional and suggests a greater respect for those in the position of slave. Second,

Peter directly addressed the slaves. Though attitudes toward slaves were not uniform, it was abnormal to address them in household codes. One would normally address the slaves through their masters. Of course, it is possible that there were no masters among Peter's audience, which would explain why Peter gave no instructions to them (cf. Eph. 6:9; Col. 4:1). Nevertheless, the custom of New Testament household codes was to directly address those in the subordinate position (e.g., Eph. 6:5; Col. 3:22). In doing so, Peter showed the value of such people as individuals.

Using a participle with the force of an imperative,[1] Peter indicated that the slaves must "submit" to their masters. The word for "slave" (οἰκέται) referred specifically to household slaves, the most common form of slave in Asia Minor. That they were to "submit" indicates that they had to follow the dictates of another, specifically their master. Peter applied the word to various situations, whether civilians submitting to the government (2:13), wives submitting to their husbands (3:1), congregants submitting to their elders in the church (5:5), or here, slaves submitting to their masters. The similarity among all of these was that there was a social situation that called for one party to be subject to the direction of another.

Slavery in the Ancient World

Kitchen notes that under Roman law a slave was "a person (male or female) owned by another, without rights, and—like any other form of personal property—to be used and disposed of in whatever way the owner may wish" (Kitchen, 1996, 1110). A significant percentage of the Roman world consisted of slaves. For example, Rome's slave population was almost a third of its overall population, and though it is hard to determine exactly, the entire empire may have had a similar ratio (Elliott, 2001, 514). There were many ways one became a slave: being conquered in war; being sold as a payment for debt; being born into slavery; selling oneself into slavery to avoid poverty; and selling one's children into slavery for financial gain (Kitchen, 1996, 1110). In Asia Minor, where Peter was writing, slaves were predominantly used within the household to perform domestic duties. Most slaves were treated relatively well, primarily because this was the best method to lead to fruitful labor (Kitchen, 1996, 1113). Nevertheless, there was no recourse for slaves against their masters, and cruel masters certainly existed, as Peter's admonition suggests. Peter's position on slavery is consistent with the broader New Testament position—namely, New Testament authors do not explicitly call for the elimination of slavery; but by humanizing and showing the value of the slave, they undermine it as an institution.

Peter noted that the slaves should be subject "with all fear." It is not clear to whom the fear is to be directed. The NIV offers one interpretive option: "Slaves, in reverent fear of God submit yourselves to your masters." The ESV offers another option: "Servants, be subject to your masters with all respect." The latter option may be defended by the close proximity of the prepositional phrase "with all reverence" to "masters." Further, the word for "fear" (φόβῳ) has a range of meaning that includes the idea of reverence appropriate to the master-slave relationship (BDAG s.v. "φόβος" 1062). On the other hand, in the opening of the household codes Peter had just called readers to fear God (2:17). This makes it likely they would associate the fear command with God, for it was uniquely given to God to be feared above all others. Read

---

1 Participle with the force of an imperative. One would expect Peter to have used an imperative verb here. Instead, he used a participle. The participle is functionally different from an imperative, though it can take imperatival force. Here, it takes imperatival force from the verbs in 2:11–12. By putting the command in the participle form, Peter is structuring the narrative, showing that slaves obeying their masters is one way that people may abstain from ungodly passions while living honorably.

this way, the command for the slaves to fear God essentially parallels the statement "for the Lord's sake" from verse 13. In both circumstances, the believer was called to obey with an eye primarily toward God.

Peter argued that the slaves must submit to both good and harsh masters. By using a correlative conjunction ("not only … but also") Peter signaled that he recognized that the readers would find the command to submit to good masters fair and logical, while the command to submit to the harsh would be more difficult. Masters in Peter's day were sometimes "good and gentle." The latter term, translated here as "gentle" (ἐπιεικέσιν), is difficult to define since it occurs infrequently in the biblical literature. One Greek dictionary defines it as "not insisting on every right of letter of law or custom" and offers the following options for translation: "yielding, gentle, kind, courteous, tolerant" (BDAG s.v. "ἐπιεικής" 371). The NIV

translated it as "considerate," but most modern translations have "gentle" (NASB, ESV, NET, CSB, NRSV). The idea seems to have been that this was a master who was concerned for the welfare of the slave.

In contrast to the "good and gentle" master was the "harsh" master. There is no clear equivalent for Peter's word for "harsh" (σκολιοῖς). English translations vary widely: "unreasonable" (NASB); "unjust" (ESV); "perverse" (NET); "harsh" (NIV, NRSV); "cruel" (CSB). The word is the origin for the word "scoliosis," referring to a crooked spine. The nonmetaphorical rendering "pertaining to being bent, curved, or crooked as opposed to straight" led to its metaphorical use: "pertaining to being morally bent or twisted" (BDAG s.v. "σκολιός" 930). Though it is hard to capture in English, Peter's point was that this master was morally crooked, not acting in an honorable way. In the verses that

A Mosaic of a Mistress with Two Household Slaves
Dennis Jarvis, CC BY-SA 2.0 <https://creativecommons.org/licenses/by-sa/2.0>, via Wikimedia Commons.

follow Peter indicated that such masters would inflict suffering unjustly. They are the opposite of the "good and gentle," for they do not care for the welfare of their slaves.

Commendable Suffering (2:19–20)

Peter distinguished two types of suffering, one that is commendable before God and one that is not.

2:19. That a Christian slave would have an unbelieving, harsh master was a very real possibility. In this verse and the next, Peter provided motivation for such servants to obey such masters. Peter provided the instruction in an intentionally poetic fashion,[2] which was designed to highlight the commendation of God toward those who obey even while suffering unjustly. The structure began in verse 19 with a positive statement of what is commendable before God; it moved to a negative statement of what is not commendable before God (v. 20a) before it moved back to a positive statement in verse 20b that mirrored verse 19.

Why should Christian slaves submit even to harsh masters? Peter answered by noting that unjust suffering was "commendable" before God. The word translated "commendable" (χάρις) is the word normally translated "grace" throughout the New Testament. For this reason, the ESV translated this clause as "this is a gracious thing." Most translations, however, recognize a distinctive use of the word to refer to what is commendable (BDAG s.v. "χάρις" 1079): "for it is commendable" (NIV); "for it is a credit to you" (NRSV); "for it brings favor" (CSB).

Commendation

The distinctive use of the word normally translated "grace" (χάρις) follows the teaching of Jesus in Luke 6:32–35, where Jesus gives three consecutive conditional sayings: "If you love those who love you, *what credit* [χάρις] *is that to you?*" (6:32); "And if you do good to those who are good to you, *what credit* [χάρις] *is that to you?*" "And if you lend to those from whom you expect repayment, *what credit* [χάρις] *is that to you?*" (6:34). Because Peter also uses this distinctive definition of the word, it appears that he may be referring back to this teaching of Jesus. Peter is effectively adding another line to Jesus's statements: "if you, as a servant, only obey when masters are good and gentle, what credit is that to you?" By obeying even unjust masters, Peter's readers demonstrate character that God rewards.

Notably, Peter generalized the admonition by using the indefinite pronoun "*someone*" (τις). This had the effect of broadening the referent beyond just slaves. Yes, slaves were commended if they suffered unjustly, but the fact went beyond that one specific historical situation and pertained to any unjust suffering. One limitation on the commendation, however, is that such commendation comes when one endures because he or she is "conscious of God." The word for "conscious" (συνείδησιν) is mostly used in the New Testament to refer to the inward faculty of the conscience (e.g., Rom. 2:15; 9:1; 1 Cor. 10:29a; 2 Cor. 1:12; 4:2; 5:11; Heb. 9:14), and some translations take it that way: "for the sake of conscience toward God" (NASB) and "because of conscience toward God" (NET). But it is better to see it used here to refer to an inner awareness about something (BDAG s.v. "συνείδησις" 967). Translations such as "because of a consciousness toward God" (CSB) and more colloquially "mindful of God" (ESV) capture this sense well.

Peter's point was that the type of unjust suffering that is commendable is the type

---

2   Intentionally poetic fashion. Achtemeier, noting both the chiastic pattern as well as the *inclusio* formed by the statement "for this is commendable," concluded that such poetic attention "shows the care with which the author has shaped these sentences" (Achtemeier, 1996, 196).

that is endured because of one's relationship to God. This does not necessarily mean that their suffering is *due to* their relationship with God (though that is certainly a possibility); rather, it is that they endure such unjust suffering, conscious that God has called them to such endurance. Understood properly, this statement places the master-slave relationship in the same light as Peter's earlier comments regarding the government-resident relationship. Just as a Christian citizen obeys the emperor because of God, so a Christian slave submits to his master because of God. In both cases, the one in power may be corrupt, but obedience is required. Nevertheless, since one obeys *for the sake of the Lord* or because he or she is *conscious of God*, then no human master has ultimate authority over a believer.

2:20. In this verse Peter envisioned two reasons one may endure suffering, and he contrasted the way God views them. Using a rhetorical question, Peter asked whether the readers thought they should receive "credit" for enduring suffering due to their own wrongdoing. The word for "credit" (κλέος) is rare in biblical Greek; it refers to "fame" or "glory" (BDAG s.v. "κλέος" 547). J. Ramsey Michaels notes that its use here is likely rhetorical in force, noting that there is no glory or renown in being known as the servant who endures punishment for disobedience to one's master (Michaels, 1988, 141). In this imaginary scenario, Peter envisioned a slave doing something opposite his master's will and having to endure a physical punishment. No one believes that such a servant deserves to receive anything positive for such behavior. On the other hand, if a servant does good and endures suffering as a result of that good-doing, Peter declared that such actions were "commendable before God." That is, such actions would result in God's good favor, leading to eternal reward (cf. Luke 6:35).

Following the Steps of Jesus (2:21)
Peter argued that unjust suffering was the inheritance of believers, for they follow in the steps of Jesus.

2:21. By beginning this verse with "for" (γάρ) Peter signaled that he was giving support for his previous assertion. Indeed, the readers may have been asking themselves, "Why does God commend good-doers when they suffer unjustly?" Peter responded to this unasked question by noting that the readers were "called to this." That they were "called" (ἐκλήθητε) highlighted their election, yet it focused not on their relationship to God, but their being chosen "for receipt of a special benefit or experience" (BDAG s.v. "καλέω" 503).

Interpreters debate what the special experience is, for Peter simply stated "for to *this* you were called." Grudem argues that "this" refers to "trusting in God while suffering for doing right" (Grudem, 1998, 136). While it is undoubtedly true that God called Peter's readers to trust amid unjust suffering, Peter's use of calling language already in this text suggests that he is speaking of a calling leading to reward (1:1–4). In other words, Peter was saying that the readers were called to *unjust suffering for good-doing, leading to eternal reward.* Thus, as Thomas Schreiner argues, Peter showed that suffering "is not a detour by which believers receive the inheritance to which they were called. It is God's appointed means for receiving the inheritance" (Schreiner, 2003, 141).

Peter explained why the readers were called to such experience: "because Christ also suffered for you." Two elements of this clause are important. First, Peter stressed that Jesus "suffered *for you*." The addition of these final two words appears unnecessary if Peter's point was simply that believers will suffer since Jesus suffered. Their inclusion points specifically to a vicarious reading, as verse 24 confirms. Accordingly, Peter was highlighting that their inclusion among unjust sufferers is due to the cross-work of Jesus Christ.

A second important element of Peter's statement was that "Christ *also* suffered."[3] Peter's logic is simple: Since Jesus experienced such suffering, his followers will experience the same. In fact, Peter highlighted that Jesus's suffering left an example. The word translated "example" (ὑπογραμμόν) referred to a "model or pattern to be copied in writing or drawing," (BDAG s.v. "ὑπογραμμός" 1036) and it was used of young children tracing the letters of the alphabet, seeking to perfectly emulate the pattern. By using this word, Peter was suggesting that Jesus's example was designed to be emulated.

The final clause of the sentence identifies a purpose—that the readers would follow in the steps of Jesus. There are two options for connecting this statement with the rest of Peter's argument. First, Peter could have been suggesting *a purpose for Jesus leaving the example*. Thus, Jesus suffered so that others would follow him, enduring unjust suffering as well. Second, Peter could have been suggesting *a purpose for which Jesus suffered*. Thus, Jesus suffered so that people would follow him, becoming his disciples. The second option is preferred, for it avoids the idea that Peter desired his followers to endure unjust suffering. Further, the idea of "following" Jesus is pervasive in the New Testament (Achtemeier, 1996, 199).

THEOLOGICAL FOCUS

The exegetical idea (Peter commanded slaves to be subject to their masters, even those who cause them unjust suffering, for in doing so they receive commendation from God as they follow the steps of Jesus) leads to this theological focus: believers should graciously endure sovereignly permitted unjust suffering, knowing that they are commended by God as they follow the steps of Jesus.

Slavery as practiced in the ancient world is no longer a dominant feature of present-world communities. For this reason, one might think Peter's admonitions would not be applicable to modern audiences. In one sense this is accurate, as the primary command ("obey your masters") cannot be directly transferred to present believers. On the other hand, Peter intended his message to reach beyond simply the slaves. Anyone who endures unjust suffering while seeking to live faithfully before God may be confident that their unjust suffering is looked at positively by God. Indeed, such believers will receive credit for such suffering, meaning they will be rewarded by God on the day of judgment.

That believers will face unjust suffering should come as no surprise, for Jesus also endured such suffering. His example leaves modern believers with an example of how to live commendable lives while enduring such suffering. Jesus was commended and rewarded by his Father, and so all those who follow in Jesus's footsteps will likewise be commended and rewarded by the Father.

An important caveat that Peter makes throughout his letter is that such suffering must be undeserved (2:19–20; 3:17; 4:15) and sovereignly allowed (1:6; 3:17; 4:19). The emphasis on undeserved suffering is given in the next few verses as Peter highlights the sinlessness and

---

3   "Christ also suffered." Due to the inclusion of this clause, Achtemeier believes a vicarious atonement reading is inaccurate. Instead, Peter was comparing the suffering of the slaves with the suffering of Jesus. An interpretive rendering of the reason for their suffering would be the following: "since Jesus suffered for them, they should suffer for him" (Achtemeier, 1996, 199). An alternative explanation is that Peter saw the suffering of believers as an evangelistic tool. Thus, just as Jesus suffered for the sake of redeeming others, so believers suffer with the hope that others would be redeemed. Schreiner argues something similar, though he makes clear that the suffering of Jesus is unique from the suffering of believers (Schreiner, 2003, 142). An interpretive rendering of this perspective is "since Jesus suffered for your redemption, you ought to suffer for the possibility of the redemption of others."

innocence of Jesus (2:22–23). That it was sovereignly allowed is highlighted by the master-slave relationship. In other words, slaves had to view their life circumstances as sovereignly directed. Just as God sometimes allowed tyrannical governments yet called his people to submit to those governments, so God allowed unjust masters, and called his servants to submit to those masters. Though we no longer have the master-slave relationship in much of the modern world, any time a believer is placed in a position where God has allowed their unjust suffering, he or she will be rewarded for enduring[4] that suffering graciously.

PREACHING AND TEACHING STRATEGIES

Exegetical and Theological Synthesis
A text like this begs us to ask the question, "Why do we even need Bible verses regulating the response of humans enslaved to others?" The very existence of this passage speaks to the dark horrors of the human heart. We belong to a people so depraved that some have undertaken to enslave others, depriving them of freedom and basic human dignities.

In this section, Peter gives commands that speak to the reality of such dark situations. His language betrays the difficulty of a life of slavery—*unjust, suffer, endure*. But Peter grounds the imperatives in the historical-theological truths of Christ enduring unjust suffering. Jesus suffered for his people, leaving an example for believers to follow when they must endure unjust suffering.

Earlier Peter dealt with the believer's new identity in Christ. Christians are born again to a living hope (1:23), now obedient children called to a life of holiness (1:15–16). This new identity links believers with Jesus and provides

the grounds for Peter's commands in 2:18–21. As Christ suffered, so believers suffer, because we share his family identity. In just a few verses, Peter provides a perspective to help believers through terrible trials. He challenges them to be "mindful of God" (2:19). He encourages them to "do good" (1:18) and tells them that enduring unjust suffering "is a gracious thing in the sight of God" (1:20). He ultimately points to the footsteps of Jesus (1:21), urging Christians to follow in them, even when (especially when) they walk through times of suffering. The gospel Jesus offers empowers believers and even *requires* believers to suffer obediently under harsh masters and continue doing good under such pressure.

Preaching Idea
Being a Slave of Christ Means Submitting to Human Masters.

Contemporary Connections

What does it mean?
What does it mean that believers should submit to human masters? First Peter 2:13–17 addressed the issue of submitting to human institutions and rulers. Here, Peter takes the idea to the extreme, applying the same principles to humans forced into slavery. It will be critical for the preacher to root the reason for submission and the need to endure unjust suffering in its proper theological basis: because Jesus endured unjust suffering, he has provided an example for us to follow. Enduring sorrows while in an unfair situation connects believers with Christ in a way that other spiritual disciplines fail to do.

What does this submission look like? First, the preacher must insist that the submission should never be against God's Word. When Daniel and his friends were subjected to unjust suffering, they submitted respectfully but

---

4   Enduring. This requires great wisdom. In the present world, there are many more avenues for recourse when injustice has been committed. Peter is not calling believers to give up their rights in all circumstances. Unfair treatment in the workplace, for instance, may be cause for a lawsuit.

also stood their ground when the Babylonian or Persian law pushed against God's law (Daniel 1; 3; 6). Being subject to a human master—be it a slave master or manager of a business—should never push one to violate biblical principles.

Second, the kind of suffering and submission pictured here is most emphatically not due to someone's sin. Getting caught stealing office supplies can lead someone to suffer a penalty on the job, but this is not at all what Peter envisions. Being mocked by your coworkers (and even your boss) because you refuse to steal office supplies like the rest of the staff may be more akin to Peter's words.

Third, Peter portrays Jesus as the ultimate example of submission and suffering here. When the soldiers gambled for Jesus's garments, when the thieves on the cross jeered at him, when the religious rulers mocked him, Jesus did not snap back or retaliate. Instead, he prayed for mercy upon them (Luke 23:34). This is what it looks like for us to live out the words of Peter in this passage.

Is it true?

Any sermon preached about slavery will naturally raise questions in the minds of modern listeners. The preacher will need to work hard to help the audience overcome a few obstacles. In order to demonstrate that being a slave of Christ means submitting to human masters, the preacher must first address why God permitted slavery in the first place. Or rather, why doesn't God just say that Christians shouldn't own slaves? It will help to remind the congregation that Peter is not addressing the slave owners here, only the slaves. Peter focuses on how to endure suffering rather than write a treatise on the rightfulness of an unfair institution. God's lack of condemnation of slavery is not to be read as an endorsement of slavery.

Second, the preacher must also carefully distinguish between nineteenth-century chattel slavery and first-century Roman slavery. He may also want to consider drawing similarities and differences with twenty-first-century slavery, whether sex trafficking or forced servitude in America or other countries. Without making these careful distinctions, the modern listener will understand "slavery" through a perception different than Peter intended.

Now what?

How does a passage written to slaves apply to twenty-first-century free citizens? Nearly all of our population lives in freedom from slavery. To those who unfortunately find themselves held against their will, the passage has direct relevance, but for the vast majority of others, how far out can we extrapolate the principle behind Peter's words and still have legitimate application?

Many have pointed to possible application in an employer-employee relationship. Indeed, the passage could have relevance in such a way, though one would have to be careful not to dumb down the issue of slavery. Serving a manager is *not* serving a slave master. After the eight-hour shift is over, the floor worker goes home to her family for the night. The manager does not have the authority to beat his employees. The employee has a worker's union and enjoys far more rights than a first-century slave.

But if these commands were true of first-century slavery, *how much more* should they be applied to an employer-employee relationship today? Employees should treat their bosses with respect, no matter if their boss is just and gentle or unfair and harsh. This passage does not restrict someone from finding a new job under a nicer employer, but for the duration of the difficult position, one can recognize that the suffering endured helps a believer relate and share an experience with Jesus.

Creativity in Presentation

In 1896, Charles Sheldon wrote the short novel *In His Steps: What Would Jesus Do?* It chronicled the lives of several believers in a church who receive a challenge from their pastor to ask the titular question of every decision they made, then follow the answer come what may. The book later sparked the WWJD movement in the late 1990s. Sheldon drew the title from the words in 1 Peter 2:21: "so that you might follow in his steps." Though the characters in his book didn't all face persecution or sorrow in the same way that Peter addressed, short examples drawn from their fictional stories may help to encourage the congregation to follow Christ. Or better, if there are other real-life examples in the congregation of individuals who lived for Christ, no matter what the consequences, this may provide helpful illustrations for the sermon too.

In regard to the suffering of the saints and believers in slavery, the preacher may want to visit websites like joshuaproject.net or prayer-cast.com, which overview many Christians being persecuted around the world. Preachers may also want to familiarize themselves (and help familiarize the congregation) with other organizations such as Children of the Night, Agape International Missions, and The Exodus Road, which help fight human trafficking all around the world. Familiarizing yourself with the testimonies and stories of such people could not only give some examples to use in the sermon but also possible videos to share. It will also help sharpen the prayer of pastors and their congregations.

The text of 1 Peter 2:21 may also provide a potential creative example to use in the sermon. As noted in the exegetical portion, the word "example" was originally used of young children tracing the letters of the alphabet. The preacher may want to connect with a preschool or kindergarten teacher in the congregation and get permission to display a few examples of children tracing letters to capture this word picture. Even having the sermon title displayed in a traceable format could draw attention to Peter's use of this word.

All of these creative illustrations should serve the text's main point, that being a slave of Christ means submitting to human masters. The sermon may be outlined as follows:

- Serve Obediently (2:18)

- Suffer Obediently (2:19–20)

- Step Obediently (2:21)

DISCUSSION QUESTIONS

1. Why didn't God just issue a command against the practice of slavery?

2. How is slavery similar and different in the first century from nineteenth-century chattel slavery? How is it similar and different from an employer-employee relationship today?

3. What is the relationship between suffering unjustly and Jesus Christ?

4. What does it look like to follow in the steps of Jesus at your place of employment?

1 Peter 2:22–25

EXEGETICAL IDEA
Jesus, in his suffering on the cross, displayed a perfect model of innocent suffering as he took the sin of the elect readers, so that they, free from sin, would follow him and live righteously.

THEOLOGICAL FOCUS
Jesus's suffering on the cross has freed believers from sin and gives them opportunity to live for righteousness.

PREACHING IDEA
Jesus's Sinless Death Leads to Life for Sinners.

PREACHING POINTERS
Transitioning from commands given to slaves, Peter provides his first-century audience the perfect example of suffering for righteousness's sake. He gives the ultimate motivation to endure persecution or unjust treatment: Jesus endured the cross, bearing sin on his body in order to provide opportunity to live righteously. No greater example can be found than the example of Jesus and the gospel.

Followers of Christ today must recognize the foundation of the cross and the gospel in order to have proper motivation for obedience. Even most believers attempt to avoid any kind of suffering at any cost. When the opposing team insults us, we repay like with like and insult back. When a coworker threatens us, we look for opportunity to bring them down. But this is not the Jesus way. This passage motivates believers to imitate Jesus, even in how we respond to suffering.

THE EXAMPLE OF CHRIST (2:22–25)

LITERARY STRUCTURE AND THEMES (2:22–25)

This section of 1 Peter is the most detailed consideration of the sacrificial death of Jesus given in the epistle. It is given within the broader discussion of the duties of slaves. Peter had just commanded the readers who are slaves to submit to their masters, even if those masters inflicted unjust suffering on them. Peter encouraged the readers that in doing this, they were following the example of Jesus, who likewise endured unjust suffering and was rewarded. This passage detailed the example that Jesus left, which highlights the following points: Jesus's suffering was unearned (vv. 22–23a); Jesus's suffering was accompanied by an attitude of trust toward God, the Righteous Judge (v. 23b); Jesus's suffering was purposeful, transferring the sins of humanity on himself, enabling believers to live righteously, and returning these believers to the God who created them (vv. 24–25).

Themes of this section include: the sinlessness of Christ; how to respond to sovereignly granted, unjust suffering; the vicarious sacrifice of Christ; and the purpose of redemption.

- **Righteous Response to Unjust Suffering (2:22–23)**
- **Vicarious Atonement (2:24–25)**

EXPOSITION (2:22–25)

In these verses, Peter described Jesus's example of patient endurance during unjust suffering. Jesus committed no sin, nor did he verbally retaliate. Instead, he entrusted his cause and his suffering to God, who had promised to judge justly. Jesus knew that his suffering was vicarious, taking the sin of God's chosen on himself, so that the chosen would be free from sin in order to live for righteousness. In all this, Jesus was acting as a servant to God's elect by seeking them as wandering sheep and returning them to their Shepherd.

Righteous Response to Unjust Suffering (2:22–23)

Despite his sinless innocence, Jesus suffered, entrusting his cause to the Father who judges justly.

2:22. This verse began Peter's exploration of the pattern Jesus left for believers who would likewise experience unjust suffering. The pattern began with an innocent sufferer. To explain Jesus's innocence, Peter provided an almost exact duplication of Septuagint Isaiah 53:9.[1] In fact, this entire passage (vv. 22–25) frequently refers to Isaiah 52:13–53:12 and is the longest consideration of the Isaiah suffering servant passage in the New Testament.

---

1   Septuagint Isaiah 53:9. Jesus's quotation differs from the Septuagint in two places. First, Peter adds "who" at the beginning, aligning this clause with the following clauses. Second, Peter substitutes a word for sin with another word for sin. Septuagint Isaiah had ἀνομίαν, but Peter has ἁμαρτίαν. The two words are equivalent, as the parallelism in 53:5 suggests. The change was likely made by Peter, who otherwise does not use νομ- stem words (Achtemeier, 1996, 200). The motivation for change may also have been influenced by the use of ἁμαρτίας in verse 24. Using the same term highlighted that though Jesus never committed sin (ἁμαρτίας), he bore the readers' sins (ἁμαρτίας).

Outside the extended reference to Isaiah 53 in 1 Peter, five other passages directly reference this text. First, Matthew noted that Jesus's healing of Peter's mother-in-law was an illustration of Isaiah 53:4: "he took our illnesses and bore our diseases" (Matt. 8:14–17). Second, the response of the crowds in rejecting Jesus, despite his teaching and signs, was used in John's gospel as confirmation of Isaiah 53:1: "Lord, who has believed what he heard from us, and to whom has the arm of the Lord been revealed?" (John 12:36–38). Third, Paul while explaining Jewish unbelief referenced the same Isaiah passage (53:1; Rom. 10:16). Fourth, Jesus himself, when giving instructions to his followers, noted that "this Scripture must be fulfilled in me: 'And he was numbered with the transgressors'" (Luke 22:35–38). Finally, the narrative of Acts indicates that an Ethiopian eunuch was reading from Isaiah 53:7–8 and required the aid of Phillip to understand its content (Acts 8:26–35).

This analysis shows that Peter's use of the text was in line with the use of the book of Isaiah in the early church. Nevertheless, Peter's use is much more extensive than the others.

That Jesus "committed no sin" supports the doctrine of the sinlessness of Christ (cf. John 8:46; 2 Cor. 5:21; Heb. 4:15; 7:26; and 1 John 3:5); nevertheless, its main function in this text is to highlight that Jesus's suffering was not due to his own actions. The second portion of the verse, "no deceit was found in his mouth," clarifies that his sinlessness was not only in act but also in speech. In relation to the pattern, only those whose suffering came despite their innocence may claim to follow the example left by Jesus.

2:23. Peter provided four statements that supported the innocence of Christ. The first two, given in verse 22, were simple statements, defending Jesus's action and speech. The two

provided in this verse further support the innocence of Jesus's speech. First, "when Jesus was insulted, he did not return insult." This focus on "insult" (λοιδορούμενος) reminded Peter's readers of the predicted humiliation of the suffering servant (Isa. 52:14; 53:3, 8, 12), as well as the mocking of Jesus (Mark 15:16–20 par.; 15:29–32 par.; Luke 22:65; Matt. 27:39; Elliott, 2001, 529). Peter's focus on the verbal nonretaliation of Jesus was purposeful, for the readers were being subject to primarily verbal persecution (2:12; 3:16; 4:4, 14).

Jesus's second righteous response was also evidenced by his lack of verbal retaliation: "when he suffered, he uttered no threats." When enduring unjust suffering, readers may have been inclined to remind the persecutor of coming judgment and looming condemnation. Jesus refused to make such retaliatory comments, which would likely be ineffective in such a context.

Though verses 22 and 24 are clearly reflective of Isaiah 53, this verse is not a quotation from that passage. Some commentators have rightly recognized an echo of Isaiah 53:7, which speaks of the silence of the lamb before its shearers. Peter's extended consideration of the verbal nonretaliation of Jesus was due to the readers' context. The most likely place readers would fail was in their verbal response to verbal assault. Thus, Peter focused on the way Jesus responded, showing how his example left a pattern for others to follow.

So far in verses 22 and 23, Peter provided evidence of Jesus's innocence through lack of sinful action, whether in word or deed. The last portion of verse 23 highlighted Jesus's positive action: "he entrusted his cause to the one who judges justly." To "entrust" (παρεδίδου) meant to give over "for care and preservation" to another (BDAG s.v. "παραδίδωμι" 762). The NLT rendering captures the sense well: "He left his case in the hands of God." Such a response matches nicely with Jesus's verbal passivity. He did not seek to argue for or fight for his cause; instead, he handed it all over to his Father, who Peter described as one who "judges justly." The clear implication is that injustice is presently taking place, but Jesus left the fulfillment of justice to his Father, who would certainly bring about a righteous end.

"His Cause" or "Himself" (2:23)

In the Greek, the verb "entrust" has no object. In such cases, it is usually contextually clear who or what the object is. The passage provides two options for the object of the verb: *himself* or *his cause*. Nearly all modern versions indicate the object as "himself" (e.g., NASB, ESV, NET, NIV, CSB, NRSV). On this reading, Jesus entrusted himself to the Father. This reading has a long history, and whether it is what Peter originally meant by the phrase, it is nonetheless true. Jesus did entrust his soul to his Father. Nevertheless, the second option appears more likely.

The most prominent Greek dictionary suggests the object is "cause" (BDAG s.v. "παραδίδωμι" 762). This appears to capture the purpose of the passage. Peter is seeking to encourage believers to leave their cause in the hand of God. Of course, this includes their own lives, but is broader than that. It also includes all their hopes, expectations, and future plans.

Throughout this verse, Peter used imperfect verbs to speak of Jesus's lack of insult, his lack of threat, and his entrusting his cause to the Father. Imperfect verbs were used to refer to action that was looked at as a process, and Peter used them here to highlight that this was Jesus's normal pattern of life, not limited to the events of the passion. In other words, Peter highlighted character qualities more than specific actions. Jesus was the type of person who when he was insulted did not insult, and when he endured suffering did not resort to threats. He always entrusted his cause to the righteous judge. Accordingly, this same pattern should be followed by the readers.

Vicarious Atonement (2:24–25)

Jesus returned the elect readers to their Creator by taking their sins on himself, freeing them to live righteously.

2:24. Continuing a focus on Isaiah 53, Peter noted that Jesus "himself bore our sins." It is not clear whether Peter was citing Isaiah 53:4, 11, or 12. Most likely, he was not intending to cite any one verse in particular but was rather generalizing Isaiah 53's themes for his readers. The word for "bore" (ἀνήνεγκεν) is used throughout the Septuagint to refer to cultic sacrifices and could be translated "offer." But it cannot bear that meaning here, because the object of the verb is "sins" not Jesus, the sacrificial lamb. Therefore, a general sense of "taking up" our sins is more appropriate to the overall context.

Peter described the sins borne by Jesus as "our sins." It is not clear why Peter switched from the second person (v. 21) to the first person (v. 24) and then back to the second person (v. 25). One suggestion is that Peter was motivated by the corporate emphasis in Isaiah 53:4–6 (Achtemeier, 1996, 203). Thus, Peter suggested that the suffering servant of Isaiah had actually borne the sin of these, his readers. Two clarifying statements highlight the specific sacrificial act of Jesus: "in his body" and "on the tree." The first highlighted the sacrifice itself, for Jesus offered his own body. The second phrase referred literally to "wood" but was used figuratively in reference to the cross. The use of "wood" (ξύλον) may have been an allusion to Deuteronomy 21:23, which in the Septuagint speaks of a man hanging on wood who was cursed by God. The allusion signified that Jesus was cursed for the sake of those he died to forgive.

Corporate Emphasis in Isaiah 53:4–6

Surely he has borne *our* griefs and carried *our* sorrows; yet *we* esteemed him stricken, smitten by God, and afflicted. But he was pierced for *our* transgressions; he was crushed for *our* iniquities;

upon him was the chastisement that brought *us* peace, and with his wounds *we* are healed. *All we* like sheep have gone astray; *we* have turned—every one—to his own way; and the Lord has laid on him the iniquity of *us all*.

The purpose of Jesus's sacrifice is given in the second portion of the verse: "so that dying to sin, we might live for righteousness." Thus, the purpose of Jesus's vicarious suffering was to make way for the elect to live righteously. To do this, he had to first free them from sin by his death. Some English versions translate the phrase "die to sins" as "free from sins" (e.g., NET, NRSV). Such a translation is possible, for the participle (ἀπογενόμενοι) may have this meaning. Nevertheless, it more likely refers to death toward something (BDAG s.v. "ἀπογίνομαι" 108). In support, such teaching echoes other apostolic doctrine, particularly Paul's consideration of the believer's death to sin and life in righteousness (Romans 6). Finally, this translation balances the phrase nicely, contrasting "dying to sin" with "living for righteousness."

Living for righteousness refers to dedicating oneself to good works. Peter throughout this letter called on readers to embrace good deeds and to live righteously (e.g., 1:15; 2:11–12; 3:10–11, 13; 4:2). Here he provided the means by which readers are to be able to accomplish this task. Simply stated, Jesus died so that readers could become good-doers and thereby bring glory to the Father. This glory is given to the Father because unbelievers see the good deeds of believers and are called to repent and trust the gospel (2:12; 3:16).

The end of verse 24 returned to considering Isaiah 53, with Peter quoting verse 5: "by his wounds you have been healed." By surrounding the statements "in his body on the tree" with reflections on Isaiah 53, Peter clearly implied that Jesus is the fulfillment of the suffering servant prophecies. The reference to "wounds" (μώλωπι) may have referred to Jesus's experience of scourging (Matt. 27:26;

Mark 15:15), but more likely was to be understood as a general reference to the entire experience of suffering Jesus endured. That the readers were "healed" should not be understood in reference to physical health; instead, it was used metaphorically to refer to the forgiveness of sins that made the reader spiritually whole (BDAG s.v. "ἰάομαι" 465).

2:25. The abrupt change of metaphors from spiritual healing to wandering sheep is consistent with Peter's penchant for abrupt metaphor shifts. Nevertheless, in this case, the shift is due to his source text, for Isaiah 53:5–6 makes the same abrupt shift. The transition may be due to Isaiah 6:10, where turning to the Lord leads to healing (Michaels, 1988, 150).

Peter spoke of the Gentiles as "sheep" who have "gone astray." John's gospel also speaks of Gentiles as sheep "not of this fold" who will be gathered to the shepherd (John 10:16). Most English versions suggest a return (NASB, ESV, NIV, CSB, NRSV) or turning back (NET, LEB) to the shepherd. But it is not clear that the Gentile readers were ever a part of the sheepfold. Perhaps the idea is that they wandered from their Creator, and now are being returned to him. It is also possible to translate the verb (ἐπεστράφητε) as "turned," for it means "to change one's mind or course of action" (BDAG s.v. "ἐπιστρέφω" 382). On this reading, Peter would be imagining the readers as wild sheep who were wandering without guidance, but who have now changed course to follow a wise shepherd (cf. Luke 15:7).

The identity of the shepherd is debated. Peter gave no direct statement concerning whether he was thinking of the Father or of Jesus as the shepherd. The latter is more likely, however, for though God is spoken of as a shepherd in the Old Testament (e.g., Num. 27:17; Psalm 23), the New Testament consistently speaks of Jesus as the shepherd (John 10:11–13; Heb. 13:20; Rev. 7:17). Further, even Peter, later in this letter, spoke of Jesus as the chief shepherd (5:4). This reading is consistent with the broader paragraph, which highlights the acts of Jesus that were necessary for the sheep to be embraced into the sheepfold.

The relationship between Jesus as shepherd and his suffering is explored elsewhere in the New Testament in a similar way as it is here. For instance, Jesus predicted, on the basis of Zechariah 13:7, that the shepherd would be struck and the sheep scattered, but he added that *"after I have arisen*, I will go ahead of you into Galilee" (Mark 14:27–28). Additionally, in the most detailed passage concerning Jesus's role as shepherd (John 10:7–18), the promise that there "shall be one flock and one shepherd" (10:16) was followed with the statement, "I lay down my life in order to take it up again" (10:17). Thus, likely due to Isaiah 53 and the gospel tradition, Peter aligned Jesus's shepherding role with his sacrifice and resurrection.

Peter highlighted the temporal shift that had taken place with the readers. Though once they were wandering without a shepherd *now* (νῦν) they had turned to their shepherd and overseer. This language is consistent with Peter's emphasis elsewhere concerning the transformation of the readers from what *they once were* to what they have *now become* (1:14, 23; 2:10). And all this is due to the work of the Messiah on their behalf. He has, by his suffering on the cross, provided a path for believers to be reconciled to God.

THEOLOGICAL FOCUS

The exegetical idea (Jesus, in his suffering on the cross, displayed a perfect model of innocent suffering as he took the sin of the elect readers, so that they, free from sin, would follow him and live righteously) leads to this theological focus: Jesus's suffering on the cross has freed believers from sin and gives them opportunity to live for righteousness.

Jesus's suffering provided an example for the slaves of Peter's audience, yet it was also designed for a broader audience, including all believers alive today. Suffering is a very real possibility in the life of the believer, and Peter shows by Jesus's example how believers are to respond when it comes. First, they must examine whether they are, like Jesus, truly innocent. They must be especially concerned to watch their verbal responses. Second, they are to entrust their cause to God, for he is a righteous judge. Though they cannot control the responses of others, they can control their own words and actions. And though it may appear that injustice will prevail, they may be sure that God, who will judge the living and the dead (4:5), will make all things right.

Jesus's example also provided a model of how innocent suffering can lead sinners to God. Of course, Jesus's suffering was endured in the place of others, while believers are never called to suffer vicariously. Nevertheless, Peter suggests that the believer's suffering may lead to the conversion of others, for it is the very people who mock and cause the believer's suffering that are the most likely to see and hear the gospel (2:11–12; 3:15–16). In this way, Jesus left an example to emulate. Believers are to suffer in hope that such suffering may give opportunity for sinners to come to God.

Believers ought to rejoice over the possibility that their suffering may result in the salvation of others. But more than that, they should rejoice in the work of Jesus that made everything possible. He took the believer's sin on himself, so that they would be free from sin and live for righteousness. Such a consideration provides motivation for godly living, as well as motivation for endurance during the times of innocent suffering. What they had to endure had already been endured in greater degree by Jesus. And he endured so that they would presently be able to endure, while living righteously.

PREACHING AND TEACHING STRATEGIES

Exegetical and Theological Synthesis
First Peter 2:22–25 makes clear that life for sinners does not come apart from the death of the

sinless Christ. All of humanity shares the same fallen condition. We are sinners in desperate need of God's grace. Our sin leads to death (Rom. 6:23). No one can escape this eternal suffering in hell by their own merits or labor.

Peter puts the theological basis for salvation fully on the shoulders of our crucified Savior. He makes it clear that, unlike all other humans, Jesus was sinless, even in the midst of unjust persecution (2:22–23). Instead of fighting on his own behalf for his innocence to be known, Jesus left the verdict in the hands of the divine court. By dying innocently, Jesus bore the sin of humankind on his own body in order that the divine exchange could take place: his righteousness becomes our own, our sin becomes his own (2:24).

Such is the message of the gospel. Paul preached the same message as Peter (Rom. 6:5–11). John emphasized the fact of Jesus's sinlessness (1 John 3:5; cf. John 8:46), as did the author of Hebrews (4:15). Before the apostles, prophets like Isaiah laid the groundwork for the gospel in passages like Isaiah 53:4–5. The sinless Savior took upon the sin of sinners. The righteous Savior exchanged the sin of sinners for his very own righteousness. This gospel cannot be earned and was not owed to us. Rather, it makes clear the perfect love of a perfect God for a very imperfect people.

Preaching Idea
Jesus's Sinless Death Leads to Life for Sinners.

Contemporary Connections

What does it mean?
What does it mean that Jesus's sinless death leads to life for sinners? In order for this statement to come together in the minds of the congregation, the preacher must convince the church of three main ideas:

1. Jesus committed no sin, even while facing persecution. This is paramount. If Jesus sinned, he would no longer be the perfect sacrifice for our sin. Even if one little curse slipped his lips, one quick nasty thought, one impure motive, this would be enough to give him a blemish, making the sacrifice unworthy (Heb. 9:14).

2. Jesus took our sin upon his body. God, in his divine plan, allowed for appropriate sacrifices to stand in our place. The Old Testament priests would often lay their hands upon the heads of the sacrificial animals, which many believe signifies a transference of guilt from person to animal (Lev. 1:4). Christ took what he did not deserve when facing the penalty for our sin.

3. Jesus exchanged our sin for his righteousness. Taking what he did not deserve, Jesus gave what we did not earn. His death allows for us to place our faith in him and die to sin and live to righteousness. The congregation must understand this concept of substitutionary atonement in order to accept and live in light of the gospel.

Is it true?
Is it true that Jesus was sinless? Is it true that his wounds can heal? These two questions challenge the minds of skeptical churchgoers. One Barna poll found that over half of Americans believe that Jesus was human and committed sins while on earth.[2] Surely some of these skeptics will be in the audience on Sunday morning. How will you convince them that Jesus was sinless?

One should not discount the Bible's testimony on the matter, for it is the highest authority (1 Peter 2:22; cf. Isa. 53:9; 2 Cor. 5:21; Heb. 4:15; 7:26; 1 John 3:5). Sometimes people are simply ignorant of the clear teaching of Scripture and only need to see the truth to believe it. For those

---

2   Barna Group, "What Do Americans Believe about Jesus? 5 Popular Beliefs," April 1, 2015, https://www.barna.com/research/what-do-americans-believe-about-jesus-5-popular-beliefs.

skeptical of Scripture's authority, point out that the testimony of Scripture accords with the testimonies of contemporaries in Jesus's time. Josephus (*Ant. xviii 3.3*) and Tacitus (*Annals 15.44*) both affirm the historicity of Jesus and support the gospel accounts. Theologically, one must note the fact that Jesus is both fully divine and fully human, enabling him to overcome sin by means of the incarnation.

But how do wounds heal? The paradox of the cross must also be explained to skeptics. First, it is important to explain what this phrase does *not* mean. It does not mean that all our diseases or sicknesses immediately vanish as Christians. Sure, God has the power to heal and he often chooses to do so, especially when we pray by faith (James 5:13–18), but there are times even in Scripture where God chooses not to heal for reasons undisclosed (2 Cor. 12:1–10; 1 Tim. 5:23). Peter's meaning (as well as Isaiah's) focuses on the healing of *sin*, not physical diseases.

Second, the healing from sin can be explained by means of the substitutionary sacrifices of the Old Testament. Sin brings the penalty of death (Rom. 6:23). God, in his gracious plan, allowed the Israelites to bring unblemished sacrifices to take their place instead of suffering the penalty for their own sin. These sacrifices were temporary and ultimately ineffective, but they pointed to the greater sacrifice of the Lamb of God, Jesus Christ. The death of Jesus is a fulfillment of the old covenant model.

Now what?

The majority of 1 Peter 2:22–25 focuses on what Jesus has done for us, but this does not mean it is devoid of application. A single line in the text provides the launching point for application: "that we might die to sin and live to righteousness" (2:24b).

Of course, being dead to sin does not mean that a believer is without sin (1 John 1:8). Romans 6:11–12 illustrates the meaning and application:

"So you also must consider yourselves dead to sin and alive to God in Christ Jesus. Let not sin therefore reign in your mortal body, to make you obey its passions." Being dead to sin means that we now have the power to live to righteousness and that we are no longer slaves to sin.

The preacher must point the congregation toward examples that demonstrate what "living sin" and "dead sin" look like. Living sin reigns and controls us. Dead sin still exists, but it has no power to dominate anymore. Consider the example of the controlling matriarch of the family. While alive, what mother says goes. She decides where to enjoy holidays, how to enjoy them, who sits where at the table. Every detail is under her control. Once mother passes, her presence is still felt at each family function, but her control no longer truly exists. It only reigns insomuch as the children allow it to reign.

Sin works in a similar fashion. Before regeneration, we were slaves to sin. After conversion, we are no longer slaves to it and should not allow it mastery over us. Gamblers were once controlled by the casinos, but now One greater than the casinos exists within them. They may *yield* to the temptation of the casino, but the sin of gambling should no longer control them. The woman given to sleazy romance novels might have felt controlled by such an addiction before knowing Christ, but upon salvation a greater love should be evident and in control of her. The preacher may want to consider using a testimony of someone freed from addiction. If there is no one within the church to give such a testimony, perhaps utilizing a resource like Christian Families Today (cftministry.org) could help.

Creativity in Presentation

Because of the heavy usage of Isaiah 52–53 in this pericope, the preacher may want to consider leaning into the Isaiah passage as an introduction to the sermon. Using a skilled orator to read the prophet's prediction, one can open the service or the sermon with a focus on these familiar words. The preacher might even want to organize the service as if it were a Good Friday service, no matter what time of year the passage is preached. If there is a certain tradition or element that the church is used to during the passion week each year, mix it into the "normal" service to give the day the feel of Good Friday. For example, some churches show a short video to begin the service or introduce the sermon, designed to reflect on the words of Scripture with creative graphics behind it. Examples can be found at worshiphouse-media.com or ignitermedia.com.

Some churches might even make use of a dramatic presentation of the death of Christ. One of the churches I (Bryan) used to work at had teens put on a short drama set to music each Good Friday. It did not replace the sermon, but was intended to complement it in a moving presentation. Such dramas can be found on YouTube (see especially those set to "Revelation Song" by Phillips, Craig, and Dean).

For those teaching the passage, the shepherding imagery may provide some occasion for creative pedagogy. If you live in a rural area, it may be possible to coordinate with a local shepherd or farmer to bring a live sheep into the classroom, or at least outside on church property. Having an explanation of what it is like to round up "straying sheep" may help bring this passage to light in an unforgettable way and will strengthen the point that Jesus's sinless death leads to life for sinners.

Preachers may want to consider the following outline to help in their preparation:

- Jesus's Sinlessness (2:22)

- Jesus's Suffering (2:23)

- Jesus's Sacrifice (2:24)

- Jesus's Shepherding (2:25)

DISCUSSION QUESTIONS

1. Explain the gospel using some of Peter's words in 1 Peter 2:22–25.

2. Do you believe that Jesus committed no sin? Why is this an important element of the gospel?

3. How does verse 23 set for us an example when we are persecuted for our faith? Have you had to face such opposition in your life?

4. What does it mean for us to die to sin and live to righteousness? What does this look like in your life?

5. What does it mean that Jesus's wounds heal us?

6. Why does Peter use shepherd imagery to describe Jesus?

1 Peter 3:1–7

EXEGETICAL IDEA
Peter instructed wives to submit to their husbands and display an inward beauty that attracts unbelieving husbands, that is honorable in God's sight, and that follows the example of prior godly saints; and Peter instructed husbands to live with their wives knowledgeably, honoring them as coheirs in the gift of life.

THEOLOGICAL FOCUS
Wives must follow the lead of their husbands, focusing on inward beauty, while husbands must live with their wives knowledgeably, honoring them as coheirs in the gift of life.

PREACHING IDEA
There's No Place Like Home . . . When Wives and Husbands Enjoy Their Proper Roles.

PREACHING POINTERS
Households of Peter's day typically upheld clear distinctions between husband and wife, child and parent, slave and free. This is true of both believing and unbelieving households. Social norms controlled much of went on in the home and how husbands and wives interacted with each other. Peter speaks to these distinctions, upholding some of them and subverting others, in order to help the Christian husband and wife live out their God-given roles in the home.

Today's society has broken down many of these cultural distinctions, especially in the Western world. No longer can it be assumed that the husband is the head of the household or that the wife stays home and keeps house while the husband works for a living. Peter's commands speak to moderns just as he did to people in his day. The biblical truths he shares are timeless in their values and transcend culture in a way that help believers in the home, whether they share the bedroom with a Christian spouse or not. The preacher will find in this passage opportunity to speak biblical truth to families of all designs.

HONORABLE CONDUCT AND CHRISTIAN MARRIAGE (3:1–7)

LITERARY STRUCTURE AND THEMES (3:1–7)

In 2:11–12 Peter commanded the readers to abstain from sinful desires and act honorably. After providing some general ways to accomplish those goals (2:13–17), Peter began giving specific directives to certain segments of the audience. This paragraph contains the second and third specific directives, both speaking to marriage relations. Beginning with the wives, Peter commanded submission to husbands, with the hope that if the husbands do not believe they will be attracted to the gospel by the wife's conduct (3:1–2). Peter then developed the nature of that attractive conduct, showing that by submitting and acting honorably in marriage, wives may follow the example of godly matriarchs (3:4–7). Turning to the husbands, Peter commanded that they live before God with considerate knowledge of their wives, and treat their wives honorably as equal heirs of eternal life. To the wives, Peter gave hope that despite their subordinate position, they may positively influence their husbands. To the husbands, Peter gave a warning, reminding them that their relationship to God is partly dependent on their relationship to their wives.

Themes of this section include the following: the husband's and wife's responsibility in marriage; the evangelistic power of a wife's character; how believers should focus on internal, character-based beauty; the example of the godly matriarchs; the spiritual equality of husband and wife; and the censure of God toward inconsiderate husbands.

- *Wives Must Follow the Lead of Their Husbands (3:1–2)*
- *A Wife's Beauty Should Be Internal (3:3–4)*
- *The Example of Holy Women (3:5–6)*
- *Husbands Must Live Knowledgeably with Their Wives (3:7)*

EXPOSITION (3:1–7)

Peter addressed the household, starting with the wife. The chief command was to submit to her husband (v. 1). While all wives must submit to their own husband, Peter holds out hope that wives with unbelieving husbands may win their husbands by the outward expression of their inward beauty of character (vv. 1–2, 4). Indeed, they must cultivate that character, while avoiding an emphasis on external beauty (v. 3). They should do this, because the holy women of old did the same (vv. 5–6). Peter then turned to address the husbands, who were commanded to live with their wives according to knowledge. More specifically, they were to treat them honorably as coheirs in the grace of life. Peter noted that their very relationship to God depended on their obedience to this command (v. 7).

Wives Must Follow the Lead of Their Husbands (3:1–2)

Wives were commanded to follow the lead of their husbands, in hope that their honorable conduct would lead to the conversion of their unbelieving husbands.

3:1. Having addressed the slave-master relationship, Peter turned to another relationship often explored in household code literature—that between the husband and wife. As Peter did throughout the household codes, he reversed the expected order, speaking to the wives and then the husbands. The statement "in the same way" (ὁμοίως) is not designed to draw a parallel between the submission of the wife to the husband and the submission of a slave to a master. Instead, it simply draws attention to the transition to the next group in the household codes. This is confirmed in that the transition to husbands in verse 7 also has "likewise" (ὁμοίως).

Peter's primary command to the wife was to "submit" (ὑποτασσόμεναι) to her husband.[1] The word commonly meant to "subject oneself, be subjected or subordinated, obey" (BDAG s.v. "ὑποτάσσω" 1042). In Peter's day such a command was uncontroversial. Submission of the wife was expected for she, as a woman, was viewed as inferior to her male husband (Achtemeier, 1996, 206). For this reason, some have suggested that Peter's command to the wives is a culturally limited command. Just as Peter was not endorsing slavery, so submission of the wife was not being endorsed either. And just as slavery has been largely done away in the modern day, so the submission of the wife should be done away as well. Others, getting at the same conclusion from a different angle, argue that Peter was addressing a unique situation—a wife married to an unbelieving husband. According to this perspective, it is not clear whether Peter would have instructed Christian wives to submit to *Christian* husbands (Achtemeier, 1996, 206–11).

In response, it should be noted that Peter reveals no belief in the inequality of women to men, as evidenced by his statement in 3:7 that wives are "coheirs of the grace of life." In this, Peter followed Jesus, who showed great respect for women in his earthly ministry (Luke 7:12–13; 8:48; 11:27–28; John 4:7–26). Further, while

it is accurate to observe that Peter had a specialized case in mind in this passage, his use of conditional language after the command ("even if some") suggests that the command was to be applied more broadly than to only unbelieving husbands. Further, since other apostolic directives to wives were not limited to unbelieving husbands (Eph. 5:22–33; Col. 3:18; Titus 2:4–5) it is likely that this should not be limited in that way either.

It is also important to make a distinction between the husband-wife relationship and the master-slave relationship (especially of the chattel form of slavery). The latter relationship was a contrivance of man and was present due to the sinfulness of the human heart. The former relationship was a partnership established at creation by God and was present due to God's gracious gifting. The latter was often based on the idea of the inherent superiority of one type of person over another. The former was not based on inequality, for both men and women were made in the image of God (Gen. 1:26–27). Peter likewise confirmed this equality of man and woman (3:7), yet such an equality of nature does not require an equality of function. As Schreiner rightly notes, "Those who argue that a different function implies inequality betray a secular worldview that identifies worth with stature and the exercise of authority" (Schreiner, 2003, 151).

The situation Peter envisioned focused on husbands who disobey the Word. The word used for "disobedience" (ἀπειθοῦσιν) may suggest more than simple rejection of Christian teaching. These husbands may have been actively opposed to their wife's newfound religion. Considering the change of life that accompanied the embrace of Christ, such a scenario is not hard to imagine. In the culture Peter was addressing, the religion of the wife was to be the

---

1 Husband. That Peter is speaking of the relationship between a wife and her husband is made explicit in that he adds "to your own husband" (ἰδίοις ἀνδράσιν). Both the word for "wives" (γυναῖκες) and "husbands" (ἀνδράσιν) could be understood as general statements about men and women. Clearly Peter is not calling all women to be subject to all men.

religion of the husband. A converted wife, then, would be rejecting the values of the culture by disregarding the religious position of her husband. It is perhaps because of her apparent insubordination to her husband regarding his religious views that Peter emphasized the need for subordination in all other areas.

> **Women and the Religion of Their Husbands**
> Plutarch (A.D. 46–119), a Greek historian and philosopher, argued that "A wife should not acquire her own friends, but should make her husband's friends her own. The gods are the first and most significant friends. For this reason, it is proper for a wife to recognize only those gods whom her husband worships and to shut the door to superstitious cults and strange superstitions" (*Conj. praec.* 19, *Mor.* 140D; trans. Elliott, 2008, 557–58).

One purpose of subordination to unbelieving husbands is given in a purpose clause: "*so that* they may be won over without a word by the conduct of their wives." The idea of "winning over" (κερδηθήσονται) suggests acquiring "by effort or investment" and often referred to fiscal interests (BDAG s.v. "κερδαίνω" 541). By the hard work of submitting in such a difficult situation, Peter envisioned an opportunity for the wife to be rewarded with the "gain" of the husband's soul for Christ.

Peter noted that in such situations the unbeliever may be won "without a word" (ἄνευ λόγου). That such a statement was not designed to denigrate the spoken word is clear from Peter's prior consideration of the power and importance of the Word (1:23–2:4). Instead, Peter was encouraging these women that even if their spoken word was proving ineffective, they were not powerless to influence their husbands. Since the wife was transformed by the word to live differently, her actions witnessed to the Word. In fact, it was likely because of the Word that the tensions were stoked between her and her husband. Yet, at the same time, that same Word produced a beauty uncharacteristic of any who had not been changed by the Word. As Peter would later say, the difference the Word produces in believers may lead the unbeliever to "ask for a reason of the hope" that is in the believer (3:15). Read in this light, Peter was not saying "don't speak the Word; live it"; rather, he was saying, "witness to the Word by living it."

3:2. In this verse, Peter clarified what type of good behavior led to the winning of the unbelieving husband: "when they see your pure and reverent life." From the English translations, one might think there are two adjectives in this sentence—"pure" and "reverent." In reality, "reverent" is a prepositional phrase, literally translated "in fear" (ἐν φόβῳ). The sense may be represented by the following translation: "when they see your pure conduct, which is accomplished in fear." The critical question concerns the identity of the one feared. It could be that the word speaks of reverence and has as its focus the husband. This would be parallel to Paul's admonition that wives are to respect their husbands (Eph. 5:33). Alternatively, it may have God as its focus, for Peter elsewhere speaks of fear in reference to God (1:17; 2:17).

Reading the phrase "in fear" in reference to God balances this passage with the prior two sections. First, Peter asked the audience to obey the emperor "for the Lord's sake" (2:13). This suggested that if the emperor commanded something in opposition to the Lord, the audience should obey the Lord. Second, Peter argued that slaves should submit to their masters and that if they suffered, they should do so "mindful of God" (2:18–19). These statements reminded the readers that their primary audience was God and that their obedience to these earthly systems of authority was required because of their relationship to God. When seen in this light, Peter's admonition that wives submit "in fear" (of the Lord) indicated the need to submit to unbelieving husbands even in difficult times *for the sake of the Lord.*

Accordingly, if an unbelieving husband were to ask a believing wife to do something against her Lord, she would have the responsibility to disobey. Though she submits to her husband, she does so under allegiance to Christ.

The parallels between 3:1–2 and 2:12 (see the following chart) suggest that this passage is a more specific example of the principles elucidated in 2:11–12. The parallel also suggests, as highlighted earlier, that the disobedience to the Word exemplified by the unbelieving husbands is more than simple unbelief. Being parallel with "speaking against you falsely," the disobedience suggests an active form of opposition. The action of the believer in both circumstances, then, is counter to one's expectations, and this surprising element is what provokes the possibility of conversion.

A Wife's Beauty Should Be Internal (3:3–4)

Peter contrasted external adornment with the God-pleasing, internal beauty of a gentle and quiet spirit.

3:3. Peter continued his instruction to the wives with a second command, bringing focus on their means of adornment. By "adornment" (κόσμος), Peter was speaking of "that which serves to beautify through decoration" (BDAG s.v. "κόσμος" 561). He began by speaking of what must be avoided (3:3) and then turned to what should be embraced (3:4). The key distinction concerned whether the adorning was *external* or *internal*. Peter commanded that wives avoid external adorning, which consisted of elaborate hair styles, gold jewelry, and extravagant

clothes. Obviously, Peter's list is not exhaustive. Neither, however, should it be taken as an open rejection of a certain hair style or a certain metal ornamentation. This latter point can be seen by a literal rendering of the passage: "let not your adorning be external, the braiding of hair, wearing gold jewelry, *or the wearing of clothes.*" Of course, Peter was not endorsing nudity. He was rejecting a heart attitude that resulted in drawing attention to oneself by elaborate external adornment. Some *types* of clothing drew attention to external adornment, just as some types of hairstyles and some jewelry choices are chosen with the goal of bringing attention to the external facets of a person.

Bust of a Roman woman, ca. 80 CE. Public Domain.

1 Peter 2:12	1 Peter 3:1–2
Keep your conduct honorable	Submit to your husbands
So that when they speak against you . . .	So that if any do not obey the Word . . .
They may see your good deeds	When they see the purity and reverence of your life
They will glorify God	They will be won

3:4. Having commanded the wives to avoid seeking to beautify themselves by means of their external appearance, Peter here considered how Christian wives should seek to beautify themselves. A roughly literal translation of the opening phrase would be "rather, let your beautification concern the hidden person of the heart." That the person of the heart was "hidden" (κρυπτός) did not mean that the attributes Peter spoke of could not be seen nor did it mean that they were intentionally kept secret. Instead, they were to be contrasted with forms of external adornment. Whereas external adornment was designed to be the first thing a person saw, the beauty of the heart was only revealed as one observed the way a person lived. In the New Testament, the "heart" (καρδίας) of a person refers to the "center and source of the whole inner life, with its thinking, feeling, and volition" (BDAG s.v. "καρδία" 508). Thus, Peter was arguing that the wife's energies for beautification should be given over to the development of inner character.

Peter specified the type of inner character that should be cultivated: "a gentle and quiet spirit." Neither of these qualities is distinctively feminine. For instance, Jesus referred to himself as gentle (Matt. 11:29) and called all his disciples to evidence that quality (Matt. 5:5). Peter himself called all of the readers of this letter to gentleness in their relation to those who question them about the gospel (3:16). To be gentle meant to avoid being "overly impressed by a sense of one's self-importance" and to evidence this with humility, living in consideration of the needs of others (BDAG s.v. "πραΰς" 861).

The "quiet spirit" (ἡσυχίου πνεύματος) spoke of the woman's spirit, not the Holy Spirit. There is some debate as to the meaning of the term "quiet" in this context. Paul used the noun form of the word (ἡσυχία) in reference to the silence of women in certain teaching contexts (1 Tim. 2:11–12). This meaning may fit the context here, for Peter had encouraged women to divert their energy away from the verbal proclamation of the gospel to the silent demonstration of that word through their honorable behavior. Nevertheless, the verbal form of the word includes the following definition: "to live a quiet life or refrain from disturbing activity" (BDAG s.v. "ἡσυχάζω" 440). Such a definition fits here nicely, and it is consistent with the way the word is used in Septuagint Isaiah 66:2[2] and 1 Timothy 2:2, the only other two times the word is used in canonical Scripture. Significantly, both uses of the word outside 1 Peter are given to both men and women. The NET captures this sense well with the translation, "gentle and tranquil spirit."

Peter described the gentle and quiet spirit as a quality that "does not fade." Taken literally, the word (ἀφθάρτῳ) refers to imperishability, and some translations take it that way (NASB, ESV, CSB, etc.). Others adapt the translation to the context, speaking of the "lasting beauty" (NET, NRSV) or the "unfading beauty" (NIV) of these character traits. Clearly Peter was contrasting the lasting beauty of the inner spirit with the fading beauty of external appearance. As Peter already mentioned, the glory of man is like a flower of grass that is destined to wither and fade (1:24). Accordingly, Peter was calling his readers to invest in that which lasts. The contrast between what is temporal and what is lasting occurs elsewhere in the letter: the "incorruptible" inheritance waiting for believers (1:4); the redemption price paid "not with perishable things" (1:18); and the readers' new birth through "imperishable seed" (1:23). Since they

---

2   Septuagint Isaiah 66:2. In at least two places (1 Clement 13:4; Barnabas 19:4) the early church used this passage, but instead of using the Septuagint's "gentle" (ταπεινόν) the authors used the word Peter used for "gentle" (πραΰς). It is possible the early church was following a different Septuagint text, or it is possible that the language of Peter had influenced these early authors. In any case, the use of the combination of these terms together suggests that these were not distinctively feminine characteristics.

are on the side of the imperishable, they must pursue that which lasts.

Peter concluded the consideration of the wife's adornment with a statement of divine evaluation: "which is precious in God's sight." The word "which" is inherently ambiguous. It could refer simply to a quiet spirit, to both the gentle and quiet spirit, or more generally to the whole consideration of adornment. Most likely Peter was referring to the entirety of the consideration of adornment, both its avoidance of external forms of beauty and the cultivation of inner beauty. It is possible Peter was echoing the thought of 1 Samuel 16:7b: "The LORD does not look at the things people look at. People look at the outward appearance, but the LORD looks at the heart" (NIV).

A subtle theme in 1 Peter is the importance of God's view compared to man's view. For example, Jesus was "rejected by men, but chosen by God" (2:4). And though believers will "be judged in the flesh" by humans, because of God's positive view of them, they will "live in the Spirit" (4:6). This theme is also implied everywhere that Peter made a distinction between who the readers were when accepted by society and who they have become because of the work of the Spirit and the Word of God (e.g., 1:14–18; 4:2–4). By focusing on God's view of the believing wives, Peter confirmed that their labor at the difficult work of cultivating a beautiful spirit would be worth all the toil. Indeed, such a spirit is "of great worth" in God's sight—the sight that really matters.

"Of Great Worth"

Peter chose a word that was used in relation to personal finance. Some translations reflect this choice: "of great price" (KJV), "of great worth" (NIV, CSB). It is likely that Peter used this word in an ironic way to contrast with the costliness of external adornment. Paul used the same word in 1 Timothy 2:9 to refer to costly garments, and the parallels with this passage are hard to miss: "women should adorn themselves in respectable apparel, with modesty and self-control, not with braided hair and gold or pearls or *costly attire*" (ESV). Thus that which is costly (forms of external beauty) is found not to be that which is actually valuable (the development of internal beauty).

The Example of Holy Women (3:5–6)

Peter encouraged wives to follow the lead of their husbands by appealing to the example of faithful women of the past who submitted to their husbands.

3:5. This verse and the next provided both a support for the command to submit and an example for the Christian wives to follow. First, Peter provided a support for his command: Christian wives should submit because holy women of the past also submitted. The designation "holy women" occurs nowhere else in biblical literature, yet by the example of Sarah referenced in 3:6 it is clear Peter was referencing the matriarchs of Israel's history (Sarah, Rebecca, Rachel, and Leah). The designation "holy" aligns these women with the Christian readers, who were likewise made holy by the action of the Spirit and the Word of God (1:2, 16, 22–23).

The chief characteristic of these holy women was their "hope in God." This hope likewise aligned them with the modern believers, whom Peter noted were "born again into a living hope" (1:3; cf. 1:21; 3:15). Thus, being both holy and hope-filled, these women provided an example for Peter's readers to follow.

Peter noted that such women were to be emulated because they "adorned themselves by submitting to their husbands." In speaking of their adornment, Peter used an imperfect verb, which revealed that this action was characteristic of the holy women. In other words, they did not do this on a solitary occasion; rather, this adornment was a regular feature of their lives. The repetition of submission brackets the discussion, clarifying that the model behavior encouraged by Peter was submission to one's husband.

3:6. In verse 5, Peter spoke generally of the "holy women of the past." In this verse, he gave a more concrete example in Sarah, Abraham's wife. There is some debate concerning the exact moment[3] Peter was recalling in the life of Sarah when she "obeyed Abraham, calling him 'lord.'"[4] It is likely that Peter did not have a specific example in mind; rather, he was referencing the attitude of life displayed by Sarah throughout the Genesis account and in popular Jewish tradition.

The conception of Abraham as the father of the Jewish people is pervasive in Jewish literature. Paul expands the designation to Gentiles in that they are Abraham's offspring through faith (Gal. 3:7). Here Peter argued that believing wives are daughters of Sarah, a natural metaphorical extension of the patriarchal image. The final statement of the verse has been understood in different ways. It is grammatically ambiguous, leading to diverse interpretations. Some believe that the clause is conditional: "you have become her daughters *if* you do what is good and do not fear anything that is frightening" (NASB, ESV, NIV, NRSV). Others, noting that a past tense verb like "you have become" (ἐγενήθητε) would be awkward with a conditional clause, suggest a causal or temporal interpretation: "you have become her daughters when you

do what is good and do not fear anything that is frightening" (NET, CSB).

The conditional interpretation is best, despite the apparent oddness of a condition following a statement of past fact. There are other New Testament examples of this same phenomena. For instance, Hebrews 3:14 says, "We have come to share in Christ, if indeed we hold our original conviction firmly to the very end" (c.f., Rom. 11:21–22; 1 Cor. 6:9–11; Col. 1:21–23; Schreiner, 2003, 157). Read this way, doing good and lacking fear are necessary conditions of being Sarah's children. This need not mean that Peter's readers earn such a commendation by their independent acts; instead, Peter's new birth theology suggests that those who have been chosen by God have been fundamentally changed by their exposure to the Word and Spirit. Those who are devoted to doing what is right and can live that way without fear demonstrate the change that has occurred in their lives.

Peter noted two characteristics of Sarah's daughters—they do what is good and do not fear anything that is frightening. The idea of "doing what is good" is consistent with what Peter said is characteristic of believers in general (2:12; 3:13; 4:19). The fact that these wives are not "frightened by anything that is frightening" is likely connected to the context Peter has been addressing. For instance, the NLT offers this helpful interpretive translation: "You are her daughters when you do what is right *without fear of what your husbands might do.*" One

---

3   Exact moment. The only place Sarah calls Abraham "lord" (κύριος) is in Septuagint Genesis 18:12. The context would be an odd one for Peter to choose however, for in this context Sarah laughed at the Lord's prophecy concerning her coming pregnancy and lied to Abraham about it. Some interpreters (Spencer, 2000) suggest Peter is referencing Genesis 12:13 and the willingness of Sarah to lie for Abraham. This too would be an odd choice, for it would draw attention to a failure in the life of Abraham. Others (Martin, 1999, 146) argue that the necessary background information comes from the Testament of Abraham, where Sarah frequently refers to Abraham as lord, obeys him, and is a model of good works. Jobes suggests that traditions like those contained in the Testament of Abraham are likely responsible for Peter's comments, though she notes that direct literary dependence is unnecessary (Jobes, 2005, 205–6).

4   "Calling him 'lord.'" There are two ways to take this clause. First, one may take the naming of Abraham as "lord" as the means of obeying: "obeyed Abraham, [by] calling him 'lord'" (NASB, ESV, NET, etc.). Second, one may take it as attendant circumstance to the verb: "obeyed Abraham and called him lord" (NIV, NRSV).

could understand why a wife in a strongly patriarchal society would fear offending her husband, a very real possibility for a believing wife. Peter was suggesting that wives should be willing to obey God, do good, and not live in fear of their husband's response. Such a state of life was only possible for those who believed in the sovereign goodness of God and who believed obedience was worth the cost of suffering.

Husbands Must Live Knowledgeably with Their Wives (3:7)

Peter commanded husbands to live knowledgeably with and honor their wives, warning husbands that God's censure is toward husbands who disregard these commands.

3:7. Peter continued the instruction within marriage by transitioning to the responsibility of the husband to his wife.[5] As noted earlier, Peter's order is opposite what would be natural in the Greek-speaking world. One would expect Peter to have spoken first to the husband and then to those dependent to him. In this case, Peter omitted instruction to children, and he placed the instruction to the wives first. This likely reflects both Peter's positive view of the agency of the wives, as well as his immediate concern to address those in his congregation who were in difficult social situations.

There does appear to be an imbalance of instruction. Women receive six verses of instruction, while men receive only one. The imbalance is accentuated by the uneven verse lengths, for in reality Peter provided four times as much instruction to women as to men, not six times as much (ninety-seven Greek words compared to twenty-five words). Further, though the length of the admonitions differs,

Peter's instructions to both are parallel in structure, as he gave two commands followed by a motivation for obedience to both groups. The difference in length is likely the result of emphasis, as Peter was focusing on those who were in difficult social positions.

Peter began his instruction to the husband with the word "likewise." This formally connects the instructions given to husbands with the instruction given to wives (3:1) and slaves (2:18). The similarity among these three groups is that each, by following the instructions given, will lead honorable lives that have the possibility of drawing others to the gospel (2:11–12).

The instructions given to husbands can be interpreted in different ways, and the English versions differ widely in translation. The first issue concerns the number of commands Peter intended to give. "Live knowledgeably with" (συνοικοῦντες) and "showing honor" (ἀπονέμοντες τιμήν) are both participles. Peter has given the commands to both the slaves (2:18) and wives (3:1) by means of a participle already, so it is expected that he would do the same here. Nevertheless, the second participle may be taken as a second primary command (e.g., "live knowledgeably with *and* show honor"), or it could be taken as the means of fulfilling the first command (e.g., "live knowledgeably with your wives *by* showing them honor"). It is best to take the command as a means of fulfilling the first, yet it should be recognized that since this is only one of many possible ways to accomplish the first command, it presents a second distinct command as well.

A second issue concerns how the two "as" (ὡς) clauses should be understood. Some versions take both with the second command:

---

5   Responsibility of the husband to his wife. Since Peter had previously discussed the case of a believing wife with an unbelieving husband, it is possible he is speaking of the case of a believing husband with an unbelieving wife. Of course, such a scenario is common in the present world, though it would be less common in Peter's day. The wife would, by custom, embrace the religion of her husband, whether in heart or simply in external observance. That the wife is not unbelieving is suggested by Peter's statement that the wife is a "coheir of the grace of life."

"Husbands, in the same way be considerate as you live with your wives, and treat them with respect *as the weaker partner* and *as heirs with you of the gracious gift of life*" (NIV; cf. ESV, NRSV). Other versions have one "as" clause with each command: "Husbands, in the same way, treat your wives with consideration *as the weaker partners* and show them honor *as fellow heirs of the grace of life*" (NET; cf. CSB, LEB). Though either translation is possible, the latter better balances the clauses and makes better sense of the word order.

A final issue of translation concerns what Peter meant by "according to knowledge" (κατὰ γνῶσιν). Some translations appear to identify the knowledge of the husband with the fact that the wife has been given a "weaker vessel." Such translations render "according to knowledge" as "treat your wives with consideration" (NET), "be considerate" (NIV), or "show consideration" (NRSV). Other translations leave the identity of the knowledge open, rendering the phrase "live with your wives knowledgeably" (LEB) or "live with your wives in an understanding way" (CSB, NASB, ESV). The latter translations are superior in that they allow the phrase "according to knowledge" to be understood in reference to God. This interpretation parallels the way "conscious of God" (stated to the slaves; 2:19) and "in fear" (stated to wives; 3:2) were used. All three phrases drew attention to the believer's duty before God. So "according to knowledge" means "enlightened by the man's knowledge of what God requires of him" (Achtemeier, 1996, 218). Though living considerately with one's wife is an *implication* of this statement; it is not the direct meaning of the statement.

"Vessel" (σκεύει) was used to refer to any type of container but was extended metaphorically to refer to the human body (BDAG s.v. "σκεῦος" 927). Peter's choice of words may strike modern ears as objectifying women, comparing the wife to a thing that could be possessed. There is no suggestion that Peter had

such a concept in mind, for the word he chose was used of both men and women (e.g., Acts 9:15; 2 Cor. 4:7; 1 Thess. 4:4). It simply referred to the human body.

That the "woman" (γυναικεῖος) had a "weaker" (ἀσθενεστέρῳ) vessel indicated that she had some form of limitation compared to the man (BDAG s.v. "ἀσθενής" 142). The nature of that limitation is not explicitly noted by Peter, suggesting that he believed it would be naturally understood by his audience. Greco-Roman thought on gender differences highlighted the distinctions between men and women, even referring to the woman as "weaker." Consider the words of Aristotle: "Providence made man stronger and woman weaker, so that he in virtue of his manly prowess may be more ready to defend the home, and she, by reason of her timid nature, more ready to keep watch over it" (Aristotle, *Oec.* 287, 333; for more on Greco-Roman conceptions of gender, see Elliott, 2001, 576–77).

The following are possible ways Peter could have thought of women as weaker than men: spiritually, mentally, emotionally, physically, or socially. The first is clearly mistaken, as Peter had recently highlighted the "holy women of old," had spoken of the spiritual agency of women married to unbelieving husbands, and would speak of the woman's spiritual equality at the end of this verse. Nowhere does the New Testament suggest any spiritual capacity distinction between men and women. Both are made in the image of God (Gen. 1:27), and in reference to spiritual things there is no difference (Gal. 3:28). The same may be said about intellectual inferiority, for such a perspective can only be read into, not out of, the New Testament.

That women are emotionally or physically weaker than men is sometimes proposed as Peter's meaning. Both perspectives conform to the Aristotle quotation given above, and both were likely assumed in the ancient world. Of course, there is a clear distinction between men and women physically. Further, it is hard to deny there are emotional differences[6] between men and women. Nevertheless, it is not clear why Peter would reference either physical or emotional weakness in this context.

That women are socially weaker than men is an attractive exegetical option in this context, both because it avoids many of the problems associated with other interpretations, but also because it fits the context quite well. On this perspective, Peter was essentially saying, "Husbands, live with your wives before God with the awareness that your wife is in a weaker (i.e., subordinate) position." This interpretation makes sense of the rest of the verse, which reminds the husbands that, despite their position, women are equal partners in reference to salvation, and that God is ready to judge the husband who treats his wife poorly. Though other options cannot be ruled out, it appears likely that Peter had social position in mind.

The second command given to the husbands was to "show your wives honor as fellow-heirs of the grace of life." Peter's choice of language suggests that what the husband should give to his wife is that "which is appropriate"[7] to the wife (BDAG s.v. "ἀπονέμω" 118; cf. 1 Clement 1:3; Martyrdom of Polycarp 10:2). What is appropriate, then, is the giving of honor (τιμή). In the context in which these words were spoken, a reader might ask, "Why does a wife deserve honor?" Peter answered such an unspoken question by noting that wives are "fellow-heirs of the grace of life." They deserve honor, for they are equal with their husbands regarding what really matters—spiritual life (cf. Gal. 3:28). Social position, Peter revealed, is not a measure of a person's worth (cf. 1 Peter 2:17).

Peter's two commands were accompanied by a final motivation for obedience: "so that your prayers will not be hindered." In the Greco-Roman world in which Peter was writing, there was little recourse for women in abusive relationships. Peter's final warning to husbands showed that Christian husbands were accountable for their treatment of their wives. Though there may be no earthly governing body that would intercede for the wife, the husband who did not honor his wife would find that his prayers[8] were hindered. While it may be true that those who treat their wives poorly will find their motivation to pray "hindered," Peter's point seems to be stronger; those who ignored God's commands would be ignored by God (Achtemeier, 1996, 209).

Due to the complexity of this verse, we have supplied an interpretive translation to bring out the meaning more fully: "Husbands, live with your wives according to knowledge God has given you, recognizing

---

6   Emotional differences. The idea that women are "weaker" emotionally may be affirmed as a truism from a certain perspective. On the other hand, other perspectives might label women as "stronger" from an emotional quotient standpoint. The reference point of Peter and his audience seems to have been the general Greco-Roman context, which considered the male's emotional state as "stronger" than that of the woman's.

7   That "which is appropriate." First Clement used this same participle with the word "honor," noting that the readers were "rendering to the older men among you the honor *that is their due*" (1 Clement 1:3). The Martyrdom of Polycarp, likewise, used the same verbal form (infinitive) with "honor" to speak of the way believers were "taught to render, as is meet, to princes and authorities appointed by God such honor as does us no harm" (10:2). These texts show that the combination of these terms speak of the honor that is due to someone in light of their status. Peter, then, indicates that a certain honor is due to wives as a result of their status as fellow heirs of the grace of life.

8   His prayers. It is not clear in Greek whose prayers are hindered. It says, "so that the prayers of you (pl.) be not hindered." It is possible that the husband's and wife's prayers are hindered, but since these instructions have been for the husband, and since he is the one at fault, it is likely that it is his prayers that are hindered. The referent is given in the plural simply because Peter was speaking to multiple husbands.

that she, as a woman, is in a weaker position. Do this by showing her honor, the honor she deserves as a fellow heir of the grace of life. Do these things so that your prayers will not be hindered."

THEOLOGICAL FOCUS

The exegetical idea (Peter instructed wives to submit to their husbands and display an inward beauty that attracts unbelieving husbands, that is honorable in God's sight, and that follows the example of prior godly saints, and Peter instructed husbands to live with their wives knowledgeably, honoring them as coheirs in the gift of life) leads to this theological focus: wives must follow the lead of their husbands, focusing on inward beauty, while husbands must live with their wives knowledgeably, honoring them as coheirs in the gift of life.

The call for wives to submit to their husbands is now countercultural. Nevertheless, Scripture reveals that it is still the way that a wife can show the inward beauty of her godly transformation. Indeed, focusing on the inward development of personal character is itself countercultural. In an age where external beauty is magnified, a wife's internal beauty may shine like the rare jewel it is. By living in this way, Christian wives may have hope for the conversion of their unregenerate husbands, may be confident of their approval by God, and may be encouraged that they follow in a long line of faithful, godly women.

Christian husbands may demonstrate their godly disposition by striving to live in a considerate way toward their wives. As they lead in the home, they must demonstrate their firm belief in the spiritual equality of their wives, giving them appropriate honor. They must do these things, not only because of the wife's spiritual equality, but also because God's ear will not incline toward those who disregard these instructions.

PREACHING AND TEACHING STRATEGIES

Exegetical and Theological Synthesis

What makes marriage work? We have all heard the statistics—more than 50 percent of marriages fail, with just as many failed marriages in a Christian home as with non-Christian couples. How difficult is it to make marriage work in a home environment where one partner is a believer and the other is not? And should society be believed when it teaches that differences between men and women amount to no more than social constructs instead of biblical design? If culture is correct, a woman can act as the authority in the household just as much as a man, and each gender (if there is such a thing!) should be considered exactly equal in all ways.

Peter's words fly in the face of such teaching. Peter speaks to a fallen world, just as preachers do today. Women in Peter's day attempted to attract attention by prettying themselves with jewelry, fancy clothes, and makeup. Sound familiar? Men considered themselves superior to women in both the household and society, living as dictators inside the home instead of humble partners in a marriage. Sound familiar?

Peter cuts through these warped ideas of masculinity and femininity by applying the gospel to Christian marriage. He connects the gospel to situations where one spouse knows Jesus and the other does not (3:1–2). The truths of the gospel cannot be force-fed into marriage, but are rather more successfully introduced by godly conduct and humble attitudes. Peter also applies the gospel to concepts of inward versus outward beauty (3:3–4). Jesus's blood transforms—inwardly. A man or woman changed by the gospel should behave differently than before, and they should recognize that the focus of their attention should be on inward beautification rather than outward adornment. Peter connects the gospel to the way husbands treat their wives (3:7). Jesus loved his church by giving himself up on the cross, humbling himself and putting his bride first. Husbands ought to honor their wives in similar fashion, recognizing that the gospel applies equally to both men and women.

Though some in our modern culture might want to eradicate all distinctions between husband and wife, man and woman, Peter's words allow for no such elimination. Rather, his words infuse the gospel into God-ordained creational distinctives in the home.

Preaching Idea

There's No Place Like Home . . . When Wives and Husbands Enjoy Their Proper Roles.

Contemporary Connections

What does it mean?

Unless we choose to deliberately ignore or twist the words of the apostle, we must recognize that Peter shows a distinction between husband and wife in the home, and that distinction includes roles based on gender. The exegesis in this commentary has shown a complementarian reading of the text rather than an egalitarian view of Peter's words.

The preacher must take care to present these roles carefully and biblically. What does it mean that the wife should "submit" to her husband? What about his claim that the woman is the "weaker vessel"? These statements could be offensive to some, or worse, potentially used to weaponize a dominant male agenda. It might help pastors to refresh themselves with the Danvers Statement, formed from the Council on Biblical Manhood and Womanhood, which affirms the complementarian viewpoint. The statement notes that "In the home, the husband's loving, humble headship tends to be replaced by domination or passivity; the wife's intelligent, willing submission tends to be replaced by usurpation or servility." Reviewing this statement before the sermon may help the preacher carefully phrase trickier parts of this controversial doctrine.

In explaining the meaning behind such statements, the preacher will want to emphasize that as anticultural as this passage might sound to the ears of moderns, it was also anticultural to Peter's original audience—except in the opposite way. Addressing wives before husbands was out of the norm, as were his commands to show honor to the wife. Whereas a modern audience reads this and takes offense at Peter's statement about women, Peter's audience likely would have read it and taken offense at his statements about *men*. God calls husbands and wives to a radical, Christlike love that fits with his original creational design of our bodies and roles.

Perspective plays a role in understanding Peter's words. In my town (Bryan), there is a yacht club that exclusively allows membership only to men. Women and children are allowed to enjoy the club's pool and restaurant, but only if accompanying a male member. Speaking to one woman in my congregation, she noted her displeasure at such sexism. Speaking to one of the men (who was also a member), he noted that the origins of such polity arose from the men's desire to be chivalrous—only men can pay for meals; women need not pay the high membership fees, but could enjoy the benefits nonetheless at the expense of the men. These two very different perspectives on the same issue demonstrate that it depends on where one comes from in relation to how one understands 1 Peter 3. The text does not change, nor does its meaning, but the preacher must be sensitive to how the text is perceived through the eyes of different individuals.

Is it true?

Should we still take literally Peter's separate gender roles in today's antigender, "woke" society? Shouldn't our "wokeness" and growing awareness of past abuses toward women cause us to re-read Peter's words in light of our cultural expectations instead of like a twentieth-century patriarchal society?

Preachers should know that if they indeed preach this passage as it reads, it may invite a firestorm of controversy, potential hurt, and confusion with a twenty-first-century audience. Because our world today views any separation between gender roles as anathema, it becomes a challenge to communicate God's truth to a progressive listener. But cultural liberalism does not change the timeless truth of God's Word, though the preacher should proceed with an extra measure of sensitivity and grace. The preacher should root the origin of gender distinctions—and thus distinction in the home—in the original created couple Adam and Eve, noting that the distinctions are prefall and not a result of sin (Genesis 1–2; cf. 1 Tim. 2:12–15).

The other question that begs to be answered in this passage is whether husbands can be won to Christ by the humble conduct of a wife. This can be illustrated with simple examples from married life. How many husbands have been won over to the benefits of lowering the toilet seat lid by a wife's incessant nagging? How many men have delighted in picking up their dirty laundry that didn't quite make it to the hamper by their wife's pestering? Few men are motivated by criticizing, nitpicking, or fault-finding. But the wise wife knows that there are better ways to get to a man's heart and mind. If this is true with toilet seats and dirty laundry, how much more does it hold true for an unbelieving husband's salvation?

Now what?

The text presents three different specific points of application for the married couple. First, verses 1–2 speak to Christian women with unbelieving husbands. They are to be respectful and holy rather than resort to nagging and bemoaning their unequally yoked situation. Women in the congregation should be encouraged to keep in prayer for their husbands, to keep coming to church and living a chaste and godly life with the hope that their conduct will demonstrate the gospel to their spouse.

The preacher will want to address specific questions of a woman in such a situation. It may help to sit down with someone living through these difficulties and get a sense of what the true issues and questions are. Many women have questions such as: How do I faithfully tithe when my husband controls the finances? What if my husband wants me to stay home on Sunday mornings? What if he wants to keep the kids home? How do I deal with my husband's mockery of my faith commitment? The male preacher—especially one who has only known a situation of Christian marriage—will want to sensitize himself with such issues before preaching the text.

The second point of application comes in verses 3–4. The internal qualities of the heart are far more important than the external adornments of the body. The preacher can pull plenty of easy illustrations from the media, with beautiful botoxed movie stars revealing their inward ugliness through their unchaste actions. The preacher may want to go on a virtual shopping spree via Amazon or an online retailer and show how much it costs to bedazzle oneself with designer clothes and jewelry, then contrast that with the relative "cost" of cultivating one's heart spiritually, with far greater and longer-lasting benefits.

Verse 7 offers the third point of application. The preacher will want to take extra care that this sermon does not "come down" upon women without addressing men. It is easy to appear chauvinistic when preaching 1 Peter 3:1–7. (It may help to keep in mind that many of the points made directly to women in the first six verses also conversely can apply to men as well—it is far more important for men to dig into Scripture than hit the gym seven times a week!) But the words of verse 7 were just as radical in Peter's day as they are in our own. Husbands need to be challenged not to act like an ape or a dictator in the household, but instead to love their wives as Christ loves the church, showing honor and deference whenever possible. There are too few examples of this in modern sitcoms, so perhaps a contrast with the Al Bundys and Homer Simpsons of the entertainment world will help illustrate the problem.

Creativity in Presentation

The text invites illustrations with the mention of Sarah's example. The teacher or preacher can follow up the exposition of this passage with real-life illustrations from the congregation. Is there a husband and wife that exemplifies Peter's words? If so, create a panel with a few couples and ask them to respond to a few questions regarding what 1 Peter 3:1–7 looks like lived out in a real-life marriage. How does the husband show understanding and honor to the wife when picking out a date-night movie? How does a wife win over her stubborn husband in his sinfulness without being a nag? Hearing from couples who have struggled to live out these commands may help others engage in the meaning of the text even more.

A testimony from a woman who saw her husband come to Christ may also encourage those in a similar situation. People need to hear the struggle of living for years, sometimes decades, in a relationship where only one person in the marriage loves Jesus. They need to hear the ups and downs of raising kids in a home with only one Christian parent. The situation is far too common to treat it only with generalities from the perspective of a pastor who may not have personally wrestled with such difficulties. In the same category, the preacher might want to even consider the testimony of a wife's struggle with the perpetual sin of a believing husband—one caught in drug or pornography

addiction, or a husband who was imprisoned for a crime, and so on. This might touch on the same principles Peter addresses in this passage.

Though this following example will not suit the Sunday morning pulpit, it may be useful for situations where a woman teaches other women. I (Bryan) heard of a pastor's wife who was teaching 1 Peter 3 to a group of teenage girls. She disappeared into her room for a few moments, then came out dressed—in her words—like a "slut." A group of teenagers seeing their forty-something-year-old pastor's wife dressed in such a way was a shock, to say the least. They all found it inappropriate, which was exactly the point. The stark contrast with the woman's normal humility and grace showed the teens just how "ugly" external beauty can be. Again, this kind of illustration would not be advisable from the church platform—and extra caution should be taken in the age of cellphones, which can forever capture and post an image with one click of a button—but it may give rise to a creative spark that could help put even more visual impact on the passage.

Each of these creative illustrations should serve to emphasize that husbands and wives most enjoy their marriage when they live within their proper roles. One potential way of structuring the passage is:

Intro: Marital Difficulties Illustrated
I. The Role of the Wife (3:1–6)
    A. A wife's conduct (3:1–2)
    B. A wife's beauty (3:3–4)
    C. A wife's example (3:5)
II. The Role of the Husband (3:7)
    A. A husband's life (3:7a)
    B. A husband's honor (3:7b)
    C. A husband's prayer (3:7c)

DISCUSSION QUESTIONS

1. Why do wives today have a hard time with understanding (and obeying) the command to "submit" to their husbands? How has this command been misunderstood and abused? How did Peter intend it to be understood?

2. What does inward beauty look like, according to Peter? How can you tell if your focus on the outward beauty is disproportionate to the inward focus?

3. How is Sarah an excellent example of Peter's point?

4. What does Peter mean by saying that husbands should live with their wives in an "understanding" way? What does he mean by calling women the "weaker vessel"? How has this been abused? What was Peter's actual intent?

5. Are these commands limited to Peter's culture, or do they apply equally to our time? If so, what does this dynamic look like in the home?

1 Peter 3:8–12

EXEGETICAL IDEA

Peter commanded his readers to cultivate positive social values and pursue righteousness, while rejecting detrimental social responses and turning from evil, so that they would acquire the blessing of loving life and seeing good days.

THEOLOGICAL FOCUS

Believers may acquire blessing by cultivating righteousness and rejecting unrighteousness.

PREACHING IDEA

God "Likes" True Social Networking.

PREACHING POINTERS

The pressure of persecution forces believers to determine their allegiance. When the heat is turned up, the church could either fracture in discord or unite stronger than ever. Peter's readers were facing the stress of persecution, which potentially could destroy their relationships with each other or cause bitterness and anger at the unbelieving world attacking them. But Peter challenged his readers to humble themselves and unite. He urged them to respond to evil with love, and by doing so to live out the call of the gospel in the midst of the hostile world around them.

Likewise, believers today face trials and temptations from many angles. Internally, many churches are fractured over mundane issues like tertiary doctrine or opinions on how to run a ministry. In our dog-eat-dog world, many believers have taken the worldly approach to trade insult with insult instead of returning love for evil. Those who desire to see good days search for them through self-help books and internet blogs instead of through God's Word.

Peter's words point to a better way of life. Through 1 Peter 3:8–12, preachers can address issues like church unity, responding to a hostile world, and pursuing the right kinds of goals in life. The passage speaks to various relationships, both in and outside the church, and orients the believer to live out the gospel in a Christlike manner.

HOW TO LIVE THE GOOD LIFE (3:8–12)

LITERARY STRUCTURE AND THEMES (3:8–12)

With the word "finally," Peter revealed that this section of text concluded the household codes (2:13–3:7). Peter began the instruction in the household codes by speaking to the readers generally (2:13–17), then developed specific instructions for specific groups within the broader readership (slaves [2:18–25], wives [3:1–6], husbands [3:7]). In these verses, he returned to general instruction for all readers.

Peter opened this general instruction with a list of social values that believers should pursue (3:8), transitioned to what natural responses should be rejected (3:9a), and then returned to what should be pursued (3:9b). To the final positive command, Peter added a motivation for obedience (3:9c) and a support for his command from the Old Testament (3:10–12). The quotation served a double purpose as a support for his immediate commands and as a sign for the conclusion of the codes (cf. 1:24–25; 2:9–10; 4:17–18).

Themes of this section include: the believer's responsibility to cultivate socially positive qualities; how the believer may love life and see good days; God's relational presence with those who are righteous; and God's relational distance from those who do evil.

- *General Instructions for All Believers (3:8–9)*
- *How to Love Life and See Good Days (3:10–12)*

EXPOSITION (3:8–12)

With pressures mounting on the outside, Peter addressed ways that believers could cultivate positive relationships within the community and outside it. Necessary to internal relations was the development of social graces—sympathy, love, and humility. Necessary to external relations was the development of the attitude of Christ—responding with blessing when cursed. The good life, as the Old Testament argued, consisted of the pursuit of good and avoidance of evil. Peter's readers, by following these directives, could be sure that God heard their prayers, even as they were sure that God censured those persecuting them.

General Instructions for All Believers (3:8–9)

Due to their new identity, Peter commanded the readers to cultivate positive social values and reject reflexive, sinful responses.

3:8. "And finally" (δὲ τέλος) signals that this material both follows closely the material that preceded and brings the list to an end. This is confirmed in that Peter closed this section by quoting the Old Testament, as he had closed other sections (1:24–25; 2:9–10; 4:17–18). He addressed these final instructions to all his readers ("all of you" [πάντες]). It is likely that verse 8 relates to relationships *within* the family of God, while verse 9 relates to relationships *outside* the family.

The instructions were given with five adjectives that lack a verb.[1] Almost all English versions include the verb "be" or "have," rightly revealing

---

1 Five adjectives that lack a verb. There are a few ways to resolve this difficulty. Perhaps Peter assumed his readers would recognize the adjectives as imperatival (Michaels, 1988, 176). Or there may be an implied imperatival

that each of the adjectives have imperatival force. The first adjective (ὁμόφρονες) is variously translated: "be like minded" (NIV, CSB), "be harmonious" (NASB, NET, LEB), or "have unity of spirit/mind" (NRSV, ESV). Though the word only occurs here in the New Testament, the conception that believers must be united in purpose is common in the New Testament (Acts 2:46; Rom. 15:5; 1 Cor. 1:10; Phil. 2:2; 4:2). The second adjective (συμπαθεῖς) refers to having sympathy for one another. This form of the word is used nowhere else in the New Testament, but its verbal form is used twice in Hebrews. Once it speaks of Jesus as one who can sympathize with our weaknesses (4:5), while the second speaks of believers sympathizing with others who were in prison by meeting their needs (10:34).

The third of the adjectives (φιλάδελφοι) speaks of "brotherly love." Many modern versions translate the adjective as "be affectionate" (NET), "love one another" (NIV, CSB, NRSV), or "show mutual affection" (LEB). These translations fail to preserve the familial aspect of the language. Peter has developed an entire motif in this letter centered on the new birth and the readers, as newfound family members, are here being called to show a familial love to one another. A translation such as "show familial love" would communicate this concept well.

Peregrine and the Love of Christians

A satirical account written in the middle to late second century about Christians confirms the extraordinary love believers displayed toward one another. Lucian, the author, was clearly no friend to Christians, and this makes his account more spectacular. In this story Peregrine joined a Christian group, pretending to be one of them to benefit from their generosity: "In some of the Asiatic cities, too, the Christian communities put themselves to the expense of sending deputations, with offers of sympathy, assistance, and legal advice. The activity of these people, in dealing with any matter that affects their community, is something extraordinary; they spare no trouble, no expense. Peregrine, all this time, was making quite an income on the strength of his bondage; money came pouring in. You see, these misguided creatures start with the general conviction that they are immortal for all time, which explains the contempt of death and voluntary self-devotion which are so common among them; and then it was impressed on them by their original lawgiver that they are all brothers, from the moment that they are converted, and deny the gods of Greece, and worship the crucified sage, and live after his laws. All this they take quite on trust, with the result that they despise all worldly goods alike, regarding them merely as common property. Now an adroit, unscrupulous fellow, who has seen the world, has only to get among these simple souls, and his fortune is pretty soon made; he plays with them" (Lucian, 1913, sec. 13).

The fourth adjective (εὔσπλαγχνοι) indicates that the readers must cultivate a "tender heart." The word speaks literally of the entrails of a person, but is used figuratively, especially in a related form (σπλάγχνον), to refer to the deepest emotional core of a person. A verbal form of the word is used at least three times in reference to Jesus in the New Testament (Matt. 9:36; Mark 1:41; Luke 7:13), each time in reference to Jesus's compassion toward those who were in a pitiable position. Paul, in Ephesians, used the same word in reference to the duties of Christians to one another: "be kind and *compassionate* to one another" (Eph. 4:32).

The final adjective (ταπεινόφρονες) obliges the readers to cultivate "humility of mind." This last virtue was often considered a vice in the

equative verb (ἐστέ). Finally, it is possible that there is an implied participial equative verb (ὄντες; Achtemeier, 1996, 222).

Greek world (BDAG s.v. "ταπεινοφροσύνη" 989). But because of the example of Jesus, who defined himself as one gentle and *humble* (ταπεινός) in heart (Matt. 11:29) and compelled his followers to be *humble* (ταπεινώσει; Matt. 18:4), humility became a badge of honor. Frequently the New Testament epistles call for such humility (Eph. 4:2; Phil. 2:3; Col. 3:12; 1 Peter 5:5).

These five virtues appear to be structured purposefully (see chiasm below; cf. Schreiner, 2003, 164). The first and fifth are similar in that they both call the readers to think in ways advantageous to the cultivation of relationships. The second and fourth are likewise parallel since having sympathy and having a tender heart are concepts that necessarily go together. The third stands alone without a counterpart and is thereby emphasized as the center point of the chiasm. The centrality of the love command given by Jesus (John 13:34; 15:12, 17) makes the centrality of this command by Jesus's chief disciple unsurprising.

Chiasm of 3:8

Have unity of mind
    Have sympathy
        Have familial love
    Have a tender heart
Have humility of mind

3:9. Two shifts occur in this verse from the last verse. First, the instruction turned from admonition to prohibition. Second, Peter moved from instructions within the assembly to instructions concerning relationships with those outside the assembly. This latter point is not made explicit, but the context of the letter reveals that the readers were experiencing hostility from those outside the assembly, and Peter's call for them to respond opposite to the way they were treated mirrors the actions of Christ expressed in 1:21–25.

Not only were the instructions Peter gave here reflective of the example of Jesus; they

were rooted in Jesus's teaching: "But I say to you who hear, Love your enemies, do good to those who hate you, bless those who curse you, pray for those who abuse you" (Luke 6:27–28; cf. Matt. 5:38–44). On the basis of Jesus's example and teaching, Peter commanded these readers to forego the natural human response to reviling. Instead of responding to curses with curses, or with evil to evil, they were to bless. Such actions, called for elsewhere in the New Testament (Rom. 12:14, 17; 1 Cor. 4:12b; 1 Thess. 5:15), provided an opportunity to draw the attention of the persecutor to the light of the believer's works.

Unnatural Christian Responses to Suffering

Rom. 12:14	*Bless those who persecute you; bless and do not curse them.*
Rom. 12:17	*Repay no one evil for evil*, but give thought to do what is honorable in the sight of all.
1 Cor. 4:12b	*When reviled, we bless*; when persecuted, we endure.
1 Thess. 5:15	*See that no one repays anyone evil for evil*, but always seek to do good to one another and to everyone.

The Greco-Roman concept of blessing (εὐλογέω) referred to speaking well of someone, but the Greek Old Testament had the additional meaning, "to ask for the bestowal of special favor" (BDAG s.v. "εὐλογέω" 408). Due to the nature of the word and Jesus's teaching, Peter appears to have been calling on his readers to pray for those who persecuted them. This would align nicely with Peter's emphasis elsewhere concerning the hope that even the enemies of the gospel will, when they see God's good works in the life of the believer, turn in repentance (2:12; 3:1).

"To this you were called" is ambiguous, for "this" could refer backward or forward. If referring back, it is saying, "you were called to respond to evil with blessing so that you may receive a blessing." If pointing forward, it is saying, "bless, because you were called to receive a blessing."

The challenge of the first interpretation is that it appears to make the reception of blessing[2] dependent on one's actions, which appears contrary to the grace-focus of the epistle (1:1–3, 12, 23; 2:4–5, 9–10; 5:10, 13). Accordingly, some interpret the passage with the reference pointing forward, with the result that one is to bless others on the basis that he or she has received undeserved blessing. Such a rendering fits well with the grace-focus of the letter and matches the way Peter uses the same phrase in 4:6 (i.e., in 4:6 "to this you were called" clearly points forward).

It is not clear, however, that a backward reference is opposed to the theology of grace expressed in the epistle. The New Testament frequently ascribes actions to believers that are necessary for their salvation (Rom. 2:6–10; 2 Peter 1:5–11; 1 John 2:3–6), yet such works are not the *cause* of salvation but the *natural fruit* of genuine salvation. So here, Peter's point was not to highlight what was required of believers to obtain salvation; rather, it was a reminder of what was necessitated of them as those who had received God's grace. This interpretation may be defended by Peter's use of the same phrase ("to this you have been called") in 2:21 where the reference is clearly directed backward.

How to Love Life and See Good Days (3:10–12)

Using a quotation from the Psalms, Peter revealed how the readers could love life, see good days, and obtain the favor of the Lord.

3:10. This and the next two verses are a direct quotation from Psalm 34:12–16 (LXX 33:13–17). The text is very similar to the Septuagint rendering, with minor stylistic adaptions (see Elliott, 1974, 612). The selection of this psalm is not accidental. As Schreiner rightly recognized, "themes that are central in 1 Peter are evident in the psalm: the suffering of God's people, their ultimate deliverance, the judgment of the wicked, and the notion that a godly life is evidence of hoping in God" (Schreiner, 2003, 166). Peter earlier referred to this psalm (2:3). It is not clear whether Peter chose this psalm because it reflected the themes of his letter, or whether Peter determined the themes of the letter on the basis of this psalm.

One of the stylistic additions to the Septuagint text is the opening conjunction "for" ($\gamma\alpha\rho$). Clearly, Peter intended this passage to inform the argument he was just making in 3:8–9, but since this quotation concludes the entire household codes, it is likely he intended it to be reflective of all the instruction from 2:11. One confirmation of this fact is that the heeding of prayers is associated with righteous activity in both 3:12 and 3:7. More significantly, the opening of the household codes with its emphasis on avoiding evil and pursuing good (2:11–12) finds a powerful parallel at the conclusion of the codes with the psalm's instruction that the righteous must "turn from evil and do good" (3:11).

The psalm opened by addressing those who "desire to love life and to see good days." It is clear that in the psalm the referent of life was the present, earthly life. Throughout the Old Testament, observance of the law led to blessing, and such blessing often resulted in the enjoyment earthly peace and prosperity (e.g., Lev. 26:1–13 and Deut. 28:1–14). Some commentators argue that Peter has adapted the meaning of the passage, substituting the concept of eternal life for the psalm's enjoyment of the present, earthly

---

2 Reception of blessing. The reception of blessing in this context refers to the reception of eternal life. While it is broadly possible Peter was speaking of blessing in this life, the overall tenor of the letter suggests that there is little that should be expected of the present life's blessings, yet there is much to be anticipated in reference to the blessings to come.

life (e.g., Elliott, 1974, 612; Michaels, 1988, 180). Such an interpretation makes sense of the broader themes of the letter, which appear to focus the reader's attention on the attainment of eternal joy (e.g., 1:7, 13; 2:12; 5:4).

A case can be made for the blessing being granted in this life, however. Grudem has made the most powerful argument in this connection, showing how throughout 1 Peter, right conduct leads to blessing in the present life (see the following chart taken from Grudem, 1988, 157). It is also possible that Peter spoke of both the present, earthly experience of life as well as the eschatological experience of life. From the Old Testament context, Peter derived the idea that good deeds generally led to positive enjoyment of life in the present (cf. 3:13–14). Yet readers were surely to also understand, in the context of this letter, that good deeds led to the promised eschatological expectation of good days in which they may fully love life (cf. Achtemeier, 1996, 226; Compton, 2019, 217–18). Thus, it is best to see a double reference here. Obedience will grant certain enjoyments in this life, characterized chiefly by fellowship with God, but also producing harmony and peace with others. Obedience is also necessary for the enjoyment of eternal life (cf. 1:9; Heb. 12:14).

How can believers enjoy both this life and the one to come? Peter answered by quoting several lines from the psalm, which included three statements of prohibition and three statements of command. He began with the prohibitions, including two in this verse. Both prohibitions refer to the use of one's tongue. The readers were to keep their "tongues from evil," meaning that they were to guard what they said. Such a command is consistent with both the action of Jesus (2:23) and the teaching of Jesus (3:9). Further, the readers were to keep their "lips from speaking deceit." Peter had already commanded the readers to put away deceit in 2:1 and demonstrated how Jesus modeled this during his passion (2:22). Accordingly, these first two commands from the psalm not only reflect the themes of 1 Peter nicely, but also demonstrate that pursuing the good life means following in the steps of Jesus.

Verse	Right conduct	Resulting blessing in this life
1:8	loving Christ	unutterable joy
1:9	continuing faith	more benefit of salvation
1:17	holy life with fear	avoiding God's fatherly discipline
2:2	partaking of spiritual milk	growing up toward salvation
2:19–20	trusting God and doing right while suffering	God's approval
3:1–2	submitting to husbands	husbands won for Christ
3:7	living considerately with wives	prayers not hindered
4:14	enduring reproach for Christ	spirit of glory and of God rests upon you
5:7	casting cares on God	(implied) he will care for your needs
5:9–10	resisting the devil	God will restore, establish, strengthen you
Chart taken from Grudem, 1988, 157.		

3:11. This verse, a continuation of the Old Testament quotation, provided the final prohibition and introduced three positive commands. The final prohibition, "let him turn away from evil," is balanced by the first positive command, "let him do good." This theme brackets the entire household codes section, for Peter began the codes with the admonition for his readers to abstain from evil and to pursue good (2:11–12). More specifically, the conception that believers are to be doers of good is pervasive in 1 Peter (2:11–12, 14, 15, 20; 3:6, 17; 4:19).

The final two positive commands go together: "let him seek peace and pursue it." Though the word for "peace" (εἰρήνην) occurs nowhere else in 1 Peter, the concept is central to many of Peter's admonitions. Peace referred to harmony and concord in relationships, particularly with the absence of hostility. By observing the cultural norms of society, Peter was calling on believers to live at peace. They were not to disrupt such peace by insubordination or by doing evil. This attribute derived from Jesus's teaching (Matt. 5:9; Mark 9:50) and resulted in the pursuit of peace becoming a dominant train of thought in the early church (Rom. 12:18; 14:19; 2 Cor. 13:11; 1 Thess. 5:13; 2 Tim. 2:22; Heb. 12:14).

Peter, following the Septuagint psalm, not only commanded the readers to live at peace, but to "seek" it and "pursue" it. The verb for "seek" (ζητησάτω) reflected the need "to devote serious effort" to the pursuit of peace (BDAS, s.v. "ζητέω" 428). The verb for "pursue" (διωξάτω) could be used to reference someone literally running after something (Matt. 23:34), but it is used here metaphorically to speak of moving with haste toward a goal (BDAG s.v.

"διώκω" 254). The combination suggests that the readers must make peace their goal and hastily strive after it with diligent effort. Peace is often unnatural; indeed, it is supernatural, the product of the believer's transformation by the Word and Spirit. Peter was calling the readers to evidence this in their lives, opening the door to gospel witness.

3:12. The final verse of the quotation distinguished two types of people—the righteous and those who do evil. As evidenced by the surrounding context, those who are righteous are those who do good works. This does not reflect a works-based approach to righteousness. Instead, it reflects the perspective already developed in the letter—the righteous are those who have been transformed by the Word and the Spirit to do good deeds.

The three statements made concerning the righteous and those who do evil all anthropomorphize the Lord.[3] The first line speaks of the eyes of the Lord, the second his ears, and the third his face. First, the eyes of the Lord are said to be "on the righteous." Setting one's eyes upon someone indicates interest in them, and here suggests watchful care. Such loving concern is consistent with his identity as the "shepherd and guardian of their souls" (2:25). That the Lord's ears are open to their prayers is a sister concept, showing that he not only looks after them but inclines toward them, desiring to hear their cries for deliverance, intervention, or blessing (cf. the contrast in 3:7).

As for those who do evil, Peter revealed that the Lord's face was "against them." The next line of the psalm, which was not included by Peter, indicates that those to whom

---

3   Anthropomorphize the Lord. To anthropomorphize means to cast something that is not human in human terms. This occurs, for example, when someone refers to their car as "my baby." In reference to Scripture, God is often presented in human terms in order that people may understand how he relates to humanity. Of course, it is not necessary that God have nostrils in order for smoke to rise from them (Ps. 18:8), for the statement simply means that he is angry. In this case, it is not clear whether Jesus (Michaels, 1988, 181) or God the Father (Achtemeier, 1996, 227) is the "Lord" referenced here, though Peter elsewhere tends to refer to Jesus as Lord.

the Lord's face is against, God will "blot out their name from the earth." This additional line was not included by Peter, likely because including it would obscure the lexical tie between the "the one doing evil" (ποιοῦντας κακά) in verse 12 and "the ones harming you" (ὁ κακώσων ὑμᾶς) in verse 13. Nevertheless, the point is clear: God's favor is on the righteous, but his disfavor is directed toward those who do evil.

THEOLOGICAL FOCUS

The exegetical idea (Peter commanded his readers to cultivate positive social values and pursue righteousness, while rejecting detrimental social responses and turning from evil, so that they would acquire the blessing of loving life and seeing good days) leads to this theological focus: Believers may acquire blessing by cultivating righteousness and rejecting unrighteousness.

Peter began the household codes arguing that believers should avoid evil and pursue good (2:11–12), and here he concludes it, giving motivation for believers to accomplish these same goals. By quoting the Old Testament, Peter was affirming that God had not changed; he rewarded people according to their faithfulness then and would do so now. The same continues to be true today. Believers who would love life and see good days, meaning those who would enjoy both the present benefits of obedience and the future eternal benefits of obedience, must embrace loving attitudes toward those within the household of faith and avoid negative responses to those outside the household of faith.

The most important thing about a person is their relationship to God. Peter here showed that one's relationship with God is based on obedience to his commands. If they are righteous, being transformed by the Word and Spirit to do good deeds, they will have the favor of the Lord, with his watchful eye on them, and his ear ready to hear their requests.

But if they are disobedient to him, they should expect his disfavor.

PREACHING AND TEACHING STRATEGIES

Exegetical and Theological Synthesis

The sinful tendency of humankind is to hold one's opinions loud and proud, no matter what the cost. When someone picks a fight, fight back. When an aggressor insults, cut deeper with your own words. These desires to be right and to be seen as the victor in any situation reveal a selfish pride deep in the heart.

Peter applies the gospel to relationships, showing how Christ in believers should change their behavior, even in unpleasant and hostile situations. Believers should act in humility and love toward one another (3:8). They should return such love even upon their enemies (3:9). Self-control and the pursuit of peace and righteousness should characterize all Christians (3:10–12). When the gospel is at work, it transforms a believer's interaction with the world.

This higher standard of social interaction is encouraged by many different biblical authors. On several occasions, the apostle Paul commands Christians to never repay back evil to anyone, but to allow the Lord to administer justice (Rom. 12:14, 17, 19; 1 Cor. 4:12; 1 Thess. 5:15). Jesus himself set the standard, not only with his own lifestyle but in spoken word as well (Matt. 5:39; Luke 6:28). These New Testament commands are nothing new; rather, they are rooted in the ethics of the Old Testament (Lev. 19:18; Prov. 20:22; 24:29–30). Living as a believer changed by the gospel requires a Christlike standard of interacting with those inside and outside the church.

Preaching Idea

God "Likes" True Social Networking.

Contemporary Connections

What does it mean?

What does it mean that God "likes" true social networking? The Preaching Idea plays on the modern obsession with attaining as many followers and "likes" as possible on social media, such as Facebook, Instagram, Twitter, and myriad others. But God's desire for Christians goes much deeper than hoping for the most followers or the most views on a video. True Christian fellowship and interaction happens in personal social interactions, and those interactions are characterized by godly responses and goals.

The preacher should define "true social networking" through the lens of this passage. Though our culture heralds self-expression, derogatory insults (as long as they make someone laugh), and arrogant opinions, Peter calls believers to interact with harmony, sympathy, brotherly love, tenderness, and humility. God smiles upon such Christlike behavior, even if it doesn't generate as many media clicks.

Additionally, internet feuds capture attention, but the preacher will want to show from the text that the Lord calls us to bless instead of curse, even for those cursing at us. True Christian behavior exudes the gospel in all circumstances, especially when the world acts in hostility toward us. God is not impressed with our ability to snap back when someone acts aggressively, but rather, the person who pursues peace and righteousness gets the Lord's attention.

Is it true?

Is it true that God "likes" social networking? To put the question another way: Does God require us to interact with the church and with the world in order to live properly? Is there such thing as a "Lone Ranger" Christian?

A world of increasingly socially isolated people may need convincing that God desires for his children to have meaningful, healthy relationships with each other. In 2020, the world went on lockdown due to the coronavirus pandemic. Many nations around the world asked or required citizens to socially isolate themselves from the rest of the population until the virus could get under control. Though the effectiveness of the social distancing, mask-wearing, and quarantining are debatable, what was surprising to some was the effect the measures had on mental health. Within a year of the pandemic, several articles released research that indicated that the isolation had negative effects on the mental health of the population (Panchal et al., 2021).

Similarly, research has also shown the detrimental effects that social media use can have on mental health (Luxton, June, and Fairall, 2012). What is supposed to bond us together ends up distressing us. Perhaps Peter intended something more for our social interactions than just what we could get on a screen. There is a direct correlation in 1 Peter 3:10–12 between satisfaction of life and proper social behavior. Contrasting hopeless avenues of relational pursuit with godly avenues may help alleviate suspicion from Peter's words.

Now what?

Though the Preaching Idea may play with modern trends in a whimsical way, application of Peter's words goes beyond a social media fast or pulling the plug on the internet community (though there may be some merit to those options!). The exegesis has demonstrated several avenues of application for the Christian's relationships.

First, the Christian should examine how he or she interacts with other believers (3:8). If the church has problems in this area, it may be time to channel the inner prophet and speak clearly against such sins in the congregational life. If the church is well aware of the board meeting that erupted into chaos last week, make a clear call for your leaders to repent. If families in the church lack love toward each other, admonish them to act like children in the family of God.

Send out a plea for humility and unity, perhaps pointing to Jesus as the ultimate example (Phil. 2:1–11).

Second, the Christian should examine how he or she interacts with unbelievers (3:9). Concrete examples help this verse come to life. How did King David react to Shimei's curses (2 Sam. 16:5–14; 19:18–23)? How did Jesus react to the thieves mocking him on the cross (Luke 23:32–43)? Historical or modern examples can also help illustrate proper application of Peter's words. Consider Elisabeth Elliott returning to the natives who killed her husband, not with anger or bitterness but with the gospel. The next time someone is rude to you in the grocery store line, instead of snapping back, pay for their groceries in full.

Finally, the Christian should examine whether he or she is pursuing life and good days in the proper way (3:10–12). Are you seeking peace? Are you controlling your tongue (and yes, social media counts here!)? Are the eyes of Christ upon you and his ears open to your prayers because of your righteousness? Encourage the church to allow the pursuit of Christ and the application of the gospel to radically transform the way they interact with others.

Creativity in Presentation

In today's world, social media dominates the landscape. Hardly a relationship begins or ends without a friend request or algorithm suggestion leading the way. In keeping with the theme of positive social interactions, the preacher may want to lean into this technology craze, using it as a foil to critique the shallowness of that culture and at the same time pointing the way to what God intends for true believers.

In a fashion similar to the prophets of old, consider using sarcasm, irony, and humor to point out how impossible it is to follow Peter's commands when only interacting via a screen. It won't be difficult to drum up a few posts or commented responses that demonstrate the opposite of sympathy, brotherly love, tenderheartedness, or especially humility. Screenshot a few pages of material to use as illustrations. (Instead of looking for these examples on the pages of your congregants, consider a more general source such as the comments from a news website or YouTube video or celebrity Twitter post, so as not to offend or embarrass anyone in the church!)

After showing a few examples of how our culture struggles to understand humility and love, write your own responses to the original post, demonstrating what it looks like to "tweet" in the family of God. Challenge congregants to purposefully respond to a controversial post with the characteristics seen in this pericope.

The preacher will not want to land the sermon in social media applications, but guide the church to interact with love and humility in face-to-face interactions. If teaching in a classroom setting, consider role-playing a few scenarios centered around workplace interactions or home life. Consider the following example to get you started: Your obnoxious neighbor is throwing a party and blasting music after midnight on a school day. You knock on the door and ask him to turn down the tunes so your kids can get some sleep. Your neighbor—obviously under the influence—begins to curse at you and insult your children. How can you respond in a 1 Peter fashion? Keep in mind: true social networking with others in your life pleases God.

Here is a possible outline for this sermon:

I.   Traits of Godly Social Networking (3:8–9)
  A. Unity of Mind
  B. Sympathy
  C. Brotherly Love
  D. Tender Heart
  E. Humble Mind
  F. Bless Instead of Curse
II. Traits of a Blessed Life (3:10–12)
  A. Keep the Tongue from Evil
  B. Turn from Evil
  C. Pursue Peace
  D. Pray

DISCUSSION QUESTIONS

1. How does the gospel encourage the kind of social interactions Peter describes in this passage?

2. What does it look like to have unity of mind with other believers? What about sympathy? Brotherly love? A tender heart? A humble mind? Can you think of an example of each of these in action in the church?

3. What does it look like for a believer to bless instead of repaying evil for evil? Can you share a positive or negative example of this in action?

4. Read Psalm 34. Why does Peter quote such an extensive section from it? How does the psalm's context inform Peter's words?

1 Peter 3:13–17

EXEGETICAL IDEA

Peter encouraged the readers that if God willed their righteous suffering, they must consider themselves blessed, fear God above all else, and be prepared for evangelistic opportunities.

THEOLOGICAL FOCUS

Believers who suffer for righteousness must consider themselves blessed, fear God above all else, and be prepared for evangelistic opportunities.

PREACHING IDEA

Turn Periods of Persecution into Opportunities for Evangelism.

PREACHING POINTERS

Peter's readers knew suffering. Nero reigned terror on Christians, feeding them to wild beasts, lighting them on fire, crucifying them. Many of Peter's readers likely knew believers who suffered death—some friends, some family. Suffering for righteousness's sake was a reality for these Christians and in 1 Peter 3:13–17, Peter speaks directly to the persecuted church. How should one facing death on a daily basis love his persecutors? What perspective should such Christians have on their sufferings and trials?

Most believers in the Western world do not know such persecution. Some have had the unpleasant experience of losing a job because of their outspoken faith, or perhaps getting sued because of their business's moral stance. Very few believers face torture and death and only some have experienced suffering truly for doing what is good. But even if modern readers have not experienced persecution to the extent of Peter's original audience, the time is coming (Matt. 24:9; John 15:20; 2 Tim. 3:12) and this text prepares Christians for such unpleasantries.

Even more than that, it puts suffering and apologetic witnessing in the correct theological perspective. Most people desire immediate escape when undergoing pressure, but Peter's view is that it should not cause us fear, trouble, or even spiritual harm. In fact, with the right perspective, believers can turn times of persecution into opportunities for evangelism.

SUFFERING FOR RIGHTEOUSNESS (3:13–17)

LITERARY STRUCTURE AND THEMES (3:13–17)

This section of text begins the second half of the body middle of the letter. The first half was composed of the household codes (2:11–3:12). This half focuses on the suffering of Christians and the coming judgment, which will vindicate the righteous (3:13–4:11).

Peter connects this half of the body middle to the other half with a question: "Who can ultimately harm you if you are passionate about doing good?" Peter expected the obvious answer—no one! Nevertheless, Peter noted that there is a real possibility that they will temporarily suffer for righteousness. The rest of the text speaks to how believers should view such suffering. First, Peter asked them to view such suffering as a blessing (v. 14a) Second, he encouraged them to fear God, not their adversaries (vv. 14b–15). Doing this will cause questions to arise in the minds of their persecutors, so Peter gave readers a third admonition: They were to be prepared to answer questions about their hope (v. 15). With this last command, Peter gave some guidance; readers were to guard their responses so that both their conduct and words witnessed to the grace of the Lord (v. 16). The final verse summarized why they should view suffering as a blessing and reminded them that suffering for evildoing received no blessing (v. 17).

The themes of this section include the following: God's protection over his saints; the blessing of suffering for righteousness; the believer's required response to persecutors; and the necessity to be prepared to verbally defend the gospel with grace and kindness.

- *Blessed Are the Persecuted (3:13–14a)*
- *Fear God, Speak for God (3:14b–3:16)*
- *God's Will and Righteous Suffering (3:17)*

EXPOSITION (3:13–17)

This section of text is often referred to as the "apologetic mandate." The name is given for a reason; nevertheless, the passage is broader than simple defense of the faith. Peter was addressing the fears of the readers. Could someone ultimately harm them as they pursued good (v. 13)? Peter responded in the negative. Nevertheless, they may endure suffering, and if they do, it is God's will that they do (v. 17). Accordingly, they should consider themselves blessed (v. 14). They also should not fear, for knowing their savior, they have nothing else to fear (v. 15). Such a response is unexpected by unbelievers, and such unbelievers may be led to ask questions about the hope that prevents the believer's fear (v. 15). Peter notes the responsibilities of believers: be prepared for the questions and answer with kindness. This winsomeness—the combination of knowledge with grace—may lead unbelievers to shame and ultimately repentance (v. 16). But even if it does not, Peter argues that it is better to suffer because one follows God's will than to suffer for doing evil (v. 17).

Blessed Are the Persecuted (3:13–14a)

Peter noted that those who suffer for doing good are blessed and no one can ultimately harm them.

3:13. While it is clear Peter began a new section here, he connected it closely with what preceded by a conjunction (καί) best translated "now" (NRSV, ESV). The conjunction is used inferentially and reveals the way that believers should respond to unbelievers harming them for the sake of the gospel. This text provides an answer to an unstated question that is likely facing the audience: If believers have God's face positively turned toward them, and if God's ear is open to their prayer, then how should believers view their present suffering?

Peter asked a rhetorical question to begin this section. There are two divergent ways to take the question. Peter could be asking, "Now who would harm believers when they are passionate about doing good?" On this reading, Peter would be addressing the ridiculousness of the thought that one should suffer for pursuing right actions. A better way of taking the phrase, however, is, "Now who could *ultimately* harm you if you are passionate for doing good?" On this reading, Peter is not addressing the irrationality of unbelievers' actions. Instead, he is addressing more central questions: How could believers experience true harm, and who could inflict such harm?

The latter interpretation makes better sense of the context, for as noted above Peter suggested a close connection between the previous context and this context. The psalm Peter just quoted teemed with eschatological overtones, making an eschatological interpretation more likely here. This reading also makes better sense of the historical context, for Peter's readers were already experiencing suffering for their honorable conduct (4:12–19); the question "Who would harm you?" makes little sense if the readers were already amid such persecution.

Finally, based on the similarities of this teaching with Jesus's teaching, it is likely that Peter was echoing the words of the Lord when Jesus spoke of not fearing persecutors, but rather fearing the Lord who would be the ultimate judge (Matt. 10:28–31 // Luke 12:4–7).

Peter assumed that his readers would be "zealous" (ζηλωταί) for good works. Being a zealot[1] for something referred to dedicating oneself with deep commitment to a particular cause. Paul spoke of his preconversion commitment to Judaism as a form of zealousness for the law (Acts 22:3; Gal. 1:14). And, in a passage quite similar to this one, Paul spoke of those Christ redeemed as a holy people "zealous to do good deeds" (Titus 2:14). The direction of the readers' passion was to be toward the "good," which clearly refers to good deeds.

3:14a. Having just mentioned that no one can ultimately harm believers, Peter quickly added that this did not mean they could not experience temporal harm. To express this, Peter used a rare form of the Greek verb (an optative[2]; πάσχοιτε), which has led to some confusion concerning Peter's meaning in this conditional clause. Often the optative verb form refers to events that are of a remote possibility. But since Peter's readers were already experiencing suffering, such a meaning is unlikely. Instead, the optative appears to express the sporadic nature of persecution. Accordingly, Peter did not doubt the reality of the persecution; instead, he gave contingency to the timing of when such

---

1 Zealot. This word would become associated with the zealots, who were intimately involved in the disturbances in Jerusalem leading to the destruction of the city in A.D. 70. It is likely for this reason numerous text-critical issues exist in this passage. It is likely that some later scribes found the association troubling and exchanged it with something consistent in thought but less offensive in terminology. The most common variant is "imitators" or "followers" (μιμηταί; KJV).

2 Optative. Peter gives this question by means of a partial fourth-class conditional statement. It is partial because the fourth-class conditional is formed by having an optative in both the protasis and apodosis of the conditional clause. In this case, the verb in the apodosis is implied. Wallace speaks of the fourth-class conditional as expressing a "possible condition in the future, usually a remote possibility" (Wallace, 1996, 699–701).

persecution would occur (cf. Achtemeier, 1996, 231; Schreiner, 2003, 171). While there may be times when persecution is absent, there will be others when it strikes with ferocity. Such periods are not always constant, and when they come, they should not be a surprise.

Peter spoke specifically of suffering endured "for the sake of righteousness." Peter had already mentioned that a believer should only suffer for righteous causes (2:20), and it is a point he would return to again (4:15). The repetition highlights the importance of right conduct. Believers should never suffer for wrongdoing, for that is antithetical to their commitment to Christ and their witness to the world. Nevertheless, believers must be prepared for suffering due to their commitment to Christ and his righteous commands. Indeed, only suffering that comes upon believers due to their right conduct could properly be considered persecution.

Peter concluded the conditional clause by quoting Jesus, who noted that those who endure persecution for righteous causes are "blessed." Some English translations have "will be blessed" (ESV), while most simply have "you are blessed" (NIV, NASB, NRSV, etc.). The difference exists because Peter did not supply a verb, leaving the reader to imply the verb. The implied verb could be future or present. In favor of the present rendering are the words of Jesus, "Blessed are you when people revile you and persecute you and utter all kinds of evil against you falsely on my account" (Matt. 5:11). It is clear that Peter was drawing from these words; consequently, it is likely that Peter was noting the present blessed status of the readers. Of course, such an interpretation does not deny the future blessing of believers, for as Jesus says in Matthew 5:11, the reward for such suffering is great reward in heaven—a theme Peter has already mentioned (1:4).

"Blessed" is sometimes wrongly translated as "happy." Such a rendering erroneously focuses on the emotional state of the believer. Instead, the focus is on the divine vantage point

from which the believer is viewed. As such, a translation like "privileged" captures the sense well (BDAG s.v. "μακάριος" 611). From the divine vantage point—the only one that matters eternally—the suffering believer is to consider himself favored. Of course, such a consideration may lead to happiness in the present. Nevertheless, it is important to keep the order correct; joy comes as a result of the believer's recognition of God's positive outlook on his life and actions, not directly as a result of the persecution.

Some might find it odd that Peter did not detail why the believer was to consider himself blessed. The likely answer is that he expected his readers to recognize the reference to Jesus's words. In the Sermon on the Mount, Jesus noted that those who suffer for righteousness should rejoice greatly (Matt. 5:12). The reason for such rejoicing is twofold: there is a great reward in heaven, and believers in past generations (i.e., prophets) also experienced such suffering. This latter point aligned Jesus's readers with saints from previous generations and gave them some confidence in their relation to the Lord. Though Peter did not mention it explicitly in this context, his readers would likely have recognized that they align both with the prophets of old and with Jesus in their suffering. In other words, if Peter's listeners were encouraged to see that they were following in the steps of the prophets, Peter's readers would have been encouraged to see that they were following the prophets *and* Jesus.

Fear God, Speak for God (3:14b–3:16)
Peter commanded the readers to reject the fear of those who persecuted them; instead, they must fear God and be prepared to graciously answer questions about their faith, with the hope that those who question may be converted.

3:14b. This verse along with the following three provide directives for how Peter's readers were to respond to suffering for righteous action.

Peter first provided two negative commands concerning how they should not respond (3:14b) and then provided a positive command (3:15a) followed by a consideration of how that positive command is to be carried out (3:15b–16). The section is concluded by a summary statement (3:17), which reinforces the positive side of suffering for righteousness.

Peter in the first half of 3:14 considered the words of Jesus as he encouraged the readers who were experiencing unjust suffering. The second half of the verse and the first half of the next reflected on the words of Septuagint Isaiah 8:12c–13.[3] Indeed, all three of the commands in this section are taken from Isaiah.

Isaiah 8:11–15

For the LORD spoke thus to me with his strong hand upon me, and warned me not to walk in the way of this people, saying: "Do not call conspiracy all that this people calls conspiracy, and do not fear what they fear, nor be in dread. But the LORD of hosts, him you shall honor as holy. Let him be your fear, and let him be your dread. And he will become a sanctuary and a stone of offense and a rock of stumbling to both houses of Israel, a trap and a snare to the inhabitants of Jerusalem. And many shall stumble on it. They shall fall and be broken; they shall be snared and taken."

The two negative commands are "do not fear the fear of them" and "do not be frightened." In order to understand what Peter means by "fearing the fear of them"[4] we must understand the context of the Isaiah quotation. God was speaking to Isaiah and his followers, who were members of the Southern Kingdom of Israel (Judah). There were many rumors about the supposed coming attack orchestrated by the leaders of the Northern Kingdom (Israel) and Syria. God told Isaiah and his followers that they should not "fear what the people feared," which likely referred to the rumors of the coming invasion. Peter embraced this command for a new context. While living under Roman rule, Peter's readers had little fear of political enemies invading; nevertheless, the principle that God's people should not fear the things unbelievers fear crosses all historical contexts. That Peter did not mention a specific object of fear suggests that he wanted to keep the principle broad. In sum, since believers were born again, they have a different view of the world and a different set of values and hopes. These lead them to different objects of ultimate concern.

Peter's second command is closely related to the first, yet it is distinct. The first calls for the readers not to live out the concerns that motivate unbelievers. The second calls for believers to reject the thoughts that lead to such concerns. Peter noted that the believers must not "be troubled" (ταραχθῆτε). This word refers to that which causes "inward turmoil," or that leads to one being "stir[ed] up, disturb[ed], unsettle[ed], [or] throw[n] into confusion" (BDAG s.v. "ταράσσω" 990). In many ways, this is the more difficult command. It is one thing not to act on anxious thoughts; it

---

3 Septuagint Isaiah 8:12c–13. The Septuagint is exceptionally close to the exact wording of this text, showing that Peter was most certainly citing it. Compare the Septuagint text (τὸν δὲ φόβον αὐτοῦ οὐ μὴ φοβηθῆτε οὐδὲ μὴ ταραχθῆτε· κύριον αὐτὸν ἁγιάσατε, καὶ αὐτὸς ἔσται σου φόβος; Isa. 8:12–13) with Peter's Greek (τὸν δὲ φόβον αὐτῶν μὴ φοβηθῆτε μηδὲ ταραχθῆτε, κύριον δὲ τὸν Χριστὸν ἁγιάσατε ἐν ταῖς καρδίαις ὑμῶν; 1 Peter 3:14b–15a).

4 "Fearing the fear of them." When quoting the Greek text, Peter modified the singular referent (αὐτοῦ) to a plural referent (αὐτῶν). The plural genitive αὐτῶν can be taken as a subjective or objective genitive. If subjective, the meaning remains the same as the Hebrew, and Peter calls for people not to "fear what they fear (cf. NIV). If objective, however, a reading such as "Do not fear their intimidation" (NASB) makes better sense. On this reading, Peter's readers are called to avoid fearing those who persecute them.

is another to reject such anxious thoughts. In the next verse, Peter identified how the readers would be able to accomplish this high order.

3:15. After Peter noted what the persecuted-for-righteousness readers should not do in the first two commands, Peter provided one positive command slightly modified from the Isaiah text—"in your hearts honor Christ the Lord as holy." By starting with a contrastive conjunction (δέ; "but"), Peter indicated that their response was to be distinct from that which stemmed from the fear and anxiety that motivated unbelievers.

By the contrast, Peter aligned "fear" with "honor" (i.e., do not fear; instead, honor). These concepts are united in biblical thought in reference to the concept of the fear of the Lord. One who fears the Lord knows who the Lord is and thus lives appropriately in light of that knowledge. Included in such knowledge is a recognition of the vastness of God's power and a recognition of the holiness of God's justice. Accordingly, Peter was tacitly acknowledging that those who fear the Lord by honoring him need not fear what the world fears. Put differently, those who fear the Lord have nothing else to fear.

The word translated "honor" (ἁγιάσατε) is closely related to the concept of sanctification (e.g., the KJV has "sanctify Christ as Lord"). To sanctify means to set something apart as holy. In this context, Peter was calling his readers to set Christ apart from the things of this world. Christ is in a class of his own, and nothing deserves the same recognition, attention, and honor as he does. Those who know him must give him pride of place in their thinking. It is only in this way that they can truly escape the fear that holds others in bondage. Indeed, Peter noted that this honor must originate in the readers' hearts. In biblical conception, the heart is the emotional, cognitive, and volitional center. The solution, then, to the fear and anxiety that naturally comes upon humanity is a robust knowledge of Christ, a knowledge that is not merely intellectual but is grounded in a wholistic commitment to Jesus.

Peter modified the quotation from Isaiah slightly. In the Isaiah passage, the text indicates that instead of fearing what the unbelievers feared, Isaiah's readers should "honor the Lord as holy." The name "Lord" in that context is the covenant name of God—Yahweh. Peter, however, said that his readers should "honor Christ as Lord." The implication was surely not missed by Peter's readers. Jesus stands in the place of Yahweh, and he deserves the same honor Isaiah's followers gave to Yahweh. That Peter could so easily substitute the name of Jesus indicates that Peter identified Jesus with Yahweh.

While avoiding fear and anxiety and while honoring Christ as Lord, the readers were to "always be prepared to make a defense." This admonition was not given as an imperative (as the prior commands were); instead, it was given as a simple adjective. By using this form, Peter noted that this is not the central command; nevertheless, it follows from the command. Most English versions supply an imperative verb ("be") to clarify the meaning. While the believers were to be honoring Christ, they were at the same time to be preparing to provide a defense. The connection seems to be the following: when a believer does not fear what unbelievers fear and honors the Lord above all else, unbelievers take notice and are apt to ask questions.

Peter noted that they should be prepared to give a defense concerning their hope. One might have expected Peter to encourage them to defend their "faith." In many ways, Peter's conception of hope is closely related to faith (cf. 1:21). Nevertheless, the choice here is intentional. Hope is "the looking forward to something with some reason for confidence respecting fulfillment" (BDAG s.v. "ἐλπίς" 319). In Peter's readers' case, this included the "living hope" that they had received as a result of Christ's resurrection when they were born again (1:3). As a result of that climactic event, they have now been encouraged to "set their hope fully on the coming grace" (1:13). Such hope undergirds the believer's life and is the source of his or her unique identity and action (1:3, 13, 21; 3:5). Unsurprisingly, then, when such hope is exposed, unbelievers are curious.

By using the words "reason" (λόγον) and "defense" (ἀπολογίαν), Peter tacitly confirmed that the hope they have is a rational hope. Some have supposed Christianity to be an emotional crutch; Peter had no such conception. He revealed that Christianity was a rational choice based on firm expectations. The word for "defense" (ἀπολογίαν) is the Greek word from which we get the word "apologetics." This branch of Christian study considers how best one may defend the Christian belief system with rational arguments. Of course, Peter had no such formal idea in mind. He simply believed that all believers, not just the intellectual elite, could give a reasoned response to those who asked them to defend the foundation of their hope.

3:16. English versions differ on the location of the end of the previous verse and the beginning of this one. Some include "yet do it with gentleness and respect" as the conclusion of verse 15 (NASB, ESV, NIV), while others include it at the beginning of verse 16 (NET, CSB, NRSV). Because its content fits naturally with the next clause ("having a good conscience"), it is here considered under verse 16.

After indicating the necessity of being prepared to defend one's hope, Peter noted two characteristics necessary for believers to have when they give their answer. The translation of the two terms is dependent on how one understands Peter's message. Either Peter is considering one's relation to God or to men. If it is to God, then a good translation would be "respond with humility and reverence." Such a translation makes excellent sense of Peter's use of "fear/reverence" (e.g., 1:17; 2:17), which is generally directed

toward God in 1 Peter. If it is toward men, then a good translation would be "respond with gentleness and respect." In favor of this translation is the purpose clause that follows, which shows that the concern of this passage is how unbelievers will respond to the answers provided by believers. Though a choice is difficult, it is best to see these admonitions as reflecting the readers' concern to be gracious and loving in verbal response.

Why would Peter need to encourage the readers to respond with gentleness and respect? Likely it was because the questioners were the same people persecuting the believers. A natural, human response is to lash out or to respond with a critical spirit. Peter, however, called for the readers to rise above such petty responses and to communicate love with both the content of their speech and their conduct.

By communicating with gentleness and respect, they would be able to "keep a clear conscience." Though not a formal command, this admonition had the force of an imperative. The conscience spoke of the "inward faculty of distinguishing right and wrong" (BDAG s.v. "συνείδησις" 967). That Peter believed the readers' conscience would bother them if they responded harshly suggests that the Spirit they received at the new birth was teaching them to respond with grace.

The purpose of responding verbally with gentleness and grace was not merely to maintain a good conscience. Peter clarified that they should speak kindly so that "when slandered, those who revile their good behavior in Christ may be put to shame." This passage highlights the type of persecution Peter's readers were facing. Peter did not speak of physical or governmental persecution; rather, he spoke of verbal and social persecution. Of course, the latter can lead to the former. Nevertheless, at this point, Peter's readers were being verbally slandered. To "slander" (καταλαλεῖσθε) refers to speaking negatively of someone and is often, as here, associated with saying something false about another (cf. 2:12).

The content of their slanderous speech is, shockingly, the readers' "good behavior in Christ." One might think that those seeking to do good would be sheltered from criticism, yet it is the very good-doing that was causing the slander. For those who have followed Peter's letter so far, this is unsurprising, for the new birth has caused a shift of values and actions. Peter highlighted this by noting that their good conduct was "in Christ."[5] The believers' new lifestyle was at odds with their former way of life (4:3). As exiles and strangers, their conduct appeared foreign and perhaps even threatening.

Peter encouraged his slandered readers by noting the possibility that their persecutors "may be put to shame." Indeed, this is the purpose for why they responded, defending their hope with gentleness and kindness. It is not clear, however, what type of shame Peter had in mind. Commentators are split between two options: a temporal humbling, leading to salvation; or an eschatological humbling, leading to eternal judgment.

The case for an eschatological humbling is partly based on the language used. The term "put to shame" was used in 1 Peter 2:6 (quoting Isa. 28:16) in a way that clearly referred to final judgment. On this reading, Peter was encouraging his readers that though they were experiencing great trouble, they must maintain their hope and defend it graciously, so that one day their enemies would hang their heads in shame before the judgment of God, admitting that the believers were innocent of such slanderous charges.

While the eschatological reading is possible, there is reason to think Peter was speaking of a temporal shaming. First, though "put to shame" can have the eschatological meaning above, its range of meaning clearly includes a type of humbling not resulting in eternal judgment (Luke 17:13; 2 Cor. 7:14; 9:4; BDAG s.v. "καταισχύνω" 517). Second, a temporal reading fits nicely with Peter's earlier admonition that his readers must "live such good lives among the pagans that, though they accuse you of doing wrong, they may see your good deeds and glorify God on the day he visits us" (2:12). As we argued in 2:12, the reference to glorifying God is a reference to the conversion of unbelievers. The parallels with that verse are strong. In both unbelievers were speaking falsely about the good conduct of believers, and in both Peter envisioned that the unbeliever would see the good deeds of the believer. If 2:12 speaks of the response of the unbeliever as glorifying God by repenting and placing his or her trust in Christ, then surely that is the meaning of this passage as well.

God's Will and Righteous Suffering (3:17)

Peter compared suffering for doing good to suffering for doing evil, noting that God sometimes ordains righteous suffering.

3:17. This verse begins with the conjunction "for" (γάρ), which connects this statement with what comes before. It is possible to read it as strengthening the prior clause, but it is best seen as reinforcing the entire thought from 3:13–17. In other words, Peter was encouraging his readers that they should endure unjust suffering, because "it is better to suffer for doing good than for doing evil." On the surface such a statement appears simplistic, yet there is a depth provided by the biblical worldview. The reason it is better to suffer for doing good is that there is an eschatological reward for such suffering (1:6; 3:14; 4:13). Suffering endured for wrongdoing, on the other hand, promises no reward. This is the second

---

5   "In Christ." Peter's conception of "in Christ" is clearly not as developed as Paul's (e.g., Eph. 1:1, 4, 7, 11, 13). Nevertheless, Peter and Paul knew one another, and it is likely that they shared theological language.

time Peter has warned his readers about the possibility that their suffering may be caused by their own sin (2:20), and he will warn them once more before the epistle is finished (4:15).

Suffering Endured for Wrongdoing

Some see eschatological implications in Peter's words. For instance, Michaels summarizes the passage this way: "If it should be God's will that we suffer, it is better to suffer now, as doers of good at the hands of evil men, than on the day of visitation, when these same evil-doers shall receive their just punishment from the eternal Judge of all men" (Michaels, 1967, 398). Such an interpretation does fit well within the eschatological thought of 1 Peter. Nevertheless, the chief liability is that the New Testament does not use the word translated "suffering" (πάσχοιτε) for God's divine judgment of unbelievers. When this fact is combined with the theme Peter has developed in the letter that believers should avoid suffering for wrongdoing (2:20; 4:15), it is more likely that he once more encourages avoidance of evil.

Peter once more addressed what would likely have been a question on the minds of his readers. The issue is a classic one. If God is for his people, and if God is sovereign, then why are God's people suffering? Peter did not directly address the question here or within the epistle more broadly. Instead, he baldly asserted that if God's people suffer for righteousness, it is only at his allowance. The verbal form Peter chose (optative) may have indicated that this is a rare occurrence, but it more likely highlighted that suffering is an occasional experience of God's people. It is not always the case that believers experience suffering for doing good, but if God so wills it, then it will take place. This would certainly have been a comfort to those who were suffering.

THEOLOGICAL FOCUS

The exegetical idea (Peter encouraged the readers that if God willed their righteous

suffering, they must consider themselves blessed, fear God above all else, and be prepared for evangelistic opportunities) leads to this theological focus: believers who suffer for righteousness must consider themselves blessed, fear God above all else, and be prepared for evangelistic opportunities.

Contrary to many common beliefs, God has not promised his followers to shield them from all suffering. Neither will passion for good deeds lead to the avoidance of suffering. Instead, good deeds may be the catalyst for suffering, and God may will that his people suffer. How then should believers think of such suffering? This text indicates that believers of all ages should consider suffering for righteousness a blessing. More specifically, they should consider themselves blessed, both because of the affirmation of their relationship with God that it brings, and because God has promised eternal rewards to those who faithfully suffer in this way.

When one endures suffering, the natural response is to fear those who cause the suffering and to fear the suffering itself. Peter provides an alternative for believers. By fearing the Lord and honoring him, believers have nothing left to fear. He is sovereign over their experiences, and though he allows temporary suffering (3:17), he has demonstrated through the gospel his love for his people (3:18), and he has promised that he would make all things right (5:10). Those who remain faithful will find that suffering for righteousness is worth the temporary pain.

One of the most unexpected blessings of suffering is the opportunity it provides for believers to share the hope they maintain. Pressure reveals the strength of the object pressed against, and in the same way, when the believer's hope is being crushed, yet they maintain their faith, this is of great interest to unbelievers. Peter expects that believers who righteously suffer may by means of that suffering see the redemption of those who cause their suffering. They simply need to live faithfully, while preparing to share their hope when they are asked.

PREACHING AND TEACHING STRATEGIES

Exegetical and Theological Synthesis

Why do good people suffer for doing good things? How can a loving God allow righteous people to endure the inflictions of evil people? Couldn't God just bless the righteous with comfort and ease of life?

Many writers of Scripture pondered such questions. Several psalms wrestle with how God seems absent when evil people prosper and righteous people suffer. Psalm 13:2 asks, "How long shall my enemy be exalted over me?" Asaph struggles with the prosperity of the wicked all throughout Psalm 73. Psalm 37 offers theological reflection on how to respond to the apparent victories of sinners.

The problem is not new. Peter speaks to a people who know the feeling of suffering for doing what is righteous. When choosing to be honest instead of deceptive means that your unethical coworker gets a promotion before you . . . when sharing the gospel lands a missionary in jail . . . when witnessing to a neighbor leads to nasty stares and a cold shoulder—these are the times when Peter's words are most needed.

Ultimately, the passage points readers to the gospel. Who is the ultimate example of suffering for righteousness' sake? *Jesus.* He demonstrates not only the proper way of enduring such oppression, but also the glory that results when it is endured faithfully. If God had a sovereign plan to use the greatest evil in the world (the death of his Son) to bring about the greatest good (the offer of salvation), how much more can we trust that God has a purpose and reason behind our righteous suffering?

Preaching Idea

Turn Periods of Persecution into Opportunities for Evangelism.

Contemporary Connections

What does it mean?

In order for the congregation to grasp the concept of using persecution for evangelistic opportunities, the preacher will need to explain several elements of Peter's words. First, the preacher must carefully distinguish between suffering for righteousness's sake and suffering for foolishness's sake. Sharing your faith during lunch break and then facing ridicule by your coworkers is suffering for righteousness's sake. Getting fired for standing on the serving counter in the middle of your shift with a bullhorn in hand, shouting the gospel at patrons would be suffering for foolishness's sake. Peter's words only apply to the former, not the latter. The preacher must encourage Christians to be wise as serpents and innocent as doves while strategically picking opportunities for active evangelism (Matt. 10:16).

Second, preachers should explain the term "apologetics" if they choose to use it in the sermon. And they should, given that the word comes from the Greek in 3:15 (see exposition). But an "apology" means something different to most modern listeners. When practicing apologetics, we do not apologize for our faith; we defend it. A brief explanation will suffice to help orient listeners.

Finally, the relationship between God's will and suffering should take prominence in the sermon. Persecution cannot be an opportunity for evangelism unless God has divinely ordained such a relationship. The preacher can point to passages such as Psalm 2:2–4, which depicts God laughing at the attempts of the enemy against his people, or Deuteronomy 32:39, which plainly states that God is sovereign over both life and death. When properly understood, God's sovereignty over suffering and evil is a comfort, easing our troubled hearts (1 Peter 3:14).

Is it true?

Can persecution really be used as an opportunity for evangelism? The preacher needs only to show a few examples in Scripture and church history to illustrate the point. The book of Acts gives several good examples to choose from. Just before he was stoned to death, Stephen preached a sermon, sharing the gospel with his persecutors (Acts 7). When Paul and Silas were imprisoned for sharing their faith, they used the opportunity to sing hymns of praise and preach to both prisoners and guards, leading to the conversion of the jailer and his whole family (Acts 16:16–40). Later in his writings, Paul even said that being in prison gave *greater* opportunity to spread the good news of Jesus Christ (Phil. 1:12–14).

This pattern holds true for Christians all over the world, today and yesterday. Nero's persecution scattered Christians throughout the world. Each Christian who fled his or her home took one essential thing with them: the gospel. The website impantokratoros.gr traces the spread of Christianity through persecution for the first four hundred years of the church's existence.[6] As Tertullian once said, "The blood of martyrs is the seed of Christians."

Many people dedicated their lives to missions work, inspired by the faith and commitment of both the martyrs and their family members who completed their unfinished task.

Now what?

This passage calls Christians to take a more active role in witnessing the gospel to others, even (or especially so) when there is persecution. The preacher should not fear challenging Christians who have never faced persecution to ask themselves: Why not? Have they hidden their faith to the extent that no one knows they are Christians? Have they failed to share the gospel as actively as they should? Persecution falls under God's sovereignty (1 Peter 3:17), so believers who have never had the experience should not be chastised from the pulpit for it, but instead encouraged to honestly reflect on the possibility that their lack of witness may have something to do with this lack of blessing.

Second, the preacher should encourage the church to be prepared to make a defense for their hope and faith. Clearly explain what this looks like. Consider showing clips from street evangelists/apologists like Ray Comfort, who fearlessly shares his faith (and defends it when challenged) to unbelievers. Point the church to helpful evangelistic and apologetic resources that will strengthen their ability to lovingly defend their faith, such as Lee Strobel's *The Case for Faith* or Josh and Sean McDowell's *Evidence That Demands a Verdict*. Christians should not only feel *encouraged* to share and defend at the end of the sermon; they should feel *equipped* to do so, or at least know that they are on the right path to being equipped.

Creativity in Presentation

If teaching this passage in an interactive environment, consider using role-play or a mock debate format to help participants grow in their skills of defending their faith. The teacher will want to use his insight into his cultural environment, in order to know which particular aspect of apologetics he should focus his training.

For example, we (Tim and I) live in an area heavily populated with Muslims. It would benefit my congregation to have focused training on witnessing and answering the objections of the Muslim population. If you do not feel equipped to lead such a training yourself, bring in an expert—either a local missionary or seminary professor or another pastor or apologist who regularly ministers to such a population.

---

6   "The Spread of Christianity through Persecutions," Holy Monastery of Pantocrator of Melissochori, https://www.impantokratoros.gr/spread-christianity-persecutions.en.aspx?__cf_chl_jschl_tk__=pmd_a5fee8081114ef-35a702967648ead9c5c4206e08-1628970037-0-gqNtZGzNAjijcnBszQi6.

Teach the people the basics of such witnessing, then pair them up and have one of them play the Christian, and one of them the Muslim. Allow them to practice what it feels like to have their faith challenged.

This type of activity can help strengthen believers in a number of important areas—be it ministry to Muslims, apologetic defense of creation, or a discussion about the Bible's reliability. Choose a topic to home in on, then train and develop missionaries from within the congregation to go out and use their skills to share the gospel. Then, put the skills to good use by evangelizing after the service. Should persecution or trials arise, turn them into opportunities for even more gospel preaching.

Preachers may want to consider the following chiastic-style outline to help with sermon preparation:

Introduction
A. Suffering for Righteousness (3:13–14a)
   B. Speaking with Respect (3:14b–16)
A¹. Suffering for Righteousness (3:17)
Conclusion

DISCUSSION QUESTIONS

1. Can you share a time when you suffered for doing what is good?

2. What does it mean to "always be prepared to make a defense to anyone who asks you for a reason for the hope that is in you"? Why do you think Peter uses the word "hope" here instead of "faith"?

3. Do you feel prepared to make such a defense? Why or why not?

4. How does God's sovereign will relate to suffering and persecution? How does it give us comfort in such times?

1 Peter 3:18–22

EXEGETICAL IDEA
Peter encouraged the suffering readers by pointing to the example of Christ, who suffered for a noble cause and was publicly vindicated.

THEOLOGICAL FOCUS
Suffering believers are to be encouraged by the example of Christ, who suffered for a noble cause and was publicly vindicated.

PREACHING IDEA
Christ's Vindication over Suffering Motivates a Christian's Victory over Sin.

PREACHING POINTERS
What motivates a believer to overcome suffering? Peter's readers must have wrestled with that very question. Why continue in the Christian faith if it only produced increased persecution and torment from maniacal dictators like Nero? When doing the right thing only gets you punished more severely, why do the right thing? Peter challenged his readers to consider Christ's example. Jesus suffered, died, and rose victorious over sin and death. His victory and perseverance through suffering motivates a Christian's victory through similar trials.

This holds true for modern Christians just as much as for those in Peter's day. Though 1 Peter 3:18–22 has more than its fair share of theological conundrums, it offers a clear path to application for believers. The preacher can encourage the church to suffer through the toughest of trials, seeing how Jesus did so first and now reigns victoriously. The passage has a bit of everything: a clear gospel message, challenging theology, and a motivating message.

CHRIST'S SUFFERING LEADING TO EXALTATION
(3:18–22)

LITERARY STRUCTURE AND THEMES (3:18–22)

This section of text continues the second half of the body middle of the letter, which focuses on the suffering of Christians and the coming judgment that will vindicate the righteous (3:13–4:11).

Having just encouraged his readers to consider themselves blessed when they suffer for righteousness, Peter here provided an example of the righteous suffering of Christ. Despite the complexity of the history of interpretation of this passage, the core message is evident by the main clauses: *Jesus suffered to bring believers to God by dying, rising, and ascending to the Father's right hand.* The middle section of the passage (vv. 19–21) highlights Jesus's postresurrection activity, which demonstrates his victory over suffering and death. The main point of the text is that despite Jesus's suffering, he was ultimately victorious.

Themes in this passage include the following: the purpose and extent of Christ's suffering and death; the postresurrection activity of Jesus in relation to the spiritual realm; the analogy of the flood waters to baptism; the function of baptism; and the rewards of Christ's obedience.

- *Suffering, Death, and Resurrection (3:18)*
- *Proclamation to the Spirits (3:19–20)*
- *Baptism and Resurrection (3:21)*
- *Seated at the Right Hand (3:22)*

EXPOSITION (3:18–22)

Though readers often get lost in the trees of this passage, the main lines of the forest are quite clear. Jesus suffered for the purpose of bringing believers to God. Peter provided three participial clauses that highlighted how Jesus accomplished this: by dying, rising, and ascending to the Father. The first and second of these were given in verse 18, while the third was given in verse 22. The interceding verses highlight Jesus's postresurrection and preascension activity. He went in the Spirit to fallen spirits, proclaiming his victory (v. 19). This was a visible demonstration to all angelic beings that Jesus had conquered and earned the right to bring believers into the Father's presence. Having mentioned Noah's generation, Peter, in what might best be described as a slight excursus, spoke of the relation between the floodwater and Spirit baptism, the latter of which is made possible through the resurrection of Jesus (vv. 20–21). Returning to Jesus's ascension, Peter showed how, despite the suffering he endured, Jesus was vindicated and ascended to a place of ultimate authority.

Suffering, Death, and Resurrection (3:18)

Jesus suffered, died, and rose to new life in the Spirit.

3:18. This verse begins the most debated passage in all of 1 Peter. To say that 3:18–22 is disputed would be an understatement. Martin Luther famously spoke of this passage: "a wonderful text is this, and a more obscure passage perhaps than any other in the New Testament, so I do not know for certain just what Peter means" (Luther, 1859, 166). The debate centers on the details of the passage, not its main point. Significantly, there is wide agreement that Peter included this text to highlight the victory of

Christ despite the suffering he endured. The main lines of the text indicate that Jesus suffered, died, rose from the dead, and is at the right hand of God with all authority granted to him. Agreement generally ends there, however. The key questions concern what Jesus did after he was "made alive in the spirit" (v. 18) and before he "went into heaven and is at the right hand of God" (v. 22). Detailed discussion of the debate occurs in the excursus below.

By the opening conjunction ("because"; ὅτι), Peter connected the work of the Messiah to the experience of the readers. Peter recognized the suffering of the readers and highlighted how they could remain faithful amid suffering. To encourage them to faithfulness, he provided Christ's example of unjust suffering. By means of this comparison, Peter offered hope that the readers' suffering might also lead to glorious vindication.

The analogy between the readers and Jesus was not intended to be entirely parallel. Jesus suffered[1] "once" (ἅπαξ), referring primarily to his sacrificial work on the cross. The solitary nature of this sacrifice elsewhere in the New Testament points to its efficacy, as there was no more need for another sacrifice (e.g., Heb. 10:10). The sacrifice was also "for sins." But, as Peter had already made clear, Jesus was innocent (2:22). Therefore, he suffered, "the righteous for the unrighteous." This introduced a second distinction between Jesus's suffering and Peter's readers' suffering. Though it was possible that the readers' suffering may lead to the salvation of others (by causing unbelievers to ask questions and hear the gospel), Jesus's suffering was vicarious. He died in the place of sinners.

The purpose of Jesus suffering was "to bring you to God." Significantly, Peter included the readers in this, as they too were the unrighteous for whom Christ died. The verb translated "bring" (προσαγάγῃ) has the implication of taking someone alongside to give access to someone prominent. Indeed, it can speak of "admission to an audience with a Great King" (BDAG s.v. "προσάγω" 875). The implication of Peter's text is that had Christ not died for the unrighteous, they could not have come to God. This is the consistent testimony of the New Testament, which highlights that Jesus's unique, sinless sacrifice in the place of sinners purchased the right for sinners to come into the presence of God (Matt. 8:17; Mark 10:45; 2 Cor. 5:21; Heb. 4:15; 1 Peter 2:23–25; 1 John 3:5).

This larger passage (3:18–22) unfolds as follows: Jesus suffered to bring people to God. Jesus did this by doing the following three things: being put to death (v. 19), being raised to new life (v. 19), and being seated at the right hand of the Father (v. 22). Though verse 22 is proximally distant from verse 19, this list of three is given in participles that highlight their logical connection. The first and last of these are uncontroversial. It is the testimony of the church that Jesus died and that he was raised to the right hand of the Father. It was his place at the right hand that gave him the opportunity to welcome believers into the Father's presence. The second of the events—the raising to life—however, has occasioned much discussion because the grammar is flexible enough to allow multiple interpretations.

Peter noted that Jesus was "made alive by/ in the S/spirit." There is debate concerning whether the Spirit refers to the Holy Spirit, the physical spirit, or the realm of the spirit. In favor of the small "s" spirit is the apparent contrast presented. Jesus was put to death in

---

1   Suffered. There is text-critical dispute concerning this passage. The reading accepted here is in later manuscripts (B K P), but not in the most ancient manuscripts. Instead of referring to suffering, these older manuscripts say Jesus "died" often adding "for sins" ($\mathfrak{P}^{72}$ ℵ A). Seeing the similarity of the Greek words, it is not surprising that somewhere along the way some manuscripts accidently switched the words ("died" [ἀπέθανεν] for "suffered" [ἔπαθεν]). The context strongly favors "suffered."

the flesh (i.e., his body died), and so he must have been raised in regard to his spirit (i.e., his human spirit was brought to life). On this reading, the main line of this passage would not speak of the resurrection of the body. Instead, it would move from Jesus's death to his intermediate, nonbodily experience and then to the right hand of the Father. It is much more likely, however, that Peter was here speaking of the physical resurrection than that he did not detail the resurrection as a step in Jesus's victorious path to ascension.

The Meaning of 1 Peter 3:18–22

The debates concerning the best interpretation of these verses begin here in earnest. There are five major interpretations of Jesus's activity after "being raised in the Spirit" and before the ascension (see the following chart).[2] Due to space constraints, it is not possible to fully detail each of the views and the criticisms leveled against them. Other resources are able to do this in greater detail (see esp., Dalton, 1965). Here, we will simply mention each of the five views and some of their difficulties.

1 Peter 3:18–22 Interpretations of "Christ Proclaiming to the Spirits in Prison"						
Views	**Where?**	**When?**	**Who?**	**What?**	**Purpose**	**Peter's Point**
Jesus Preached through Noah	Earth	Noah's day	Humans of Noah's day	Gospel	Christ also preached to a hostile society	Proclaim the gospel in the midst of a hostile society
Second Chance for the Rebellious	Sheol/Hades/Hell	Before the resurrection	Humans	Gospel	Giving a second chance for repentance	Wicked dead are given a second chance
Release of Righteous Dead	Sheol/Hades/Hell	Before the resurrection	Humans	Gospel	Releasing Old Testament saints	Old Testament believers are vindicated by Christ
Victory over Rebellious Humans	Sheol/Hades	Before the resurrection	Humans	Victory	Announcing Christ's victory	Jesus suffered unjustly but was vindicated
Victory over Fallen Angels	Sheol/Hades or the Heavens	Before or after the resurrection	Fallen angels	Victory	Announcing Christ's victory	Jesus suffered unjustly but was vindicated

---

2   Chart by Patrick Schreiner (https://twitter.com/pj_schreiner/status/1282667110091587584), used by permission.

In favor of the Holy Spirit is the fact that the New Testament elsewhere connects the resurrection to the Spirit of God (Rom. 1:4; 8:11). On this reading, the dative noun is more likely to be taken as referencing agency: "made alive *by* the Spirit" (CSB, NKJV). The greatest hindrance to this interpretation is that it breaks the apparent parallelism of the dative nouns.[3] Nevertheless, there is no grammatical rule that demands the nouns be used in the same way. It is best to see Peter using the first dative to indicate realm (Jesus died in the realm of the flesh) and the second to indicate agency (but he was made alive by the Spirit; cf. NIV). It is significant that the exact same interpretive difficulty is best resolved in this same manner in 1 Timothy 3:16, where it is indicated that Jesus "appeared in the flesh, but was vindicated by the Spirit."

In sum, this verse highlighted that Jesus suffered with the intent that believers would have access to God. This came about by means of the death and resurrection of Jesus. The resurrection spoken of here was no mere temporary, intermediate state. Instead, it was the glorious resurrection by the Spirit into incorruptible life.

The first view is the most creative and traces back to as far as Augustine (*Epistles* 164.6.15–17), and still has some modern advocates (Grudem, 1988, 211–48). It argues that the passage speaks of Jesus's past preaching in the days of Noah. Accordingly, the passage says nothing about Jesus's postresurrection or intermediate existence. Instead, it refers to Jesus's preincarnate ministry of motivating prophets to proclaim his word. Support for this position is often taken from 1 Peter 1:11, which speaks of "the Spirit of Christ" predicting the Messiah's suffering and subsequent glory. On this reading, Noah was inspired by the Spirit of Jesus to preach to his preflood contemporaries. The greatest challenge to this interpretation is its failure to fit into the context of the passage at hand. If this reading is accurate, then verses 19–21 are a parenthetical observation, seemingly disconnected from the main point, which was Christ's suffering, death, resurrection, and ascension in glorious victory. Additionally, the position fails to explain why Peter noted that Jesus "went," when he did not go anywhere. Few interpreters have found this position convincing.

A second view is that Peter was detailing Christ's spiritual appearance to the wicked dead, particularly the deceased generation of Noah, and offering them a second chance at repentance. According to this view, since so many died without a knowledge of the gospel, it is fitting that Jesus descended to their place of punishment, providing a way of escape for them. This view is often defended by a particular understanding of 1 Peter 4:6, where Peter noted that the gospel was "preached to the dead." As we will say in our exegesis of that passage, however, that passage refers to believers who have died. Accordingly, the NIV is right to translate it "preached to those who are *now* dead." Outside of the fact that such a postmortem opportunity for repentance is outside the scope of the theology of the New Testament (e.g., Heb. 9:27), this view falters in that it fails to adequately explain why Peter speaks specifically of the people in the days of Noah.

A third view of Jesus's activity is that he went in the spirit to the righteous dead who were being held in Sheol (e.g., Calvin, *Institutes* 2.16.8–9). On this view, the righteous dead were

---

3   Apparent parallelism of the dative nouns. It is also possible that the first dative is agency. But this would require that "the flesh" refer to humankind. Thus, "he was put to death by men and was raised by the Spirit."

temporarily separated from God, awaiting the pronouncement of God's victory. Having accomplished the victory through his vicarious death, Jesus was able to visit them, declare his victory, and (in some interpretations) bring them with him to the presence of the Father. This has been a popular view throughout church history, and is often referred to as the "harrowing of hell." The chief liability of this view is that it depends on a view of the afterlife that is not clearly taught in the Scripture. Additionally, this view fails to give an adequate reason why Peter speaks of the days of Noah.

The fourth is similar to the second, though it has a different purpose for the proclamation. Whereas in the first view the proclamation was one of gospel hope and the possibility of repentance, on this view Jesus's message to the dead of Noah's day was one of condemnation. He was confirming to the wicked spirits of unjust men that their judgment had been secured. The significance for Peter's readers was that just as Noah was maligned yet ultimately on the right side, so they too are in the same situation. One day their persecutors will likewise recognize the judgment that has befallen them. Unfortunately, though giving a reason for referencing Noah, this position still falls short of giving an adequate reason Peter referenced the generation of Noah.

The final view is the one that appears most likely contextually and theologically. On this view Jesus entered the place of judgment to proclaim a message of victory over his enemies. The difference between this view and the last is the identity of the enemies. On this interpretation, the enemies are fallen angels. Thus, the message was not salvific, nor did it offer a chance to repent. Instead, it was a declaration that the judgment initiated against the fallen angels was secured by the final victory of Christ. This provided a message of hope to Peter's audience in two different ways. First, they could hope for final vindication over their enemies like Jesus, who also suffered righteously. Second, because Jesus has been victorious over all of the spiritual forces and is at the right hand of the Father, then believers have all the more confidence during their own spiritual exile.

The major hurdles to this interpretation are not exegetical. In fact, this interpretation fits perfectly well with Peter's text, as the following exegetical commentary will show. The major difficulties are conceptual. Such an interpretation fights against the naturalism of our age which finds conceptions of angels and a spiritual realm difficult to comprehend. Peter's readers, however, would have had no trouble with such ideas. The book of 1 Enoch[4] is instructive. This apocryphal work was known in the early church (cf. 2 Peter 2:4; Jude 6), and it puts forward the ancient view that in Genesis 6 the "sons of God" were fallen angels who cohabitated with humans, producing unnatural offspring. As Schreiner rightly notes, "this interpretation was standard in Jewish literature in Peter's day" (see 1 Enoch 6–19; 21; 86–88; 106:13–17; Jubilees 4:15, 22; 5:1; Damascus Document 2:17–19; Testament of Reuben 5:6–7; Testament of Naphtali 3:5; 2 Baruch 56:10–14; cf. Josephus, *Antiquities of the Jews* 1.73; Schreiner, 2003, 188).

---

4   1 Enoch. Enoch is clearly pseudepigraphical (written by someone other than the author mentioned). Nevertheless, the Ethiopian church considers it canonical. The content is purported to be about the life and teaching of Enoch (Gen. 5:18–24). For more information on this book, see Hiehle and Whitcomb (2016).

Selections from 1 Enoch

6:1–5a "And it came to pass when the children of men had multiplied that in those days were born unto them beautiful and comely daughters. And the angels, the children of the heaven, saw and lusted after them, and said to one another: 'Come, let us choose us wives from among the children of men and beget us children.' And Semjaza, who was their leader, said unto them: 'I fear ye will not indeed agree to do this deed, and I alone shall have to pay the penalty of a great sin.' And they all answered him and said: 'Let us all swear an oath, and all bind ourselves by mutual imprecations not to abandon this plan but to do this thing.'"

7:1 "And all the others together with them took unto themselves wives, and each chose for himself one, and they began to go in unto them and to defile themselves with them."

10:11b–14a "And the Lord said unto Michael: 'Go, bind Semjaza and his associates who have united themselves with women so as to have defiled themselves with them in all their uncleanness. And when their sons have slain one another, and they have seen the destruction of their beloved ones, bind them fast for seventy generations in the valleys of the earth, till the day of their judgment and of their consummation, till the judgment that is for ever and ever is consummated. In those days they shall be led off to the abyss of fire: and to the torment and the prison in which they shall be confined for ever.'"

This reading has the advantage of answering a question the other interpretations failed to address—namely, why mention Noah? Noah was mentioned because Peter had a larger goal in mind, and Noah was on the path of explaining that larger narrative. The point of this passage is that Jesus suffered, died, and rose to new life. In that resurrected life, he went to the fallen angels of Noah's day and proclaimed a message of vindication. Then Jesus ascended to the Father, with all angels, authorities, and powers subject to him. The example of Noah and the fallen angels was designed to show that even the rebellious angelic realm is now fully subject to Jesus and the victory he gained through suffering. Now, the readers need not fear even the spiritual realm, for their redeemer Jesus has decisively won the victory and won them access to the Father. The way he did so is powerfully instructive, for he won by suffering and being rejected. In the same way that Jesus gained ultimate victory, so Peter's readers would likewise gain their victory.

Proclamation to the Spirits (3:19–20)

Jesus, in the Spirit, proclaimed a message of victory to spirits imprisoned since the days of Noah.

3:19. The relative pronoun that starts this verse ("in which also"; ἐν ᾧ καὶ) refers to the Spirit[5] from the prior verse. Since this refers to the Holy Spirit, it is best to see this as indicating agency:

---

5   Refers to the Spirit. Interpreters disagree on the correct interpretation, depending on their view of the interpretation of the whole passage. Some argue that it refers to the spiritual realm (Michaels, 1988, 205–6). Thus, Jesus went in the spiritual realm to the spirits. Others argue that the relative pronoun indicates the circumstances or time ("at that time" or "in relation to this"; NIV). Following the normal use of the relative, it is most likely Peter was referencing something just mentioned. In this case, it would be the Spirit from the prior verse.

"by which Spirit he went and made proclamation." Thus, what Jesus did after the resurrection was done through the agency of the Holy Spirit. By the language of the passage, it is clear Jesus went to a distinctive location. As noted in the excursus, the location is debated. Some see it as hell, others as Sheol, and still others as a location of the imprisoned fallen angels. One's view of location is determined chiefly by the audience Jesus was addressing. In the interpretation championed here, Jesus went to the place of judgment reserved for the fallen angels.

When Jesus arrived, he "made a proclamation." The verb for "proclaim" (ἐκήρυξεν) is used elsewhere for the verbal expression of the gospel (e.g., Matt. 24:14; Col. 1:23; 1 Thess. 2:9), but it is also used in a more general sense for any spoken message (cf. Rom. 2:21; Gal. 5:11; Rev. 5:2). Most significantly, Peter used a different word in this letter for the proclamation of the gospel (εὐαγγελισθέν; cf. 1:25). The word Peter chose here (ἐκήρυξεν) had the sense of a "proclamation that is divine in origin" (BDAG s.v. "κηρύσσω" 543). Whether by his own divine authority, or from the authority of his Father, Jesus was making a divine announcement.

The group Jesus proclaims his message to are called "spirits in prison." Though the word for "spirit" (πνεύμασιν) may refer to humans, this is far from its normal meaning in the New Testament. In the only place it speaks of humans in the New Testament, it explicitly clarifies that it does so (Heb. 12:23). Additionally, Peter used another Greek word (ψυχαί) to refer to the spirit of a human (3:20). Though the word for "spirit" (πνεύμασιν) used in this text does not normally refer to humans, it is often used for spiritual beings, especially evil spiritual beings (Matt. 8:16; 12:45; Luke 10:20; 1 Tim. 4:1; Heb. 1:14; Rev. 3:1; 5:6; 16:14; Forbes, 2014, 124).

Peter noted that Jesus's audience was "in prison" (ἐν φυλακή). The term refers to a place where people are guarded, with the idea that they should not be able to escape (Brown, 1971, 4:624). This term is a chief reason to reject the interpretation that these are Old Testament saints. This same word is used in Revelation 20:7 to refer to the prison Satan will be locked in for the thousand years. Obviously, then, the type of prison being considered is not physical; it is a prison strengthened by God's omnipotence to restrain the activity of evil spirits. Jesus went to this domain and made a proclamation to these prisoners.

Peter does not mention why the spirits were imprisoned. This suggests that Peter expected his readers to know the broader context of the discussion. Two other passages speak of a situation where angels sin and are judged by being imprisoned. First, Jude 6 speaks of "the angels who did not keep their positions of authority but abandoned their proper dwelling—these he has kept in darkness, bound with everlasting chains for judgment on the great day." Second Peter 2:4 likewise speaks of a similar judgment: "God did not spare angels when they sinned, but sent them to hell, putting them in chains of darkness to be held for judgment."

In each of these passages, angels sinned, were imprisoned, and awaited a future day of judgment. Clearly then, teaching of this sort was known by Peter and the early church. And the best interpretation of these passages comes from the text of 1 Enoch, as noted above. Jude clearly knows of the book of Enoch, for he quotes it directly (v. 14). If we read 1 Peter in light of these texts, then the "spirits in prison" are the ancient fallen angels who have been imprisoned by God since the time of Noah and are awaiting the final judgment.

3:20. Peter continued to describe the spirits Jesus proclaimed a message of victory over. He highlighted that they were the ones who "in former times did not obey when God patiently waited in the days of Noah during the building of the ark." As noted above, this timeline fits perfectly with the interpretation that the "spirits" are the angels who sinned by cohabitating with human women, bearing children with them. According to the Genesis account (Genesis 6), this activity preceded the flood and was a significant factor that led to God's decisive, worldwide judgment.

The English translation "God waited patiently" represents a more literal "the patience of God waited." By making "patience" (μακροθυμία) the subject of the sentence, Peter emphasized God's patience. Despite the depth of wickedness, God patiently waited during the building up of his wrath. Paul, in Romans 2:4, indicates that God's patience (μακροθυμίας), his delaying the coming judgment, is because such forbearance is designed to "lead to repentance." Though Peter makes no positive mention of God's grace here, Peter elsewhere calls Noah a "preacher of righteousness" (2 Peter 2:5), and the reference here to God's patience likely refers to God's activity of calling sinners to repentance, even while the ark was being built. In the same way, God's patience was waiting in Peter's readers' day as the final judgment was being prepared. The parallel would likely have been recognized by Peter's readers: just as Noah preached God's mercy while the coming judgment was ever approaching, so Peter's readers have opportunity to preach God's mercy as the final, cataclysmic judgment is ever approaching.

Peter then turned his attention to the ark that Noah built, which he noted preserved the

Building the Ark, by James Tissot. Public domain.

life of eight people. Peter clarified that eight people is only a "few" (ὀλίγοι). Significantly, this is the same word Jesus used when he spoke of the "few" that find the narrow path to eternal life (Matt. 7:14). The point seems to be that despite God's extensive patience and the proclamation of grace that accompanies that patience, only some will respond positively to biblical truth. They, as the community of those who are being saved, should not be surprised at their small number. Instead, they should rejoice even more that they are included in those who are being saved.

Those who were saved in Noah's day were "saved through water" (διεσώθησαν δι' ὕδατος). This appears to be an odd way of describing Noah and his family's survival on the ark. One might have expected Peter to have said they were saved "from the water." The key to understanding this is the recognition that Noah and his family were not primarily saved from the flood, but from the wrath of God. It was the flood that appeased the wrath of God, allowing Noah and his kin to have a fresh start. In this way, Noah and his family were actually saved from wrath by means of the new life made possible by the floodwaters.

Baptism and Resurrection (3:21)
Peter highlighted the divine intent of baptism, how it functions, and the basis of its efficacy.

3:21. The syntax of this verse is rather complex.[6] Michaels's translation captures the meaning well: "This water—or baptism, which corresponds to it—now saves you" (Michaels, 1988,

194–95). Peter was comparing the waters of the flood and the waters of baptism. "Correspond" (ἀντίτυπον) does not suggest an equality between the two; instead, it highlights a symbolic or typological connection (BDAG s.v. "ἀντίτυπος" 90; Heb. 9:24). The flood of Noah's day was to be viewed as a pattern that was in some way evidenced also in Christian baptism.

On the surface the similarity of these two appears only related to their connection with water. Nevertheless, there is a deeper connection. The destructive, deadly floodwaters of Noah's day were the means by which God cleansed the world of sin. In a similar way, it is through a death symbolized in baptism that sin is done away in the life of the believer. Thus, Peter can say "baptism saves you . . . through the resurrection of Jesus Christ." This latter clause, separated by a parenthetical clarification (not by physical washing, but by an appeal for a good conscience), is crucial to recognizing what Peter was communicating. The ultimate parallel is represented in the following chart (cf. Elliott, 2001, 669):

Few persons (eight)	You (few persons)
Were saved	Are now saved
Through water	Through the resurrection of Jesus

Peter was addressing the underlying reality that baptism pictures. As Paul indicated in Romans 6, physical baptism pictures the death, burial, and resurrection of the believer with Christ:

---

6   Rather complex. There is debate concerning what the relative pronoun that begins this verse refers to. It could refer to the whole previous clause ("eight souls were saved through water"), or more likely simply "water." The presence of textual issues is likely due to the awkwardness of the syntax. Some mss replaced the nominative pronoun (ὅ) with the dative (ᾧ), which leads to an easier translation: "by which water." Other mss eliminate the relative altogether. It is best to keep the relative, both in light of the textual witnesses (including A B C K P Ψ) and the fact that it is the more difficult reading. Another difficulty concerns the nominatives "baptism" (βάπτισμα) and "corresponds" (ἀντίτυπον). Since the relative appears to indicate the subject, which is the proper subject? On the reading given above, "baptism" stands in apposition to "this water" as does "correspond."

"Do you not know that all of us who have been baptized into Christ Jesus have been baptized into His death? Therefore we have been buried with Him through baptism into death, so that as Christ was raised from the dead through the glory of the Father, so we too might walk in newness of life" (NASB). Baptism was the physical picture of the spiritual reality of the death and resurrection of the believer.

Because the phrase "baptism saves you" may be open to various misunderstandings, Peter clarified that such salvation comes "not as a removal of dirt from the body." Peter's point was that baptism is no mere external event, which only involves the cleansing of the physical body. Such an act could not save, for it could not take away God's wrath. Put simply, it was not the act of baptism that saved them; rather, it was the spiritual reality that they experienced prior to baptism, which led them to being publicly identified with Christ through physical baptism.

The power of this baptism lay not in its removal of dirt from the body, but in its "appeal to God for a good conscience." Two interrelated issues cause interpretive difficulty in this text. First, there is debate concerning the meaning of the word translated "appeal" (ἐπερώτημα). The word only occurs here in the New Testament, and only occurs once in the Septuagint (Dan. 4:7). That Septuagint reference is not helpful, however, for its meaning, "decree," is clearly not applicable in this context. Outside of biblical literature, the word refers to contractual arrangements in which one "pledges" or "promises" obedience to the stipulations of the contract (for detailed references, see Dalton, 1965, 224–28). Some English translations define the term this way: "pledge of a clear conscience" (NIV, NET, CSB). Another way of defining the word, however, is to look at the noun's verbal form (ἐπερωτάω), which occurs with regularity in the New Testament. The verbal form clearly means "to ask for" (BDAG s.v. "ἐπερωτάω" 362). Accordingly, an appropriate definition of the noun form would be "appeal" or "request." Some

English versions also reflect this definition: "appeal for a good conscience" (ESV, NRSV, NASB, LEB).

Before deciding on which definition is best, it is important to observe the second exegetical difficulty, for it is related to the prior one. The genitive noun clause "good conscience" (συνειδήσεως ἀγαθῆς) can be taken as an objective or subjective genitive. If subjective, the following are the options: "a good conscience pledge" or "a good conscience appeal." The problem with both of these interpretations is that they appear to make the reception of salvation subsequent to having a good conscience. The text would then read, "baptism saves you by a good-conscience appeal/pledge." In the first case, God would grant salvation on the basis of a good-conscience appeal; and in the second, he would grant salvation on the basis of the believer's pledge to live faithfully.

The objective genitive reading avoids these difficulties. On the objective genitive reading, Peter is either saying baptism saves as "a pledge for a good conscience" or "an appeal for a good conscience." The former is exegetically possible, and it captures the biblical emphasis on the necessity of obedience in the life of a believer. Further, it is likely that the early church required a statement of Christ's lordship and their obedient intent at one's baptism.

On the other hand, the reading "an appeal for a good conscience" makes best sense of 1 Peter overall, and this text in particular. The contrast Peter presented was that baptism did not wash the physical body, but it did accompany an appeal to God to cleanse the conscience. In other words, the effective power is not the outward washing, but the personal, inward call of repentance and faith made possible because of the resurrection of Christ. Those who partake of this baptism are those who have called on God to make them new, which he does by giving them new birth. Thus, the baptism Peter spoke of is spiritual baptism, which physical baptism publicly illustrates.

Coming back to the broader analogy Peter was presenting, we now see how the flood is a picture of baptism. In both, the righteous are saved because the wrath of God is averted from them and a new path to life is opened to them. In the case of the flood, Noah and his family responded in faith, building the ark and entering it. The new path was opened by the cleansing water of the flood, washing away sinful humanity and providing a place for righteousness to once more dwell. In the case of baptism, believers respond in faith by recognizing their need for cleaning and submitting to baptism, which represented identity with Jesus's death, burial, and resurrection. The new path is provided because of the resurrection of Jesus to new life, which opens the door for believers to share in resurrection life through the new birth.

Seated at the Right Hand (3:22)

Having finished his proclamation, Jesus ascended to the right hand of God, with all powers subject to him.

3:22. To understand the significance of this verse, it is necessary to step back and see what Peter has been leading to in this broader passage. The main theme of the passage is Jesus's suffering, which was done for the purpose of granting believers access into God's presence (v. 18). By means of a number of participles, Peter indicated how Jesus accomplished this. First, Jesus died (v. 18). Second, he was raised from the dead (v. 18). Third, after going to the imprisoned spirits and making a proclamation of his ultimate victory (vv. 19–20), "he went into heaven" (v. 22). The participle in verse 22 concerning Jesus's ascension is the second time in the passage that a verb of movement was used (3:19, 22). The effect is to indicate that there were two parts of his journey; he had to make proclamation before ascending to the Father.

Having entered heaven, "Jesus is at the right hand of God." The location of Jesus is significant for two reasons. First, because Jesus is now with the Father, he can give us access to the Father. Jesus acts as an advocate who has gone before believers to prepare the way for their meeting with the king. It should be remembered that the word Peter used for "access" in verse 18 (προσαγάγῃ) suggested exactly this nuance. Jesus entered heaven for the express purpose of preparing the believer's reception into the presence of the Father (cf. Rom. 8:34).

Jesus's location is significant for a second reason: the right hand is a position of power, authority, and especially honor. It is a position widely recognized to be granted to the Messiah (Ps. 109:1), one that Jesus claimed to be his own (Matt. 26:64; Mark 14:62; Luke 22:69), and a position spoken of consistently in the New Testament in reference to Jesus (Matt. 26:64 // Mark 14:62 // Luke 22:69; Mark 16:19; Acts 2:33; 5:31; 7:55–56; Rom. 8:34; Eph. 1:20; Col. 3:1; Heb. 1:3; 8:1; 10:12; 12:2). Because of Jesus's place at the right hand, some believe the participial clause that follows is a clause reflecting result: "is at the right hand with the result that angels, authorities, and powers are made subject to him." More likely, however, the clause is temporal: "after angels, authorities, and powers were subjected to him, he went into heaven and is at the right hand of God." This reading incorporates verses 19–21 and shows why Peter believed it was necessary to elucidate the first step (i.e., the victorious speech to the fallen angels) in Jesus's journey to the right hand of God.

Though Peter used three separate words for the spiritual beings (angels, authorities, and powers), each of the terms refers generally to the beings who inhabit the spiritual realm. No hierarchy among the terms has been discerned, and Peter likely used all three for rhetorical purposes; namely, by stacking the terms, Peter highlighted that all the spiritual realm has been subject to Christ.

THEOLOGICAL FOCUS

The exegetical idea (Peter encouraged the suffering readers by pointing to the example of Christ, who suffered for a noble cause and was publicly vindicated) leads to this theological focus: suffering believers are to be encouraged by the example of Christ, who suffered for a noble cause and was publicly vindicated.

Christians are often discouraged when they consider the suffering they have endured or are destined to endure for righteousness. Though Scripture calls for joy in suffering for righteousness (Matt. 5:10–12; Rom. 5:3–5), in practice being joyful is difficult. One way to remain faithful in such suffering is by observing the example of Christ. He endured unjust suffering, yet he did not do so aimlessly. He knew that suffering was the will of the Father, and that by such suffering others would be redeemed.

In a similar though unparallel way, believers may also suffer for the sake of the redemption of others. When believers suffer for righteousness, this produces a curiosity in the lives of unbelievers. This curiosity may lead to questions, and questions to conviction, and conviction to conversion. Though the believer may not vicariously suffer for others as Christ did, he may view his suffering as a means by which God can draw unbelievers to himself. In this way, Christ's example of suffering for a noble cause—suffering for the sake of the redemption of others—provides an example for believers to follow in their own suffering.

Jesus not only suffered for a noble cause; he was also publicly vindicated. The analogy is not hard to see. Just as Jesus, though suffering unjustly, was ultimately vindicated, so believers too have hope that one day their righteousness will be visibly manifested to all. Though believers may not be able to sit at the right hand of the Father (a place reserved for Jesus), they can be encouraged that the rewards for their suffering will be worth the difficulty they have endured.

PREACHING AND TEACHING STRATEGIES

Exegetical and Theological Synthesis

Death and taxes: the two constants in life. Since the creation of the first humans, death has ruled the world. No human, animal, or any other living thing can escape its clutches. The Old Testament sacrificial system attempted to provide relief for the problem of sin, but the blood of animals was ineffective (Heb. 10:4) and ultimately served to exacerbate the problem (10:1).

All that changed with the death, burial, and resurrection of Jesus Christ. Peter relates that Jesus suffered only "once" for sins, the righteous for the unrighteous (3:18), solving the problem that thousands of sacrificed animals could not. Though the text of 3:18–22 provides numerous theological and exegetical possibilities, whatever Peter intended for us to understand, Jesus was victorious over death and sin. He now reigns at the right hand of God, with all angels, authorities, and powers subjected under his feet (3:22).

Because of Christ's sacrifice, the righteous dying for the unrighteous (3:18), now humanity has hope. Men and women can put their faith in Jesus for the forgiveness of sins and for the promise of victory over both sin and death. As Jesus died and was raised again, so will Christians too. The short pericope that ends 1 Peter 3 magnifies the victorious travels of Jesus after his death and gives hope for the believer for a similarly victorious outcome, even in the midst of suffering.

Preaching Idea

Christ's Vindication over Suffering Motivates a Christian's Victory over Sin.

Contemporary Connections

What does it mean?

The question "What does it mean?" can apply to nearly every phrase of this passage. First Peter 3:18–22 is not only the most debated in the epistle, but is likely one of the most debated in all the New Testament. Many questions can arise from such a complex and controversial passage, so preachers can help the congregation by giving a clear explanation not only of the common options of interpretation, but also of their final position in the matter (assuming they have one).

First, boil down the issues to a few main questions that the sermon will attempt to tackle. When I (Bryan) taught this passage, I asked three main questions: (1) Where did Jesus go? (2) Who are the spirits in prison? (3) What did Jesus say to them? My goal was that my congregation would know my position on each of these questions by the end of the sermon, and my hope was that they could articulate why.

If the teacher or preacher will work through main interpretative possibilities, also consider giving an outline or chart that helps the audience follow along (see the chart in the exposition). Remember: You have been studying this passage for an entire week (at least!). Most members of your congregation read it for the first time at the top of your sermon. Go slow, be clear, explain as if 100 percent of the people have never heard it and 50 percent don't care.

Is it true?

The pastor-teacher faces quite the challenge with 1 Peter 3:18–22. Nearly every sentence begs to be asked the question: Is it true? Is it true that Jesus went and proclaimed victory to the fallen angels in Sheol? Is it true that fallen angels cohabitated with women in the time of Noah? Is it true that baptism saves? With so many questions, where does the preacher start?

Truthfully, no preacher will ever be able to "prove" Jesus's descent to Sheol, or the angelic interpretation of Genesis 6, or any other thing in this passage for that matter. In this particular pericope, time should be spent not on proving the interpretive exegetical decisions at every turn, but instead focus on Peter's *purpose* for writing these words.

Believers ought to look to Christ's vindication over sin as a motivation for their own victory over suffering. Is it true that his victory over sin provides such motivation? Of course! It can be "proven" by encouraging the congregation to see the connection between Christ and Christian. Jesus suffered, died, and was raised. Believers too suffer in persecution, die daily to their sins, and will rise again one day (Gal. 2:20). The more Christians identify with the experience of Jesus, the more he will motivate their present-day living.

Now what?

It is all too easy to get caught up in the minutiae of theological details and arguments in a text such as this one and forget that the purpose of preaching and teaching is not to inform but to change hearts and actions. If people leave without a pathway to transformation, the preacher has failed his job.

But what application can come from such a controversial text? The application here centers around motivation: Christ's vindication over suffering *motivates* a Christian's victory over sin. With a lack of imperative in the paragraph, the preacher should lean on the connection with verse 17. Verse 18 begins with the word "for," connecting verses 18–22 (the work of Jesus) with verses 13–17 (the suffering of the readers). What motivates a believer to be faithful during suffering? Jesus was faithful. What hope does a believer have during such times? Jesus suffered and resurrected and experienced vindication and glory; a believer should recognize that such hope awaits them as well.

Consider an Olympic hopeful, training in the pool day after day. Swim training is nothing but hard work. Mile after mile, lap after lap, working every muscle in the body. Practices are unforgiving and can feel hopelessly difficult. What motivates such suffering? It is not just the possibility of a gold medal. For motivation, Olympic hopefuls also look toward those who have been through similar suffering and succeeded during practice. Michael Phelps swam the same lanes and suffered the same agony of training, to his eventual glory. Katie Ledecky did her laps and put in her time, to experience the joy of winning. Those who have been through suffering and experienced the victory can motivate those who are currently in the thick of trials.

Creativity in Presentation

Theology need not be dry or boring. Preachers must take care to present such a theologically complex passage in a way that engages the congregation. The text might be exciting for pastors to consider the various avenues of interpretive possibilities, but they should not imagine that every congregant shares that same enthusiasm without a little work on his part to help them along.

To put the sermon into perspective, the preacher might want to consider using a "dialogue partner" with a song or a creed. The Apostles' Creed famously includes the line "he descended to hell" after "was crucified, died, and was buried." The preacher can have the congregation recite the creed, then zero in on that line, asking (rhetorically) what it means. This can lead into the sermon text. The creed acts as a foil for preachers as they work through the text, always keeping the question of "What does that mean?" in the background of the message. If not the creed, then consider using a song like "Creed" from Rich Mullins, which also clearly mentions the descent into hell in one of the lyrics.

Assuming the preacher mentions several different possible interpretations and understandings of the passage, the preacher may want to rewrite the text in a summary at the end, once he has explained his opinion. This is not a replacement of the biblical text, merely a clarification of its meaning. For example, instead of "in which he went and proclaimed to the spirits in prison" (v. 19), the preacher might say, "Jesus went to Sheol and proclaimed victory to the punished angels from Noah's time." It will help the congregation know clearly where the preacher falls in his understanding of the text.

Whatever you do, make sure to keep the emphasis in the proper place. The pulpit should not be devoid of application, even in a theology-heavy sermon (*especially* with such a sermon). One simple way to outline the sermon might be:

- Introduction: Apostles' Creed
- 3:18–22: Interpretive Possibilities
- 3:18–22: Connection to Context
- Application
- Closing: Revisit the Apostles' Creed

Using Apocryphal Texts in a Sermon

Using an apocryphal text like 1 Enoch in a sermon can be tricky business. Besides the general unfamiliarity with such documents, many congregants may struggle with the appropriateness of using a noninspired text to illustrate a biblical point. But the preacher can use 1 Enoch and other apocryphal texts as long as he keeps a few basic principles in mind.

First, clearly explain that apocryphal texts such as 1 Enoch are not inspired Scripture. The preacher need not dive into a half-hour discussion on the doctrine of inspiration and canonicity, but a simple explanation up front will help congregants understand that the preacher is not quoting 1 Enoch in the same way he would quote James or Romans.

Second, remind listeners that many noninspired books can provide useful information for sermons and biblical understanding even today. C. S. Lewis's *Mere Christianity* is not inspired, but it sure is helpful. Edwin M. Yamauchi's *Persia and the Bible* is not Scripture, but it illuminates a great deal about the Bible times. Give listeners a few analogies with other resources like these to help them see that an uninspired text can still find a place in a sermon without introducing heresy to the church.

Third, use apocryphal texts sparingly and strategically. Do not give the congregation the impression that you did your devotions in 1 Enoch during the week. Nor give them the impression that *they* should have done their devotions in 1 Enoch! Listeners might accept a few extra-biblical examples, as long as they clearly see how they relate to and illuminate the text. Too many apocryphal references are like too much pepper on a steak—it can ruin the whole meal.

Finally, find a way to project the text. The congregation did not bring their pseudepigrapha alongside their *ESV Study Bible* to church with them. Make sure to have the text presented to them in an easy fashion for best results.

DISCUSSION QUESTIONS

1. What does it mean that Jesus "went and proclaimed to the spirits in prison" (v. 19)?

2. What does Peter's reference about Noah refer to (v. 20)?

3. In what way exactly does baptism save (v. 21)?

4. How can you summarize Peter's meaning in your own words? Is there room for disagreement on this issue between Christians? Why or why not?

5. How do Peter's thoughts in verses 18–22 connect to verses 13–17? How does this motivate application for believers?

1 Peter 4:1–6

EXEGETICAL IDEA
Peter commanded the readers to prepare to suffer for righteousness, knowing that such suffering is evidence of their cessation from sin, their obedience to the will of God, and their positive outcome in the future judgment.

THEOLOGICAL FOCUS
Believers must prepare to suffer for righteousness, knowing that such suffering is evidence of their cessation from sin, their obedience to the will of God, and their positive outcome in the future judgment.

PREACHING IDEA
Believers Must Arm Themselves to Suffer While Abstaining from Sin.

PREACHING POINTERS
Living righteously has consequences, both pleasant and unpleasant. Peter's readers learned quickly that sometimes living out the Christian life drew attention in all the wrong ways. Not only did they suffer persecution from Nero, but abstaining from the social connections of their life before Christ brought fallout as well. Believers found themselves maligned and suffering over their choices to cease from sin.

Christians today feel the same heat of persecution from colleagues and family members who don't understand their new lifestyle. Abstaining from alcohol leads the believer to incur great ridicule from his old drinking buddies. Abstaining from sex before marriage brings plenty of mockery from a woman's sorority sisters. Openly sharing the faith brings outright persecution and even shunning from certain family members. Christians face suffering for living like Jesus. Through the words of 1 Peter 4, preachers can challenge believers to persevere through such difficulties. Pointing the believer to Christ's example encourages the Christian to abstain from sin, even when the consequences continue to pile up in his or her social life.

CEASING FROM SIN AND THE FUTURE JUDGMENT
(4:1–6)

LITERARY STRUCTURE AND THEMES (4:1–6)

There is one central command in this text: "arm yourselves for suffering" (v. 1). The rest of the text highlights the importance of this mental foundation. According to the text, the suffering they are enduring comes about because they have abandoned their former ways of life (vv. 3–4). The response of their unbelieving friends is first surprise and then mockery (v. 4). It is in this way that suffering indicates the cessation of sin, for the reason they suffer in the flesh is not because they have sinned but because they have stopped sinning. Despite the present circumstances, however, Peter ended the text encouraging believers to have a long-view mindset. Those who believe the gospel and are transformed by it experience suffering in this age, but will live in the Spirit. On the other hand, those who, following the natural course of the world, mock believers, will experience God's censorious judgment (v. 6). With rhetorical flair, Peter compared the "judgment" of men (i.e., what they think) with the judgment of God (i.e., the duty of executing justice), implicitly minimizing the former in light of the latter.

Themes of this section include the following: the believer's attitude toward suffering; the reason believers suffer in this age; the believer's duty to abandon the former way of life; the surprising nature of the believer's conversion; the apparently irrational response of unbelievers to the believer's conversion; and the judgment of God compared to the judgment of man.

- *Ceasing from Sin (4:1–2)*
- *The Gentile Way of Life (4:3–4)*
- *Present and Future Judgment (4:5–6)*

EXPOSITION (4:1–6)

Peter commanded readers to think the way Jesus thought about suffering—namely, that suffering was the prerequisite to the glory the Father had promised. By embracing such suffering, readers would show that they were done with sin. Even more, they would show that they had embraced God's will for their lives. Their unbelieving neighbors would respond to their changed lives first with surprise and then with vilification; God will judge them for such actions.

Ceasing from Sin (4:1–2)

Believers must be mentally prepared, knowing that those who are through with sin and embrace the will of God will suffer.

4:1. Peter began this text by connecting it with the prior text (3:18–22): "therefore, since Christ suffered in the flesh." The "therefore" highlights that what follows is an implication drawn from Christ's suffering. Broadly stated, the connection between the passages is as follows: since Christ suffered in the flesh and received a reward for his suffering, so believers should prepare to suffer, knowing that they too will receive a reward (cf. Schreiner, 2003, 199).

Peter continued to emphasize the connection between the believer's experience and Christ's experience. Since Jesus suffered in the flesh, so believers should expect nothing less than suffering in the flesh. This is made clear here by the emphatic "you also." The believer's suffering is not identical to Jesus's (as Peter has already made clear). Nevertheless, the source of the suffering is the same: the unbelieving world, when confronted with righteousness, reacts negatively, inflicting suffering on those who display God's righteousness.

Peter's command is that the readers would "arm themselves" (ὁπλίσασθε). The language is intentionally militaristic, picturing a warrior donning armor to defend from incoming attacks (BDAG s.v. "ὁπλίζω" 716). That which Peter commanded them arm themselves was not a weapon or armor; it was a mental attitude (BDAG s.v. "ἔννοια" 337). Though weapons and armor are essential to a battle, so is the mental preparation of the warriors. It is this latter element that Peter emphasized here. Believers must think of themselves as in a war, and they must be prepared to suffer as Christ suffered. Believers who blithely go through life not considering the cost of discipleship will experience great hardship when their faith inevitably brings them into conflict with the world and its value system. Those, however, who study the life of Christ, knowing that believers must follow his steps, will be mentally prepared for the battle and will not be able to be ambushed.

Peter gave two reasons believers ought to mentally prepare to suffer. The first—since Christ also suffered—has already been mentioned. The second reason is given in the last clause: "since the one who suffered in the flesh has ceased from sin." Though the verb "ceased" (πέπαυται) has the literal sense of stopping an activity, it can also be used to refer to being "through with" something (BDAG s.v. "παύω" 790). The perfect tense of this verb (which indicates a past action with ongoing results) is consistent with this interpretation. On this reading, Peter was saying that "the one who is willing to suffer shows that he is through with sin." When this verse is read in light of the rest of the letter, and especially the following verses, the sense becomes clearer. Peter was saying that those who suffer are through with sin, because the suffering they are experiencing is a result of their being through with sin! In other words, when believers abandoned

their former way of life, causing shock to their neighbors, they elicited mocking from those same neighbors. Their commitment to continue on the path of righteousness, despite suffering, is evidence that they have "ceased from sin."

> ### Ceasing from Sin: A Second Reason to Suffer?
>
> Some do not see Peter's statement ("since the one who suffered in the flesh has ceased from sin") as a *reason* that readers ought to be through with sin. Instead, they argue that this clause indicates the content of thought that the believer must have in mind (Calvin, 1994, 121; Kelly, 1969, 166; Achtemeier, 1996, 278; Davids, 1990, 148). A translation like the following makes this interpretation clear: "Since Christ suffered in the flesh, arm yourselves with the same thought he had: those who suffer in the flesh, cease from sin." This is exegetically possible, as the ὅτι can have this meaning. One advantage of this reading is that it avoids having two grounds for the command (because Christ suffered and because you cease from sin). Further, it avoids any interpretive difficulty resulting from the phrase "ceased from sin." On the other hand, the major problem with this interpretation is that it appears to cast doubt on the sinlessness of Jesus. Clearly Jesus did not suffer in order to cease from sin (2:22). On the whole, it is better to see this as a second ground for why the readers should obey Peter's command.

4:2. The grammatical form that begins this sentence (εἰς τό with an infinitive) can either signal purpose or result. Additionally, it is not clear whether it refers back to the verb from verse 4a "arm yourselves" or the verb in 4b "ceased." This results in four options:

1. "arm yourselves so that you no longer live for human desires but God's will"
2. "arm yourselves with the result that you no longer live for human desires but God's will"
3. "he ceased from sin with the result that

he no longer lives for human desire but God's will"

4. "he ceased from sin so that he no longer lives for human desire but God's will"

Each of the options is exegetically possible and may be defended by the theology of the letter. Nevertheless, the last option appears most likely. On this reading, Peter was noting that believers prepare to suffer because they know that those who suffer in the flesh do so because they are through with sin, intending now to no longer live by the motivations of mankind, but to devote themselves to God's will.

Peter noted that people who make this commitment do so for the "time remaining in the flesh." Whether this refers to the time before the coming of the Lord or the time before death makes no difference. The point is that mortal life is temporary, and the choice one makes extends throughout that life.

Peter provided only two options for the direction of one's life. Either one lives according to "humankind's desires," or he or she lives according to the "will of God." The implication is that these are opposed to one another, so that one cannot choose to do both. As Peter will indicate in the coming verses, it is the choice to follow God's will that causes the rejection the readers face. Again, this is why choosing to suffer evidences the finality of the believer's choice against evildoing.

The Gentile Way of Life (4:3–4)

Peter contrasts the previous life of the believers with their current life, while considering the unbeliever's response to the changed life of the believer.

4:3. This verse gives the reason (γάρ) Peter's readers should be done with the desires of men and should live for the will of God. Peter began with a temporal indicator: "for the time which has passed is enough." By means of this clause, Peter divided the readers' lives into two sections. There was the period prior to their embrace of Christ, and there is now a time after that. Peter has already spoken of them "living the rest of their lives" for the will of God. As a motivation for continuing that, Peter reminded them of their life prior to Christ. By saying that the time was "enough," Peter was rhetorically signaling that the time was overly sufficient. There is now no more time for such living.

Their previous life is defined as "carrying out the will of the Gentiles." As the list of sins they used to partake of evidences (e.g., idolatry), the readers were and still are ethnically Gentile. Accordingly, Peter was using this term as a general reference to those who are not believers. The NIV translation "pagans" rightly captures the sense.

The list of vices presented here characterize "the will of the pagans" and is representative of the past life of the readers. The vices divide into three unequal categories. The first two refer to sexual vices, the middle three with alcohol and partying,[1] and the last to idolatry. Peter was not seeking to be comprehensive with this list; rather, he was displaying those characteristics that once were evidenced in the lives of the readers, but were now to be rejected, for they were not in accordance with the will of God. That the list appears weighted toward drinking and partying may appear initially odd. Understood in context, however, it makes perfect sense. These were the places where social connections were made and reinforced. Believers, due to their new birth,

---

1   Alcohol and partying. Some translations take the middle term of the three (κώμοις) in reference to sexual sin (e.g., "orgies" in the ESV). This is a possible rendering, but since Peter had mentioned sexual sin with the first two words, and since the vices preceding and following this vice are both related to alcohol, this one is likely to be taken that way as well.

rejected these, and thereby opened themselves to censure by their prior relations.

4:4. Peter began this verse with a grammatical construction (preposition with relative pronoun; ἐν ᾧ) that is debated in every place Peter used it (1:6; 2:12; 3:16, 19). The most likely interpretation here is that it refers back[2] to the lifestyle encapsulated in the entire vice list Peter just referenced. The ESV rendering with an addition captures this sense well: "With respect to this [lifestyle]."

What interests the pagans is that the believers no longer "join them in their reckless, wild living" (NIV). The way Peter spoke of the pagans' lifestyle is colorful. Literally, he spoke of the readers' lack of "running[3] with them into the same flood of wickedness." That the pagans "run" toward the rushing stream of iniquity indicates their excitement. That what they are running to is a rushing stream or flood of wickedness portrays the pagans sprinting to a flowing river and diving in with enthusiasm. The content of the rushing river is hard to translate in English. The word used (ἀσωτίας) is a negated form of the word most commonly used for salvation (σωτηρία). It has the sense of prodigality or waste, even of lacking salvific quality (BDAG s.v. "ἀσωτία" 148; Achtemeier, 1996, 283). The overall image is of people sprinting toward and leaping into that which carries them away from salvation.

Unbelievers are "surprised" (ξενίζονται) that believers no longer join them in this activity. Surprise refers to causing "a strong psychological reaction through introduction of something new or strange" (BDAG s.v. "ξενίζω" 684). Believers, when they embraced Christ and experienced the new birth, were transformed, abandoning their former ways in favor of living for God's will. Such a reversal shocked the believers' companions, who could not have expected this sudden change of direction.

The response of unbelievers to the shocking reversal of the believer's life is blasphemy[4] (βλασφημοῦντες). This word refers primarily to verbal disrespect. Most English translations indicate that the verbal disrespect is directed toward believers: "they malign you" (NASB, ESV); "they vilify you" (NET); "they heap abuse on you" (NIV). On this interpretation, Peter was saying that pagans observe the reformation of the believer's life and respond in mockery. But because "blasphemy" is used more frequently in reference to God (BDAG s.v. "βλασφημέω" 178), it is possible that the verbal disrespect is directed toward God.

A mediating position understands the verbal disrespect to be directed primarily toward believers, yet the net effect is blasphemy of God, for he is the one who has done the renovating work in their life. A parallel would be Jesus's question to Paul on the road to Damascus, "why do you persecute me?" (Acts 9:4). When Peter was attacking the church,

---

2   Refers back. Achtemeier argues that the relative has no direct referent, but it has both general retrospective and anticipatory elements. He suggests multiple translations that would fit the context, though none would capture the fullness of Peter's meaning: "'therefore,' 'because of this,' or 'at,' 'by this'" (Achtemeier, 1996, 283). Few have followed Achtemeier, for it is much more likely that Peter had a single referent in mind, which is the normal use of the relative. Further, taking the referent in regard to the list of vices is both exegetically possible and makes good contextual sense.

3   "Running." The analogy to running is complemented by the previous phrase, which indicated that the readers once "walked" in the ways of the pagans (πεπορευμένους; v. 3).

4   Blasphemy. Some suggest that the participle is attendant circumstance and should be translated as follows: "they are surprised . . . blasphemers!" (e.g., Michaels, 1988, 233). This is grammatically possible, but even as Michaels himself later suggests (234), there are better ways to interpret the passage (as suggested in the commentary).

he was attacking God. In the same way, when unbelievers speak against God's sanctified people, especially when their attack centers on sanctification, such unbelievers are verbally disrespecting God.

There are two ways to take the reference to blasphemy. The first is to take it with verse 4, resulting in the following interpretation: "they are surprised, and so they blaspheme." The second takes the participle with the following verse, resulting in the interpretation, "because they blaspheme, they will give an account." The difficulty in choosing between these interpretations is that both are consistent with what Peter is saying in this text. Whatever choice is made, the other interpretation is implied.

Present and Future Judgment (4:5–6)

Though unbelievers have their way presently, God will judge all men according to his standard.

4:5. Despite the present circumstances, Peter wanted to encourage his readers that all would be made right in the end. Those who were persecuting them "will give an account" (ἀποδώσουσιν λόγον). Such language was clearly and intentionally judicial, as the following statement, "ready to judge," indicates. By using the same word he used back in 3:15 (λόγον), Peter provided a powerful contrast. Though the readers would be asked to provide a reason for their hope before mere mortals, unbelievers will be required to give an account (λόγον) before their Creator.

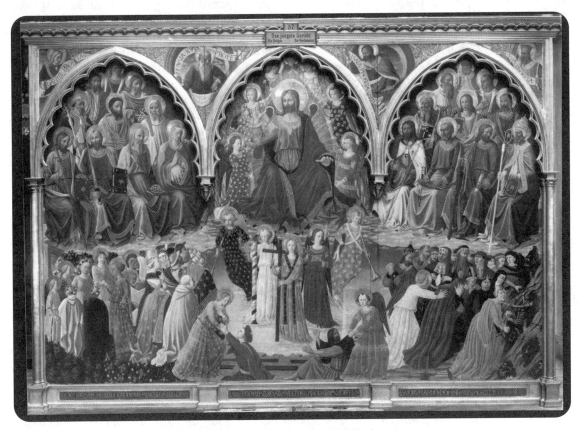

Last Judgment by Fra Angelico. Public domain.

That Peter had in mind the judgment at the eschaton is made clear by the designation "the living and the dead." He added that this judge is "ready," suggesting the imminency of the coming judgment. Believers have hope that the day is approaching, while unbelievers have increasingly shortened time to prepare for such a judgment.

The identity of the judge is not clear. On the one hand, Peter's sermon recorded in Acts 10:42 clearly states that Jesus has been appointed by God to be the judge of the living and the dead. On the other hand, Peter usually speaks of the Father as judge in this letter (1:17; 2:23). In light of Peter's prior sermon, the judge being Jesus is most likely, though a decision does not significantly influence the meaning of this passage.

4:6. Having spoken of the judgment of the "living and the dead" in verse 5, Peter added further consideration of the "dead." Before addressing the content of this verse, it is necessary to consider the identity of whom Peter was addressing when he spoke of the dead. This has been debated since ancient times. One early interpretation considered the dead as spiritually dead. On this reading, Peter was saying that the gospel was proclaimed to those who are spiritually dead so that they might be given life in the Spirit. Undoubtedly, the Scriptures do speak of unbelievers as being spiritually dead (John 5:25; Eph. 2:1, 5; Col. 2:13). Nevertheless, two facts militate against this view. First, Peter gave no indication that he was referencing the spiritually dead here. In fact, his use of the "living and the dead" in verse 5 suggests that the use of "dead" here has the same meaning there—the physically dead. Second, this reading does not adequately explain why Peter mentioned the judgment of men in the flesh.

Another interpretation of the dead is that they are those who have died and are presently in judgment. This view is normally combined with a particular reading of 3:19, whereby Christ went to the spirits of the dead and proclaimed a message of repentance, offering them a second chance. Interpreters who embrace this view differ on the full identity of the dead, whether it includes only those from Noah's day, only those who did not hear the gospel message, only those prior to the gospel proclamation, or all the dead. Though this view has ancient adherents, it fails for numerous reasons. Foremost, the message of a second chance appears to work directly against Peter's overall message in this letter broadly, and in this passage specifically. Throughout the letter Peter encouraged faithfulness and an eternal reward. To suggest that those who were temporally unfaithful will be received by God positively would certainly work against that argument. Second, the view that Peter proclaimed a message of repentance to the human dead has already been demonstrated to be an inferior interpretation in our consideration of 3:19 above.

The best view of the identity of the dead is that they are those who were alive when the gospel was preached to them, but who have since died. Some English versions capture this sense well with the addition of the word "now": "the gospel was preached to those who are *now* dead" (NIV, CSB, NET). The following analysis, based on this identification of the dead, will demonstrate that this is the most exegetically fitting interpretation.

Peter began this verse with a conjunction and strengthening phrase ("for this reason"; εἰς τοῦτο γάρ) that signaled he was building an argument from the prior point.[5] Because all people—the living and the dead—will give

---

5   Prior Point. Not all interpreters agree that Peter was pointing back. Some, for instance, argue that Peter was pointing back with "for" (γάρ), but he was also pointing forward with "this reason" (εἰς τοῦτο; Achtemeier, 1996, 286). While this is possible, it appears exegetically awkward, and a simpler explanation exists, as defended in this commentary (cf. Grudem, 1988, 178).

account to God, the gospel[6] was also[7] preached to them prior to their death. The purpose of the proclamation was that such people would "live by the Spirit," even though "judged in the flesh." Here Peter once more contrasted the Spirit and flesh (πνεύματι; σαρκί). And as in 3:18, the flesh (σαρκί) should be taken as referring to location (in the flesh) while spirit (πνεύματι) should be taken as referring to agency (by the Spirit).

The critical point Peter emphasized here is made evident by two parallel clauses: "according to men" (κατὰ ἀνθρώπους) and "according to God" (κατὰ θεόν). Despite the fact that humanity judges those who believe the gospel as inferior and liable to punishment, God judges them as worthy of eternal life given by the Spirit. Such a contrast encapsulated the distinction between the way God judges and the way man judges. Though from a human point of view, Christians were foolish, from a divine point of view their choice of Christ evidenced supreme wisdom.

It is quite likely that Peter addressed this point because unbelievers were mocking believers, noting that believers died just as unbelievers died. From a mortal point of view, Christians lost much because of their faith. This passage, then, serves as an encouragement and reminder. When the final judgment is made, those who were considered losers according to humanity's scorecard will be found to be the victorious ones. The opposite, then, is implied though not directly stated. Peter had already addressed the fact that unbelievers would have to give an account, but here he focused not on the unbeliever's coming judgment, but on the believer's coming vindication.

THEOLOGICAL FOCUS

The exegetical idea (Peter commanded the readers to prepare to suffer for righteousness, knowing that such suffering is evidence of their cessation from sin, their obedience to the will of God, and their positive outcome in the future judgment) leads to this theological focus: believers must prepare to suffer for righteousness, knowing that such suffering is evidence of their cessation from sin, their obedience to the will of God, and their positive outcome in the future judgment.

Suffering should not come as a surprise to believers. Jesus suffered, and believers are called to follow the same path (2:21). It is because they pursue the standard of the righteousness of Christ, imitating his holiness, that they experience such suffering. Indeed, experiencing such suffering gives evidence that the believer has embraced the will of God and is therefore through with sin.

There are two directions humans may pursue. The first is natural to humanity and is spoken of as the "desires of the pagans" (v. 3). The other is unnatural to humanity and consists of the "will of God" (v. 2). Believers, due to their embrace of the gospel and the new life it grants, have definitively turned toward the latter and away from the former (vv. 3–4). This turning elicits a persecution response from unbelievers, who are shocked by such an abandonment of one's former life and pursuits (v. 4). Such a response is not the exception but the rule.

Believers may despair, knowing that the whole of humanity finds them abnormal, unnatural, and worthy of censure. Nevertheless, believers should maintain their steady walk of

---

6   Gospel. The verb used here (εὐηγγελίσθη), speaks of proclaiming good news. It is passive, and it is possible that either God, Jesus, or the readers are the intended proclaimer. Most likely, however, it is designed to be general, so that it could refer to whoever preached the gospel to them.

7   Also. Though most English versions translate this as "even," it is most likely to be translated "also." The translation "even" suggests some extended extent to which the gospel was preached. On the other hand, "also" suggests that the gospel was not only preached to unbelievers, but it was also preached to those who became believers and have subsequently died (Dubis, 2010, 137).

faith, knowing that man's judgment is not consistent with God's judgment. Though men have already judged believers as inferior according to their standard (v. 6), God has already approved them, because they have responded to the gospel. Their good behavior in Christ is both the catalyst for their persecution as well as their confirmation that they have been accepted in the beloved. At the final day, when God judges all men according to his perfect, righteous standard, believers will live by the Spirit, while unbelievers will have to give account of their actions, including their blasphemy against God's people.

PREACHING AND TEACHING STRATEGIES

Exegetical and Theological Synthesis

People love sin. Humans rarely need convincing that bad behavior is enjoyable or entertaining. Stop in a frat party and you will see smiles and hear laughs, even as students fall over themselves in a drunken stupor. No one needs to teach children to misbehave or talk back. It comes naturally and—if we are honest—children seem to enjoy misbehaving more than obeying.

It is when someone pushes against this flow of sin that they stand out. Jesus did, and it earned him the cross. Believers must recognize that the gospel at work in their lives means abstaining from certain sins and behaviors that once characterized them in their ungodliness (1 Peter 4:1–2). This will mean severing many social relationships, sometimes to emotionally devastating effect. Jesus warned that disciples must be willing to surrender relationships with both family and friends for the sake of the cross (Luke 14:26; cf. Mark 10:29–30). Living as a Christian has consequences.

Peter calls believers to a high standard, one that comes with a high cost. But if the gospel has truly changed a believer, that change entails a transformed lifestyle, one that takes him or her out of their previous manner of living and thrusts them into a lifestyle characterized

by holiness and righteousness. Peter has already shown that sometimes the impact of such gospel living will draw people to Christ (3:1, 15–16). But other times, a gospel life will draw mockery and persecution from those not yet in the light of Christ.

But once again, Jesus stands as the perfect model for believers to follow. He rejected the ways of the world and lived without sin. He not only sets the standard for the believer, but his righteousness becomes our own upon our acceptance of the gospel (3:18). Peter ties together these gospel threads to encourage believers to endure the suffering that a godly lifestyle sometimes attracts.

Preaching Idea

Believers Must Arm Themselves to Suffer While Abstaining from Sin.

Contemporary Connections

What does it mean?

What does it mean to "arm oneself to suffer"? Picture a warrior gearing up for battle, whether a Greek or Persian with metal battle armor protecting the body, or a modern-day soldier wearing tactical gear and covered in camouflage. Soldiers suit up in order to reduce their vulnerability and protect their body. Peter's militaristic language in verse 1 commands believers to be armed not with physical gear but with a mental attitude, an inner preparedness, spiritually ready to face the oncoming battle. Just as soldiers suffer in war, so Christians ought to think of themselves geared up to fight and, most likely, to suffer. Arming oneself to suffer is a mental preparation, a spiritual readiness to face hardship and reject the world's values and increase one's faith in Jesus Christ.

The preacher must also be prepared to explain the relationship between arming oneself to suffer and abstention from sin. Peter calls for a radical distancing from the old sinful lifestyle. That "social distancing" leads to mockery, confusion, and sometimes outright persecution from unbelievers who do not understand the change in a believer. The preacher should help the church realize that to abstain from sin oftentimes acts as a magnet, attracting attention in ways that will challenge one's commitment to the faith. But Christians should be willing to suffer nonetheless, for after all it is the way of Christ (4:1).

Is it true?

Some congregants might not readily see the connection between abstaining from sin and persecution. A few brief testimonies might help make the point. Scripture offers several—Peter and John found themselves imprisoned just after the founding of the church (Acts 4); Paul suffered extensively upon his conversion to Christianity (2 Cor. 11:21–33); the exorcism of the slave girl in Acts 16 caused a stir in the community when her owners saw how much revenue they were losing.

The preacher might also use the testimony of people in the congregation for a powerful effect. A few short, three-to-five-minute prerecorded or live stories of people experiencing persecution simply for not caving in to the cultural norms will suffice: a businessman who was demoted because he refused to continue to participate in the unethical practice of his partners; a doctor who was sued because she refused to perform a gender-reassignment surgery; a college student who faced ridicule from both peer and professor for taking a stand in his faith. Any testimony that draws a connection between persecution and faith will help illustrate Peter's point and convince the church that faith and suffering are uniquely tied together for the believer.

Now what?

The passage offers two simple points of application that can have deep impact on a believer's life. First, the Christian ought to *abstain from sin*. Peter specifically mentions a number of social sins that characterized Gentiles during his time: sensuality, passions, drunkenness, orgies, drinking parties, and lawless idolatry. One need only to look at a secular college campus to illustrate any numbers of these vices.

When I (Bryan) first moved to Michigan, I took my kids to a secondhand bookstore. What I failed to realize at the time was that the drive would take me right past Michigan Stadium on game day. Behind every sidewalk on our slow, traffic-clogged drive was a house filled with partying college students. Some were dressed in revealing outfits. Others were clearly drinking, reveling in their intoxication. The drive ended up educating my children more than I anticipated!

Most cities have a college nearby. Those that don't surely have a bar. Using Peter's examples to point out a few of these places of debauchery and licentiousness can provide relevant, local impact to a congregation.

The second point of application is to *arm yourself for suffering*. Once one abstains from sin, one needs to also mentally prepare for the mockery and ridicule that will follow from the social connections that defined life before Christ. Just like an army officer might share with his cadets the horrors of war, steeling their minds for the trials to come, so a pastor must be real with his people, helping them to count the cost of taking up their cross.

Creativity in Presentation

One of the clearest launching points for a creative presentation is Peter's central command to "arm yourselves" (4:1). The commentary pointed out the purposefully militaristic flavor of the command. Preachers might want to show pictures of modern and ancient tactical gear that adorned soldiers before battle. Better yet, have a congregant who is active in the military or law enforcement join you on stage as a living illustration of Peter's analogy. Be careful not to press such an illustration too far by allegorizing each piece of gear ("the bulletproof vest is the Word of God . . . the helmet represents prayer . . ."). Surely

Peter's point is more general than that. But the striking visual of the extent that a soldier will go to prepare for battle helps the Christian to know that similar mental and spiritual preparations are needed to ready oneself for spiritual warfare.

In verse 4, Peter uses another visual that has potential to capture the imagination of the church. Peter speaks of unbelievers showing surprise that the believer does not "join them in the same flood of debauchery." As the commentary pointed out, the text literally reads, "running with them into the same flood of wickedness." Many film clips illustrate the horrors of trying to outrun a tidal wave. One can think of older films like *Deep Impact* (1998) or newer, more realistic movies like *The Impossible* (2012), where a family tries to reconnect after a devastating tsunami in Thailand. Images of people running *from* a tidal wave are common; one cannot think of someone running *toward* such a deadly force of nature.

But that is Peter's point. Unbelievers run *toward* the tidal wave of wickedness. Juxtaposing the images or short clip of people fleeing from a tsunami with the actions of unbelievers in their sin could conjure up the mental images Peter uses in this verse. If someone on staff is skilled in graphic design, perhaps consider reversing some of the images to show a person running toward the oncoming flood.

Each of these creative illustrations should serve the greater point that believers need to prepare themselves to suffer, all while carefully abstaining from sin. Preachers may want to modify the following outline for their sermon:

- A Present Command: Cease from Sin (4:1–2)

- A Past Consideration: Gentilic Living (4:3–4)

- A Future Condemnation: Penalty of Judgment (4:5–6)

DISCUSSION QUESTIONS

1. What kind of suffering does Peter envision here? How does the suffering come about?

2. How should Christians "arm" themselves in their thinking to prepare for suffering?

3. What sins have you left behind in your old way of life, leading to persecution from old colleagues, friends, and family members?

4. What does Peter mean when he speaks about "the gospel that was preached even to those who are dead"?

5. When you have to give an account to God (v. 5), what do you think God will say?

6. If you have never experienced suffering for your faith, why might that be?

1 Peter 4:7–11

EXEGETICAL IDEA

Peter commanded the readers to live rationally in light of the last days by loving, serving, and being hospitable to one another, for by doing so their prayers would be heard, and they would glorify God.

THEOLOGICAL FOCUS

Believers must live rationally in light of the last days by loving, serving, and being hospitable to one another, for by doing so their prayers will be heard, and they will glorify God.

PREACHING IDEA

Maximize Your Vertical Relationship with God by Deepening Horizontal Relationships with Believers.

PREACHING POINTERS

Peter's words to the first-century church conveyed an urgency not only due to the situation of persecution of his readers, but due to the dispensation in which they lived. Peter told them that "the end of all things is at hand" (4:7a), driving the commands that followed. The believers were urged to increase the effectiveness of their prayers by strengthening the quality of their relationships with each other and their impact on the local church. This would help them live as end-times believers, righteously prepared to meet their Savior when he comes.

If this was true of Peter's readers, it is all the more true and even more urgent two thousand years later for the modern church. This built-in urgency heightens the impact of the sermon from the very first phrase of the text. Peter provides other motivations for the church as well. Who doesn't want an increased prayer life? Who doesn't want to glorify God? Every believer wants both, and these motivations, placed within the pressure cooker of the end-times perspective, sound a clear alarm for believers to allow the gospel to work through their lives with powerful results.

HOLY LIVING IN THE ASSEMBLY (4:7–11)

LITERARY STRUCTURE AND THEMES (4:7–11)

This section of text concludes the second half of the body middle of the letter, which has focused on the suffering of believers and the coming judgment. This concluding section highlights how believers are to live in light of the coming judgment.

The phrase "the end of all things is near" provides the context for Peter's instructions throughout this section. Peter provided one command—live sensibly in these end times—which was to be carried out in three ways: love one another, be hospitable to one another, and serve one another. To each instruction he gave additional information, whether giving a reason to obey the command (v. 8), showing how to obey the command (v. 9), or even giving examples of how the command could be obeyed (vv. 10–11). He also gave two major reasons to obey the commands. First, they should live sensibly for the sake of their prayers (v. 7). In other words, God's ear would incline toward those who obeyed these commands. Second, they should live sensibly because it is through this way of life that they could glorify God through Jesus Christ (v. 11).

Themes of this section include: how believers should live in light of the ever-approaching eschatological end of this age; the believer's responsibility to his fellow believer; the centrality and power of love; the twofold gifts of God (speaking and serving); and the way the believer may give glory to God in his or her life.

- *The End of All Things (4:7)*
- *Love and Be Hospitable (4:8–9)*
- *Serve One Another (4:10–11)*

EXPOSITION (4:7–11)

As Peter's readers considered the quickly coming climactic conclusion to this age, Peter encouraged them to live rationally in light of that coming end. By doing so, they would demonstrate their righteousness, and God would attend to their prayers (4:7). The most important activity they could engage in was loving one another, for through this means they would keep harmony. When love is exercised, sins are covered and relational challenges are passed over (4:8). Other ways to love one another included showing hospitality (4:9) and using spiritual gifts, whether speaking or teaching gifts (4:10–11a). By using such gifts as God desired, believers would be able to direct all praise to God, who was the rightful recipient of it (4:11b).

The End of All Things (4:7)

Peter argued that since the eschatological end is approaching, his readers must live sensibly for the sake of their prayers.

4:7. Peter connected this section with the last by means of a conjunction (δέ) that signaled an advancement of the argument. Having just spoken of the judgment of the living and dead, Peter here noted that "the end of all things is near." "The end" translates a Greek word (τέλος) used here in the sense of "a point of time marking the end of a duration" (BDAG s.v. "τέλος" 998). In combination with the emphatically placed "all things" (at the beginning of the Greek sentence) and in light of 4:6, the meaning is clearly the end of this age, when all things are brought to their intended end and God judges humankind.

That this is "near" (ἤγγικεν) suggests it is an event that is close in chronological proximity (BDAG s.v. "ἐγγίζω" 270). The verb was given in the perfect tense, suggesting that the end has already begun, and yet is still awaiting its final culmination. Because of the work of Jesus, the last days have been inaugurated and the conclusion is awaiting its consummation (cf. Jobes, 2005, 275–76; cf. the language of the nearness of the kingdom; Matt. 4:17; 10:7; Mark 1:15; Luke 10:11). Peter was not intending to set an expected date for the coming eschatological conclusion of world history. Instead, he encouraged his readers to view history from the perspective of God's timetable. The coming of Jesus to suffer, die, and rise set in motion the plan that will conclude with the culmination of all things in Christ. It is for this reason that the New Testament speaks of this age as "the last hour" (1 John 2:18) and the church members as those on whom the culmination of the ages has come (1 Cor. 10:11).

How then are his readers to live if this is truly the last hour? This is the question Peter answered in these verses. He said, "therefore [since this is the last hour] be sensible and sober." Peter's commands demonstrate that the time period between the beginning of the end and its final culmination might be quite large. In other words, Peter did not suggest dramatic actions that gambled on the divine timetable; instead, he commanded the readers to continue to live relatively normal, though sanctified, lives.

The two commands "be sensible and sober" (σωφρονήσατε καὶ νήψατε) are to be understood together, as their meanings overlap significantly. The effect of using both is to emphasize the command. Though the latter verb can speak of sobriety as opposed to drunkenness (and may contrast the behavior of the pagans in 4:4; BDAG s.v. "νήφω" 672), its combination here with "be sensible" (σωφρονήσατε) produces an interpretive translation, "think rationally." The sense then was, "because you know the end is near, live rationally in light of that truth."

Peter provided an incentive for his readers to act sensibly, but translators differ on how best to interpret his meaning. The underlying Greek

has a simple preposition with the plural noun "prayers" (εἰς προσευχάς). Some translations suggest that the preposition indicates purpose: "act sensibly for the purpose of prayer" (NASB) or simply "for prayer" (CSB). This interpretation suggests that the purpose of their acting sensibly is so that they are able to pray effectively. Prayer as a hedge against the attacks of the spiritual enemy in the New Testament (e.g., Matt. 26:41) makes this interpretation attractive.

Other translations suggest another, more contextually sensitive interpretation: believers were to act rationally in accordance with the nearness of the end "for the sake of prayer" (NET, NRSV) or more explicitly, "for the sake of your prayers" (ESV). On this reading, Peter used the preposition to signal that the actions of the readers would determine God's response to their prayers. Those who committed themselves to thinking seriously and acting faithfully would find God's "ears open to their prayer" (3:12). Earlier Peter instructed husbands that they must show their wives honor so that their "prayers would not be hindered" (3:7). In each of these passages, God's ear is inclined toward those who are obedient, but is closed to those who continue in rebellion against him.

Love and Be Hospitable (4:8–9)

Peter noted two ways his readers could live sensibly in light of the coming end: loving one another, and being hospitable to one another.

4:8. The commands throughout the rest of this passage (vv. 8–11) are given as either participles or predicate nominatives. This revealed that loving (v. 8), showing hospitality (v. 9), and serving (vv. 10–11) are all means of living rationally in light of the end of all things.

The first command Peter gave was to "maintain love toward one another." By using the word "maintain" (ἔχοντες) Peter clarified that he believed the readers already had this quality and simply needed to maintain it. Translations differ on how to translate the adjective that modified "love" (ἐκτενῆ): whether Peter asked them to "maintain love constantly" (e.g., CSB, NRSV, LEB) or whether he asked them to "maintain fervent love" (e.g., NIV, ESV, NASB). In combination with "maintain," it seems best to understand Peter to have called the readers to maintain their love constantly. This would be necessary for Peter's readers, who not only faced the internal relational issues common among all people but who were also exposed to intense external pressures. In such circumstances, there was a need for readers to actively maintain their love for one another.

Centrality of Love in Jesus's Teaching

Matt. 22:36–40 "Teacher, which is the great commandment in the law?" And he said to him, "You shall love the Lord your God with all your heart and with all your soul and with all your mind. This is the great and first commandment. And a second is like it: You shall love your neighbor as yourself. On these two commandments depend all the Law and the Prophets."

John 13:34–35 A new commandment I give to you, that you love one another: just as I have loved you, you also are to love one another. By this all people will know that you are my disciples, if you have love for one another.

Peter noted that the command to love is "above all" (πρὸ πάντων) the other commands he provided here. This is consistent with the rest of the New Testament, where the centrality of the love command is well known (Rom. 12:9; 1 Cor. 13:1–7; 16:14; Eph. 5:2), deriving from Jesus himself (Matt. 22:37–40; John 13:34–35). That Peter emphasized the love command here indicates that the chief way that the readers would obey the command to take seriously the remaining time they had until the end was to love one another.[1]

As Peter had done elsewhere in the letter (1:24–25; 2:9–10; 4:17–18), he added support with an Old Testament citation (Prov. 10:12b)[2]: "for love covers a multitude of sins." By using the authoritative text, Peter provided two means of support for his command. First, the call to love is consistent with what godly people have been saying for generations. Second, love was and continues to be a means by which sins are "covered." The word translated "covered" (καλύπτει) means "to cause something not to be known" (BDAG s.v. "καλύπτω" 505). Peter was saying that love is willing to overlook the offences of another party for the sake of unity (see sidebar "Whose Sins are Covered?"). As a congregation being assailed from outside, the internal unity of the congregation was essential to their overall health. By loving one another, the relational fractures natural to human relationships in a fallen world would be mended.

---

1 Love one another. Peter did not address the need for love for those outside the Christian assembly. He did, however, address the need to honor those outside (2:17). Achtemeier suggests that "Love for those outside the community, or for those who do evil, as enjoined by Jesus (Matt. 5:43–48), falls outside the purview of this letter, perhaps because of external and internal pressures exerted by the sporadic persecutions Christians were undergoing at this time" (Achtemeier, 1996, 295).

2 Proverbs 10:12b. Peter normally followed the Septuagint renderings of passages, but here he departed from it. The Septuagint reads, "but friendship covers all who are not fond of strife" (NETS; πάντας δὲ τοὺς μὴ φιλονεικοῦντας καλύπτει φιλία). Because of the nearly identical use of this passage in James 5:20, it is most likely that the passage was well known in the ancient church. Accordingly, the non-Septuagint rendering is likely due to the dependence on a tradition that developed from the Hebrew form of Proverbs 10:12b.

Whose Sins Are Covered?

There are three options concerning whom Peter may have referred to when speaking of "covered" sins:

1. The sins of the one loved are covered, because love causes them to repent.

2. The sins of the one loving are covered by the acts of love.

3. The sins of the one loved are covered by the fact that they are loved.

The first option is possible, and it is similar to the way the same proverb is used in James 5:19–20: "My brothers, if anyone among you wanders from the truth and someone brings him back, let him know that whoever brings back a sinner from his wandering will save his soul from death and will cover a multitude of sins" (ESV). Such an interpretation would be fitting in this epistle as well, for the external pressures against the church may lead some of its members to begin wandering. The response of believers should be to love the wandering one constantly, seeking to draw them back to Christ, where such a wanderer may find renewed forgiveness.

Though the second option has some ancient support (2 Clem. 16.4; Clement, *Quis div.* 38; Origen, *Hom. Lev.* 2.4.5; Tertullian, *Scorp.* 6), the letter of 1 Peter clearly indicates that the sins of humanity are done away by Christ (1:18–19; 2:24–25; 3:18). Ultimately, the interpretation that a person's acts of love could do away with sin lessens the sacrifice of Christ and suggests that people may contribute to their own salvation.

The third interpretation is best. On this reading, it is because one is loved that his or her sins are looked

over by the one who loves them. The strength of this position is that it is consistent with the context of the Proverbs quotation, which has this doublet: "hatred stirs up conflict, but love covers all wrongs" (10:12). Proverbs is saying that hatred brings conflict to the surface, while love is willing to overlook offences. This interpretation is further evidenced elsewhere in the New Testament, where believers are called to love and forgive (Matt. 18:21–22; 1 Cor. 13:5).

4:9. The second way Peter's readers were to be sensible in light of the last times concerned hospitality.[3] Though not widely considered a chief virtue today, in the ancient world hospitality was highly valued. And though hospitality was essential for the dissemination of the gospel (3 John 7), the emphasis here was more likely the need for hospitality in hosting church families for worship (cf. Rom. 16:23). Opening one's doors for other believers may have opened the Christians up to greater attention from their unbelieving neighbors. Further, even without the external pressures, being hospitable is taxing on those who engage in it.

Due to the inherent challenges involved with hospitality, Peter added that believers must be hospitable "without grumbling." The word translated "grumbling" (γογγυσμοῦ) refers to "an utterance made in a low tone of voice" (BDAG s.v. "γογγυσμός" 204). One would grumble when he had a complaint that he did not want to publicly make known. Such grumbling suggested internal dissatisfaction and, when left to fester, would lead to disunity. Peter sought to avoid this by noting that when believers were hospitable, they must guard their hearts against hidden complaints. Most likely, this was to be understood in relation to the last command. If

---

3   Hospitality. The command to be hospitable did not come as a participle, as the other two commands of this section do (vv. 8, 10). It is likely that the adjective "hospitable" is to be taken as a predicate nominative with an implied participial equative verb (ὄντες; Achtemeier, 1996, 298).

a believer found evidence of discontent rising in her heart, she should love her fellow believers, covering over their offences.

Serve One Another (4:10–11)

Peter addressed the final way his readers could live sensibly in light of the coming end: by serving one another with the gifts God provided them.

4:10. Having spoken of the need for believers to live sensibly in light of the last days by loving one another and by being hospitable, Peter provided a final directive: "serve" (διακονοῦντες) one another with the gift (χάρισμα) you have been given.

That they were to serve using the "gift" suggested that their opportunity and means of serving were based on God's grace. In fact, the word for "gift" (χάρισμα) derives from the word for "grace" (χάρις). Thus, it was by God's grace that each was given a gift. The note of individuality communicated two things. First, Peter was now turning from the duty of all believers to the duties of individual believers. A second point, communicated by the word "each," is that every believer had been given a gift. Paul elsewhere noted that God granted to each believer a special gifting to accomplish God's purposes for the building up of the church (Rom. 12:3b; 1 Cor. 12:7, 11; Eph. 4:7).

Peter further clarified that the grace was "varied" or "diverse" (ποικίλης). Though Peter would organize the gifts into two broad categories (speaking and serving), it is clear that there are numerous specific gifts under each broad category. No two lists of spiritual gifts in the New Testament are identical (Rom. 12:6–8; 1 Cor. 12:4–11, 28; Eph. 4:11), and this suggests that they were not designed to be exhaustive. They are likely not exhaustive because they can't be exhaustive. God's gifts truly are varied.

That each believer was given a gracious gift designed to aid the body indicated two things. First, believers would never be able to boast about their own abilities, for in any way that they have benefited the larger body of believers, this has been accomplished only due to God's grace. Second, believers now have a "stewardship" over this grace. That believers are "stewards" of the grace of God indicates that each believer has a responsibility to manage his or her gift well. Though the modern Western world has done away with household stewards, the concept is still quite understandable. A steward is one who "is entrusted with management" and will consequently be held responsible for his or her actions. Accordingly, this command to steward the gift of God should be looked at both as a privilege and a responsibility (Schreiner, 2003, 214).

4:11. Two categories of spiritual gifts were referenced by Peter: speaking and serving. The speaking gifts included public proclamation, whether by preaching, teaching, or evangelism. Under this gifting would certainly be the gifts necessary for the role of pastor-teacher and evangelist, though the gifting need not be limited to those who would fill official roles. Those who were given speaking gifts were to recognize that their exercise of this gift meant that they spoke the "very words of God." The point was not that their words became God's words; rather, their words were to accurately represent God's words. A heavy weight of responsibility rests on the shoulders of those who are given the task of relaying the message of a sovereign—more so when the one speaking is the Creator God.

The second category of spiritual gits concerned serving gifts. The number of gifts that could be classified under this category are innumerable. They include anything done for the sake of Christ. Those whose gifts fall under this rubric are to do their acts of service "through the strength God provides." In other words, they must recognize their dependence on God for the ability to accomplish what they desire to do.

Peter encouraged readers to exercise their gifts appropriately "so that in everything God may be glorified through Jesus Christ." That God would receive glory is inherent in the gifts, for both categories of gifts are given in such a way that humans are not able to take credit for their success. If God grants fruit from the speaking gifts, it was ultimately his words that were effective, even if the believer was the instrument who communicated those words. If God grants fruit from the serving gifts, it was ultimately the strength of God that caused the increase, even if it was the believer who carried out the act of service. And even if the exercise of the gifts does not result in fruit, God receives the glory for the obedience demonstrated by his servants in the exercise of the gifts. Significantly, the glory comes to God through Jesus Christ. This addition highlights that Jesus makes possible the life that brings glory to God.

There are indications that this phrase concerning God's glory should not simply be limited to the exercise of the gifts. First, it occurs at the very end of the body middle of the letter, concluding 2:11–4:11. Second, it is accompanied by a doxology. Third, Peter made the statement expansive, indicating that God would be glorified "in everything." Accordingly, it seems best to interpret the phrase as a conclusion to all of 2:11–3:7.

The final clause of this verse is the first of two doxologies in 1 Peter. This doxology is present to conclude the body middle, while the second concludes the entire letter (5:11). It is not clear whether the doxology refers to Jesus or to the Father. In favor of Jesus is the fact that his name is the closest referent to the relative pronoun that begins this clause ("to him"). Nevertheless, the prior clause indicates that God receives glory *through* Christ, suggesting the Father is the referent. Despite this latter point, the location of the relative pronoun directly following Jesus's name shifts the weight considerably to Jesus being the referent.

The doxology is not a wish: "may glory and dominion be his forever and ever." Instead, it is a statement of reality: "to him belong glory and dominion forever and ever." "Dominion" references the "exercise of ruling ability" (BDAG s.v. "κράτος" 565) and complements the earlier indication that Jesus was raised to the right hand of the Father (3:22), where it was commonly known that Jesus would rule (Ps. 110). Peter concluded the doxology with a strong personal indication of his agreement with the statement: "amen."

THEOLOGICAL FOCUS

The exegetical idea (Peter commanded the readers to live rationally in light of the last days by loving, serving, and being hospitable to one another, for by doing so their prayers would be heard and they would glorify God) leads to this theological focus: believers must live rationally in light of the last days by loving, serving, and being hospitable to one another, for by doing so their prayers will be heard and they will glorify God.

The resurrection of Jesus from the dead fundamentally changed reality. It ushered the next age into this age, and signaled that the final days were upon humanity. Knowing this monumental shift has taken place, believers must live rationally in light of the coming end. The correct response is not extreme asceticism or indulgence, for no precise date has been set. Instead, the correct response is to commit to faithful living among the community of God's people.

The primary task is to love one another, for it is by means of love that offences are overlooked and unity maintained. Additionally, believers must show hospitality to one another, building a network of close relationships, even as the world seeks to ostracize and expel believers from broader society. Finally, believers must use their God-given spiritual gifts for the betterment of the community. If one has received a speaking gift, the believer must use it with the awareness that he represents God's words by his words. If one has received a speaking gift, the believer must use it, relying on the strength of God.

Believers who live sensibly in the light of the last days have been given two major motivations to continue in faithfulness. First, because of believers' faithful living, motivated by God's Spirit, God has promised to incline his ear toward their prayers. Second, as they live faithfully they may be assured that God receives the glory through their right actions. Because they have been transformed by the work of Christ to do good and exercise their spiritual gifts, God receives the glory from their transformed life. Thus, a believer's good works are not chiefly evidence of their own goodness but evidence of the righteousness granted to believers because of the redemptive work of Christ. As good deeds flow from the life of the believer, attention is drawn to Christ, the one who made righteous acts possible, and consequently glory is given to the Father, who sent the Son to redeem a people.

PREACHING AND TEACHING STRATEGIES

Exegetical and Theological Synthesis
First Peter 4:7–11 provides the theological framework for end-times living for believers. Believers who have been changed by the gospel (v. 6) ought to live in such a way so as to glorify God (v. 11) and increase the effectiveness of their prayers (v. 7). Peter's audience was already well on their way with their love for one another, so Peter urged a continuance of this behavior (v. 8). Persecution often drove people to flee from one city to another, and traveling missionaries and preachers needed a safe place to stay when entering new towns. Thus, hospitality was an essential ministry among the early church (v. 9). As the church continued to grow despite the persecution, Christians also needed to use the unique

gifts that the Holy Spirit provided them in order to benefit the body of Christ (v. 10).

Peter's commands align with those of the other apostles, but especially the words of James. James noted the nearness of the Lord's coming as a motivation for his exhortations (James 5:8). He too made explicit the connection between righteousness and the effectiveness of one's prayers (5:16), finishing his short letter with similar words about covering a multitude of sins (5:19–20). One wonders whether Peter had leaned on James in the opening verses of his pericope!

Peter's comments culminate in a doxology. All gospel living ultimately points to the glory of God. Peter writes that "in everything God may be glorified through Jesus Christ" (1 Peter 4:11). He tops off these words with an outpouring of praise to the Lord. By focusing on God's glory, Peter not only shows the way in which believers should live, but also the ultimate goal of such living.

Preaching Idea
Maximize Your Vertical Relationship with God by Deepening Horizontal Relationships with Believers.

Contemporary Connections

What does it mean?
What does it mean to maximize your vertical relationship with God by deepening horizontal relationships with believers? In this preaching idea, "vertical" refers to someone's relationship with God, whereas "horizontal" refers to someone's relationship with other believers. Like James (5:16), Peter shows a connection between one's effectiveness in prayer and one's godliness. Loving, serving, and being hospitable all enhance the effectiveness of a person's prayers.

How does this work? A family analogy might help illustrate the concept. My children are much more likely to be "heard" when they treat one another with respect and dignity throughout the day. When they fight, bicker, complain, annoy, and act up, their request to go out to McDonald's for dinner will fall on deaf ears. But when they get along, play nicely together, and help out around the house, their mother and I are much more eager to take them out for a treat.

It is not that God is unable to hear the prayers of sinning Christians. Rather, he is much more ready to take action for those who follow him by loving others. Believers live as children who please their Father when they actively edify the church through use of their spiritual gifts, keep themselves under self-control, and demonstrate love by showing forgiveness.

Is it true?

Is it true that deepening relationships with other believers can enhance your prayer life? Scripture is replete with examples that show that certain prayers are more effective than others, usually due to the godliness of the person praying. James 5:16 speaks of the prayer of a righteous person having great power. Jesus says in John 9:31 that God hears the prayers of God-fearing people who do the Lord's will, but not the prayers of the sinners. Psalm 34:15 indicates that the Lord's ears incline toward the cries of the righteous.

But will the church believe this? The preacher might lend some proof to the formula by illustrating the power of prayer through examples in church history. Many examples of testimonies can be found online, such as

at the pastor's forum at https://www.9marks. org/article/pastoral-forum-stories-of-an-swered-prayers. The pastor may also want to give examples using a prayer journal or another method of keeping track of how God answers prayers. Use the time as an opportunity to teach the spiritual discipline to the congregation.

The sermon may need to answer another "Is it true?" question: Is it true that "the end of all things is at hand" (4:7)? How can it be that the end is at hand when Peter wrote these words nearly two thousand years ago? In what sense did he mean this? Here is where knowledge of Greek may help a congregation, as the perfect tense suggests the end has already begun, but still awaits that final culmination. The preacher may want to show a chart representing general end-times events in order to demonstrate that the Bible views the time after Christ's death and resurrection as the "end times." Though we often think only of events future to us as the "last days" or "end times" (such as the tribulation or millennial kingdom for some theological perspectives), the Bible speaks in broader terms.

Now what?

Peter does a nice job organizing the text for application, giving three main commands with two primary results. The first command is to "keep loving one another earnestly" (4:8). He relates this to love covering sins (cf. Prov. 10:12b). When I (Bryan) do premarital counseling, I

Old Testament   **The End Times**

always warn that husbands and wives *will* offend one another in their marriage. If it hasn't happened yet, it is only a matter of time. Love means releasing these offenses, at times even if the spouse has not apologized. We don't bring them up again. We don't weaponize them to win an argument. We don't allow them to cause bitterness in the marriage. We love by applying the gospel of Jesus Christ to every aspect of life, including when we feel offended. How much greater is the offense Jesus incurred from us— yet he has forgiven our sins! How much more should we be willing to love others by forgiving them?

Second, Peter commands believers to "show hospitality to one another without grumbling" (4:9). For anyone who has ever hosted others for any length of time, the "without grumbling" part of this command is probably the most difficult. Like fish, guests in the home begin to stink after three days. It is easy to be excited about the idea of hosting a small group, or opening your guest room for a missionary for the month, or boarding the youth intern for the summer. But when their annoying habits begin to surface, Peter's command becomes all the more important to remember. Love the guest by serving them without grumbling or complaining, remembering that it is your Christian duty to do so.

Third, Peter encourages believers to "serve one another, as good stewards of God's varied grace" using each one's spiritual gifts (3:10–11). The Holy Spirit has given each genuine believer at least one spiritual gift to build up the body of Christ by edifying one another. Point out the varied gifts in your congregation. Make sure to emphasize some of the lesser-appreciated gifts, like hospitality and service. Consider even spotlighting a few humble servants in the church as prime examples of those who use their gifts for the building up of the church.

Creativity in Presentation

Peter organizes this paragraph into three main applications with two results: love, show hospitality, and serve—resulting in effective prayer and glory to God. If the preacher wishes to preach the text in a nonsequential fashion, this might make a good sermon outline. If the preacher chooses to follow more carefully Peter's train of thought, the sermon outline may look as follows:

I. Introduction: Who wants to have a more effective prayer life? (4:7)
   A. The command to love (4:8)
   B. The command to show hospitality (4:9)
   C. The command to serve (4:10–11a)
II. Conclusion: Who wants to glorify God? (4:11b)
   A. The preacher can then close with the doxology in 4:11c.

One creative way to engage the church through Peter's text is to bring to life the various gifts mentioned in verses 10–11, complementing Peter's point with other spiritual gifts as well. Make a list of areas of service in the church, coinciding with different spiritual gifts mentioned in the New Testament. For example:

Ministry	Spiritual Gift(s)
Children's Sunday School Teacher	Teaching; Administration; Service
Greeters	Hospitality
Fall Festival Setup/Cleanup	Service; Helps

After highlighting areas of service and the spiritual gifts best suited with each area, have leaders ready after church to integrate eager believers into each ministry. Consider putting on a "ministry fair" by highlighting each major church ministry at separate booths or tables in the church lobby.

Some teachers might want to utilize a "spiritual gifts inventory" to help novice believers discern where their gifts lie. Such inventories can sometimes limit or misdirect believers, so urging them to consider their passions and talents and then "trying out" areas of ministry that seem intriguing may be a better method of discerning one's gifts. Either way, believers should feel equipped to not only identify their own spiritual gifts, but to know where and how to put them into practice in the church after listening to this sermon.

DISCUSSION QUESTIONS

1. What does Peter mean when he says, "the end of all things is at hand" (4:7)? How can this be, since this was written nearly two thousand years ago?

2. Describe the connection between horizontal relationships with believers and vertical relationship to God through prayer. How can it be that prayer is more effective when we love one another properly?

3. What does Peter mean when he says that "love covers a multitude of sins"? Give an example of this in everyday life.

4. How can we show more hospitality to one another without grumbling?

5. What spiritual gift has God given you? How have you been using it?

HONORABLE SUFFERING AS THE FLOCK OF GOD
(1 PETER 4:12–5:14)

This section doubles as the closing of the body of the letter (4:12–5:11) and of the letter proper (5:12–14). Having encouraged the readers to consider their identity in the body opening (1:13–2:10) and having exhorted the readers to live faithfully to that identity throughout the body middle (2:11–4:11), Peter turns to final encouragements to faithful living and endurance through suffering in the body closing (4:12–5:11).

This portion of the letter divides into three sections. The first (4:12–19) summarily reminds the readers of some of the themes addressed earlier: the unsurprising nature of suffering, the readers' blessedness when enduring suffering, the avoidance of suffering for wrongdoing, and the need for faithfulness in light of the coming judgment. The second section (5:1–5) once more addresses intercommunity responsibilities, whether of the elders (vv. 1–4), of the "youngers" (v. 5a), or of the whole congregation (v. 5b). The third section (5:6–11) provides final advice, addressing the believer's need for humility (vv. 6–7), attentiveness (v. 8), and perseverance (v. 9). The body letter closes with a statement of confidence in God's goodwill toward believers and a doxology of praise (vv. 10–11). The body closing is followed by a short letter closing (5:12–14), which includes a recommendation note concerning the letter carrier (v. 12), a statement of greeting from the church in Rome (v. 13), and a final prayer of peace for the readers (v. 14).

This major section, Honorable Suffering as the Flock of God, is broken into three preaching units: Suffering as a Christian (4:12–19), The Flock of God (5:1–5), and Final Admonitions (5:6–14).

1 Peter 4:12–19

EXEGETICAL IDEA

Peter commanded the readers to not be shocked or ashamed at suffering for righteousness; instead, they were to entrust themselves to God, rejoicing in suffering—because they knew that those who suffer for righteousness glorify God, are blessed in this life, and are vindicated in the next.

THEOLOGICAL FOCUS

Believers must not be shocked or ashamed at suffering for righteousness; instead, they are to entrust themselves to God, rejoicing in suffering—because they know that those who suffer for righteousness glorify God, are blessed in this life, and are vindicated in the next.

PREACHING IDEA

Flip the Script of Honor and Shame by Rejoicing in Righteous Suffering.

PREACHING POINTERS

If nothing else, the exposition of 1 Peter has established that the original readers experienced great persecution and suffering. They knew the difficulties of living life as a Christian and paying dearly for it. What kind of encouragement does a group like this need? Peter connects suffering to surprising phrases like "rejoice," "be glad," and "you are blessed." This upends expectations for his readers, giving them a new and renewed disposition to face their problems.

Believers today are not exempt from trials or persecution. In fact, they are to expect them (2 Tim. 3:12). When the cake shop owner is sued for refusing to compromise moral principles, how should she handle such suffering? When a college professor mocks a Christian student for his belief in God and the Bible, how should the student interpret this trial? How do third-world believers suffering physical imprisonment and even death react to such persecution? First Peter 4:12–19 reorients the minds and hearts of believers in any age going through righteous suffering, giving hope and promise to overcome such trials.

SUFFERING AS A CHRISTIAN (4:12–19)

LITERARY STRUCTURE AND THEMES (4:12–19)

This passage begins the body conclusion and repeats many of the themes mentioned previously in the letter. The passage may be divided into two contrasting options, with an exhortation at the end. The first contrast is that the readers should not be surprised at suffering; instead, they should rejoice in suffering, for those who follow the path of Christ's suffering will rejoice exceedingly at his coming (vv. 12–13). Indeed, those who suffer in this way are blessed, because such suffering shows that the Spirit is within them (v. 14). The second contrast is that the readers should not suffer for shameful evil; instead, they should suffer for righteousness, with the result that they bring glory to God (vv. 15–16). This is even more important as the day of judgment approaches, for those who glorify God will be vindicated, while those who do evil will be judged (vv. 17–18). The final exhortation is that believers must entrust themselves to a righteous God as they engage in good deeds (v. 19).

Themes of this section include the following: the believer's expectation of suffering for righteousness; why believers should rejoice at suffering; the honor of suffering for righteousness and the opportunity it provides to bring glory to God; the frightening nature of the coming judgment for those who are ungodly; and the need for believers to commit themselves to God's good and providential care.

- *Expect Suffering and Rejoice (4:12–14)*
- *Suffer as a Christian (4:15–18)*
- *Entrust Oneself to a Faithful God (4:19)*

EXPOSITION (4:12–19)

Peter warned his readers that they should expect coming fiery trials, which are designed to prove their faith (4:12). To the degree that such trials include suffering, to that same degree the readers should rejoice, for they will be rewarded at Jesus's return (4:13). Indeed, such trials also evidence their right standing with God, since it is those possessed by the Spirit who suffer in such ways (4:14). Of course, no reward awaits those who suffer for doing evil (4:15). Such people should be ashamed, but those who suffer for Jesus should hold their heads high, for their suffering results in God's glory. And since the end is near and the judgment is ready to begin, Peter reminds readers that it is with difficulty that they reach their final redemption. Those who do not believe the gospel, however, have no hope in the judgment to come. Accordingly, though they have been given a difficult path of suffering, they must endure with hope, knowing that they serve a faithful Creator.

Expect Suffering and Rejoice (4:12–14)

Peter's readers must not be surprised at suffering, but must rejoice in it, knowing that such suffering is evidence of blessing and leads to further blessing.

4:12. That this verse begins a new section of 1 Peter is evidenced both by the preceding doxology, which closed the last section, and the vocative "beloved" that begins this section (cf. 2:11). By calling the readers "beloved" Peter reminded them of their status as God's precious loved ones. This will be necessary to remember in light of the coming exhortations.

Old Testament Passages on Fire Purification

Ps. 66:10	For you, O God, have tested us; you have tried us as silver is tried.
Prov. 27: 21	The crucible is for silver, and the furnace is for gold, and a man is tested by his praise.
Zech. 13:9	And I will put this third into the fire, and refine them as one refines silver, and test them as gold is tested.
Mal. 3:1–4	Behold, I send my messenger, and he will prepare the way before me. And the Lord whom you seek will suddenly come to his temple; and the messenger of the covenant in whom you delight, behold, he is coming, says the Lord of hosts. But who can endure the day of his coming, and who can stand when he appears? For he is like a refiner's fire and like fullers' soap. He will sit as a refiner and purifier of silver, and he will purify the sons of Levi and refine them like gold and silver, and they will bring offerings in righteousness to the Lord. Then the offering of Judah and Jerusalem will be pleasing to the Lord as in the days of old and as in former years.

Peter asked readers not to be surprised by the "fiery trial" they were enduring.[1] The nature of this trial is debated. Some have suggested the text references actual burning of Christians, perhaps even the persecution of Nero who infamously used Christians as torches for his parties (Tacitus, *Ann.* 15.44). Such a literal interpretation of the phrase is unlikely, however, in light of Peter's use of similar fire imagery in 1:7 to refer to purification.

The background to such imagery is surely the Old Testament (Ps. 66:10; Prov. 27:21; Zech. 13:9; Mal. 3:1–4; Johnson, 1986). Particularly instructive is Proverbs 27:21 in the Septuagint, which uses this same word for the metallurgic purification of gold.

That Peter had in mind a purifying fire is confirmed in that "it comes upon you to test you." The word for "test" refers to "an attempt to learn the nature or character of something" (BDAG s.v. "πειρασμός" 793). Accordingly, the fiery trial was designed to prove the character of the one enduring the test. That the verb "comes upon" is passive is likely to be taken as a divine passive. It is God who allows the test, which is designed to prove the character of those tested. Throughout the New Testament, God is pictured as one who allows tests and trials to strengthen his people (Rom. 5:3–5; James 1:2–4). Romans 5:3 is particularly close to the present context, for it notes that believers should rejoice in their suffering because they "know that suffering produces perseverance."

That believers would experience suffering and testing should come as no "surprise." What they are experiencing, Peter said, is not something strange or unknown. There are several reasons Peter's readers should not be surprised. First, the Old Testament predicted that God would refine his people, cleansing them for further good works (Ps. 66:10; Prov. 27:21; Zech. 13:9; Mal. 3:1–4). Second, Jesus predicted that his followers would experience great suffering (Matt. 10:24–25; John 15:18–21). Third, though unbelievers were surprised at believers' behavior (4:4), believers should not be surprised at unbelievers' behavior. Since Jesus was treated poorly, and since they were following Jesus, they should expect the same treatment.

---

1 They were enduring. Though some versions suggest the trial may yet come to the readers (e.g., ESV, CSB, LEB), the text, by means of the preposition with dative (ἐν ὑμῖν), suggests that such trials are already present.

4:13. Peter called the readers to an unnatural response to suffering: "rejoice." Once more, however, he clarified that rejoicing should be limited to those times when someone suffers for the right reason. In this case, they should rejoice insofar as[2] they "share Christ's suffering." That is, to the degree that their suffering is based on their obedience to Jesus, they should rejoice to the same degree. The reference to "sharing in Christ's suffering" is not meant to indicate that believers may sacramentally or mystically join with Christ in his suffering. Such a phrase simply indicated that believers share the same *type* of suffering. In other words, Jesus suffered because of righteousness, and now believers share in that same form of suffering. A passage describing the early church's joy at suffering is recorded in Acts 5:41 and shares many characteristics with this passage: "The apostles left the Sanhedrin, rejoicing because they had been counted worthy of suffering disgrace for the Name" (NIV).

Having spoken of their present need for rejoicing in trials, Peter turned to consider the role that their present rejoicing would have on their future rejoicing. Indeed, they rejoiced now "in order that" they should "exceedingly rejoice" when Jesus returns. That the referent of the "revelation of his glory" is the second coming of Jesus is confirmed by the similarity of this passage with 1:7, which concluded by speaking of the revelation of "glory and honor when Jesus is revealed" (cf. 1 Cor. 1:7; 2 Thess. 1:7; 1 Peter 1:13). The emphatic "exceedingly rejoice" was created by an artful combination of two words, likely derived from Jesus's teaching on the same topic (Matt. 5:12). By doubling the terms, Peter highlighted that the future rejoicing would be much greater than the present rejoicing.

A question remains: In what way did present rejoicing lead to future rejoicing? Some argue that present rejoicing demonstrated belonging to Christ. Accordingly, those who could rejoice in suffering had reason to believe that they would rejoice all the more when Christ returned (Schreiner, 2003, 220). More likely, Peter was commanding the readers to respond appropriately to suffering now, with the goal that they would maintain the faith and not fall to the pressures that mounted against them (Achtemeier, 1996, 306). As elsewhere in this letter, the call to faithfulness and endurance did not militate against the new birth; rather, it demonstrated evidence of that new birth. That is, those who were truly redeemed would respond positively to Peter's command, enjoying both the joy in this age and the multiplied joy in the one to come.

4:14. In this verse, Peter considered an experience that was quite likely already true for his readers: "if you are insulted[3] for the name of Christ." To be "insulted" (ὀνειδίζεσθε) referred to verbal reproach and once more highlighted that the suffering endured by the Anatolian church was primarily verbal in nature. The suffering being considered was "for the name of Christ," which signified that it was for the person of Christ. Again, this highlighted that the suffering that was to be commended was connected to the believer's relation to Christ.

---

2   Insofar as. The preposition (καθό) can refer to degree (as in the interpretation above) or it can be causal. On the causal reading, Peter was saying, "rejoice since you share Christ's suffering" (cf. Elliott, 2001, 774). More likely, Peter was highlighting that their rejoicing should be consonant with the degree to which their suffering was the result of their obedience to Jesus.

3   "If you are insulted." Achtemeier argues that this might be translated "since" or "when." Nevertheless, as Wallace rightly notes, Peter used the construction that suggested possibility for a reason (he had other options to say "since" or "when"). In this case, as Wallace noted, changing the text to "since" or "when" turns "an invitation to dialogue into a lecture" (Wallace, 1996, 692).

Jesus and Blessing

The use of the word "blessed" confirmed that Peter was echoing the teaching of Jesus from the Sermon on the Mount. After giving six blessings (also known as beatitudes), Jesus noted a seventh: "blessed are those who are persecuted because of righteousness" (Matt. 5:10). Jesus went on to personalize the statement for the readers: "Blessed are you when people insult you, persecute you, and falsely say all kinds of evil against you because of me. Rejoice and be glad" (5:11–12a). The correspondence between Jesus's teaching and this passage is strong. First, both spoke of a divine blessing granted to believers for the sake of enduring persecution. Second, both used the same word to refer to verbal insult (ὀνειδίζω). Third, both indicated that the suffering was due to Jesus ("name of Christ" [1 Peter 4:13] and "because of me" [Matt. 5:11]).

Despite the maltreatment, believers who experienced such verbal assault were "blessed." As noted in our consideration of 3:14, the meaning of "blessed" is best understood as "divinely favored" (BDAG s.v. "μακάριος" 2a, p. 611). In other words, the readers should look at their suffering as a mark of divine privilege. In what way were the readers the recipients of divine privilege? In the Sermon on the Mount (see sidebar), the persecuted are privileged in two ways: because of their great heavenly reward and because they are persecuted in the same way as the prophets of old (Matt. 5:12). The first was a future reward, the second a present. The present reward was not simply the knowledge that they were persecuted like others, but rather that righteous people in the past experienced the same thing as they are. In other words, by recognizing that righteous people had experienced verbal attack, they had reason to believe they were likewise righteous. In sum, the reward was a confidence that they were rightly related to God.

Peter provided the same answer to the question "how are the readers recipients of divine privilege" as Jesus did. Of course, Peter had already considered the eternal reward in verse 13. Here he considered the present reward: "the spirit of glory and of God[4] rests on you." Based on the similarity of the language used here with Isaiah 11:1–3 in the Septuagint, interpreters believe Peter was echoing that text. There Isaiah said that "the branch of Jesse" (i.e., Jesus) "will have the Spirit of God rest on him" (καὶ ἀναπαύσεται ἐπ' αὐτὸν πνεῦμα τοῦ θεοῦ). What Isaiah spoke of as a future event, Peter spoke of as a present event. That it referenced Jesus and now references the readers is either based on the union of believers with Christ, or on the fact that believers who follow in Jesus's footsteps may expect some of the same blessings Jesus received.

In sum, Peter encouraged the readers that they were presently being blessed by the presence of the Spirit in their lives. The logic of the passage works this way: "by suffering persecution you show that the same spirit that resided with Jesus resides with you, since he was likewise persecuted for righteousness." Read this way, Peter's present reason for rejoicing was

---

4 "Spirit of glory and of God." This phrase is grammatically difficult. Three main interpretations exist. First, as we have translated it here, there are two phrases, both referencing the same Spirit, who is at one time spoken of as a Spirit of glory and another time as the Spirit of God. Second, the καί can be taken as ascensive, leading to the translation "the Spirit of glory, even the Spirit of God." This translation differs only in that it explicitly identifies the latter with the former, something left unstated in the first interpretation. The final interpretation understands the first phrase as distinct from the second: "the eschatological glory and the Spirit of God rests on you." The glory spoken of there would be the glory just referenced in verse 13. This final interpretation has much to commend it. Nevertheless, the meaning of the passage differs little based on how one interprets these, for both reference the glory believers receive and the Spirit they receive.

the same as Jesus's reason for rejoicing. In both cases, their experience of suffering identified them with those who were righteous and suffered before them.

Suffer as a Christian (4:15–18)

Peter argued that believers should not suffer because they do evil, but they should honor God through good deeds, leading to honorable suffering, for the time of judgment is coming.

4:15. Though Peter had addressed the possibility of suffering for wrongdoing before (2:20; 3:17), here he explicitly warned the readers that they must avoid the sinful activities that lead them to public censure. Specifically, none of the believers should "suffer as a murderer or a thief or an evildoer or as a meddler." The first two activities forbidden by Peter were straightforward. The Old Testament as well as the first century Greco-Roman morality denounced murder and theft. The third, using a Greek word (κακοποιός) that combines the words for "bad" (κακός) and "doer" (ποιέω) references any type of wrongdoing.

The final forbidden activity presents "one of the most difficult interpretive problems in the New Testament" (Schreiner, 2003, 223). The primary challenge is that this is not only a *hapax legomena* (a word that occurs only once in the Greek New Testament), but also a word that occurs nowhere else in extant Greek literature prior to Peter's use. By defining the word by its parts ("overseeing" [ἐπίσκοπος] and "what belongs to another" [ἀλλότριος]), most English translations speak of someone who is a "meddler" (ESV, NASB, NIV) or "busybody" (NKJV).

The chief liability of the "meddler" view is that it seems like an odd addition to sins like murder and theft. Accordingly, interpreters have sought other definitions. Nevertheless, in the Greek Peter did set this activity apart from the rest by adding "or *as*" (ἢ ὡς). The addition seems to indicate that the final element is distinct from the others. Likely, it highlights that

this item is in a category less serious than the others (cf. Jobes, 2005, 289). Why then was it added? Though it may rank lower on the scale of serious sins, it has an overly large impact on the Christian community. Those who meddle in other people's lives attract the attention of others. Peter throughout this letter has essentially argued that believers should seek to live harmoniously within society, being its best members. They could do this by submitting to government (2:13–17) and maintaining right relationships within the household (2:18–3:12). If attention was to be drawn to the Christian community, it should be because they were recognized as great citizens or because of their distinctive Christian behavior. In sum, meddling drew harmful attention to the Christian community. That Peter addressed the issue likely indicates that he had some awareness that this was a problem, whether in Asia Minor particularly or in the churches of God more generally.

Meddlers?

Because the other sins listed here are considered serious, meddling in other people's affairs appears problematic to many interpreters. This has led to other interpretations. A few scholars have suggested "revolutionary" (Moffatt, 1928, 157–58). In Peter's day, being a revolutionary would certainly be a serious offence, and it would have elicited great suffering at the hands of fellow citizens, who desired to keep peace with Rome. Few have embraced this interpretation, however, for there is little textual evidence to support it. A more defended suggestion is that the word refers to an "embezzler" (e.g., Achtemeier, 1996, 310). Such an interpretation suggests that believers were in a social position of looking into the affairs of others (e.g., a steward) and may be tempted to take what was not rightfully theirs. Calvin suggested another interpretation, when he said the word referred to a "covetous" person (Calvin, 1994, 137). This reading is a more specific form of meddling, for it is looking into the affairs of another with a covetous eye.

4:16. Though believers must not suffer shame by acting as evildoers, they should not be ashamed if they "suffer as a Christian." This is one of the few times the word "Christian" (χριστιανός) is used in the New Testament. The only other two times are in Acts; the first (Acts 11:26) highlighted that the term was first used of believers in Antioch, while the second (Acts 26:28) showed that the term had apparently become more widely known, as Agrippa used it while speaking with Paul. The term likely derived from unbelievers who sought to describe believers as those who are committed to one called the "Christ." Significantly, then, unbelievers recognized that Christians were distinct. In regard to this passage, Peter was saying that believers should not be ashamed when they suffer, since in suffering *they follow Christ.*

The mention of shame is significant. In the Middle Eastern culture in which this letter was written, the honor-shame dynamic is hard to overemphasize. The greater honor one received, the greater social standing one had. The opposite applied to shame, for the more shame directed toward someone, the less their social position. As a result of believing in Christ, readers had embraced positions that lowered their social standing and attracted societal shame. Nevertheless, Peter asked the readers to view the issue in the opposite way. Though they were openly shamed by unbelievers, they should not actually feel ashamed. They certainly should not fold to pressure and change their actions (cf. where shame leads to potential apostasy Mark 8:38; 2 Tim. 1:8, 12, 16; 2:15). They should feel no shame, because they lived by a new standard, an eternal one that would one day be revealed to all.

That the believer should feel honored when shamed was suggested by Peter's command: "instead of experiencing shame, glorify God by bearing the name 'Christian'" (Michaels, 1988, 170).[5] In other words, Peter's readers were to live as Christians, upholding the name of Christ. As they did so, their behavior would be distinctive, drawing the negative attention of society. The society, for its part, would shame them, seeking to get them to change their behavior. Instead of feeling ashamed, the readers should accept such dishonor as a way to glorify the One who made them different. Because of their transformed perspective, they recognized that the more shame they experienced, the more glory God received through Christ.

4:17. This verse provides the grounds for why believers should obey the admonitions offered in verses 12–16:[6] "for the time has come for judgment to begin at the household of God."

---

5   "Bearing the name 'Christian.'" There is a textual variant in this verse, leading some versions to say "glorify God in that matter" (KJV, NKJV). The textual variant was not listed in the United Bible Society's fourth edition, because the committee did not think it was a viable option. In the fifth edition, however, it was included. The fifth edition began using an advanced computer-based method for determining the best readings, which indicated that "in that part" (ἐν τῷ μέρει τούτῳ) was the better reading. Though the fifth edition gives the reading a B rating (suggesting some level of confidence), using classical text-critical methods the reading presented in the text above is better, partly because of its congruence with the context, as well as its much broader textual support (e.g., 𝔓⁷² ℵ A B Ψ).

6   Verses 12–16. That this verse provides the grounds for Peter's advancing argument is clear. Precisely what it grounds is not. There are five options, which are here listed in order from less likely to most likely (list modified from Forbes, 2014, 160):

   1. "Suffering as a Christian" from verse 16a
   2. "Not being ashamed" from verse 16b
   3. "Glorifying God" from 16c

The judgment being referenced is the final judgment of all humanity (cf. 4:5). Since the main verb is not supplied, the reader could supply a perfect verb ("the time of judgment *has come*" [CSB, NRSV, NKJV]) or a present verb ("*it is* time for the judgment" [LEB, ESV, NIV]). The former is supported by the broader context, which indicated that the end of all things has begun (v. 7).

Possible Old Testament Echoes in 1 Peter 4:17

Commentators suggest two Old Testament passages as possible sources for Peter's language here: Ezekiel 9:6 and Malachi 3:1–4. Ezekiel 9 is often compared to the present passage because of lexical similarity. In Ezekiel, God was judging his own people and indicated that the judgment should "begin from my holy places" (NETS; ἀπὸ τῶν ἁγίων μου ἄρξασθε). Such language is similar to Peter's "begin with God's household" (τοῦ ἄρξασθαι τὸ κρίμα ἀπὸ τοῦ οἴκου τοῦ θεοῦ). Despite the similarity of language, the contexts are quite distinct. In Ezekiel the focus of the judgment is on those who do not bear God's mark and thus are not a part of God's people. In Peter's text, the focus of the judgment is on the people of God.

For this reason, Malachi 3:1–4 is often viewed as a more likely echo. Though there are few linguistic commonalities, there does seem to be some theological overlap. Both passages reference the "house of God," though Malachi refers to it as the temple (3:1). Further, both speak of the purifying work of God among his people by means of the Messiah (3:1–3). Finally, both passages speak of the coming judgment of the wicked and the righteous, emphasizing God's positive relation to the righteous in the judgment (3:5).

If Peter was referencing Malachi, he recast it in a new light. The temple is no longer a place but a people—a theme evident elsewhere in the New Testament (1 Cor. 3:16; 2 Cor. 6:16; Eph. 2:19; 1 Tim. 3:15; Heb. 3:6). Further, the "sons of Levi" in Malachi have now become believers of any heritage. Both of these shifts are present earlier in the letter, where Peter maintains that believers are "living stones" that are "being built into a spiritual house to be a holy priesthood" (2:5). As suggested when we considered Peter's use of Israelite language for the readers in 2:4–10, it is likely Peter was drawing parallels between the people of God in this age and those who will one day experience the fullness of what is anticipated by the Old Testament prophets. In this way Peter was noting that the days of the end, though still future, are in an important sense already upon humanity.

The judgment begins at the household of God. Of course, judgment need not imply a negative verdict, nor is the term limited to a simple judicial verdict. In this case, judgment references the process whereby God differentiates those who are righteous from those who are not. Accordingly, the type of judgment expected by believers and unbelievers is different. For believers, the type of judgment they undergo is a purifying type, which reveals the nature of their new birth. They are, in the earlier words of Peter, going through a "fiery ordeal" that comes upon them to "test them" (v. 12). The positive result of such testing is the purification of the believer, confirming their possession of the Spirit of God (v. 15) and providing them immense hope as they face the prospect of coming eschatological judgment (vv. 13, 16). In sum, Peter was arguing that believers have already entered into the process of

---

4. The thought of the prior two verses (15–16)
5. The whole thought from verses 12–16

The final option seems most likely in light of how well it flows with the context, highlighting both that the readers should avoid evil (v. 15) and pursue those things that glorify God (v. 16). These are themes Peter has been arguing since 2:11–12.

final judgment. In their case, God is refining them, showing them to have been made righteous by the work of the Spirit of God.

Peter throughout this letter avoided direct consideration of the fate awaiting those who disobey and do not believe the gospel. The latter portion of this verse comes close, yet even here he entertained their end by comparing it to the judgment experienced by believers. Peter provided a lesser to greater argument: "if the judgment begins with us, what will be the outcome for those who do not obey the gospel of God?" The assumption is that since the judgment of believers, who are loved and chosen by God, is difficult, the judgment of unbelievers will be even more difficult. The reason for the judgment is clear: they "do not obey the gospel of God." Obedience and belief go together in Peter's thought (cf. 2:8; 3:1), for it is those who believe who are changed to become obedient.

4:18. As Peter has done elsewhere in the letter (1:24–25; 2:9–10; 4:8), he supported his just stated point with an Old Testament citation. Peter was quoting from Septuagint Proverbs 11:31,[7] which serves to support verse 17 by restating its central message in different words.

The quotation was fitting grammatically as well as thematically. Both verses 17 and 18 were given in a parallel fashion (e.g., parallel if/then statements, parallel questions, parallel comparisons). Accordingly, Peter aligned the "righteous" of verse 17 with "us" from verse 16. In other words, Peter noted that the readers were those whom the proverb indicated were righteous. Both Peter and the proverb note that the righteous are saved, though it is not clear whether they were saying the righteous are "scarcely" (ESV, NKJV) or "with difficulty" (NASB, NIV, CSB) saved. The challenge is that the adverb can have either of these two meanings (BDAG s.v. "μόλις" 657). In favor of the first, Peter may be following Jesus in highlighting the few who find the path to life (Matt. 7:14).

Nevertheless, Jesus in that same context argued that the path to life was difficult, naming it the narrow path. Accordingly, the difficulty of salvation is not an idea unique to Peter. This second interpretation appears to be more contextually sensitive. For Peter's readers, their experience of new birth led to a change of values, which brought about social persecution. Added to this, Peter's readers were fighting against their own remaining sinful inclinations. They had found the path of salvation a difficult one. Nevertheless, the comparison Peter presented highlighted that their position was envious, especially as one considered the position of the "ungodly" and "sinner."

The question asked concerning the unbeliever is literally where he "will appear," but the meaning is better expressed by the interpretive translation, "What will become of the ungodly and the sinner?"[8] In sum, Peter was asking, "If the ones God loves and who are righteous must pass through great difficulty on their path of salvation, what sort of severe judgment is reserved for those who are disobedient?" The net effect of the two parallel clauses was to confirm the

---

7   Septuagint Proverbs 11:31. The Hebrew of this passage is distinct from the Greek. The NIV translates from the Hebrew text: "If the righteous receive their due on earth, how much more the ungodly and the sinner!" Bruce Waltke offers an interpretation of the Hebrew, which would be consistent with the Septuagint translation and with Peter's quotation. In his words, the Hebrew proverb "probably implies a distinction between the present remedial punishment of the righteous 'in the earth' and the future penal punishment of the wicked" (Waltke, 2004, 1:514; cf. Carson, 2007, 1041–42).

8   "What will become of the ungodly and the sinner?" Dubis challenges this argument, suggesting that the sense is better captured by a specific answer to the question of where someone will appear: "the sinner and ungodly will not appear in the world to come" (Dubis, 2001, 95).

difficulty of the present life of the saints, yet at the same time to show that such a life was far more desirable than that of those who do not believe.

Entrust Oneself to a Faithful God (4:19)
Peter encouraged the readers to do good and entrust themselves to God, because they know that he is both sovereign and faithful.

4:19. In light of the reality ("so then"; ὥστε καί) that the judgment began with the household of God, Peter commanded suffering readers to "entrust their souls to a faithful creator." To "entrust" meant to commit "someone to the care or protection" of another (BDAG s.v. "παρατίθημι" 3b, p. 772). In this case, Peter was calling suffering readers to commit themselves to God. Of course, they had already done so through their new birth; yet Peter was calling them to persevere.

Why should they have entrusted their souls to God? One reason given concerned God's role as faithful creator. While the mention of God's creative activity seems initially odd, it served to highlight the power of God and his ownership over creation. All that was created was by his design, and this should have given encouragement to believers as they sought to follow the path he indicated was right.

But he is not merely a creator, he is a *faithful* creator, meaning he is one who is ultimately dependable. Though life may be volatile, Peter was saying that the readers could commit themselves to him, knowing that he had their best in mind. Peter was not, however, providing a rosy view of the Christian life. Despite God being faithful, suffering was often "according to his will." This statement both excluded suffering for evil (for that is surely outside God's will), and it clarified that suffering is sometimes the will of God for his people.

The final statement of this verse—"do good"—may be combined with the command "entrust yourselves" in various ways: "entrust while doing good" (ESV, NET, CSB); "entrust and continue to do good" (NIV); "entrust in doing what is right" (NASB, LEB, NKJV). The first and second option distinguish entrusting from doing good, while the third indicates that it is by doing good that one entrusts himself to God. Whichever translation is chosen, the net effect is similar. Suffering believers were to entrust themselves to God even while they continued to do good, the very thing that was causing their suffering.

THEOLOGICAL FOCUS
The exegetical idea (Peter commanded the readers to not be shocked or ashamed at suffering for righteousness; instead, they were to entrust themselves to God, rejoicing in suffering, because they knew that those who suffer for righteousness glorify God, are blessed in this life, and are vindicated in the next) leads to this theological focus: believers must not be shocked or ashamed at suffering for righteousness; instead, they are to entrust themselves to God, rejoicing in suffering, because they know that those who suffer for righteousness glorify God, are blessed in this life, and are vindicated in the next.

The believer's natural response to suffering for righteousness is shock. Why would someone verbally assault another person who was trying to do right? Understood rightly, however, such persecution against believers is the natural response of the unbeliever to the behavior of believers. Because good behavior reminds unbelievers of the moral law they would rather forget, they persecute and seek to shame believers, hoping to revert believers to the lifestyle they abandoned at their new birth.

To the degree that a believer follows in the steps of Jesus, he should rejoice in such suffering for two reasons. First, it is proof that the believer has become indwelled by the Spirit of God (v. 14). Second, by enduring suffering for righteousness one reveals his membership in the household of God and confirms that great joy awaits him at the return of Jesus (v. 13).

Despite the suffering, the believer must commit to entrusting himself to God, while pursuing good deeds (v. 19). This means setting aside one's own interests and concerns and welcoming the suffering that is experienced because of identifying with Jesus. Doing so is not foolish, for God is faithful and powerful, sovereign over the suffering of his people. Further, by doing so the believer may honorably bring glory to God by his transformed life, drawing attention to the Father who granted him new life.

All of this is essential for believers living after the coming of Christ and before his final return. Such believers live in the last time, and they know the final judgment has already begun (v. 17). In their case, the process of judgment is restorative, refining them to become more like Christ. Accordingly, though suffering is not to be sought, it is not to be feared. God wills it for the good of his people. On the other hand, the enemies of believers are moving quickly toward their utter destruction. And though believers may wish to escape their present suffering, they have hope for future glory. Unbelievers, however, enjoy many pleasures today but will experience devastating judgment at the coming of Jesus.

PREACHING AND TEACHING STRATEGIES

Exegetical and Theological Synthesis

It is all too easy to lose focus during trials in life. Though we might leave Sunday morning worship on a spiritual high, it all comes crashing down on Monday when reality hits us at work and the all-too-familiar persecution heats up again. A few times in his letter, Peter addressed the believer's perspective during persecution. He spoke of the function of trials to test a believer's faith in 1:6–7. He pointed to the example of Christ, who was rejected by men but precious in God's sight (2:4–8, 21–25; cf. 3:18–22). Several times he briefly noted the tendency of unbelievers to criticize and speak evil of believers

(2:12; 3:9; 4:4). In 4:12–19, Peter addresses the issue of persecution at length, offering surprising advice to his readers.

Peter upends expectations by associating positive terminology and actions with a negative concept of suffering. Suffering, he says, should not surprise a believer and is not at all strange (4:12). Twice in verse 13 he tells his readers to "rejoice" and once he says, "be glad." Neither of these words comes to mind first when the average believer undergoes a difficult trial. Yet suffering both identifies the believer more with Christ by a similar experience and anticipates the glory to be revealed one day.

Peter also notes that the believer is "blessed" when suffering persecution (4:14). Most will wonder whether or not they did something wrong or are suffering punishment or a curse from God. But the apostle's reason for the blessing is quite the opposite: Persecution is a good indication that the Spirit of God indwells a person. Persecution confirms salvation. Because of this, it should result in greater glory to God (4:16) and a greater trust in his faithfulness (4:19). The "theology of suffering" points believers in a helpful direction to not only survive the trials of life but to thrive through them, growing in relationship to Christ.

Preaching Idea

Flip the Script of Honor and Shame by Rejoicing in Righteous Suffering.

Contemporary Connections

What does it mean?

What does it mean for Christians to flip the script in honor and shame by rejoicing in righteous suffering? To "flip the script" means to reverse expectations in a conventional social situation. A husband might try to flip the script by making the wife feel guilty after she tries to confront him on something that offended her. In the Old Testament, Esther flipped the script on Haman by turning a celebratory feast into an occasion for Haman's hanging. Elisabeth Elliot flipped the script after her husband was murdered by the Auca tribe in Ecuador, when instead of it driving her off the mission field it motivated her all the more to share the gospel with this lost tribe. Olympic athletes flip the script when the analysts expect them to lose, yet instead they mount a dominant performance over their competitors. To flip the script is to act unexpectedly when everyone else behaves status quo.

Apply this to the concept of shame and honor. Believers were being shamed for living holy. They were scorned for doing good works and separating themselves from the pagan norms of the culture. Unbelievers expected to shame believers out of Christianity. Flipping the script meant that Christians—instead of allowing shame to dissuade them from godly living—determined to consider it an honor to suffer for Christ. The suffering, then, had the opposite effect. Instead of destroying their faith, it strengthened their faith.

Apart from the Preaching Idea, the preacher may also need to explain a few important concepts in the text to help the church understand Peter's intended meaning. In verse 17, Peter indicates that "it is time for judgment to begin at the household of God." Clarify the difference between the judgment of unbelievers and that of believers. One has a negative verdict; one has a positive verdict. Believers have already entered their process of judgment with the trials they endure having a purifying effect on them.

Preachers may also want to clarify Peter's quotation of Proverbs 11:31 in verse 18. In what way is salvation difficult for the righteous? By highlighting Jesus's teaching, preachers can help align and illustrate Peter's meaning. Jesus preached at the Sermon on the Mount, "For the gate is narrow and *the way is hard* that leads to life, and those who find it are few" (Matt. 7:14, emphasis added). Being a Christian is no walk in the park, at least not on this side of heaven.

True believers ought to expect and anticipate suffering and persecution.

Is it true?

Is it true that believers can actually rejoice while suffering? A few illustrations in other areas of life will help prove the notion more plausible.

I (Bryan) used to swim in high school. Swim practices were rarely what you would call "fun." Most of the practice consisted of lap after lap after lap (after lap), back and forth, working every muscle in the body, for two straight hours. It was not fun; it was suffering. But suffering had a purpose—the glory of the medal on race day. Suffering brought strength and stamina to the body. Suffering bonded the swimmers in the pool together. We would all "enjoy" complaining about how tough practice was when we got on the bus at the end of the night. Many times we found ways to joke and goof off between laps. If there can be rejoicing and glory and enjoyment while suffering through sports conditioning, certainly there can be rejoicing in other areas of life as well.

One of the reasons Peter encourages believers to rejoice in suffering is that believers then share in Christ's sufferings and will have a greater gladness when Christ returns in glory (4:13). Military cadets endure the suffering of boot camp because they know great war heroes have suffered the same trials before them. They consider the glory of graduation once basic training is over. Remembering that Christ suffered and considering the glory that is to come helps Christians endure unpleasant trials in this life.

Now what?

How do we rejoice in sufferings? Peter shows that the ability to rejoice comes from two related factors: the knowledge that our sufferings reflect the sufferings of Christ, and the knowledge that our sufferings bring blessing and ultimate glory. In other words, believers are encouraged to look at the past (Christ's sufferings) and the future (blessing and glory) to manage their present trial.

Rightly understood, Peter is not advocating for a love of suffering, as if in some twisted sense we should enjoy the trial itself. Rather than rejoicing in the trial, we rejoice *through* the trial, in Christ. The route to rejoicing in hardship begins at the cross, and Jesus has paved the way. The preacher should also remind the believer that identifying with Jesus through suffering is a privilege only granted on this side of heaven. In eternity to come, there will be no more suffering and hence, no more blessing of this unique union with Jesus.

Preachers should also paint the church a clear picture of what suffering for sin looks like (4:15). The man caught in adultery and suffering an ugly divorce cannot whine about alimony payments, child support payments, or a messier love life. He has brought such suffering upon himself. The businessman caught embezzling should not blame money or business partners for the legal woes he suffers. He asked for it. Christians should be taught to distinguish between righteous suffering and its counterpart.

Creativity in Presentation

Early in his letter, Peter illustrated the tested nature of faith with an example from the world of metallurgy (1:7). Peter returns to a similar image in 4:12, this time in relation to enduring persecution and trials (cf. Prov. 27:21). The preacher might want to draw an example from fire assays to illustrate the point. Mining companies and refineries use the fire assaying process to value and extract precious metals from ore. A sample is heated and treated with chemicals in a process that determines the relative purity of a precious metal in the sample. Likewise, believers are similarly tested in their faith, not through literal fire and chemicals but through the heat of persecution. The preacher might want to show some images of such a process to help the church envision the process as it relates to their Christian lives.

Later in the passage, Peter also speaks about "busybodies" or "meddlers" (1:15) who suffer for their evil. A classic example in television is Marie Barone, the overly nosey mother in the show *Everybody Loves Raymond*, played by Doris Roberts. She has no problem walking into her son's house at all hours of day or night, sticking her nose into everybody's business as if it's her own. Many plots from the show center around the trouble she brings on herself and the family as a result of her meddling. Using an example from this sitcom or another similar show gives a clear picture of the kind of person Peter envisioned. When illustrating, be careful not to lose the bigger picture of rejoicing in righteous suffering.

Preachers can structure the sermon in accordance with the theme of suffering:

- Suffer Expectantly (4:12)

- Suffer Joyfully (4:13–14)

- Suffer Righteously (4:15–18)

- Suffer Faithfully (4:19)

DISCUSSION QUESTIONS

1. What kinds of "fiery trials" were the first-century believers facing? What kinds of trials do believers face today?

2. What motivates a believer to rejoice in sufferings? How does this rejoicing connect to Christ's sufferings?

3. What is the difference between suffering as a Christian and suffering as a sinner?

4. Explain the relationship between shame and honor for believers. How does this relationship help believers face persecution?

5. How does God's faithfulness as creator motivate believers suffering persecution?

1 Peter 5:1–5

EXEGETICAL IDEA
Peter detailed duties within the community: elders must shepherd willingly and eagerly, serving as examples to the flock, nonelders must submit to the elders, and all must show humility to one another.

THEOLOGICAL FOCUS
Believers have duties within the community: elders must shepherd willingly and eagerly, serving as examples to the flock, nonelders must submit to the elders, and all must show humility to one another.

PREACHING IDEA
Humble Elders Lead Humble People toward a Humble Shepherd.

PREACHING POINTERS
Peter is near the end of his letter. He has addressed the issue of suffering in multiple parts of his writing. He applied Christian identity to various spheres of life, including what it looks like to act godly toward the government, in a master-slave relationship, and in the home between husbands and wives. Peter now turns to address the church, helping both the leaders (elders) of the church to understand what it looks like to lead and what it looks like for the followers to follow that leadership. Proper relationships within the church are essential if the Christian community is going to persevere under persecution.

Today, if the church is to succeed in her mission, such proper relationships remain essential. Too many examples abound of domineering or abusive pastors and leaders. The headlines are smeared with shepherds who have taken advantage of sheep by stealing money from the offering or worse, by leveraging their position for sexual satisfaction. Peter's words cut through this kind of unbiblical crassness and show what a true church leader ought to look like. He also addresses the congregation, encouraging a similar humility that reflects a submissiveness to both God and human leader. Churches today would do well to pay attention to Peter's admonitions to the flock.

THE FLOCK OF GOD (5:1–5)

LITERARY STRUCTURE AND THEMES (5:1–5)

This passage consists of the middle portion of the body closing (4:12–5:11). Three groups of people were addressed: the elders, the younger, and the entirety of the congregation. Peter addressed the elders with an extended introduction, showing how he was also an elder and a partner in suffering. Such an introduction served to strengthen his admonitions concerning shepherding the flock of God. Faithful shepherds, Peter argued, would receive a worthy reward. The younger were given one simple yet often difficult command: follow the leadership of the elders. Finally, Peter addressed the whole congregation, encouraging them to act with humility toward one another. To this command he added an incentive: God gives grace to the humble.

Themes of this section include the following: the duties of elders in the household of God; the duty of those under the leadership of elders in the household; the duty of believers to one another; and the outsized reward for faithfulness in the duty of shepherding.

- *The Motivations and Duties of an Elder (5:1–4)*
- *The Duty of God's People (5:5)*

EXPOSITION (5:1–5)

For the first time since the introduction of the letter, Peter here referred to himself. His comments show that he, as a fellow-elder, a fellow-sharer in suffering, a fellow-partaker in glory, was speaking to the elders as equal brothers in the faith (5:1). His directive was straightforward: shepherd the flock God gave you oversight over (5:2). Such shepherding

required willingness, eagerness, and humility (5:2–3). Faithful shepherds, Peter revealed, would receive great reward at the return of Jesus (5:4). Peter then addressed the "younger," referring to those who were not elders, and he called them to follow the lead of the elders (5:5). Peter's final directive concerned all the readers: "clothe yourselves with humility toward one another" (5:5).

The Motivations and Duties of an Elder (5:1–4)

On the basis of his own calling, Peter commanded the elders to shepherd willingly and eagerly, providing an example to the flock, so that they would receive eternal reward.

5:1. It is debated whether this passage begins with a conjunction "therefore" (NASB, ESV, NET; $\mathfrak{P}^{72}$ A B; NA^{27}) or whether the conjunction is absent (NIV, CSB; P 33. 81. 307*. Byz. NA^{28}). The lack of the conjunction makes the passage easier to understand, for the conjunction seems to suggest a connection between 5:1 and the previous verses that is not easy to determine. But for that very reason, it is likely original, since there is motivation for eliminating the conjunction but very little reason to introduce it. Possibly, Peter was continuing a consideration of Ezekiel 9, which notes that the judgment of the household begins with the elders (Jobes, 2005, 300). The connection would then be summarized as follows: "so, since the judgment begins at the household of God, the members of the household should act rightly." The exhortations for elders and those under their care, then, is based on the knowledge that the judgment of God's people is already underway.

The first exhortation is directed toward the "elders" (πρεσβυτέρους). The word for "elder" could simply refer to older people in the congregation, yet it is clear Peter has a more specific identification in mind. Throughout the New Testament, the leaders of the church are called elders (e.g., Acts 11:30; 20:17; 1 Tim. 5:17; Titus 1:5; James 5:14). In this passage, the elders are called to shepherd and exercise oversight among the congregation (v. 2). Further, they are given a portion to lovingly rule over (v. 3). It is then to the pastors that Peter first speaks.

Up to this point, Peter had only spoken of himself when he noted his authorship of the letter (1:1). The first-person address here, then, is both unexpected and emphatic. Peter noted three things concerning himself, each of which added to the power of his words. First, he called himself a "fellow-elder" (συμπρεσβύτερος). This term appears to have been one coined by Peter and is simply the combination of the words "elder" with the word for "with." Thus, he is an "elder with them." Such a designation does not suggest that Peter was a pastor within the assembly there; rather, it was Peter's way of identifying with those he was exhorting. Peter was one with those who sought to shepherd the flock of God. As the gospel of John indicates, some of the last words of Jesus to Peter before the ascension were "feed my sheep" (John 21:15–17). It is probable that Peter was echoing these words, reminding the readers that he too was tasked with shepherding God's people. In this shared role, Peter was passing down his lived wisdom to his readers.

Second, Peter called himself a "witness of the sufferings of Christ." The term "witness" can be used in more than one way (BDAG s.v. "μαρτύρομαι" 619). Some read it as referring to Peter's role in giving eyewitness to the suffering that Jesus endured. This is a possible reading. Of course, Peter may not have seen Jesus on the cross, but he did observe the suffering Jesus endured from the religious leaders of his day. Such social rejection is similar to the type of rejection Peter's readers were facing.

A better way of reading "witness," however, refers to Peter not as an *eyewitness*, but to Peter as a *proclaimer-witness*. In other words, Peter was not saying that he was a *witness of* Jesus's suffering; he was saying that he was a *witness to* Jesus's suffering. In support of this reading is the fact that there is only one Greek article joining these first two descriptors. This suggests that those Peter were writing to were not merely fellow elders, but they were also fellow witnesses of the suffering of Christ. Clearly, readers did not see the suffering of Jesus, but if they were leaders of the congregation, they were tasked with witnessing to that suffering.

Peter's final description of himself concerned his role as a "sharer in the glory that is to be revealed." In two other places Peter referred to "glory" and "revealed" together. The first spoke of the testing of faith, which results in "praise, glory, and honor at the revelation of Jesus" (1:7). The second spoke of rejoicing in suffering knowing the coming abundance of joy "when his [i.e., Jesus's] glory is revealed" (4:13). Taken together, these passages indicate that the glory is the glory of Jesus, which will be made manifest at his coming. Believers may share in this glory if they endure the trials of life, showing their new birth by obedience to Jesus.

Despite his apostolic identity (1:1), these three descriptions show that Peter provided an example the elders could follow. He, like them, was a shepherd of God's people. He, like them, had been called to witness to the sufferings of Jesus. He, like them, was anticipating the glory that he would share with Christ at Jesus's return. Thus, having established himself as one tasked directly by Jesus with the same duties as these elders, Peter moved forward with his exhortation.

5:2. The chief command Peter gave to the elders was to "shepherd the flock of God." The metaphor of shepherding, though common in an agrarian world, was drawn primarily from the Old Testament, which pictured God as the shepherd of his people (e.g., Pss. 79:13; 80:1; 95:7; Ezek. 34:31). And though the leaders of Israel are sometimes referred to as shepherds (e.g., Num. 27:17; Isa. 63:11), it is in the New Testament that the idea expands in significance. Jesus spoke of himself and was spoken of as a shepherd, who not only had sheep in Israel, but also among the Gentiles (Matt. 10:6, 16; Mark 6:34; 14:27–28; Luke 12:32; John 10:1–18). It was to Peter specifically that the task of shepherding God's people was passed (John 21:16). The metaphor of a pastor as a shepherd took root in the early church (e.g., Acts 20:28; Eph. 4:11), and Peter referred to it here.

The metaphor should not be overread. Peter was not seeking to make analogy between the people and sheep, as though the readers are dumb and prone to wander. Instead, the metaphor highlighted the need for leaders among God's people. This is clarified by the participle "exercising oversight,"[1] which means to "accept responsibility for the care of someone" (BDAG s.v. "ἐπισκοπέω" 379). Peter was saying that the elders must shepherd *by* (participle of means) accepting the responsibility granted to them of guiding the congregation.

The rest of this verse and the next highlight how the elders are to shepherd through their exercise of oversight. Three sets of contrasting attributes are presented, with the first being what the elders must avoid and the second being what they must do. The first set of attributes indicated that the shepherds must lead "not under compulsion but willingly." To act under compulsion (ἀναγκαστῶς) meant to act in a way that was not self-willed.[2] The opposing attribute, and the one that Peter commended, is that elders must lead "willingly." To this positive attribute Peter added "according to God" (κατὰ θεόν). The shortness of the prepositional phrase opens it to interpretive debate. Two options are possible:

1. "Shepherd willingly, which is God's will." On this reading, the prepositional phrase modifies the willing shepherding, and indicates that the Lord requires willing shepherds.
2. "Shepherd willingly in a way God desires." On this reading, the prepositional phrase highlights the way that the shepherd ought to approach his task.

The first option is to be preferred, for the location of the prepositional phrase directly after "willingly" suggests that the phrase modifies the willing service. This sense is the most common one adopted in English translations: "as God would have you" (ESV, NRSV, CSB) or "as God wants you to be" (NIV).

The second contrasting pair noted that shepherds must exercise oversight "not for shameful gain but eagerly." The word Peter used for "dishonest gain" is only used here in biblical literature, but an adjective to which it is related (αἰσχρός) is used three times in the New Testament to refer to things that are shameful (1 Cor. 11:6; 14:35; Eph. 5:12; Silva,

---

1 "Exercising oversight." This passage helps us understand the roles of leadership in the early church. Though some have made fine distinctions between elders, pastors, and bishops, this passage suggests they refer to the same position. First, the overall passage is speaking to the elders of the congregation, and it commands them to "shepherd" (the term from which we get "pastor") by "exercising oversight" (the term from which we get bishop; cf. Calvin, 1994, 145).

2 Self-willed. It is not clear what circumstances would cause one to serve as an elder under compulsion. Perhaps Goppelt and Davids are right to say that the elders were appointed by the congregation, and therefore may not have self-chosen the role. Of course, in a socially hostile situation like the one Peter was writing to, becoming a leader in the congregation would only highlight the elder as a person to target (Goppelt, 1993, 345; Davids, 1990, 178).

2014, 1:18). Peter was likely not indicating that elders in the church were engaged in lucrative activities that were shameful; instead, it appears that the engagement in shepherding *for the sake of financial gain* was what was shameful. Those whose eyes have shifted from the eternal reward to the temporal may also be tempted to shift their ministry goals toward temporal rather than eternal goals.

Instead of doing the job to get the salary, elders were to serve "eagerly." It is important to recognize that Peter did not contrast getting paid for the work with working for free. He did not say, "don't shepherd for gain, but do it freely." Accordingly, it is clear Peter was not arguing against paying elders in the church (cf. Matt. 10:10; 1 Cor. 9:3–14; 1 Tim. 5:17–18). Though the elder may have been paid, that is not why he engaged in the work. He did the work "eagerly," out of an inward passion to accomplish the task God put before him.

5:3. The final contrasting pair showed that elders were "not to lord it over those allotted to their care but to be an example to the flock." It is almost certain that Peter was referring to the words of the Lord when he wrote this passage. In Mark 10:35–45 (see sidebar), Jesus provided a lesson on leadership to the disciples, indicating that though the Gentiles considered one who "lorded over" (κατακυριεύουσιν) others to be a leader, his disciples were to lead through service to others. The greatest was not the one who had the most servants under him but the one who, despite being in a position above others, placed himself under others in service.

The elders were commanded not to lord over those "allotted to their care." The word translated here as "allotted to their care" is used in the New Testament to refer to an item used to determine the will of God (i.e., a lot that is cast; e.g., Acts 1:26b). It is also used to refer to that which has been appointed by lot

or assigned by someone (e.g., Acts 8:21; Col. 1:12; BDAG s.v. "κλῆρος" 548). It is this latter sense that is used here. The elders have been granted by God a portion of the people of God to shepherd. Knowing this helps the elders to avoid lording over others, for they are not the ultimate master.

> **Jesus's Memorable Lesson on Leadership**
> James and John approached Jesus, asking to sit at his right and left hand in the kingdom. Jesus's response was memorable to the disciples, who were disturbed at the audacity of the brothers. Jesus responded to the brothers and then spoke to the entirety of the disciples (including Peter):
> "You don't know what you are asking," Jesus said. "Can you drink the cup I drink or be baptized with the baptism I am baptized with?" "We can," they answered.
>
> Jesus said to them, "You will drink the cup I drink and be baptized with the baptism I am baptized with, but to sit at my right or left is not for me to grant. These places belong to those for whom they have been prepared." When the ten heard about this, they became indignant with James and John. Jesus called them together and said, "You know that those who are regarded as rulers of the Gentiles lord it over them, and their high officials exercise authority over them. Not so with you. Instead, whoever wants to become great among you must be your servant, and whoever wants to be first must be slave of all. For even the Son of Man did not come to be served, but to serve, and to give his life as a ransom for many." (Mark 10:38–45)

Instead of domineering over those in their charge, shepherds are called to "be an example to the flock." Domineering leaders cannot serve as examples, for there can only be one at the top. Servant leaders, however, by sacrificing their own desires for the sake of others may show others how to serve. Peter was likely remembering Jesus's words from Mark 10:45. After noting that his disciples must lead not through domineering, Jesus told them that great leadership is accomplished through service. He then offered himself as an example: "For even the Son of Man did not come to be served, but to serve, and to give his life as a ransom for many." Following Jesus, the elders in Asia Minor were able to best lead their congregations by providing an example of selfless service to the congregation allotted to their care. As Davids notes, "Being an example fits well with the image of 'flock,' for the ancient shepherd did not drive his sheep, but walked in front of them and called them to follow" (Davids, 1990, 181).

5:4. By observing these commands,[3] shepherds have great hope of receiving reward when the "chief Shepherd appears." The reference to "appearance" (φανερωθέντος) speaks of the second coming of the Lord (cf. Col. 3:4a; 1 John 2:28; 3:2b). That Jesus is referred to as a chief Shepherd (ἀρχιποίμενος) indicates that Jesus still guides his people. It further suggests that those who work as undershepherds will give an account of their treatment of the sheep in their care. Peter here envisioned a positive outcome of the judgment, but underlying this positive assessment is the incipient warning that the judgment could be negative.

Though elders must not serve for temporal gain, they should seek after the reward Jesus brings for faithful shepherds: the "unfading crown of glory." Indeed, the word for "receive" (κομιεῖσθε) is stronger than simple granting; it refers to receiving something as a reward for work accomplished (BDAG s.v. "κομίζω" 3, p.

557). Thus, it is those who have labored hard in the way Peter has suggested that will receive this reward. That it is a crown invokes the athletic competitions so popular in the ancient Greek world. Much labor and self-discipline was necessary to become the recipient of such a reward (cf. 1 Cor. 9:24–27). This crown, however, is not like those crowns, for those wreaths were made of perishable flowers. The crown Peter has in mind is imperishable.[4]

In this letter Peter intentionally highlighted eternal things that last, comparing them to things that do not last. The coming inheritance will not perish, spoil, or fade (1:4), and is compared to gold that perishes (1:7; cf. 1:18). The seed that brought them redemption was an imperishable seed (1:23), compared to the perishable seed that gives life to flowers and grass. The beauty of a godly wife is described as unfading and is glorious in God's sight (3:4), and it is contrasted to the beauty sought after by means of external adornment. Here Peter provided another contrast. Elders may seek after the rewards of this life (whether financial gain or power over others), or the rewards of the next. Those in this life will perish, while those in the next will endure.

Peter described the reward as a "crown of glory." The genitive "of glory" could be taken in more than one way. It could simply mean "glorious crown" or "a crown which is glory." The second reading takes the genitive as epexegetical, describing what the crown really is. In other words, believers will not literally receive a crown; rather, they are "crowned" in a metaphorical sense with glory. A key question concerns whether this reward is specifically reserved for elders. Two facts indicate that it is not unique

3   By observing these commands. Forbes rightly notes, "The use of καί and the future indicative, κομιεῖσθε in the main clause, following the imperative focus of vv. 2–3, virtually makes vv. 2–4 a conditional sentence where vv. 2–3 form the protasis and v. 4 the apodosis. In other words, the reward spoken of here is dependent upon exercising oversight in the appropriate manner" (Forbes, 2014, 169).
4   Imperishable. The word used here likely refers to an amaranth flower, which was known for its color remaining steadfast (BDAG s.v. "ἀμαράντινος" 49). The use here is clearly figurative, however.

to them. First, all believers will receive glory at the return of the Lord (1:7). Second, Peter used the singular "crown of glory," and if he were referring to individualized rewards we would have expected him to use the plural ("you [pl.] will receive crowns of glory"; Michaels, 1988, 287). Elders, like the rest of God's people, will be rewarded with eternal life for the obedience that springs from the new birth.

Crowns in the New Testament

This is not the only passage where the New Testament speaks of crowns as rewards. A passage exceptionally close to this one in meaning is 1 Corinthians 9:25: "Everyone who competes in the games goes into strict training. They do it to get a crown that will not last, but we do it to get a crown that will last forever" (NIV). No identification of the type of crown is indicated there, but other passages do identify the type of crown received. Paul speaks of a *crown of righteousness*, which will be given to him, but also to all that love the Lord's appearing (2 Tim. 4:8). James speaks of a *crown of life*, which will be given to all that love the Lord (1:12). Likewise, Revelation speaks of the *crown of life* that will be given to those who overcome (Rev. 2:10).

In each case, the crown is best viewed as a metaphor. For example, Paul elsewhere noted that the Thessalonians were his "crown of rejoicing" (1 Thess. 2:19). Clearly he meant this metaphorically, to indicate that they were what gave him opportunity to rejoice. In Psalm 103:4 David indicates that God "crowns" him with "love and compassion." In other words, God grants love and compassion to David. In the same way, Paul was noting God's gift of righteousness, while James and John were referencing God's gift of life. Peter, in this text, is arguing that God gives glory to faithful elders at his return.

The Duty of God's People (5:5)
Peter commanded those under the elders to follow their lead and for all believers to show humility to one another.

5:5. Having just addressed the "elders," Peter turned to address the "younger." The use of the term "likewise" (ὁμοίως) indicates that the instructions to these "younger" is part of the broader category of which the previous instruction was a part. In other words, Peter was addressing roles in God's household, starting first with the "elders" then the "younger" and afterward he would speak to the entirety of the congregation (v. 5b).

The identity of the "younger" is one of the more complicated interpretive issues in 1 Peter. On the one hand, the word itself refers to those who are of younger age (BDAG s.v. "νέος" 669). On the other hand, the word appears to be the opposite of the "elders," which in this context refers not to age but to position of authority. Based on these facts, two major interpretations are understood: (1) the reference is to young people generally;[5] (2) the reference is to all in the church who are not elders.

Peter Davids champions the view that it refers to young people. He suggests that Peter took advantage of the ambiguity of the term, having it mean an ecclesial position in 5:1–4, but then having it refer to "older people" in 5:5. The younger, according to Davids, were the most likely to act brashly and cause the community difficulty. Such actions are based on immaturity, and so the younger people needed to follow the direction of those who were older and wiser (Davids, 1990, 183–84).

More likely, Peter was using "younger" in a figurative sense, to refer to all those who were not elders in the church. The language of "elder" and "younger" is able to be adapted for use here because the elders were generally taken from

---

5 Young people generally. The NASB and the LEB have "younger men." The limitation to young men appears to be based on the fact that they would have been the ones addressed in such a command (cf. Dubis, 2010, 163–64).

the older people, and those not in leadership were generally from the younger generation.

The command given to the younger was to "be subject to the elders." This is the fifth time Peter used the term "submit" (ὑποτάγητε; 2:13, 18; 3:1, 5). It referred to obeying the dictates of one who has a position of authority over oneself. The other uses of this term referred to established social situations (government, master-slave, marriage), and the use here gives further confirmation that the early church was likewise an established social entity. Those under the care of the shepherds had a duty to follow the direction of their loving guides. Of course, such authority was not absolute. Only to the degree that the shepherd was following the Chief Shepherd should he be obeyed. As Paul said, "follow me as I follow Christ" (1 Cor. 11:1).

Having addressed the "elders" and the "younger," Peter finally addressed "all" (πάντες) of the household of God. The command to "clothe yourselves with humility" is given with a verb that is nowhere else used in biblical literature (ἐγκομβώσασθε). It is likely that the verb derives from a noun (ἐγκόμβωμα), which refers to an apron donned by servants when they were about to engage in servile tasks (Achtemeier, 1996, 333). On this reading, Peter was calling all believers to clothe themselves like servants in order to serve one another.

Jesus famously donned an apron and washed the feet of the disciples (John 13:4). Peter was among those whose feet were washed (13:6), and this memorable event likely was the source of this admonition. The remembrance supports two elements of the broader context. First, Jesus set an example for the disciples, the very thing Peter was calling the elders to do for the congregation. Second, Jesus's action motivated all believers. If Jesus, the greatest of all, did this, then they had no excuse not to do it for one another.

Jesus Washing Peter's Feet by Ford Madox Brown. Public domain.

Each of the three commands requires humility. The elders must act in humility as they lead the flock, providing examples of self-sacrifice and service. The younger must submit to the leadership of the elders, which requires a humble consideration of one's own place within the assembly. Finally, each member must don the clothing of service for the sake of one another, an inherently humble act. It is for this reason that the final statement of this section ("because God opposes the arrogant, but gives grace to the humble") applies to all three commands, not simply the final command.

As Peter has done throughout the epistle, he concluded this section with support from the Old Testament. In this case, he cited the Septuagint form of Proverbs 3:34. The point of the citation was to show that God has always opposed the proud and arrogant and has given grace to the humble. The application of the proverb to the present text is easy to see. Elders who are arrogant and domineering will find God opposing them, while elders who serve humbly will receive grace. The members of the household under the elders' care will find that their humility in accepting the leadership of their shepherds will reflect the way that God responds to them. If they oppose the elders, God will oppose them. If they humbly accept such leadership, they will be shown grace. Finally, each member will find that to the degree he or she is puffed up, so God will oppose him or her. On the other hand, to the degree that he or she is humble, so God will give grace.

THEOLOGICAL FOCUS

The exegetical idea (Peter detailed duties within the community: elders must shepherd willingly and eagerly, serving as examples to the flock, nonelders must submit to the elders, and all must show humility to one another) leads to this theological focus: believers have duties within the community: elders must shepherd willingly and eagerly, serving as examples to the flock, nonelders must submit to the elders, and all must show humility to one another.

The church is an assembly of redeemed sinners who need direction so that they may function efficiently. The fuel that runs the church is humility, and everyone needs it. The elders, following the example of Jesus, are to put others first, walking ahead of the sheep, guiding them (v. 2). By their self-sacrifice and service, they are to provide an example that all believers may follow (v. 3). Their motivation for service must be sincere, not for any temporal gain (v. 2). They must be willingly desirous to give themselves to the work, knowing that God will reward those who show themselves faithful (v. 4).

Those who are not elders must also show humility. It is not always easy to follow the direction of another. Sheep may not always know why the shepherd chose the path they are on. Nevertheless, believers are called to follow God-honoring elders, knowing that the elders are shepherds seeking to follow the Chief Shepherd. By humbly following the leader God has assigned, believers receive the grace of God (v. 5).

Finally, all believers—elders and non-elders—must put on the garments of service in humility. Like Jesus, they must serve all people.

If Jesus was not too significant to don the clothes of service, then no mere mortal may reject the towel. It is through humble service that one finds oneself the recipient of God's grace; it is through selfish ambition that one finds oneself opposed by God.

PREACHING AND TEACHING STRATEGIES

Exegetical and Theological Synthesis

Peter's address to church leaders and congregants showcases an ideal relationship between the two parties. In our fallen world, this ideal does not always manifest itself—a reality Peter was well aware of. Peter recognizes the fallen nature of the leader. Too many church leaders stick around in their positions due to some persuasive force acting in their life—be it because dad was a pastor, the pressures of using that seminary degree, or because some other leader in the church pushed them into such a position. But Peter says that true leaders are not to serve under compulsion but willingly (5:2a).

To their shame, other church leaders are in the business to make money, make a name for themselves, or garner a following. This is an unfortunate manifestation of pride, self-idolatry, and the ugliest parts of our sin nature. But Peter speaks directly against this self-serving tendency in the ministry (5:2b). Other leaders are more narcissistic and lead with an iron fist, a "my way or the highway" approach to ministry (5:3). This kind of leadership can be incredibly damaging, as abusive and manipulative leaders exist to serve themselves, leaving the carcasses of burned-out and trampled congregants in their wake. Peter tempers this kind of abuse by putting Christ on a pedestal as the perfect example of what shepherding looks like (5:4).

In this way, Peter is once again able to point readers back to the gospel. A pastor's identity as a Christian transformed by the gospel should be seen in the way he leads the church. Christlikeness is the most important aspect of church leadership. Though the world may point to the need for business savvy, type-A personality, or the right people on the team (all of which may be of great use to a church), Scripture points to the humble heart of a shepherd who abandons any self-interest for the sake of the flock. This is the gospel way.

Preaching Idea

Humble Elders Lead Humble People toward a Humble Shepherd.

Contemporary Connections

What does it mean?

What does it mean that humble elders lead humble people to a humble Shepherd? Elders are the leaders of the church, elsewhere called overseers (1 Tim. 3:1; Titus 1:7) and pastors (Eph. 4:11). Though Peter does not explicitly use the word "humble" in connection with the role and character of a church elder, his ideal description of them certainly points in this direction. Elders should not serve for shameful gain or with domineering leadership, but rather lead as examples, with Christ as their ultimate example. How did Jesus lead? With humility, of course (Phil. 2:1–11)! If church elders take their cue from Jesus, they will not lead with arrogance or with an iron fist, but rather lead with godly character, putting the needs of others before their own. In other words, they will lead with humility.

But humility does not just apply to the church leaders; it should also apply to those under the charge of the elders. Peter here calls these people "younger" (5:5). And in his address to them, he does indeed explicitly speak to their need for humility. Humble followership willingly follows the example and leadership direction of the elders, as long as they lead in accordance with the Word. If a layperson disagrees with the direction of the church, that disagreement should be voiced through the appropriate channels, with tones of love and grace. They should realize that God set the leaders in charge for a reason, and though the leaders do not always act perfectly they (ideally) direct the church in the best direction.

Humble leaders and humble congregants alike should reflect the humble Chief Shepherd who set the example for them. This keeps the earthly shepherds/elders in check. It is far too easy for pastors to get big heads about the success of "their" ministries. They must always keep in mind that even if the church calls them the "lead" or "senior" pastor, they are not, in actuality. There is one true Chief Shepherd who leads his church perfectly. That alone should keep us humble.

Now what?

The application of this passage is twofold: one part for the church leaders, one part for the rest of the congregation. The preacher should state at the outset that the principles here do not just apply to elders/pastors. *Any* church leader should serve willingly, not greedy for their own gain but being an example to those under his or her care. This will help the application fall on committee leaders, ministry leads and other individuals in various positions in the church.

The preacher might illustrate both positive and negative examples of church leadership through news clippings. Unfortunately, it will not be difficult to find such stories of pastors gone wrong. Chuck DeGroat's book *When Narcissism Comes to Church: Healing Your Community from Emotional and Spiritual Abuse* (2020) speaks to the pain of pastors exercising domineering control over congregations and other leaders. The preacher may want to share an excerpt from this resource, or perhaps a clip from *Christianity Today*'s podcast "The Rise and Fall of Mars Hill," which chronicles the story of a pastor who succumbed to the temptations of arrogance and control, leading to the downfall of a massive ministry.

The second pathway of application lies in the congregation. The preacher should seek to answer the question: What does it look like to follow with humility and be subject to the church leaders? It is important to emphasize that subjection does not mean blind followership, especially if leaders lead in a direction that strays from the Bible. But consider highlighting a few faithful examples of what this looks like within the congregation itself. Who among the members has humbly followed, perhaps even in cases where minor disagreements existed? Preachers must walk a fine line here between preaching the message of the text and not sounding like they expect blind loyalty from church members. Exemplify the message of 1 Peter 5 by preaching with humility. Use restraint by not leaning in too much to the shepherd/sheep analogy and making it seem like the congregation consists of a bunch of dumb farm animals. Do not pretend to exemplify verses 2–3 perfectly—the congregation will see right through that lie. Instead, point people to Jesus, the perfect example of what a church leader should look like.

Creativity in Presentation

One way to illustrate Peter's goal of earthly shepherds receiving an "unfading crown of glory" is to have a creative person in the church construct a crown similar to what a victor might have received back in Peter's time. Most crowns back then were not made of gold and precious stones, unless you were a king; they were usually woven of flowers and grass. Construct a crown of such materials several days before the sermon and let the flora dry and wither. Pull a volunteer from the crowd and set the crumbling crown on their head to illustrate the fading glory of earthly rewards. Contrast that with the unfading crown

of glory in store for the obedient leaders of God's church.

The preacher may also want to encourage the congregation to visualize and pray for the character and responsibilities of the present leaders of the church. I (Bryan) am always surprised when members of my church do not know who their leaders are. After all, we put their pictures on the website! But this is not enough for most people. Call the leaders to the front of the auditorium. Introduce them one by one and spend time praying for them as they carry out God's mission. Then, when preaching verse 5, ask the laypeople in the congregation to stand and take a moment to pray for them as well. If you are really brave, consider having the laypeople in the congregation lay hands on the leaders, or vice versa. It is all too easy to use a passage like 1 Peter 5 to beat up on unruly leaders and stubborn congregants. Instead, use it as an opportunity to build meaningful relationships between leaders and followers. These relationships should highlight the fact that humble elders lead humble people toward a humble Shepherd.

Here is one possible outline for this passage:

I. The Job Description of Elders (5:1–4)
   A. Shepherd God's Flock
   B. Exercise Oversight Willingly
   C. Shepherd Eagerly
   D. Be an Example
II. The Job Description of God's People (5:5)
   A. Be Subject to the Elders
   B. Clothe Yourself with Humility

DISCUSSION QUESTIONS

1. How does Peter's description of elders fit with the popular view of what pastors/leaders should look like in the church today?

2. If you're a church leader, how do you match up with Peter's description of your character in verses 1–3? If you're a layperson, how do you match up with Peter's description of your character in verse 5?

3. What does it look like for a leader to "domineer" over those in his charge? What does the opposite of this look like?

4. Why is it important that Peter emphasizes the role of the Chief Shepherd in verse 4? How does that help our understanding of how leadership dynamics within a church should function?

1 Peter 5:6–14

EXEGETICAL IDEA

Peter gave final admonitions noting the need for humility, watchfulness, and enduring faith while the readers waited for God's coming climactic redemption.

THEOLOGICAL FOCUS

Believers must continue in humility, watchfulness, and enduring faith as they wait for God's climactic redemption.

PREACHING IDEA

Stand Firm in Faith, Watching for Christ's Coming and Wary of Satan's Schemes.

PREACHING POINTERS

The first-century church had suffered a lot. Persecution from Rome reached a pinnacle under Nero's leadership. In just five short chapters, Peter addressed the identity and calling of a believer under such circumstances. Now, at the close of his letter, he offered final words of instruction for the Christians. The devil still prowls the streets. Believers will continue to suffer. But Peter urged his readers to stand firm in their faith, awaiting the final glory of Christ's second coming.

The final sermon of any series can be a momentous occasion for the congregation. The preacher should feel the electric charge of Peter's closing instructions and translate that to a high-energy call to the church. If Peter's words were true back then, they are still so today: the devil continues to prowl, believers continue to suffer persecution, but *Jesus will return in glory!* This final passage gives believers hope for the future as they face the trials of the present day.

FINAL ADMONITIONS (5:6–14)

LITERARY STRUCTURE AND THEMES (5:6–14)

This section of text closes both the body letter (5:6–11) and the epistle as a whole (5:12–14). It is connected with the prior section by the link of humility. Nevertheless, Peter transitioned from considering roles in the community (5:1–5) to here considering how the community will survive until the coming of the Lord (5:6–14). The first command Peter gave was to be humble, giving one's concerns to God and waiting for the Lord to act in his good time (5:6–7). The second command was to be watchful, for the enemy is seeking people to destroy (5:8). The third command indicated how they were to overcome their great enemy: maintain steadfast faith (5:9). Through humility, watchfulness, and steadfast faith, believers would endure until God himself concluded their temporary struggle (5:10–11). The conclusion to the letter follows, including a confirmation of the truthfulness of the letter, a final admonition to steadfast faith, and a recommendation for the letter carrier (5:12). It further included the greeting of Mark and the church in Rome (5:13), and concluded with a call for mutual harmony and a prayer of peace (5:14).

Themes of this section include: how and why believers should humble themselves; the constant threat spiritual forces pose against believers; the need for perpetual vigilance in the face of spiritual danger; how to resist the devil; and the coming grace of God that will make all things right.

- *Be Humble (5:6–7)*
- *Be Watchful and Faithful (5:8–9)*
- *God's Climactic Redemption (5:10–11)*
- *Final Remarks (5:12–14)*

EXPOSITION (5:6–14)

Peter continued the theme of humility, noting the paradoxical truth that those who humble themselves will be exalted (v. 6). The way they were to do this was through prayer, laying their burdens on the Lord, the one who cares for them (v. 7). In addition to embracing humility, Peter's readers were to be watchful and sober-minded. These were necessary because their spiritual enemy—the devil—was seeking to devour the unsuspecting (v. 8). They could and must resist their enemy. Nevertheless, they were not unique in their struggle, for believers across the globe were experiencing the same sorts of trials (v. 9). Such trials, however, were only temporary, for God would come and make all things right (vv. 10–11). Peter concluded the letter by endorsing the letter carrier and reaffirming the message of the letter, which spoke of the grace of God (v. 12). Peter called the readers to stand firm in that grace. After sending greetings, Peter closed the letter with a prayer wish of peace to all those in Christ (vv. 13–14).

Be Humble (5:6–7)

Peter encouraged the readers to humble themselves by submitting to God's will and casting their care on God.

5:6. This verse is transitional, connecting with the previous verses by the word "therefore" and the continuation of the theme of humility. The new section no longer considers the roles of believers within the church (5:1–5); rather, it addresses the believer's need for perseverance in light of hostile enemies seeking to destroy their faith.

Peter had just indicated that God gives grace to the humble (5:5). In light of this, he

279

commanded the readers, "therefore humble yourselves under the mighty hand of God." Read in context, Peter was likely referring to submitting to God's will in suffering. Numerous times throughout this letter Peter had noted that God may will the suffering of his people (1:6; 2:21; 3:17). It is clear that the readers were presently enduring suffering, and so Peter called them to humble themselves before God, seeking his grace, which he freely bestows on those who humble themselves.

"The mighty hand of God" is a phrase used throughout the Old Testament in reference to God's deliverance of Israel from Egypt (e.g., Exod. 3:19; 32:11; Deut. 5:15; Dan. 9:15). Its use here suggests God's positive intention for their suffering. Yes, he is allowing them to go through difficulty, but he is the one who redeemed the people from Egypt, delivering them safely from the enemies that surrounded them. In the same way, he would deliver these saints. Thus, they were not simply submitting to suffering, as those resigning themselves to a poor life. Instead, they were submitting to temporary suffering, knowing that their God was a God of deliverance. This reading is confirmed by the next clause, which indicates the reason believers should humble themselves: "so that God may exalt you in due time."

Jesus argued that the humble *would* be exalted (Matt. 23:12; Luke 14:11; 18:14), yet many have found Peter's command to "be humble *so that* you may be exalted" contradictory. Those who seek to be exalted surely cannot be humble, can they? Those who find this contradictory misunderstand the nature of the humility called for. They believe the reader should look at themselves as lowly, but

Peter wanted them to stop looking at themselves at all. Instead, the humility called for is one where the readers looked to God, submitting to his will,[1] not their own. As they did so, they would recognize that those who follow Christ would be exalted. This may serve as a motivation for their obedience, but it did not negate the fact that their humility was found in their submission to God and their rejection of their own pursuits. Indeed, their exaltation would be "in due time" (NET, NIV, NRSV) or "at the proper time" (NASB, ESV, CSB). This time is determined by the sovereignty of the Lord, who would, according to verse 10, bring their suffering to an end.

5:7. One significant means by which believers may humble themselves was given by Peter: "casting all your care on him." The participle "casting" is literally used of throwing an object, but it is used metaphorically here of taking one's weight of concerns and transferring them to God (BDAG s.v. "ἐπιρίπτω" 378). Indeed, what is cast is one's "anxiety" or "worry" (BDAG s.v. "μέριμνα" 632). Read in context, this likely refers to the concerns over the persecution they are facing. Will it continue? Will it increase? How will the next round of persecution be different than the last? Such thoughts are to be cast, through prayer, on God. That casting one's anxieties on God is humbling oneself is evident, for those who do so reveal their dependence.

The last clause of the verse provides a motivation for prayerfully releasing one's cares: "because God cares for you." In other words, Peter was encouraging the readers to humbly submit their life situation to God

---

1   Submitting to his will. This interpretation may be confirmed by an observation of how James used the same passage. After quoting Proverbs 3:34, James said, "Submit [ὑποτάγητε] yourselves therefore to God." It is likely that Peter's "humble yourselves therefore" and James's "submit therefore" are equivalent. In both, the idea is that since God opposes the proud and gives grace to the humble, then one ought to submit to God's way of life, rejecting the prideful disposition of seeking one's own way.

in prayer, releasing themselves of the worry concerning what is to come. They could do this because they knew that God cared for them; that is, God had a sovereign plan for them. This belief was grounded in all the positive descriptions Peter gave at the beginning of the epistle: the readers are elect, chosen in Christ to be God's holy people.

Humility, Exaltation, and Resisting the Devil in James and 1 Peter

Peter's admonition in 5:5–9 is quite similar to the admonition given by James 4:6, 7, 10.

But he gives more grace. Therefore it says, "God opposes the proud but gives grace to the humble." Submit yourselves therefore to God. Resist the devil, and he will flee from you. . . . Humble yourselves before the Lord, and he will exalt you.

It is doubtful, in light of the differences in the passages, that either one of these letters was written in recognition of the other. Nevertheless, their similarity suggests that this teaching was common in the early church. By means of bookending the consideration of resisting the devil with the consideration of humility, James clarifies that resisting the devil is dependent on humility.

That these themes were common in the early church is not surprising, since both the command to humble oneself (Matt. 23:12) and the need to be watchful (Luke 22:31) are themes from Jesus's teaching.

Be Watchful and Faithful (5:8–9)

Peter warned the readers to be spiritually vigilant and to be strong in faith in order to resist the devil.

5:8. The two commands of this verse are to be considered together: "be watchful and vigilant." This was the third time Peter called for the reader's "watchfulness" (νήψατε). The

other two times concerned their need for watchfulness at the coming grace when Jesus returns (1:13) and their need for watchfulness in prayer (4:7). The word is literally used of sobriety, but is throughout 1 Peter used in a figurative sense (BDAG s.v. "νήφω" 672). The figurative sense is derived from the literal, however, for those who are drunk are not able to think seriously and be prepared for the things that are coming. The connected command to "watchfulness" is close in meaning and can also be translated "be watchful." The combination of two related words serves to strengthen the command. This second word, translated here as "be vigilant," was used by Jesus in eschatological contexts (Matt. 24:42–43; 25:13; Mark 13:34–35, 37; Luke 12:37), as it is used here. Peter, as he drew the letter to a close, reminded the readers of their need for vigilance as the end approached.

Their watchfulness should focus on their "adversary, the devil" who sought their destruction. The term "adversary" was a courtroom term, referring to someone who "brings a charge in a lawsuit" and thus acts as an "accuser" (BDAG s.v. "ἀντίδικος" 88). However, this accuser is dishonest, for he is titled "the devil," which literally means someone who "engages in slander" (BDAG s.v. "διάβολος" 226). Such a title is a fitting description of Satan, elsewhere known as the "ruler of this world" and the one to whom unbelievers (often unwittingly) follow (Eph. 2:2). This devil slanderously accuses believers, just as unbelievers slanderously accuse believers. Indeed, Peter may be suggesting that the assaults they are experiencing are fundamentally spiritual.

Their adversary was "walking around as a roaring lion." The lion is well known as a powerful and fearful animal in ancient as well as modern thought. By picturing Satan as a lion, Peter presented him as a powerful foe. That he is roaring suggests that he is seeking to induce fear in the hearts of God's people, just as a lion's roar naturally induces fear in the hearts of all within the range of its sound. Thomas Schreiner suggests that the roar should be identified with the persecution of God's people. Nevertheless, "the roaring of the devil is the crazed anger of a defeated enemy" (Schreiner, 2003, 242). He releases persecution against God's people, seeking to provoke fear in them, leading them to abandon Christ. Despite this, he knows—as do all the fallen spirits (3:19)—that his days are numbered.

Lions in the Ancient Near East

Because of the increase in human population and the decrease in its normal habitat, the lion is no longer a resident of the Middle East. In biblical times, however, lions were present in the forested regions surrounding Israel. As Fowler notes, "Due to its unmatched power and majesty, the lion leant itself to artistic and literary expression" (Fowler, 2000, 811). Often the lion represented majesty and power, as with the "lion of the tribe of Judah" (Rev. 5:5). But other times, as here, the lion was pictured as a source of fear, a powerful predator that threatened to destroy.

5:9. Having called the believers to humble themselves (v. 6) and to be vigilant (v. 8), Peter provided a third command, which flows from the consideration of the reader's chief enemy: "Resist him." To "resist" meant to be "actively opposing pressure or power" and could be translated "to fight back against." The way that the readers were to do this is revealed by the adjective "strong in faith,"[2] which the NIV captures nicely with "standing firm in faith." In other words, the readers can fight against the plans of the enemy by their commitment to Christ and the new life he has provided them. Those whose faith remains strong need not fear the impotent roar of the conquered lion.

Peter added a reason to obey the command just given: "because you know that the same types of suffering are being endured by your brotherhood throughout the world." On the surface, this appears to be a strange motivation for standing against the devil. Nevertheless, Peter gave the motivation purposefully. The readers were in danger of solitary thinking, imagining themselves to be the only ones experiencing suffering for Christ. These words reminded the readers of what they already knew—suffering is the experience of all God's people. Even at their present time, believers throughout the world were enduring the same types of experiences of suffering. Of course, it was not the recognition that others were going through hardship that encouraged Peter's readers. It was simply that their Christian experience was not unique.

God's Climactic Redemption (5:10–11)
God, to whom all dominion belongs, will complete the redemptive work he began.

5:10. This verse and the next serves as a conclusion to this short section (5:6–11). Peter was

---

2   "Strong in faith." It is possible that the adjective is to be taken as descriptive of the readers: "those who are strong in faith, resist the accuser." On this reading, Peter was singling out some of the readers as strong in faith and able to stand against the devil, while others in the congregation were not able to do so. While such a reading is possible, it seems best to take Peter as indicating the way that every one of his readers may resist the devil.

essentially saying, "Be humble, be watchful, resist the devil, and after you have done these things for a little while the God of all grace will make all things right."

In this verse God was described in two ways. First, he was called the "God of all grace." This was a way of emphasizing the graciousness of God. To the degree that grace exists, it exists because it has its source in God. Second, he was "the one who called you into his eternal glory in Christ." That this glory is eternal highlights the nonending life that believers are called to obtain. They do not receive it, however, without Christ. Though Peter does not appear to have a developed "in Christ"[3] theology as is reflected in Paul's writing, this use of "in Christ" is consistent with such theology. Only because of the believer's relationship with Christ does he or she have the hope of eternal glory.

"Calling" in 1 Peter

The term for calling (παρακαλέω) is used numerous times in 1 Peter. The word can mean "encourage" and it is used that way a few times (2:11; 5:1). It is also used a few times in reference to calling upon someone (1:17; 3:6). The key uses of the term are in reference to God's calling the readers to certain experiences. First, God called the readers to holiness through imitation (1:15). Second, God called the readers "out of darkness and into his marvelous light" (2:9). Third, he called them to suffer, since Christ also suffered (2:21). Fourth, he called them to bless those who persecute them (3:9). Finally, here Peter noted that God called readers to an eternal glory in Christ (5:10). The text of 1 Peter suggests

that these callings are not distinct; rather, those who experience one call receive them all. Those who are called to holiness and eternal glory are also called to suffer and bless their persecutors. No one may have one without the others.

The action God takes, due to his grace and his purpose for those he called, is to "restore, establish, strengthen, and establish" believers. These four descriptions are difficult to translate, for the terms overlap in meaning. The first, translated here as "restore" (καταρτίσει) refers to God's work in restoring the readers to wholeness after their significant trials (Achtemeier, 1996, 346). The second (στηρίξει) and third verbs (σθενώσει) describe God's strengthening of the readers. The final verb, translated here as "establish" (θεμελιώσει), is used literally of laying a foundation for a building, but is used here figuratively to reference God's providing "a secure basis for the inner life and its resources" (BDAG s.v. "θεμελιόω" 449). Together, the verbs indicate that God will pick up the battered believers after their time of trial and provide all that they need for their enjoyment of eternal glory.[4]

Because the verbs are in the future tense, they do not describe a prayer wish (which would require an optative verb), but a statement of future reality. In essence, these are statements of promise from God. Further, the future tense in connection with the phrase "after a little while" indicates that these blessings will come after their time of trial. Nevertheless, Paul Achtemeier rightly notes, "The fact that the verbs are

---

3   "In Christ." It is not clear whether this prepositional phrase is to be taken with the verb "God called you in Christ" or with the object "into his eternal glory in Christ." The word order may favor the latter, but the lack of the article favors the former (Michaels, 1988, 302). Davids may be right that commentators debate for no reason, for "Peter made no distinction—both the calling and the glory are in Christ" (Davids, 1990, 195).

4   Enjoyment of eternal glory. Michaels helpfully notes that the absence of God's victory over the devil is intentional: "The devil fades out of the picture as abruptly as he came into it. The reason is that the real issue in this passage is not warfare against the devil, but a firm and unshakable commitment to God and to the consequences of God's call" (Michaels, 1988, 303).

also what is needed during the suffering, that is, strong and unshakable confidence in God, is perhaps not accidental. Christians are already to show the kind of reality that will be theirs at the time of the eschatological fulfillment" (Achtemeier, 1996, 346).

The use of the phrase "after a little while" may defend Achtemeier's point, for Peter noted in 1:3–7 that believers were granted new birth, granted an inheritance, and were being guarded by God's power until the day of salvation. Before that day, however, they must endure "for a little while" (1:6). Accordingly, the beginning and end of the letter are bookmarked by statements concerning the "little while" of suffering, which are accompanied by statements concerning God's sure intention to finally redeem his elect. Since God is promising that he will do these things in the future for the readers, it assumes the power of God will preserve them safe until the final day.

Peter noted that the time of their suffering before exaltation would be a "little while." As elsewhere in this letter, Peter was not establishing a particular time for the coming of the Lord. The "little while" was meant as a contrast between the "eternal glory" they would have. In other words, their present time of temporal suffering would lead to an eternal reward of glory. In essence, Peter was making them aware of their investment: suffering for a short period, leading to glory for eternity. Of course, the length of suffering may be eighty or more years, but compared to the span of eternity, such is but a "little while."

5:11. Peter concluded the body of the letter with a doxology. Though the prior doxology (4:11) is debated concerning its ultimate referent—Jesus or the Father—this one is clearly written of the Father. Interpreters differ on what verb Peter implied, whether it was a statement (indicative;

"to him belongs the power" NET) or whether it was a prayer wish (optative; "to him be the power" CSB, ESV, NIV). In favor of the former is the fact that Peter used the indicative in the prior doxology (4:11) and had just used the indicative in the prior verse. Thus, Peter was not indicating that power should be God's; rather, it was a statement of fact that God was the one who had all the power. Such a statement offered praise to God and gave readers confidence that God could do what he promised. The doxology ended with a statement of affirmation: "amen."

Final Remarks (5:12–14)
Peter concluded the letter, giving greetings, encouraging faithfulness, and offering a prayer of peace.

5:12. The conclusion of the letter begins here with a statement of the letter carrier, Silvanus. While it is possible Silvanus was an amanuensis (i.e., a scribe) for Peter (Keener, 2021, 393–402), the language of this statement ("through Silvanus") confirms only that he carried the letter (Richards, 2000). The name Silvanus (Silas is an abbreviated form of the same name) was too common to say for certain that Peter spoke of the same man who was noted in other Pauline letters (2 Cor. 1:19; 1 Thess. 1:1; 2 Thess. 1:1), was known to have traveled extensively with Paul (Acts 15:40; 16:19–29; 17:4–14; 18:5), and was described as a prophet (Acts 15:32) and leader of the early church (Acts 15:22). What is clear is that Peter considered Silas to be a faithful brother. Such a statement was not merely for flattery's sake, but it served as an endorsement for the churches to welcome Silvanus as he traveled with the letter (cf. Rom. 16:1–2; Eph. 6:21–22; Col. 4:7–8).

The purpose of Peter's "short letter"[5] was to "exhort and declare that this is the true grace

---

5   "Short letter." Peter's statement that he wrote "briefly" is a statement generally given in letters of the time and does not actually reflect whether the letter was actually short (cf. Heb. 13:22). Michaels notes three possible

of God." The duplication of verbs indicated that Peter's purpose was to both testify to the truth as well as exhort readers to live in light of the truth. The referent of "this" was likely not to be limited to any one passage; it referred to the entirety of the letter. On the basis of this truth, he exhorted the readers to action.

One primary action needed was to "stand firm" in the grace just presented. Of course, Peter's audience was walking through troubled times. They were enduring social rejection and being pressured to abandon their newfound way of life. Peter here reminded them of the grace he had addressed throughout the letter. God had chosen them; they were granted new birth through the death, burial, and resurrection of Jesus; they were a part of God's program that he was enacting; they were promised an inheritance that will never fade. Because of the hope springing from such truths and the resolve naturally flowing from such promises, Peter called the readers to "stand firm." To not do so would be to deny grace, apostatizing from the faith. Affirming the need for perseverance did not negate God's sovereignty in election, for as Schreiner notes, "grace does not cancel out the imperative but establishes it" (2003, 249–50). In the language of 1 Peter, one may say that those who have truly been embraced by Christ have been given new life in the Spirit and have thereby been fundamentally changed. Such people will heed the call for endurance and persevere.

5:13. In a letter conclusion, one would normally note greetings from those present with the letter writer. Peter noted two parties. The less controversial one is Mark, who is described as Peter's "son." This Mark was likely the John Mark known throughout the New Testament (cf. Acts 12:25; 13:13; 15:37–39; Col. 4:10; 2 Tim. 4:11; Philem. 24). John Mark's mother's home was one of the meeting places of the early church (Acts 12:12), and this would have provided opportunity for Peter to have met and established a strong relationship with this younger believer. The testimony of church history is that Mark's gospel originated with Peter (Eusebius, *Hist. eccl.*, 2.15.1–2), suggesting just the sort of figurative father-son relationship revealed in this letter.

The second party that sent greetings was designated "the elect lady of Babylon." Though some early commentators suggested that this referred to Peter's wife, it is doubtful that he would associate her with "Babylon" nor that he would refrain from using her designated name. More likely, the reference was to a church. The letter of 2 John used the same type of reference, calling the church a lady (vv. 1, 13). Such a designation was feminine because "church" (ἐκκλησία) is a feminine noun. The introduction of this commentary addressed the various places Babylon could refer to. It was concluded there that the location was Rome. Thus, the church in Rome was sending greetings to the churches of Asia Minor.

Peter clarified that the church in Rome was "likewise chosen." By means of this description, Peter bookmarked the entire letter with the theme of election. The readers were elect according to the foreknowledge of God (1:1); and in like manner, all the way across the empire, God had chosen another group of believers. By means of this description, Peter reminded readers that they were not alone. Though they could at times feel like an isolated,

---

reasons to make this claim. First, it could be a roundabout way of apologizing for the length of the letter. Second, it could be a muted notation that the letter could have been longer. Third, "The fact that δι᾽ ὀδίγων follows close on the ὀλίγον παθόντας, 'suffered a little,' of v 10 may suggest that the issues addressed in the epistle, although serious, should be kept in perspective: a 'few lines' are sufficient answer to a 'little' suffering" (Michaels, 1998, 308). Of the three, the second appears to be the most likely.

rejected band of weary travelers, they had to remember that God was at work throughout the world, choosing people for himself.

5:14. Peter concluded the letter with one final command and a prayer wish. The final command was to "greet one another with a kiss of love." The love-kiss was an innocent sign of affection, comparable to a handshake today. The command reinforced the importance of maintaining unity in the congregation. By wishing the readers peace, Davids suggests that Peter was invoking the Hebrew concept of *shalom*, asking that the readers would have "the fullness of health and good relationships both among them and with God" (Davids, 1990, 205). Such peace may only be found in relation to Jesus and thus, Peter limits the prayer wish to those "in Christ."

THEOLOGICAL FOCUS

The exegetical idea (Peter gave final admonitions noting the need for humility, watchfulness, and enduring faith while the readers waited for God's coming climactic redemption) leads to this theological focus: believers must continue in humility, watchfulness, and enduring faith as they wait for God's climactic redemption.

Though God has made great and precious promises, he has also indicated that the culmination of those promises is reserved for the future. How then can believers maintain their faith while they wait for the redemption promised? First, believers must submit to God's will, humbling themselves to follow his directives. God has promised that he will exalt those who humble themselves, but he has not indicated when he will do so. Believers should expect to endure hardship during the time in waiting. Instead of responding with anger or confusion, believers are to respond by casting their anxieties on God, who has shown without a shadow of doubt that he cares for them. The lack of immediate redemption leads to difficulty, providing opportunities for believers to submit to

God's will and recognize their need for his enduring care.

The second activity that will lead to perseverance is watchfulness and vigilance. This is especially the case since Satan is presently wandering the earth seeking ways to destroy the faith of believers. And though his roar is significant, Jesus has taken away his bite. The Lion of the tribe of Judah was victorious by becoming a sacrificial lamb. Such truth does not resolve the believer of the duty to be watchful, but it encourages her as she watches. Yes, there is an enemy who seeks to destroy her faith, yet through Christ she has the power to overcome, just as Jesus overcame.

The third way to maintain faith is by resisting the devil. This suggests more than merely defending oneself against his attacks. Instead, the believer is to positively battle against Satan by becoming strong in the faith. This suggests that the weapon that Satan fears most is the believer's trust in the promises of God. Those who maintain such strong trust are incapable of being swayed from their firm foundation. As believers endure, they are to remember that their experience is not unique. Believers all over the world are experiencing the same things. All believers will suffer, and all believers will be redeemed.

The redemption of believers is no mere hope-wish. It is a promise of God, who has indicated that he will make all things right, strengthening believers to stand firm in the final day. Of course, this implies that he will strengthen them in the present to remain faithful until they reach that final day. Their difficulties may last many years, though in the light of eternity it will be but a "little while" until they enter into the eternal glory promised them when they were united to Christ through faith.

This letter presents the testimony of Peter for readers of all ages. What he presented is the true grace of God. Accordingly, believers must stand firm in it, while cultivating relationships among believers as they await the final day of redemption when they will truly and finally be at peace with God, one another, and the new world God will establish.

PREACHING AND TEACHING STRATEGIES

Exegetical and Theological Synthesis

First Peter 5:6–14 offers more than just a few closing instructions. In his final words, Peter gives a clear summary of the correct posture of a believer during times of persecution. Humility in light of God's sovereignty should, above all, characterize believers in crisis (5:6–7). The prayers of a suffering Christian do not go unheard by the omnipresent God who loves his children. This should bring comfort to the believer.

Believers should not only rest in the present sovereignty of God but look forward to the eternal glory in Christ that will forever change the landscape of the universe (5:10–11). As Peter has made abundantly clear throughout his letter, Christians have been called and chosen for a new identity through the gospel. This calling by the God of grace is a calling into eternity, a permanent calling that cannot be undone by the enemies of the cross.

Peter also challenged believers to adopt the posture of a watchman, keeping a lookout for the devil and his schemes (5:8–9). They should recognize that other Christians suffer similar persecution, which should bind together God's children in a common plight, despite Satan's plots against them. This posture of humility and dual perspective of watchfulness—for the devil's schemes and the Lord's return—should orient believers in the proper way to endure the trials of this world, in Peter's time and in ours.

Preaching Idea

Stand Firm in Faith, Watching for Christ's Coming and Wary of Satan's Schemes.

Contemporary Connections

What does it mean?

A great deal of 1 Peter requires careful explaining to understand the theological content of the apostle's letter. If there was confusion earlier, there is clarity here. Peter packs several commands into a few short verses in order to leave his readers a clear path forward. Most of these commands are clear-cut; the preacher can focus more on application rather than interpretation.

But there is, perhaps, a word that may need special attention from the pulpit: "Your adversary prowls around like a roaring lion, seeking something to devour. Resist him" (5:8b–9a). Some Christians have obsessively overread this into every aspect of life. Satan is attacking my children's school system; Satan caused my health problems; Satan made my car break down; Satan made me burn my Christmas cookies. Others, perhaps in reaction to this overreading, have swung too far in the other direction. No thought of Satan and his schemes ever comes to mind. The devil has no agenda—or worse yet, some erase him altogether as a figure of speech in the mind of the biblical writers.

The preacher must carefully draw the line between both extremes. Satan is real and active, yet he is likely unconcerned over the condition of your Christmas cookies. Settle the verse in its context. The believers of Peter's day were in danger of being devoured by falling to temptation as a result of heavy persecution. Satan (and perhaps by extension, his demons) can cause believers to fall away from faith using trials like suffering. Likewise, believers today can fall away from faith when the going gets tough, becoming yet another snack for the devil. By preaching the verse in its context, pastors avoid extremism and rightfully apply it for the church.

Is it true?

It is near-impossible to convince a skeptic of the existence of Satan. Many apologetics resources exist to "prove" or confirm the rationality of God's existence. But what about Satan's existence?

If preachers wish to solidify the thought that there exists an evil being whose purpose it is to thwart God's plans, they must ultimately rely on the Bible to help. Noting passages like Matthew 4:1–11, where Jesus faces temptation by Satan and interacts with a personal being, will help demonstrate that the Bible does indeed view the devil as a real creature. Other passages like Job 1–2 and Zechariah 3 show that the devil is not just a New Testament concept created with figurative, flowery language, but that the very earliest books of the Bible give testimony of his reality.

The preacher should keep away from personal testimonies or popular books (even Christian books) that claim to have seen or experienced satanic or demonic entities. Many of these have no basis in biblical truth and at best are subjective. Instead, seek to demonstrate the Bible's clear message about Satan's existence and activity among believers today. Do not minimize Satan's existence, but also be careful not to give him glory. He is but a created being, a defeated and subservient enemy to God.

Now what?

How should believers stand firm in the faith, watching for Christ's coming and wary of Satan's schemes? Peter gives three specific applications in this paragraph that will help a preacher apply the passage.

First, believers should humble themselves under God's hand while casting anxieties upon him (5:6–7). One thinks of a doctor-patient relationship. When undergoing surgery, or perhaps treatment for a potentially deadly disease, the patient endures the suffering while the doctor prescribes and watches over the treatment. There must be a level of trust in the doctor's knowledge and abilities. Worrying about the disease will not heal. When undergoing surgery, the patient must literally submit her entire body to the surgeon in order to obtain the desired

results. Believers ought to cast all anxieties on the heavenly physician, knowing that the suffering they endure is purposeful, common, and not outside of God's plan.

Second, believers should be sober-minded and watchful of Satan's schemes (5:8). Sobriety invites analogy with alcohol and drunkenness. A night watchman prone to drinking will not be successful stopping thieves or spotting suspicious activity. A security guard at a college sports stadium will be less capable and can even be a danger if he or she has had a few drinks before starting work. Likewise, believers should be as vigilant as a sober watchman, always prepared for temptation and threats to a life of godliness.

Third and finally, believers should resist Satan by standing firm in the faith (5:9a), keeping in mind that millions of believers worldwide suffer the same persecution (5:9b) and that Christ will eventually return in glory to reign forever (5:10–11). One might envision this on a horizontal and vertical line of sight. Horizontally, we see other believers suffering in similar ways, encouraging us that we do not endure this trial alone but that it is a common feature of Christian experience. Vertically, we look to the heavens and eagerly anticipate the return of Christ, knowing that he will come soon to put an end to this misery. These horizontal and vertical perspectives help believers stand firm and endure the sufferings of this world.

Creativity in Presentation

Peter's admonition to "cast all your anxieties on" Christ reminds me (Bryan) of times around the campfire during my days as a teenager in youth group. Often, retreats would end with visual representations of our emotional and cognitive decision to commit to Christ and repudiate a life of sin. Whether writing our sins upon a notecard and nailing it to a wooden cross on the stage or tossing sticks into the campfire thath represent said sins, sometimes a physical action could help internalize a command such as this one.

In verse 8, Peter compares the devil to a prowling, roaring lion, ready to devour someone. Certainly, getting a lion in the church would push the bounds of both wisdom and safety—whether it was caged or not! Instead, the teacher might consider a short video clip highlighting the power and terror of these beasts. Most people only encounter lazy lions sunbathing behind fences in a zoo, but a short visual reminder of their fury might put Peter's words into sharper perspective.

To illustrate other brothers and sisters in Christ suffering around the world for their righteousness (v. 9), the preacher could play a testimony or compilation of testimonies from persecuted Christians. Voice of the Martyrs (persecution.com) and other similar mission organizations could provide a few options for the preacher. Better yet, a testimony from one of the church's supported missionaries would hopefully bring home the reality that many Christians face on a daily basis. We must all stand firm in the faith, watch for Jesus's coming, and remain wary of Satan's schemes. The passage can be outlined according to the structure of the Preaching Idea:

- Stand Firm in the Faith (5:6–7)

- Be Wary of Satan's Schemes (5:8–9)

- Watch for Christ's Coming (5:10–11)

- Final Remarks on 1 Peter (5:12–14)

DISCUSSION QUESTIONS

1. What hope does Peter give in this section for believers suffering persecution or trials?

2. In what way does the devil prowl around like a roaring lion? In Peter's original context, what does it mean that he seeks to devour people?

3. How are verses 6–11 a great summary of the theology and message of the entire letter of 1 Peter?

4. Who is "she who is in Babylon"? To what extent does it matter?

5. What is your top takeaway from the letter of 1 Peter? How has this book impacted your identity as a believer and the way you face suffering?

REFERENCES

Achtemeier, Paul J. 1996. *1 Peter*. Hermeneia. Minneapolis: Fortress.

Agnew, Francis H. 1983. "1 Peter 1:2—an Alternative Translation." *CBQ* 45:68–73.

Baldick, Chris. 1996. *The Concise Oxford Dictionary of Literary Terms*. Oxford: Oxford University Press.

Bateman, Herbert W. 2017. *Jude*. Evangelical Exegetical Commentary. Bellingham, WA: Lexham Press.

Beare, Francis Wright. 1947. *The First Epistle of Peter*. Oxford: Blackwell.

Beekman, John, John Callow, and Michael F. Kopesec. 2018. *The Semantic Structure of Written Communication*. Dallas: SIL International.

Best, Ernest. 1970. "I Peter and the Gospel Tradition." *NTS* 16:95–113.

_____. 1982. *1 Peter*. New Century Bible Commentary. Grand Rapids: Eerdmans.

Bridges, Jerry. 1978. *The Pursuit of Holiness*. Colorado Springs: NavPress.

Brown, Colin. *The New International Dictionary of New Testament Theology*. Grand Rapids: Zondervan, 1971.

Brox, Norbert. 1993. *Der Erste Petrusbrief*. 4th ed. Evangelisch-Katholischer Kommentar zum Neuen Testament 21. Zurich: Benzinger.

Calvin, John. 1994. *Hebrews and 1 & 2 Peter*. Grand Rapids: Eerdmans.

Campbell, Constantine. 2009 *Verbal Aspect and Non-indicative Verbs*. Studies in Biblical Greek 15. New York: Lang.

Carson, D. A. 2007. "1 Peter." In *Commentary on the New Testament Use of the Old Testament*, edited by G. K. Beale and D. A. Carson, 1015–46. Grand Rapids: Baker Academic.

Chin, Moses. 1991. "A Heavenly Home for the Homeless: Aliens and Strangers in 1 Peter." *TynBul* 42:96–112.

Compton, Bruce. 2019. "1 Peter." Class Notes. Detroit Baptist Theological Seminary.

Dalton, William J. 1965. *Christ's Proclamation to the Spirits: A Study of 1 Peter 3:18–4:6*. Analecta Biblica 23. Rome: Pontifical Biblical Institute.

Davids, Peter H. 1990. *The First Epistle of Peter*. 2nd ed. New International Commentary on the New Testament. Grand Rapids: Eerdmans.

DeGroat, Chuck. 2020. *When Narcissism Comes to Church: Healing Your Community from Emotional and Spiritual Abuse*. Downers Grove, IL: InterVarsity Press.

Dubis, Mark. 2001. "First Peter and the 'Sufferings of the Messiah.'" In *Looking into the Future: Evangelical Studies in Eschatology*, edited by David W. Baker, 85–96. Grand Rapids: Baker Academic.

_____. 2002. *Messianic Woes in First Peter: Suffering and Eschatology in 1 Peter 4:12–19*. Studies in Biblical Literature 33. New York: Lang.

_____. 2010. *1 Peter: A Handbook on the Greek Text*. Waco, TX: Baylor University Press.

Elliott, John H. 2001. *1 Peter*. Anchor Yale Bible. New Haven, CT: Yale University Press.

_____. 2005. *A Home for the Homeless: A Social-Scientific Criticism of 1 Peter, Its Situation and Strategy*. Eugene, OR: Wipf & Stock.

Fanning, Buist M. 1990. *Verbal Aspect in New Testament Greek*. Oxford Theological Monographs. Oxford: Clarendon.

Feldmeier, Reinhard. 2008. *The First Letter of Peter*. Waco, TX: Baylor University Press.

Forbes, Greg. 2014. *1 Peter*. Exegetical Guide to the Greek New Testament. Nashville: B&H Academic.

Fowler, Donald. 2000. "Lion." In *Eerdmans Dictionary of the Bible*, edited by David Noel Freedman, 811. Grand Rapids: Eerdmans.

France, Richard Thomas. 1998. "First Century Bible Study: Old Testament Motifs in 1 Peter 2:4–10." *Journal of the European Pentecostal Theological Association* 18:26–48.

Glenny, W. Edward. 1987. "The Hermeneutics of the Use of the Old Testament in 1 Peter." ThD diss., Dallas Theological Seminary.

Goppelt, Leonhard. *A Commentary on I Peter*. Edited by Ferdinand Hahn. Translated by John E. Alsup. Grand Rapids: Eerdmans, 1993.

Greaux, Eric James. 2003. "'To the Elect Exiles of the Dispersion . . . from Babylon': The Function of the Old Testament in 1 Peter." PhD diss., Duke University.

Green, Joel B. 1997. *The Gospel of Luke*. New International Commentary on the New Testament. Grand Rapids: Eerdmans.

Grudem, Wayne A. 1988. *The First Epistle of Peter: An Introduction and Commentary*. Tyndale New Testament Commentary 17. Grand Rapids: Eerdmans; Leicester: InterVarsity Press.

———. 2018. *Christian Ethics: An Introduction to Biblical Moral Reasoning*. Wheaton, IL: Crossway.

Gundry, Robert H. 1964. "The Language Milieu of First-Century Palestine: Its Bearing on the Authenticity of the Gospel Tradition." *JBL* 83:404–8.

———. 1967. "'Verba Christi' in I Peter: Their Implications Concerning the Authorship of I Peter and the Authenticity of the Gospel Tradition." *NTS* 13:336–50.

———. 1974. "Further Verba on 'Verba Christi' in First Peter." *Bib* 55:211–32.

Hemer, C. J. 1978. "The Address of 1 Peter." *Expository Times* 89:239–43.

Hiehle, Jonathan Alan, and Kelly A. Whitcomb. 2016. "Enoch, First Book of." In *The Lexham Bible Dictionary*, edited by John D. Barry et al. Bellingham, WA: Lexham Press.

Horrell, David G. 2002. "The Product of a Petrine Circle? A Reassessment of the Origin and Character of 1 Peter." *JSNT* 24 (4):29–60.

Jobes, Karen H. 2002. "Got Milk? Septuagint Psalm 33 and the Interpretation of 1 Peter 2:1–3." *WTJ* 63:1–14.

———. 2005. *1 Peter*. Baker Exegetical Commentaries. Grand Rapids: Baker Academic.

———. 2012. "'Got Milk?' A Petrine Metaphor in 1 Peter 2.1–3 Revisited." *Leaven* 20 (3):5.

Jobes, Karen H., and Moshe Silva. 2000. *Invitation to the Septuagint*. Grand Rapids: Baker.

Johnson, Dennis E. 1986. "Fire in God's House: Imagery from Malachi 3 in Peter's Theology of Suffering (1 Pet 4:12–19)." *JETS* 29:285–94.

Judge, E. A. 1996. "Slavery in the New Testament." In *New Bible Dictionary*, edited by J. D. Douglas, D. R. W. Wood, N. Hillyer, and I. Howard Marshall, 3rd ed., 1113–14. Downers Grove, IL: InterVarsity Press.

Keener, Craig S. 2021. *1 Peter: A Commentary*. Grand Rapids: Baker.

Kelly, J. N. D. 1969. *A Commentary on the Epistles of Peter and of Jude*. Black's New Testament Commentaries. London: Black.

Kendall, R. T. 2010. "The Literary and Theological Function of 1 Peter 1:3–12." In *Perspectives on First Peter*, edited by Charles H. Talbert, 103–20. Eugene, OR: Wipf & Stock.

Kitchen, K. A. 1996. "Slavery in the Old Testament." In *New Bible Dictionary*, edited by J. D. Douglas, D. R. W. Wood, N. Hillyer, and I. Howard Marshall, 3rd ed., 1110–13. Downers Grove, IL: InterVarsity Press.

Levinson, Bernard M. 2020. "The Significance of Chiasm as a Structuring Device in the Hebrew Bible." *Word & World* 40:271–80.

Louw, Johannes P., and Eugene Albert Nida. 1996. *Greek-English Lexicon of the New Testament: Based on Semantic Domains*. 2nd ed. New York: United Bible Societies.

Lucian. 1913. *Works*. Edited by A. M. Harmon. Loeb Classical Library. Cambridge: Harvard University Press.

Luther, Martin. 1859. *The Epistles of St. Peter and St. Jude*. Translated by E. H. Gillett. New York: Randolph.

Luxton, David D., Jennifer D. June, and Jonathan M. Fairall. 2012. "Social Media and Suicide: A Public Health Perspective." *American Journal of Public Health* 102 (Suppl 2):S195–S200. https://www.ncbi.nlm.nih.gov/pmc/articles/PMC3477910.

Martin, T. W. 1999. "The TestAbr and the Background of 1 Pet 3, 6." *ZNW* 90:139–46.

McCartney, Dan G. 1989. "The Use of the Old Testament in the First Epistle of Peter." PhD diss., Westminster Theological Seminary.

———. 1991. "Λογικός in 1 Peter 2, 2." *ZNW* 82:128–32.

Michaels, J. Ramsey. 1967. "Eschatology in I Peter III. 17." *NTS* 13:394–401.

———. 1988. *1 Peter*. Word Biblical Commentary. Waco, TX: Word.

Miller, Timothy E. 2018. "Echoes of Jesus in the First Epistle of Peter." PhD diss., Midwestern Baptist Theological Seminary.

———. 2019. "The Meaning of 'Milk' in 1 Peter 2:1–3." *Detroit Baptist Seminary Journal* 24:63–80.

Moffatt, James. 1928. *The General Epistles, James, Peter, and Judas*. Moffatt New Testament Commentary. London: Hodder & Stoughton.

Page, Sydney H. T. 2010. "Obedience And Blood-Sprinkling in 1 Peter 1:2." *WTJ* 72:291–98.

Panchal, Nirmita, Rabah Kamal, Cynthia Cox, and Rachel Garfield. 2021. "The Implications of COVID-19 for Mental Health and Substance Use." KFF, Feb. 10, 2021. https://www.kff.org/coronavirus-covid-19/issue-brief/the-implications-of-covid-19-for-mental-health-and-substance-use.

Perdelwitz, Richard. 1911. *Die Mysterienreligion und das Problem des 1. Petrusbriefes*. Religionsversuche und Vorarbeiten 11. Giessen: Töpelmann.

Porter, Stanley E. 1993. "Did Jesus Ever Teach in Greek?" *TynBul* 44:199–235.

Pryor, John W. 1986a. "First Peter and the New Covenant (1)." *RTR* 45 (January):1–4.

———. 1986b. "First Peter and the New Covenant (2)." *RTR* 45 (May):44–51.

Reeves, Michael. 2021. *Rejoice and Tremble: The Surprising Good News of the Fear of the Lord*. Wheaton, IL: Crossway.

Richards, E. Randolph. 2000. "Silvanus Was Not Peter's Secretary: Theological Bias in Interpreting Δια Σιλουαψου . . . Εγραψα in 1 Peter 5:12." *JETS* 43 (3):417–32.

Runge, Steven E. 2010. *Discourse Grammar of the Greek New Testament: A Practical Introduction for Teaching and Exegesis*. Peabody, MA: Hendrickson.

Rupprecht, A. 1976. "Slave, Slavery." In *The Zondervan Pictorial Encyclopedia of the Bible*, edited by Merrill C. Tenney, 5:453–60. Grand Rapids: Zondervan.

Schreiner, Thomas R. 2003. *1, 2 Peter, Jude*. New American Commentary. Nashville: Broadman & Holman.

Selwyn, Edward Gordon. 1946. *The First Epistle of St. Peter*. London: Macmillan.

Silva, Moisés, ed. 2014. *New International Dictionary of New Testament Theology and Exegesis*. 2nd ed. Grand Rapids: Zondervan.

Simpson, John A., ed. 1991. *The Oxford English Dictionary*. 2nd ed. Vol. 19. Oxford: Clarendon.

Spencer, Aída Besançon. 2000. "Peter's Pedagogical Method in 1 Peter 3:6." *BBR* 10 (1):107–19.

Spicq, Ceslas. 1966. *Les Épîtres de Saint Pierre*. Sources Bibliques. Paris: Gabalda.

Thompson, Michael. 1998. "The Holy Internet: Communication between Churches in the First Christian Generation." In *The Gospels for All Christians: Rethinking the Gospel Audiences*, edited by Richard Bauckham, 49–70. Grand Rapids: Eerdmans.

Tov, Emanuel. 1997. *The Text-Critical Use of the Septuagint in Biblical Research.* 2nd ed. Jerusalem: Simor.

Trench, Richard Chenevix. 1871. *Synonyms of the New Testament.* 7th ed. London: Macmillan.

Turner, Nigel. 1978. *A Grammar of New Testament Greek: Style.* Edited by James H. Moulton and Wilbert F. Howard. Vol. 4 of 5 vols. Edinburgh: T&T Clark.

Vlach, Michael. 2010. *Has the Church Replaced Israel? A Theological Evaluation.* Nashville: B&H Academic.

Wallace, Daniel B. 1996. *Greek Grammar beyond the Basics.* Grand Rapids: Zondervan.

Waltke, Bruce K. 2004. *The Book of Proverbs.* 2 vols. New International Commentary on the Old Testament. Grand Rapids: Eerdmans.

Warden, Duane. 1989. "The Prophets of 1 Peter 1:10–12." *ResQ* 31:1–12.

Williams, Travis B. 2011. "Reconsidering the Imperatival Participle in 1 Peter." *WTJ* 73:59–78.

———. 2014b. "The Divinity and Humanity of Caesar in 1 Peter 2,3: Early Christian Resistance to the Emperor and His Cult." *ZNW* 105:131–47.

Winer, Georg Benedikt. 1882. *A Treatise on the Grammar of New Testament Greek.* Translated by W. F. Moulton. Edinburgh: T&T Clark.

Woan, Susan Ann. 2008. "The Use of the Old Testament in 1 Peter, with Especial Focus on the Role of Psalm 34." PhD diss., University of Exeter.

KERUX COMMENTARY SERIES

———————

1 & 2 Kings: A Commentary for Biblical Preaching and Teaching
David B. Schreiner & Lee Compson

Psalms, Volume 1: The Wisdom Psalms: A Commentary for Biblical Preaching and Teaching
W. Creighton Marlowe & Charles H. Savelle Jr.

Jeremiah and Lamentations: A Commentary for Biblical Preaching and Teaching
Duane Garrett & Calvin F. Pearson

Zephaniah–Malachi: A Commentary for Biblical Preaching and Teaching
Gary V. Smith & Timothy D. Sprankle

Ephesians: A Commentary for Biblical Preaching and Teaching
Gregory S. MaGee & Jeffrey D. Arthurs

Philippians: A Commentary for Biblical Preaching and Teaching
Thomas S. Moore & Timothy D. Sprankle

Colossians and Philemon: A Commentary for Biblical Preaching and Teaching
Adam Copenhaver & Jeffrey D. Arthurs

Hebrews: A Commentary for Biblical Preaching and Teaching
Herbert W. Bateman IV & Steven Smith

1 Peter: A Commentary for Biblical Preaching and Teaching
Timothy E. Miller & Bryan Murawski